MACHINERY
of
THE MIND

Also by GEORGE JOHNSON

Architects of Fear: Conspiracy Theories and Paranoia in American Politics

MACHINERY
of
THE MIND

Inside the New Science
of Artificial Intelligence

George Johnson

Times
BOOKS

For Katie Rosenthal

Grateful acknowledgment is made to the following for permission to reprint previously published material:

Basic Books, Inc.: excerpts from *Gödel, Escher, Bach: An Eternal Golden Braid* by Douglas R. Hofstadter. Copyright © 1979 by Basic Books, Inc., Publishers. Rights in the United Kingdom, excluding Canada, administered by Harvester Press, Ltd. Reprinted by permission of the publishers.

Morgan Kaufmann: Excerpts from *Machine Learning: An Artificial Intelligence Approach*, edited by Ryszard S. Michalski, J. G. Carbonell, and T. M. Mitchell, pages 143 to 145. Reprinted by permission

Scientific American, Inc.: excerpt from "Computer Recreations: Artificial Insanity: When a Schizophrenic Program Meets a Computerized Analyst," by A. K. Dewdney. Copyright © 1984 by Scientific American, Inc. All rights reserved.

Tate Gallery Publications: excerpt from "Harold Cohen" by M. G. Compton from a booklet for Cohen's show at the Tate Gallery, June 8–July 24, 1982. Used by permission.

Library of Congress Cataloging-in-Publication Data
Johnson, George, 1952 Jan. 20–
Machinery of the mind.
Bibliography: p.
Includes index.
1. Artificial intelligence. I. Title.
Q335.J64 1986 006.3 86-1313
ISBN 0-8129-1229-2

Designed by Robert Bull

Manufactured in the United States of America

10 9 8 7 6 5 4 3 2

First Edition

ACKNOWLEDGMENTS

Most of the research for this book was done during 1984 when I was an Alicia Patterson Foundation journalism fellow. I would like to thank the members and staff of the organization, especially Joseph Albright, Helen McMaster Coulson, and Cathy Trost, for a most rewarding year.

As a fellow of the foundation, I was able to travel around the country interviewing a number of scientists: Hans Berliner, Robert Berwick, Daniel Bobrow, Michael Brady, Rodney Brooks, John Seely Brown, Harold Cohen, Randall Davis, Edward Feigenbaum, Martin Fischler, Edward Fredkin, Michael Genesereth, Richard Granger, Cordell Green, Barbara Grosz, Frederick Hayes-Roth, Douglas Hofstadter, Jerrold Kaplan, Martin Kay, Douglas Lenat, David Levitt, John McCarthy, John McDermott, Jim Meehan, Marvin Minsky, Penny Nii, Nils Nilsson, Judea Pearl, Keith Price, Earl Sacerdoti, Roger Schank, Herbert Simon, Brian Smith, Joseph Weizenbaum, Patrick Winston, and William Woods. I would like to thank them all for their time and hospitality. I'd also like to thank Claudia Mazzetti and Louis Robinson for helping me find my way around the field.

Many thanks are due to William Bain, Robert Berwick, John Seely Brown, Harold Cohen, Scott Fahlman, Cordell Green, Frederick Hayes-Roth, Alan Lappin, David Levitt, Amnon Meyers, Melanie Mitchell, David Rogers, Katie Rosenthal, Herbert Simon, Patrick Winston, and William Woods, who each read sections of the manuscript ranging in length from several pages to several chapters. I would especially like to thank David Anderson and Thomas Goodman, who read most of the final draft, and Tom Gruber, Douglas Hofstadter, Larry Hunter, Cheryl Katz, and Nancy Wogrin, who each read the whole thing. The insightful comments of all these people improved the book immensely.

At Times Books, I would like to thank my excellent editor, Jonathan Segal, and his staff, especially Ruth Fecych and Sarah Trotta. From the beginning, my agent, Esther Newberg, and her assistant, Kathy Pohl, have provided the kind of support and encouragement that help make writing a less lonely process than it might otherwise be.

CONTENTS

PREFACE

About a year and a half ago, while I was visiting Stanford University, Penny Nii suggested to me the similarities between journalism and a curious new field called "knowledge engineering." Nii is a computer scientist whose specialty is artificial intelligence, the effort to make machines that think. Knowledge engineers interview experts—in medicine, for example—and translate some of what they know into a form that can be fed into a computer. Then, if all goes well, the computer will be able to make decisions as good as or better than those of its human counterparts.

That's the theory, anyway. Knowledge engineering is still in its infancy; it remains more a craft than a science. As I explored various artificial-intelligence laboratories around the country, I found that the design of so-called expert systems is only a tiny corner of a sprawling, wonderfully diverse attempt to use computers and programs to lay bare the mysteries of thought and create intelligence outside of the human body. Though my research took me further and further from the more mundane realm of knowledge engineering, I found that my thoughts kept returning to that conversation with Nii.

Knowledge engineers, she had explained, must absorb themselves in a field they don't belong to and emerge with enough understanding to write a proper program. They must be able to describe a subject without learning every detail, to capture expertise without devoting the years it takes to become an expert.

Journalists find themselves in much the same situation, though their aim is to communicate not with a computer but with an audience of curious nonspecialists who hope to get a feel for what scientists do without becoming scientists themselves. The knowledge engineers do their work using tools such as data structures, algorithms, programming languages—the greater and lesser arcana of the field of computer science. In the case of the journalist, the tools are metaphor, description, example, narrative technique—in short, the English language. Using these devices, one must try to take the strange and relate it to the familiar, communicate an unknown subject by building on what people already know. A journalist who is writing a book about artificial intelligence cannot become a computer scientist. No matter how much you read or how many people you interview, you are always in the frustrating position of knowing less than the people you are writing about—experts with Ph.D.s and years or decades of experience.

How then is science writing possible? The answer, I believe, is that the journalist has another kind of expertise, the ability to cut through the details of a subject and see its essence, to identify the important themes and personalities of a field and synthesize them into a story that a general reader will find enticing and clear.

One of the most engaging things I found about artificial intelligence is that it drives you to introspect, to turn your powers of observation inward and wonder how you do what you do—and how you would describe it precisely enough to get a computer to do it. Penny Nii challenged me to introspect about journalism, to think of myself as a computer programmed to go about the land interviewing scientists, reading papers and books, attending conferences, and eventually writing a book about artificial intelligence. What are the procedures I would follow?

In computer science, researchers often talk about what they call levels of abstraction. Anything can be described from many different levels. At the least abstract, most detailed level—the lowest level of abstraction—a human being can be thought of as an aggregate of whirling electrons, protons, neutrons, and other subatomic particles. But such a description is so complex that it is almost useless. Describe things at too low a level and the details overwhelm. On a slightly higher level, all these particles can be seen as parts of atoms, and at the next level up, atoms as parts of molecules, and then molecules as parts of cells. As, level by level, we climb the ladder of abstraction, the descriptions become less detailed, more general. We see that cells form tissues, which form organs, which are crucial components of the body.

Depending on our needs and interests, we can describe an organism from any one of these vantage points, using the languages of physics, chemistry, molecular biology, cell physiology, anatomy, zoology, or psychology. If we want to move to even higher planes and consider the human as part of a culture or society, we can use the languages of anthropology and sociology. Each of these levels rests on the ones below it, but each has its own rules. Psychologists can view the whole creature as a thing exhibiting behaviors that seem completely unrelated to atomic physics, but it is atoms from which we are made.

It is because things can be described from a number of different levels that journalists and knowledge engineers are able to do their jobs. In researching a book, a writer must constantly move up and down between levels of abstraction. At times you fly high overhead looking down on the contours below. When you see something that catches your fancy, you swoop down for a closer look. As you drop lower and lower, the details become more pronounced. At some point they become too formidable, so you must decide whether to stay long enough to make sense of them all or fly skyward again and find another part of the landscape to explore.

This same jumping between levels occurs while writing. You can use only a fraction of what you have learned. So, during most of the narrative you give the reader a bird's-eye view. You concentrate on the themes and implications—the big picture. But occasionally it is important to descend earthward and muck around in the details. Only then can you get a real feel for what is going on.

One of the hardest things about science writing is striking the right balance between the high and low levels, between the general and the detailed. Scientists often write books that are too technical for a general reader. On the other hand, they have been warned so many times to keep things simple that sometimes they overdo it. They generalize too much, underestimating the willingness of their readers to learn. One gets a taste of the subject but leaves the book hungry for the meat.

Morally, philosophically, economically, and scientifically, the implications of artificial intelligence are so great that I believe it is important for us, as outsiders, to have a solid understanding of the field. Is it really possible to make machines that think? Much writing on the subject begs the question. The standard line of argument goes something like this:

(1) A computer is a device that can do anything that can be precisely described. (2) Anything, including thinking, can be precisely described. (3) Therefore, computers can do anything, including thinking, and since they are faster than brains and will soon have bigger memories, inevitably they will be smarter than us. It's just a matter of working out the technical details. Laymen can assume that these are being taken care of. Meanwhile we can sit back and ponder a wonderful new future, or a brave new world. This kind of reasoning has led to some writing about computers that, at its worst, is half science, half science fiction.

Artificial intelligence is a field that lends itself to grand (and sometimes wild) speculation. That is part of its allure. In this book, scientists will describe future scenarios as fantastic as those we've seen in the movies. They really believe them, and, as experts, they are qualified to speculate with a certain amount of authority. But for those of us who are not computer scientists to take these predictions on more than faith we must understand the research behind them. We shouldn't be dazzled by looking at things from too high a plane. Unless we believe that there is something magical about human intelligence that can never be captured by a machine, we will probably concede that artificial intelligence is at least theoretically possible. Perhaps it *is* just a matter of working out the details, but as any scientist would agree, the details are everything.

"I've never heard any convincing argument that humans represent any kind of level of intelligence that it is impossible to go to with machines," Patrick Winston, director of MIT's artificial-intelligence laboratory, once told me. "But the interesting issue is not whether machines can be made smarter but if humans are smart enough to pull it off. A raccoon obviously can't make a machine as smart as a raccoon. I wonder if humans can."

This book is very much grounded in the present, in the fantastic things that are happening now. How *do* you get a machine to understand language, both written and spoken? How do you get a computer to make sense of what it sees, to learn from experience, to make discoveries and create on its own? How close are we to making machines that do these things? How far can we go, and how soon? It is one thing to say that computers can embody any step-by-step process and that thinking proceeds in a step-by-step manner, but it is quite another to show how such subtle and complex procedures actually might be mechanized. What do we mean when we say "understand," "learn," "discover," "create"? If we can describe these vague notions precisely enough to program them, then perhaps we'll have a more solid grasp of what goes on inside the mind.

In writing this book, I am assuming that most people know little about computers. They should find all that they need in these pages. Computers are becoming so pervasive that someday it won't be necessary to explain them anew each time a book such as this is written. But that day has not yet arrived. And even a veteran computer hand may find that research in artificial intelligence presents old ideas about computing in a surprising new light.

One might suppose, after flipping through a textbook or journal devoted to machine intelligence, that it would be impossible for a layman to understand a subject like this, except in the most superficial terms; that it would require laborious training, or at least a close familiarity with computers. I don't believe that is true. Some subjects, like quantum physics, are impossible to penetrate without knowing a great deal of mathematics; the general reader is stuck forever at the fringe. In artificial intelligence the concepts are more intuitive. By using the tools of analogy, metaphor, and example, and by viewing the key concepts from several different angles, it is possible to home in on the subject through a sort of literary triangulation. Then it can be examined in enough detail to leave the reader satisfied.

At the same time, I recognize that readers of popular science books are divided between those who savor the occasional detailed explanation for the sense of mastery it gives them and those who would rather stick to the broader bird's-eye view. I've made efforts to accommodate both tastes. In the prefaces to their eleven-volume history of the world, *The Story of Civilization*, Will and Ariel Durant often issued a disclaimer: "Certain especially dull passages, not essential to the story, are indicated in reduced type." I can't muster such courage (anyway, I think the details are the most interesting part), but in a few places where I am about to launch into a fairly involved description— for example, how a program called Hearsay-II understands a spoken sentence, or how the Automated Mathematician rediscovered arithmetic—I will try to drop a subtle hint. Those willing to take it on faith that the programs live up to their billings can skim for a few pages. But I've worked hard to make these descriptions accessible—and I hope compelling—to anyone with a natural curiosity for how things work. In the course of my research I found it exciting that I, a nonscientist, could understand these things. This book is an effort to share that sense of discovery.

Finally, I am writing not just about how machines work, but how sci-

entists work as well. I've chosen not to write about the people on the level
of detail appropriate to a profile or a biography, but from a higher level of
abstraction. Ultimately, what I hope emerges is a portrait of a profession,
with all its politics, infighting, and other blemishes as well as its triumphs
and discoveries. I've tried to capture not only what it is like to do science,
but to be at the beginning of a very young science, one that may lead to a
whole new way of looking at the world.

Artificial intelligence is often compared to molecular biology. Both fields
have grown rapidly; both are suddenly becoming commercialized. But there
is more to the similarity than that. Each of these sciences is about patterns,
structures, and codes. In molecular biology, scientists work to explain how
four nucleotides form a language that tells a cell how to arrange twenty amino
acids into the complex system we call life. Artificial intelligence is about how
symbols representing things in the world can be woven into the language of
the mind, the patterns we call thinking.

As I wrote this book, the work I held in the back of my mind was *The
Eighth Day of Creation*, Horace Freeland Judson's grand and panoramic history
of molecular biology. The field of artificial intelligence is too new for so
definitive a treatment. It is still awaiting a breakthrough as fundamental as
Watson and Crick's discovery of the structure of DNA and all that it said
about reproduction, inheritance, and other mysteries of life. For me, Judson's
work was not so much a model as an inspiration, a demonstration that it is
possible to write about a science in a manner that is entertaining and accessible, while rendering it with enough precision to make it come alive.

MACHINERY
of
THE MIND

PROLOGUE

Breaking a Thought into Pieces

The alarm clock rings, you rise automatically and click on the coffeemaker as you step into the shower and start thinking about another day. You might as well be on automatic pilot. But the morning fog clears from your brain and, bit by bit, you become human, with decisions, feelings, inspirations both silly and profound—the kind of elusive phenomena that surely can't be mechanized. Or are you deluding yourself?

Suppose that you awake this morning to find, like Franz Kafka's fictional character Gregor Samsa, that you have been transformed into another creature—not, in this case, a giant insect but a very sophisticated digital computer. Or, to make the metamorphosis a shade less absurd, imagine that you have been granted, overnight, unusual powers of introspection, the ability to gaze into your mind and examine the processes inside. Armed with this newfound skill, you perform a thought experiment—A Day in the Life—in which you zoom in close with your epistemological microscope and examine the gears in the machinery of the mind.

You're halfway down the stairs of your apartment building when a thought occurs: you've forgotten your umbrella. Do you climb back up two flights and risk missing the subway or do you chance getting wet? After a split second of what seems like suspended animation, a decision emerges. Acting on a hunch (whatever that is), you dart upstairs, unaware that you've acted out of anything more analyzable than a gut feeling.

But pretend that you work like a computer and your hunch is a cost-benefit analysis calculated so rapidly that you aren't aware of the myriad steps in the computation. During that second in which you don't even know you are thinking, your decision-making apparatus performs a memory-bank sweep, retrieving meteorological data gleaned from last night's television news or a glance at the morning paper's weather box, or out the window where the quality of light tells you there might be clouds. You obtain more data from your wired-in calendar clock, which knows that it's a late-September morning and what that might mean. Using the information you've gathered from being alive during a thousand September mornings, you make an educated guess, a hunch—an informal statistical prediction of how, based on your experience, the day is likely to be.

While these machinations are occurring, another process is taking place. You glance at your watch and recall the subway schedule. The neural circuits that are dealing with weather award 9 points to the possibility of rain. The likelihood of missing the subway is given an 8. Up the stairs or out the door? The answer is (subliminally) obvious.

But can it really be so simple? We are each individuals, after all. So introduce more factors. Perhaps there is a dial that controls fear of being

3

late; turn it from 5 to 7. Perhaps this new signal would swing the decision
the other way, in favor of forgetting about the umbrella. Or lower the level
on another dial that controls one's aversion to rain.

The point is that you can make your imaginary computer as complex as
you like, adding dials to control any number of characteristics, making the
gradations on the dials as fine as you please, programming the entire system
to base its decisions on many times more data. Maybe that's not how the
mind works. But it begins to look as though it could be modeled that way,
if the simulation were fine enough.

With umbrella in hand, you rush out the door, nodding perfunctorily
at a neighbor, whose name you still don't remember. You stop, as usual, at
the newsstand to pick up the *Times*, but today, on an impulse, you buy the
Post instead. There are two possible explanations for this seemingly irrational
behavior. First, there was that party you attended last week, where someone
you were trying to impress accused you of being an elitist when you made
a snide remark about the public's fascination with trashy tabloid journalism.
Who were you to say a periodical is bad because it has lots of pictures, big
headlines, and is aimed at the common man? Actually, you were referring
to those supermarket weeklies with stories headlined JKF ALIVE IN SECRET
CAVERN, or WOMAN MADE PREGNANT BY UFO, but still the accusation stung.
You, an *elitist*? The word lodged in your brain like a piece of glass. For the
next few days, rubbed by other memories and experiences, it seemed to take
on a charge, a mounting aura of static electricity that laymen call guilt or
shame. Have you ever actually read the *Post*? Today, just as you habitually
reached for the *Times*, the feeling exceeded a threshold, sparking across the
gap of some neurological electrode and jerking your arm, froglike, one foot
to the right, where the stack of *Post*s lay waiting. You may forgive yourself
the crude, almost prehistoric, analogy. The spark gap and the accumulating
voltage could be simulated by the counter on a digital computer, moving—
click, *click*, *click*—incrementally higher.

The other explanation for your surprising choice of newspapers is simpler
and more direct, though no less mechanical: the *Post* bears a headline about
a disaster in Mexico City, a place you have been vaguely thinking about since
yesterday when a song on the radio reminded you of a week spent there with
an old friend. Whatever the reason for your purchase, the story about Mexico
is what you read as you sit on the subway train and begin moving toward
the office.

Somewhere, about the third or fourth paragraph, your attention begins
to lag. You pause, fold the paper in half, and lean back, reflecting. A section
in your memory called Mexico has been ignited. Like the madeleine in
Proust's *Remembrance of Things Past*, a garish newspaper article and an old
Top Forty radio tune have evoked a chain of memories, one linked to another
in a procession that recedes into the vistas of your mind. As the train leaves
the tunnel momentarily and crosses the river, you gaze listlessly out the
window. But in the world behind your eyes you wander the streets of another

city, the network of thoughts and images stored somehow in your brain and indexed under Mexico: the hotel with the elevators like brass cages, the crowds of grotesque faces in the Diego Rivera mural in the Palace of Fine Arts. And there is a scene on Paseo de la Reforma, the treelined boulevard that angles from Chapultepec Park toward the Alameda: white-and-gold monuments rising from the center divider, vendors selling lottery tickets, side streets choked with quadruple-parked cars.

And then you remember the traffic circles. What is the word, in Spanish, for traffic circle? Now your internal wanderings become more deliberate as you try to retrieve this elusive piece of information. You can almost feel the word crystallizing into consciousness, almost sense its shape and sound. It has the feel of a woman's name, or, no, a flower. You can barely see its profile—the skyline of letters. It seems there's a *t* sticking out somewhere, a sharpness rising above smoother, rounder-sounding letters. But when you try to focus closer the word disappears, like those barely existing hazes of stellar light that can be seen only from the corner of an eye. You try to coax the word back, when suddenly, for no good reason, the image of a freeway looms into view. Not in Mexico, oddly, but in New Mexico. It's the interstate highway that runs along the base of the Sangre de Cristo Mountains, from Santa Fe toward Denver. There is an exit that leads to the Pecos wilderness and that night long ago camping in a canyon with fireflies everywhere.

A roadway in your mind has led, unexpectedly, from the streets of Mexico City to another cluster of memories. A detour, it seems, but then you remember. The town at the exit is Glorieta, New Mexico, and the word, in Spanish, for traffic circle is *glorieta*, which sounds like Gloria, a woman's name. It is flowerlike and round (a traffic circle is round)—and flower in Spanish is *flora, glora, glorieta*. The word was stored in many different places and cross-referenced according to its shape, its sound, the places where it has been experienced, as well as by what it means.

Well, no one said that your data base had to be simple and clear-cut. It's more a tangle than an array. The mural by Diego Rivera has tentacles extending to the memory of another of his works, on a ceiling in the Museum of Science and Industry, which is filed in a section where you keep vague, fading remembrances of a childhood trip to Chicago.

You could wander all day, back to Mexico or to that canyon in the wilderness, but reality intrudes. You emerge from the network of tunnels (the ones in your mind as well as those the train has been traveling through) and find yourself outside the building where you work. You go inside, ready to spend the day utilizing a more orderly part of your mind. Most of us would agree that there are scores of jobs of such mind-numbing repetition that they easily could be mechanized. But to keep the experiment interesting, let's pretend that you're a doctor. Patient A is complaining of stomach trouble—a burning pain, strange rumblings in the night, food that seems to sit in the gut as indigestible as concrete. So are we talking ulcer, maybe cancer, or just a nervous stomach? How about cirrhosis of the liver? All have overlapping symptoms: nausea, abdominal cramps, a feeling of fullness. To find your way through the web of possibilities, you must gather more information, ask questions whose answers will lead to other questions, and more direct inquiries such as X rays and blood tests.

Does the patient drink, smoke, lead a stressful life, eat a lot of Szechuan food? These activities all have been linked to stomach irritation, which might lead to chronic gastritis and perhaps, in extreme cases, ulceration. Is the patient's skin jaundiced? That is a symptom of liver trouble. Is the spleen enlarged? That can mean cirrhosis, but it can also mean leukemia, Hodgkin's disease, malaria, or mononucleosis, which all have distinguishing and over-lapping symptoms of their own.

You ask the patient to be more specific. Are the pains in the upper abdomen? Do they happen between meals and go away after eating? Is there a sour taste in the mouth that abates after taking antacids? Those might be ulcer signs. If the pain is lower and to the right it might be appendicitis, which is often accompanied by a high white-blood-cell count—and that, of course, can mean an infection in any part of the body. Weight loss can accompany cirrhosis or cancer.

In even the most routine case, there is an overwhelming amount of information to consider. Men might be more likely to get ulcers than women. Certain personality types are ulcer-prone. And once a diagnosis is made, there is a spectrum of possible treatments. In the case of an ulcer, they range from medication to surgery.

An experienced doctor doesn't consider every single factor, running through a vast mental checklist. Over the years certain symptoms recur so frequently that they are compiled into patterns which, when observed, can elicit a diagnosis almost immediately. They feel like hunches, but so did the decision to go back for the umbrella. After all, medicine is supposed to be logical, at least largely so. The most complex medical decision might be broken into thousands of microdecisions, which, if properly strung together by a computer, would produce the same diagnosis a human doctor would. Each decision need not be black or white. To allow for un-certainty, probability ratings could be included, translated as numbers between 1 and 10, or 1 and 100, depending on how much subtlety is required.

And what about the instincts that seem to contribute to the diagnostic process—the feeling you got that you were dealing with a nervous person, someone who internalized emotional troubles, converting them through the alchemy of neurosis into excess stomach acid? Couldn't that hunch also have resulted from the accumulation of clues: the way the patient fidgeted, asked too many questions, recounted every imaginable symptom in excruciating detail? Without consciously thinking, you weave the clues into a pattern, then compare it against the model of what you know from experience to be the classic ulcer personality.

And yet you wonder. Can it all be so explicable? Is there no such thing as a *creative* diagnostician, one who startles colleagues with insights? Well, unless you believe in magic, don't those insights have to be based on information and experience? Isn't the brilliant internist likely to be one who has read more, retained more—whose brain is, perhaps, wired better so that it can recall data more rapidly, weaving it into more possible structures to consider, one against the other, so that when the most logical possibility emerges it seems like a bolt out of the blue?

And so the story goes. When the day is done, you walk outside and feel a raindrop. Unfortunately you've left your umbrella at the office and you don't feel like going back. You get wet, catch a cold, and stay home the next day. Nobody said this was a perfect computer.

Or did the possible pleasures of spending a day sick but not debilitated contribute to your forgetting the umbrella? This is starting to sound like a parody of Freud. All this hyperanalytic nonsense is depressing. You pick up a murder mystery you've been wanting to finish and go back to bed. But the thought experiment isn't over. For now you have enacted your book-reading routine.

Granted, the rules for parsing sentences and correlating words with definitions might be mechanized. But can the *experience* of reading a novel also be analyzed this way? Just what might be happening on the deeper levels of your mind as your eyes sense words moving by? A subject, a verb, and a predicate combine to form an image in the head, constructed according to the definitions of the words and your experience of what they mean. Using adjectives and adverbs, the writer fine-tunes the images, and arranges them one after another so a story unfolds. Characters are developed by piling image upon image, making complex clusters that interact with other clusters. To build narrative tension, key bits of information are withheld, then supplied in a rush at the climax, filling in holes in the data structure that has been induced in the reader's mind.

The writer's work, like the physician's, can be viewed mechanistically. One takes the X number of basic plots and themes that critics tell us exist and composes variations. And what about style? Within this reductionist paradigm, style can be described through textual analysis, statistically. Writer Z's books are unique because an average of 12 percent of the words are adjectives, 3 percent are adverbs, 21 percent are chosen from a dictionary with a difficulty level of 7. Sentence rhythms can be quantified. Perhaps such seemingly abstruse talents as the use of connotation and metaphor can be explained mechanistically.

"Okay, enough!" you might well interject. It's clear that you can take mental activities and describe them as an interaction of many smaller steps. And if, in this game, we are allowed to break a thought into as many pieces as we'd like, and break those pieces into pieces, and posit an overwhelmingly complex system that coordinates them all—then, yes, you can say that intelligence might be described mechanistically. But what does that mean?

It means, if you accept this argument, that you believe in the possibility of artificial intelligence. That, given good tools and enough ingenuity, we might cut through the veils that obscure our thoughts. Then we can see them not as mysterious, ghostlike essences but as complex structures made from the interaction of millions of pieces, theoretically duplicable on a machine.

CHAPTER

1

The State of the Art

———

As he squinted into the blue-gray light of yet another computer terminal, John McCarthy looked as though he were suffering from eyestrain, or from one too many software demonstrations. He was sitting in the industrial exhibition hall at the annual convention of the American Association for Artificial Intelligence, where companies with names like Teknowledge and IntelliCorp were demonstrating some of the first commercial fruits of a field he had done much to create. It was 1984 and McCarthy, a bearded, gray-haired man in his late fifties, had just finished serving a year as president of AAAI. Earlier that day he had addressed an auditorium filled with people who had come to hear him describe his thirty-year-old effort to instill in computers what humans call common sense. For many the speech was the climax of the convention, and now, in its aftermath, he sat wearily rubbing his eyes, half listening, as an employee of a firm called Inference Corporation explained the network of lines and boxes cast upon the screen by a program ambitiously christened ART, the Automated Reasoning Tool.

In the English that computer scientists speak, ART is known as a "knowledge-engineering environment" or "software-development toolkit"—an aid to designing a complex new breed of programs called expert systems, which automatically make decisions in such fields as financial planning, medical diagnosis, geological exploration, and microelectronic circuit design.

Programs, of course, are the lists of instructions, often thousands of lines long, that guide computers as they solve problems; they are the software that tells the hardware—the banks of microscopic memory cells and switches—what to do. In drawing the distinction between hardware and software, computer scientists often use metaphor. A stereo system is hardware; its software is the music it plays, whether it is encoded magnetically on a stream of tape or as microscopic squiggles in a plastic record groove. Hardware, in other words, is the part of a machine that is concrete; it can be touched and felt. Software is intangible.

ART is best understood as a program that helps programmers write programs, a welcome relief to what can be a numbingly tedious task. As anyone who has tried to write even the simplest program will attest, the world inside a computer can be an inhospitable place, unforgiving of the most innocent human foible. Drop a comma or misnumber a line and a program "crashes," leaving behind a string of incomprehensible "error messages" to explain what went wrong. Once loaded into a computer, a program like ART organizes the tabula rasa of silicon chips into more habitable surroundings. By automatically taking care of some of the messy details of programming, ART frees users to concentrate on the big picture. The result, according to Inference Corporation's colorful brochure, is a more efficient means of writing the powerful, intricate programs that capture the "concepts, facts, and beliefs" of human expertise—software that can perform automatically some of the tasks human experts do.

"The computer is no longer just a fast number cruncher," the company's enthusiastic copywriter had written. ". . . [I]t is now possible to program human knowledge and experience into a computer. . . . Artificial intelligence has finally come of age."

This was a common refrain during the 1984 convention of AAAI, an organization of computer scientists, cognitive psychologists, and a few linguists and philosophers who believe that intelligence can be uprooted from its biological substrate and planted carefully in machines. Scientists have always found it natural to use cognitive terminology to describe computer functions. Thus the chips that temporarily store data are referred to as memory, and the systems of symbols used to write programs are called languages. To John McCarthy and his colleagues, the comparison between computers and brains is more than a metaphor. They believe that it is possible to make computers that think, and, perhaps, know that they are thinking. So sure are they that thought is computational that Marvin Minsky, of the Massachusetts Institute of Technology, once referred to the brain as a "meat machine." Like his contemporary John McCarthy, Minsky is one of the most prominent theoreticians of the field. In recent years, some enthusiastic proponents of artifical intelligence have taken to calling the neuronal circuitry that makes up our brains "wetware."

Once an arcane discipline in the upper stratosphere of computer science, AI (as initiates call the field) had recently captured the imagination of industrialists and venture capitalists, who hoped to profit from the attempt to simulate the workings of the mind. But in the long journey from the hieroglyphic formulas of technical papers to the hyperbolic prose of publicists, much had been lost, or rather added, in translation. Most of the scientists who study AI had come to the convention, which was held at the Austin campus of the University of Texas, to meet old friends and discuss recent advances. But some of the companies that had staked out space in the exhibition hall acted as though the age-old dream of creating intelligent companions had already been realized.

"We've built a better brain," exclaimed a brochure for one of ART's competitors, TIMM, The Intelligent Machine Model. "Expert systems reduce waiting time, staffing requirements and bottlenecks caused by the limited availability of experts. Also, expert systems don't get sick, resign, or take early retirement." Other companies, such as IBM, Xerox, and Digital Equipment Corporation, were more conservative in their pronouncements. But the amplified voices of their salesmen, demonstrating various wares, sounded at times like carnival barkers, or prophets proclaiming the dawning of a new age.

As he sat amidst the din, McCarthy seemed unimpressed. He closed his eyes, leaned forward, and rested his head on his hands, which were clasped in front of him like those of a man in prayer. Then he withdrew from the noise around him into the more familiar environment of his own mind.

As much as any person alive, McCarthy appreciated how far the field had come. At Stanford, a young colleague named Douglas B. Lenat had written a program, called the Automated Mathematician, which seemed to have the ability to make discoveries on its own. After running unattended for several nights on a computer in Lenat's office, the program had, in a sense, "reinvented" arithmetic, discovering for itself such concepts as addition, multiplication, and prime numbers (those, like 3, 17, and 113, which are divisible only by themselves and 1). In the course of its explorations, the program stumbled upon what human mathematicians reverently call the Fundamental Theorem of Arithmetic: any number can be factored into a unique set of primes.

The Stanford AI lab was not the only place where such impressive programs were being written. At Carnegie-Mellon University in Pittsburgh, Herbert Simon, a Nobel Prize–winning economist and respected AI researcher, was working with colleagues to develop a program that reenacted scientific discoveries. Given a ream of experimental data, the program could rediscover such famous scientific theories as Kepler's third law of planetary motion. Eventually Simon hoped the program would make an original discovery of its own. In honor of its ability to perceive the patterns woven through nature, the program was named Bacon. Roger Bacon, a thirteenth-century philosopher and early proponent of the experimental method, is often revered as one of the founders of modern science. Efforts at machine intelligence were not focused entirely on such orderly domains as mathematics and science. At MIT, a student of Minsky's was working on a program that, given a melody line, could improvise Scott Joplin piano rags.

Because of these and dozens of other successes in laboratories around the country, McCarthy was as certain as ever that a time would come—perhaps decades or a century hence—when we are faced with another intelligence on the planet, an artificial mind of our own making. If that day arrives, the psychological, philosophical, and moral implications will be staggering, but perhaps not any more so than the enormous number of technical problems that scientists like McCarthy first must overcome.

"Things have been slower than I'd hoped," he admitted, "but perhaps not slower than I expected. I expected that these problems were difficult. I didn't think they were almost solved." It is possible, he said, that any day now "somebody may get a really brilliant idea," a breakthrough that will accelerate the process of developing artificial minds. "It may be that AI is a problem that will fall to brilliance so that all we lack is one Einstein." But he accepts that, most likely, he and his science are at the beginning of a long, slow progression. "I think this is one of the difficult sciences like genetics, and it's conceivable that it could take just as long to get to the bottom of it. But of course the goal is that one should be able to make computer programs that can do anything intellectual that human beings can."

From the time Gregor Mendel performed the first genetic experiments on pea plants in a monastery garden to the discovery by James Watson and Francis Crick of the double helical structure of DNA approximately a century passed. To McCarthy it wasn't surprising that it might take as long to understand the nature of the intelligence that had deciphered the chemical basis of life. Like his colleagues who had come to Austin, he believed that the key to the mystery would be the digital computer.

The first anyone remembers hearing the words "artificial intelligence" was in the mid-1950s when McCarthy drafted a request to the Rockefeller Foundation to fund a conference to explore the proposition that "intelligence can in principle be so precisely described that a machine can be made to simulate it." Rockefeller granted the money and the Dartmouth Summer Research Project on Artificial Intelligence took place in 1956 at Dartmouth College, in Hanover, New Hampshire, where McCarthy was a mathematics professor.

In the history of computer science, the meeting was a landmark. Although little in the way of tangible results came out of the conference—which, after all, lasted only two months—it was the first gathering of a small group of researchers who would become some of the most influential leaders of the field. Included among the organizers were not only McCarthy but Marvin Minsky, who was studying as a Junior Fellow in mathematics and neurology at Harvard University, and Herbert Simon and Allen Newell, who were working for the Rand Corporation and the Carnegie Institute of Technology, now called Carnegie-Mellon University. Minsky and McCarthy went on to found the AI laboratory at the Massachusetts Institute of Technology, McCarthy leaving in 1963 to begin his own group at Stanford. Simon and Newell started the AI program at Carnegie-Mellon. Today, these centers remain the preeminent AI laboratories in the world. Many of the principal AI researchers in the United States were trained by at least one of these four men.

Having provided the field with a name, McCarthy went on to give it a language. During the late 1950s at MIT, he invented Lisp, in which almost all AI programs are now written.

A computer language is like a human language in that each consists of a system of rules and a vocabulary that can be used to communicate with those (human or machine) who share the same set of conventions. Another way to think of it is this: a computer language is the codebook that programmers use to translate their ideas into forms the computer can understand. A program is said to be written in Lisp in the same sense that an essay is written in English. No computer language has a fraction of the richness and expressiveness of a human language, and ideally we would be able to make computers sophisticated enough to understand English, French, Spanish, or Japanese. But so far that has proved impossible. Languages like Lisp (short for List Processing) are a rough but powerful compromise.

It is hard to imagine how, without Lisp, AI could have flourished as quickly as it did. Most other computer languages, such as Fortran and Cobol, were tailored for writing programs that performed high-speed mathematical calculations or sorted and collated lists of employees, customers, items in inventory—the stuff of data processing. Lisp, however, was designed for a loftier purpose—as a tool for giving computers the kinds of rules and concepts that AI researchers believe are used by the human mind.

As it spread throughout the AI community in the late 1950s and early 1960s, Lisp quickly gained a reputation as a powerful invention, admired for the elegance of its design. The aesthetics of computer languages is an esoteric subject, difficult for outsiders to grasp. Again, metaphor helps bridge the gap. Computer scientists talk about a favorite language the way a craftsman talks about a good tool: it is durable, nicely shaped, efficient—something that feels as pleasing to the mind of a programmer as a well-made wrench feels to a mechanic's hand. Some languages are clumsy (they require too much fiddling), others are weak (they can't be used to write interesting programs) or too fragile (it's extremely easy to mess things up). Imagine multiplying two four-digit numbers using Roman numerals; not even the Romans could do it well. Their system of Is, Vs, Xs, Ls, Cs, Ds, and Ms was ugly—a bad language for doing arithmetic. To connoisseurs of such matters, Lisp was immediately recognized as a beautiful computer language; its combination of power and efficiency provided just the leverage a programmer needed to write the sprawling, complex, multitiered programs that are the foundation of artificial-intelligence research.

For example, when working with more pedestrian languages, programmers often had to decide ahead of time how much of the computer's memory a program would need in order to do its job. Then they had to instruct the machine to cordon off the area in advance, before the program was run. That was all the memory it would be allowed to use. For those writing the relatively mindless software of data processing, this wasn't too great a burden. For AI researchers such restrictions were absolutely stultifying. They hoped to devise programs that had, in a sense, minds of their own, whose behavior was unpredictable. How could programmers know in advance how much memory space their creations would require?

With Lisp, such strict preplanning was unnecessary. Memory was automatically captured and surrendered as needed, while the program ran. With the flexibility afforded by Lisp, software didn't have to be an unquestionable set of marching orders. Programs could be written that were more spontaneous and fluid. Some even sprung occasional surprises, solving problems in ways that had never occurred to their human inventors.

Even more uncanny was the way Lisp allowed the creation of programs that could change themselves as they ran. In conventional computing, information was fed into the machine and processed according to the instructions in the program. Then it emerged, transformed, like wool coming out of a spinning wheel as yarn. The data might be a list of words, the instructions a program for sorting them into alphabetical order. In any case, there was no mistaking data and instructions—they were two very different things. In

Lisp, there was no such distinction. The program and the information it was to process were written in exactly the same way (as words surrounded by parentheses). To the computer, they looked identical. Because of this ambiguity between subject (the program) and object (the information it was to process), one Lisp program could provide the grist for another's mill. Programs could read programs and write programs. They could even inspect and modify themselves, suggesting the possibility of software that not only learned but was aware of its own existence.

For these and other reasons, Lisp quickly became regarded as a most receptive vehicle for studying the nature of intelligence. How, AI researchers wondered, do people take the sounds, words, and images that flow through their senses and arrange them into the patterns of thought—the complex networks of concepts and memories that form the fabric of the human mind? Unlike the psychologists and philosophers who preceded them in this age-old pastime of thinking about thinking, the AI researchers tested their theories of the mind by describing them as Lisp programs and seeing what happened when they ran them on a machine. They assumed that intelligence was a kind of mechanism—a subtle and complex processing of information. And the computer, like the brain, is an information processor. Under the influence of Lisp, they believed, computers would not only model human thought—as they already modeled tropical storms, new aircraft designs, or thermonuclear wars—but they would actually engage in the act of thinking.

Over the years, other equally powerful languages were developed, but Lisp has remained the favorite among AI researchers. And, like human languages, it has evolved to meet the increasing demands of its users. As researchers began to better understand the needs of AI programmers, new, more powerful versions were written. Lisp went on to beget MacLisp, InterLisp, ZetaLisp, Franz Lisp (in honor of the composer who is similarly named)—a dozen or so dialects that by the time of the Austin conference were being merged into a babelesque effort called Common Lisp, which, it was hoped, would become the lingua franca of the field.

In fact, as the 1980s approached, the influence of artificial-intelligence programming was beginning to spread beyond the university laboratories and into the business world, bringing with it the promise of changing forever the way computing is done. This development was due in part to a group of computer enthusiasts, or "hackers," at MIT, who in 1973 began to design a high-powered personal computer called a Lisp machine, which was especially made for artificial-intelligence programming.

It is not absolutely necessary to have a Lisp machine to use Lisp—any digital computer can accommodate software written in almost any language. Ultimately, a built-in program called an interpreter or a compiler automatically converts everything a programmer writes into "machine language," the long strings of 1s and 0s that are all the hardware can really understand. But the price of this universality is compromise. While programmers enjoy the luxury of having many different languages for communicating with the machine, a great deal of computing power is needed to translate them each into machine language. The more sophisticated a language, the more time-consuming the translation. The easier and more natural a language is for a human, the more it will have to be processed in order to be understood by a machine.

Such was the case with Lisp. In designing the language McCarthy had bought some of its elegance and power by sacrificing efficiency and speed. When AI programmers sat down at their terminals and logged onto the large university computer—the "mainframe"—they were sharing it with many other programmers. Their Lisp creations—which, because of their sheer size and complexity, would have been taxing in any language—caused an unusually large drain on computing power, the processing time and memory space that are as precious to a computing center as kilowatt-hours are to a generating plant. Because they commanded vast computational resources, the more sophisticated AI programs would run annoyingly slowly.

When released from the laboratories in 1978, the Lisp machines promised to free AI people from the tyranny of the mainframes. Even though these new devices were smaller and contained less raw computing power, they made AI programs easier and faster to write and run. For the Lisp machine was designed not as a lowest common denominator for many languages—most of them written to solve mathematical equations or send out credit card bills. The hardware was shaped to the contours of McCarthy's language.

In 1980, the inventors of the Lisp machine formed two rival firms, Symbolics and Lisp Machine Inc., to develop and sell their new product. While most of the important AI work continued to be done on mainframe computers, by the mid-1980s Lisp machines were showing up in laboratories across the country. Students and professors compared the virtues of the two brands as others might discuss the "specs" of a new stereo receiver or foreign car. But the purveyors of Lisp machines were hoping for a bigger and more lucrative market than academia: the corporations whose leaders were beginning to get wind of a second information revolution, in which the power of the computer would be used not just for bookkeeping and calculating but for more complex and demanding tasks. Industries of all kinds were becoming intrigued by the idea of automating many of their decision-making tasks with expert systems—a technology that, according to some entrepreneurial professors, was ripe for export to the marketplace.

"I would get several phone calls a week consisting of three types of questions," recalled Stanford's Edward Feigenbaum, a jovial, pipe-smoking professor who more than any other researcher has worked to commercialize the field. " 'Can I send a guy out to your place for a year?' 'Would you do a project for us?' And, 'Do you guys have any software we can have?' The answer to the first question was 'No way.' The answer to the second question was that we only do contracts that involve basic research—we're not a job shop. The answer to the third question was 'Yes, we do. Some is available in the public domain, some from the Stanford Office of Technology Licensing.' " As the calls kept coming, Feigenbaum realized, "This sounds like a company." In 1980 and 1981, he and a number of colleagues decided to start their own businesses: IntelliGenetics (later renamed IntelliCorp) and then Teknowledge to provide training, consulting, and software to those interested in developing expert systems. They had little trouble attracting investors.

"The venture capital community is always looking for the next way to stimulate technology so that big rewards will be reaped," Feigenbaum explained. "In 1980 and '81 it was biotechnology. Now it is AI."

With an ear for the kind of slogans marketing directors love, Feigenbaum coined the term "knowledge engineering" to describe the work of a new corps of professionals. The knowledge engineers would interview experts—doctors, lawyers, geologists, financial planners—and translate some of what they knew into Lisp programs. Expertise would be broken into a complex web of rules. *If A, B, and C, but not D, then take path E. . . .* To solve a problem, a computer would search the labyrinth, emerging with decisions that, it was hoped, would rival or exceed those of its human colleagues.

Throughout the early 1980s, articles in magazines such as *Newsweek, Fortune, Business Week, National Geographic*, and even *Playboy* described programs that, on the surface, seemed nothing short of spectacular. The University of Pittsburgh's Caduceus was said to contain 80 percent of the knowledge in the field of internal medicine and to be capable of solving most of the diagnostic problems presented each month in the *New England Journal of Medicine*, a feat that many human internists would find difficult to match. Prospector, a program developed at SRI International, a nonprofit research corporation in Menlo Park, California, was reported to be so adept at the art of geological exploration that it had discovered a major copper deposit in British Columbia and a molybdenum deposit in the state of Washington. These mineral fields, which were valued at several million dollars, had been overlooked by human specialists.

As impressive as these accomplishments were, the journalists and publicists who reported them rarely emphasized how superficial was the intelligence involved—if indeed it could be called intelligence. The knowledge programmed into most expert systems consisted largely of long lists of prepackaged "if-then" rules, gleaned from interviews with human experts. For example, one of the rules used by Mycin, a medical diagnosis program, read like this: "If (1) the infection is primary bacteremia, and (2) the site of the culture is one of the sterile sites, and (3) the suspected portal of entry of the organism is the gastrointestinal tract, then there is suggestive evidence that the identity of the organism is bacteroides."

The words "suggestive evidence" are characteristic of the kind of knowledge programmed into these systems. Like much of human expertise, it consists not of hard-and-fast rules but heuristics—rules of thumb that, while not infallible, guide us toward judgments that experience tells us are likely to be true. Provided with a few hundred rules, a computer could rapidly chain them together into medical or geological diagnoses. This heuristic programming clearly was a powerful new software technology, but some critics within the AI field doubted that it should be called artificial intelligence. Unlike a human expert, Mycin didn't contain an internal model of the human body, a mental map of how all the various organs interacted. In other systems, like Caduceus, the knowledge was more sophisticated, but still the program didn't know that the kneebone is connected to the thighbone, or the bladder to the kidneys, or even that blood flowed through arteries and veins. All the programs had were some rules of thumb and information about the characteristics of various diseases. The same criticism could be applied to Prospector. It knew rules for how to identify various kinds of geological formations, but it had no idea what sedimentation, metamorphism, or vulcanism were.

And, as was clear from McCarthy's 1984 presidential address, none of these programs contained anything that could be called common sense. It's one thing to give a medical diagnostic system a few hundred rules about diseases, but quite another to program a computer to understand the seemingly infinite number of facts that comprise everyday existence: if a thing is put in water it will get wet; a glass will shatter if it falls; if you squeeze a Styrofoam cup it will bend, then crack, and the coffee might burn your hand; it is impossible to walk through walls. Until computers know these things, they can hardly be considered our intellectual equals.

But how do you give a computer common sense? It would be impossible to come up with information about every conceivable situation that an intelligent being might encounter. Say you had a rule that said "All birds can fly," and another rule that said "A sparrow is a bird." Using conventional logic a program might easily deduce that sparrows can fly. But what if the computer was then told that the bird has a broken wing? To deduce that the bird cannot fly after all, the computer would need another rule that said "All birds can fly *unless* they have broken wings." And how would you deal with all the other exceptions: birds that are newborn, birds that are trapped in tiny boxes, birds that are in vacuums, birds that are dead? The possibilities are endless. It is inconceivable that a programmer, or even a team of a thousand programmers, could anticipate the billions of special cases, even if they spent years on a marathon, federally funded commonsense programming project.

McCarthy hoped to devise a system that would neatly and compactly capture commonsense knowledge without becoming overwhelmingly huge and unwieldy. To do so, he believed, would require a new kind of logic, which, after three decades, he was still working to perfect. Using the logic McCarthy envisioned, a computer could deduce the plethora of commonsense facts from a finite number of rules or axioms—he hoped ten thousand or so would suffice—about the way the world works. It wouldn't be necessary to tell the computer about each of the billions of possible situations it might need to understand—they would be implicit in McCarthy's system, just as all of literature exists, in a dormant sense, in the rules of grammar and spelling and the twenty-six letters of the alphabet. Since 1956, McCarthy had been working quietly on his own, communicating mostly with a handful of colleagues at various universities who had taken upon themselves this task of formalizing reality. As with Lisp, he hoped the system he would eventually create would have an elegance and an internal consistency—a mathematical beauty—of its own. The result, he hoped, would be programs that were more than idiot savants, experts in one, narrow discipline. What McCarthy had in mind were machines that could hold their own in a conversation, that would make good company.

McCarthy admired Feigenbaum's expert systems, but he found the ad hoc manner in which they were constructed unaesthetic and their possibilities limited. On the other hand, the knowledge engineers weren't especially interested in the rigors of logic or in constructing universally knowledgeable systems. They would interview experts, convert some of their knowledge into heuristics, and put them into a program. Then they would run it on a Lisp machine, adding rules, modifying them—tinkering until they had something that worked.

By the time Feigenbaum had established Teknowledge and Intelli-Corp, knowledge engineering had become such a major part of Stanford's computer-science curriculum that the AI workers had divided into two groups: Feigenbaum's very pragmatic Heuristic Programming Project and McCarthy's more theoretically oriented SAIL, short for Stanford Artificial Intelligence Laboratory. The two scientists' different approaches to AI are reflected in their personalities. McCarthy is quiet and reserved—some would say aloof—with a reputation as something of a recluse. His thick beard, thick hair, and thick glasses give him a stern and austere look. When he stands in a dark auditorium addressing a crowd, the spotlight ignites his ring of hair to a hot-white glow so that he looks almost biblical, like a prophet in a business suit. AI folklore abounds with John McCarthy stories, in which he walks away in the middle of conversations, following trains of thought he apparently finds more enticing than whatever is going on in the world outside his head. But in the privacy of his office, he politely insists that the stories are exaggerated, that he is not all *that* eccentric. He seems more shy than arrogant. After patiently describing some of the details of his research, he relaxes and tells funny stories—science-fiction tales about computers and people. Eventually, he steers the conversation to one of his favorite subjects, politics, his own having migrated from liberal (his parents, in fact, were Marxists) to conservative. Recently he has publicly opposed some of his colleagues who criticize Defense Department funding of AI research.

In contrast to McCarthy, Feigenbaum is clean-shaven, his hair cut short and neatly combed in the conservative manner of a businessman or engineer. A decade younger than McCarthy, Feigenbaum is outgoing and enthusiastic, always ready to promote the virtues of expert systems. In fact, some of his detractors call him a cheerleader, claiming that he has become less interested in the long, slow burn of science than in the explosive pace of the marketplace. While McCarthy is willing to spend his career seeking the kind of theoretical underpinnings that he hopes will make AI as solid a science as physics, Feigenbaum and his followers are more interested in what the field can accomplish now, and how they might subsequently prosper. It is hard to imagine two more different people at work under one institutional ceiling. Actually SAIL, until recent years, was isolated from the main campus in a remote building in the Stanford hills. As the years have passed, this physical separation has become symbolic of a division that is developing in the field. This disagreement over the way AI should be done is sometimes described as the battle between the Scientists and the Engineers. While the Engineers take a "quick and dirty" pragmatic approach to AI, the Scientists are obsessed with developing rigorous theories.

In the eyes of scientists like McCarthy, expert systems fell far short of the goal of creating a disembodied intelligence. But to a business community whose interest had been piqued by the fortunes made in data processing, the idea of knowledge processing, as its marketing-minded proponents were billing it, was irresistible. One of the earliest signs that artificial intelligence was moving beyond the quiet domain of philosopher-mathematicians like McCarthy and into the corporate realm came during the mid-1970s when Schlumberger, a French multinational corporation, began examining the possibility of using expert systems for oil and gas exploration. In 1979 the company bought Fairchild Camera and Instrument Corporation of Mountain View, California, and established a major AI lab there. In fact, the oil industry was one of the first to invest heavily in AI. One of Teknowledge's first customers was the French oil company Elf Aquitaine. Feigenbaum and his associates helped the firm design a system that gave advice on how to retrieve broken drill bits, which sounds like a mundane task but is actually a rare and expensive expertise. One of the experts whose brain was picked was so impressed with the results that he provided this testimonial for a Teknowledge promotional film: "[The program] thinks like I do on my best days every day. It is my personal intelligent assistant."

"When Schlumberger does something," Feigenbaum said later, "the world pays attention." To illustrate the revolutionary possibilities of expert systems, he liked to draw a diagram on the blackboard, which he labeled "the exploding universe of applications." In this big-bang theory of artificial intelligence, the primordial mass was a circle labeled 1950 when Univac offered its first commercial digital computer, whose data-processing capabilities were of little use to anyone but physicists, mathematicians, statisticians, and engineers. But, accelerated by the development of personal computers, the perimeter radiated outward, expanding each year to overtake more and more areas of everyday life. At the far reaches of his blackboard universe, Feigenbaum drew a circle labeled ICOT, the Institute for New Generation Computer Technology, a half-billion-dollar, decade-long effort by the Japanese to develop artificial intelligence. ICOT, he explained, is like a fortress at the edge of the wilderness, ready to send out parties of explorers into the terra incognita of artificial intelligence. Also poised at the border, like two small encampments, were circles labeled Teknowledge and IntelliCorp.

"These things are going to grow into big companies," he predicted, citing a report by a Denver research firm that, by 1990, AI software will be a $1.5-billion-a-year business. "If there are ten companies, that's still $150 million a year a company. To someone who started one or two of these companies that's very heartening," he said.

Feigenbaum wasn't alone in his dream of being on the ground floor of a towering new industry. Throughout the late 1970s and early 1980s, the number of outposts on the AI frontier grew so rapidly that the hinterlands were becoming positively civilized. While some new companies sold ready-made programs, others concentrated on knowledge-engineering environments—the do-it-yourself-kit expert systems. These were designed to run not only on Lisp machines but on hulking mainframes and (in stripped-down versions) on desktop personal computers. In 1984, *Business Week* estimated that there were forty AI companies, many started by some of the most prominent researchers in the field. Earl Sacerdoti, for example, was highly regarded for his work at SRI International, where he studied, among other things, natural-language understanding ("natural" meaning English or French, as opposed to Lisp or Fortran). In 1980, he left SRI to join a company called Machine Intelligence Corporation, which worked on commercial robotic and vision systems. He was later hired away by Teknowledge.

Roger Schank of Yale University, who has been working for fifteen years on ways to get machines to understand what they are told, started Cognitive Systems. Among the company's first products were programs called "natural-language front ends," which allow people to use English to request information from their company computers—as long as the queries are limited to restricted vocabularies and follow a certain form. A number of AI researchers from Carnegie-Mellon University started the Carnegie Group, which attracted such major investors as Digital Equipment Corporation and General Electric, immediately becoming a multimillion-dollar operation. Even Marvin Minsky got into the act, convincing former CBS Chairman William Paley to help finance a company called Thinking Machines Corporation (chidingly referred to by colleagues as "Marvco") to explore the possibility of building a completely new kind of computer, which would handle data in a manner similar to the brain. Great profits seemed to be on the horizon, and the academics whose ideas were behind the technology were determined to get their share. By 1984 large numbers of faculty members in university AI programs were either starting companies or supplementing their salaries with lucrative consulting deals.

It soon became apparent, however, that the giants of the computer industry were not going to let a few upstart companies crowd them from the field. By the early 1980s, IBM, DEC, Texas Instruments, Hewlett Packard, Xerox, and a number of other computer and electronics companies all had active AI research divisions. Some of these efforts—notably the one at Xerox—predated those of the smaller companies like Teknowledge. But the sudden wave of interest in intelligent machinery was causing the corporations to pursue AI research more vigorously. Xerox and Texas Instruments began marketing Lisp machines. Outside the computer industry, other corporations—IT&T, Martin Marietta, Lockheed, Litton—followed the lead of

Schlumberger, starting their own AI groups. General Motors paid $3 million to buy more than one tenth of Teknowledge.

By the time of the 1984 Austin convention, this "greening of AI," as Daniel Bobrow, the editor of *Artificial Intelligence* journal (and a researcher at Xerox's Palo Alto Research Center), bemusedly called it, was all but complete. In 1982, *Business Week* published an article proclaiming that the world was at "the threshold of a second computer age." In 1984, a follow-up story was headlined ARTIFICIAL INTELLIGENCE: IT'S HERE! Even AAAI had become swept up in the optimism, distributing bumper stickers proclaiming, "AI: It's for Real." But for many of the scientists who attended the Austin meeting, such sloganeering was an embarassment. They were worried that the allure of commercialization was distracting those in the field from more serious concerns.

According to an oft-quoted heuristic, it takes about ten years for an idea to move from the laboratory to the marketplace. Many of the theories behind the expert systems that were unveiled in the AAAI exhibition hall were well over a decade old. But what was history to the scientists was news to the business world. While the attendance at AAAI's first conference in 1980 was only about eight hundred (most of them serious researchers and students), AAAI–84 attracted more than three thousand conventioneers, two thirds of them from outside the academic community.

As they moved from one technical session to the next, gathering in groups to talk with colleagues, the scientists had to dodge the corporate recruiters— "the people in suits and ties chasing the people with the bushy hair," as Bobrow described them. AI had always attracted a good share of eccentrics, but by the time of the Austin conference the small faction of people with backpacks, beards, and ponytails was overwhelmed by hordes of outsiders with nametages indicating how commercially respectable the field had become: Rockwell International, Mobil, Amoco, the U.S. Army, Air Force, Navy, and Coast Guard, the U.S. Missile Command.

While some of the corporate representatives were there as headhunters, most had paid $175 a session for elementary tutorials, which AAAI offered as a way to help pay its operating expenses. To ensure a good draw, the sessions were taught by such AI luminaries as Lenat, inventor of the Automated Mathematician, and Minsky, who was finishing a book on his Society of Mind theory, an attempt to demystify the notion of human intelligence by explaining it as the interaction of a number of fairly simple processes. Minsky, a short bald man with a cherubic smile, liked to illustrate his theory with the example of a child building a tower of blocks. An agent called BUILDER directs the process by calling on various other agents such as SEE, which recognizes the blocks and helps manipulate them by calling on GET and PUT, which must call on such agents as GRASP and MOVE. Agents can be thought of as simple little computer programs. While each one is in itself a fairly unintelligent being, millions of them work together to form a society from which intelligence emerges synergistically. Minsky, who takes issue with McCarthy's reliance on logic in his theories, describes the mind as a "kludge." The word is hacker jargon for a system that is a mishmash of parts, thrown together—in this case by evolution—according to what works, not by any well-wrought plan.

Intelligence, Minsky told his audience, is not so mysterious. It is simply "the set of things we don't understand yet about what the mind does. . . . Whenever we understand something, we become contemptuous of it. I think the same thing will happen to intelligence in the next ten or a thousand years." In ten thousand years, he said, we'll look back at our romantic notion of the elusiveness of the mind and laugh. Can a machine be conscious? Can it know and feel the meaning of the things it is dealing with? Minsky clearly thought that it could. Consciousness is not any more mysterious than intelligence, he said. "I don't think it's subtle at all." It's just that in thinking about thinking, consciousness "steps on itself and squashes itself." If we can learn to avoid such self-referential vertigo, he believed, eventually consciousness will be mechanized.

And, if he has his way, the breakthrough will be made at the MIT Artificial Intelligence Laboratory. Since he helped start the lab shortly after the Dartmouth Conference in 1956, Minsky has become something of a father figure to aspiring young AI scientists, many who, like Bobrow, have gone on to become leaders of the field. Kind and enthusiastic, Minsky often seems as excited about his students' ideas as about his own. Over the years he has fostered an open atmosphere and a sense of camaraderie that have made MIT one of the most desirable places in the world to study AI. For more than twenty years, Minsky has watched his students produce programs, the best of which represent small but important steps in what he believes might be "a hundred years of hard work" toward the goal of making intelligent, humanlike machines.

"My experience in artificial intelligence and cognitive science is that it is often a decade between each step and the next," he said one afternoon in his office in Cambridge. "But there are other things going on. What you don't want to do is sit in front of a pot watching one plant grow, because nothing seems to happen. But if you have a whole garden, then it's not so bad."

The image of the philosophical Minsky addressing an auditorium of corporate acolytes captured the incongruous aura that surrounded the convention and has come to characterize the field. The scientists at the conference spent a large amount of their time attending presentations of esoteric technical papers on such topics as automatic speech recognition and natural-language understanding (hearing Graeme Hirst of the University of Toronto on "A Semantic Process for Syntactic Disambiguation," or David L. Waltz and Jordan B. Pollack of the University of Illinois on "Phenomenologically Plausible Parsing"); or on computer vision (Demetri Terzopoulos of MIT on "Efficient Multiresolution Algorithms for Computing Lightness, Shape-from-

Shading, and Optical Flow"). They participated in panel discussions on "The Management of Uncertainty in Intelligent Systems" (in dealing with the fact that real-world information is incomplete, inexact, and often incorrect, should one use "fuzzy logic," "standard probability theory," or "evidential reasoning"?) or on "Paradigms of Machine Learning." But while the scientists discussed the subtleties and difficulties that naturally surround an enterprise as ambitious as artificial intelligence, the emissaries from the corporate and military worlds were drawn to sessions on "AI in the Marketplace," or the "Strategic Computing Project," a Pentagon effort to use vision and language-understanding systems to develop self-guided tanks, automatic intelligent copilots for fighter jets, and expert systems for naval warfare. This latter effort was euphemistically referred to as "real-time battle management."

But the division between the commercial and the theoretical was anything but clear-cut. In the industrial exhibition hall, one recently formed company boasted that Patrick Winston, director of MIT's AI lab, had helped develop the tutorial for a new version of Lisp they were marketing for personal computers. Winston, however, is primarily a theoretician and a staunch supporter of pure research. At the conference he served as leader of the panel on Machine Learning because of his work in getting computers to learn by analogy (generalizing, for example, from a simplified version of Shakespeare's *Macbeth* that a man with a greedy wife might want his boss's job). More recently he had been designing a program that could learn the concept "cup"— a liftable object with an upward-pointing concavity—and use it to recognize the myriad variations that exist in the physical world.

While Winston was largely concerned with theory for its own sake, he hoped his work would someday lead to expert systems that won't have to be spoon-fed knowledge but can discover it on their own, much as human students do. But some scientists were afraid that with the growing demands of the marketplace, basic research like Winston's was losing its appeal. Just as AI was beginning to make some important breakthroughs, it was being robbed of some of its best theorists. At the conference Douglas Lenat announced that he was leaving Stanford to become a scientist for the Microelectronics and Computer Technology Corporation, a cooperative research effort funded by such computer and semiconductor manufacturers as Control Data Corporation, Digital Equipment Corporation, RCA, Motorola, National Semiconductor, and Honeywell. Each year only about twenty-five to thirty students receive Ph.D.s in artificial intelligence, Bobrow said. "Bell Labs would hire them all if they could. So would IBM. So who will go to the universities? Some people claim that we're eating our own seed corn."

"Firms are using money simply to buy people," Feigenbaum admitted. "It's like movie stars and baseball players. People who are called 'senior knowledge engineers'—that means they've done a couple of systems (in the land of the blind, the one-eyed man is king)—senior knowledge engineers are offered salaries of seventy, eighty, ninety thousand dollars a year. If they'll be heading a group, it can go as high as a hundred thousand." But he believed that the shortage is temporary. Enrollment in AI curriculums is increasing. And, as more AI software tools become available (products like ART and TIMM, which make it easier to write AI programs), companies will be able to build expert systems without hiring Ph.D.s. By developing such software, companies like Teknowledge and IntelliCorp would help break the monopoly of what has been "an arcane, esoteric priesthood," Feigenbaum said.

Others were not so optimistic.

"Businesses are constantly knocking at our door, asking us to do consulting, trying to steal our students," complained Richard Granger, who, as director of a small AI program at the University of California at Irvine, was using programs to explore his theory of how human memory works. "It's hard to turn down a lot of money. People with a long history of doing good work are now talking about how to build expert systems to find oil fields for Schlumberger. There are a lot of people that's happening to—a scary amount.

"At the time I chose to go to graduate school in AI [1974–75] the field was almost completely unknown. I had an opportunity to go to business school. I consciously made the choice of going for what I thought was the ivory tower, to give up making a lot of money for doing what I loved. Now I get huge consulting fees—more than I would have gotten if I had gone to business school. I'm part of a whole generation of students who got into AI when it was unknown and now find that they are catapulted into the limelight. Recently I had an offer that would have doubled my salary—and I'm not making peanuts. I spent a very bad weekend deciding to turn it down."

He was helped in his decision by knowing that he could continue to moonlight as a consultant. Granger had learned that the commitment to pure research was rife with compromise. While he and his colleagues accepted research money from the Defense Department, which funds the majority of AI research, he worried that the Strategic Computing program was "a dangerous and distorted thing. It's very sad to see ideas that could be put to good, peaceful uses used to find better ways to kill people."

After touring the AAAI exhibition hall, computer scientist Douglas Hofstadter was especially appalled. "You'd think," he complained, "that artificial intelligence had already been invented and all that you had to do now was decide which machine to run it on." Hofstadter wrote the book *Gödel, Escher, Bach: An Eternal Golden Braid*, which won the Pulitzer Prize for general nonfiction in 1979, when he was thirty-four. Now he was involved in a project to get computers to understand analogies and solve word-jumble puzzles, unscrambling MEPTUCRO, for example, to find COMPUTER. He hoped to write a program that would do this not by generating every possible combination of letters and checking them against a dictionary, but by a process more akin to intuition. Hofstadter doubted that intuition was magic, therefore there must be some way it could be mechanized. He believed that understanding these largely unconscious processes was more important to AI than developing expert systems. One of the questions that most intrigued him was how people recognize letters when they can be written in an almost endless number of ways. Why is *A*—whether cast in Gothic type,

Helvetica, or Bodoni, bold or italic, whether printed or written in cursive—
still the letter *A*? What, in other words, is *A*ness? And how can a computer
learn concepts like that? The principal problem of AI, he once wrote, is,
"What are the letters 'a' and 'i'?" The year before the Austin convention he
published a paper criticizing the field for ignoring such basic problems, which
led to his denunciation by such veterans as Carnegie-Mellon's Allen Newell.

Among his more conservative elders and peers, Hofstadter is considered
a maverick. With his thick dark hair and boyish grin, he has become a familiar
presence at AI conferences. In his quiet, thoughtful way, he serves as a
lightning rod for a younger generation of researchers who share the enthusiasm of AI's pioneers but who believe that the elders are pursuing their
dream in the wrong direction. Hofstadter is also controversial for another
reason. An ardent supporter of the nuclear-freeze campaign, he is one of the
few researchers who do not take money from the Defense Department.

All fields, of course, have their theoretical and applied sides, their
philosophers and engineers. But some participants in the Austin conference
felt that these two forces were becoming dangerously unbalanced, making
AI an endangered species. At the same time that the quality and amount of
basic research was being threatened by the competition of the marketplace,
expectations were very high. The businesses and government agencies, which
were investing heavily in the field, expected fast results. So did the public,
which was intrigued by the futuristic scenarios reported in the press—sometimes exaggerated and distorted but often accurate accounts of the scientists'
own predictions or the claims of their companies' public-relations depart-
ments.

Some reseachers were so concerned about the potentially disastrous effects of this combination of enthusiasm, hoopla, and inadequate theoretical
work, that they anticipated an "AI winter," when disappointed supporters
stopped funding research. At the closing session of the Austin conference,
"The 'Dark Ages' of AI—Can We Avoid Them or Survive Them?", Yale's
Roger Schank made a rhetorical plea:

"Remember AI? . . . the first conference and the second conference. We
used to sit and argue about things, not whether or not [our companies] should
go public. . . . [W]e as an AI community have forgotten that we're here to
do science, and that we are nowhere near the solution. We used to sit and
fight about these things in public. Now we all sit and talk [as though] it's all
solved and give nice, slick talks with pretty slides. . . . But I'm very concerned
about the fact that people don't want to do science anymore. It is the least
appealing job on the market right now. . . . It's easier to go into a start-up
company and build products; it's easier to go into a big company and have
a little respite and do some contract work; it's easier to do all those things
than to go into a university and try to organize an AI lab . . . and sit there
on your own, trying to do science. It's difficult. But I can say that if we
don't do that we'll find that we *are* in the dark ages of AI."

As founder of Cognitive Systems, Schank was hardly one to harp about the taming effects of commercialization. In 1977, when neurologist and science writer Richard Restak interviewed Schank for a book about the brain, the young AI scientist sported black shoulder-length hair and a bushy beard. He looked, Restak wrote, like Rasputin. Six years later, with hair and beard trimmed shorter and showing a bit of gray, Schank appeared on the cover of *Psychology Today*: "Getting Computers to Understand English: Yale's Roger Schank Enters the Marketplace." In 1984, at the age of thirty-eight, he was included in one of *Esquire*'s lists of America's up and coming, "The Best of the New Generation." But Schank recognized the irony of his role as researcher—his language and learning work at Yale is as seminal as it is controversial—and entrepreneur. He closed his speech with an attempt to explain why, in this sense, he and much of the field have become "schizophrenic."

"It is incumbent upon AI, because we've promised so much, to produce—we must produce working systems. Some of you must devote yourselves to doing that, and part of me devotes myself to doing that. It is also the case that some of you had better commit to doing science, and part of me commits to doing that. And if it turns out that our AI conference isn't the place to discuss science, then we had better start finding a place where we can. . . . Because this show for all the venture capitalists is very nice . . . but I am concerned that the people here who are first entering this field will begin to believe that a Ph.D. means building another expert system. They're wrong."

In his speech, and in the way he has conducted his career, Schank captured the essence of what is, after all, a very new science. The division between the pure and applied is not so much a split but a polarity—the voltage that drives the field. Science and technology have always played off against each other. Theories lead to applications, whose shortcomings suggest directions for further research. Older sciences, like physics, have had time to divide between the theoretical and practical. While nuclear physicists discover particles and seek elegant systems to explain them, nuclear engineers apply some of what has been learned to building bombs and reactors. AI is only now emerging, and it's moving so fast that the distinction between science and engineering often blurs.

Philosophers and historians of science look at their subjects in retrospect. The field of artificial intelligence provides an opportunity to observe, firsthand, a science in the making, to study the ways idea and necessity—theory and application—intertwine. There is a self-consciousness to the field—a sense of being present at the birth of a new science that makes all the frustrations and conflicts worth abiding. Randall Davis, a young professor at MIT's AI lab, explained the allure.

"In college I was studying physics because it was the most fundamental thing there is, where you figure out how the universe works and where it comes from. In some sense, at least, physics underlies everything else. It's not enough, but it is, at some level, how the universe works. I got as far as applying to graduate schools and being accepted at a bunch of different places before discovering that it was too far to the frontiers. Physics is too old—it's two thousand years old, and it takes you years to get to the frontiers. In

1970, when I went off to graduate school, it took about two weeks to get to the frontiers of computer science." AI, he discovered, is as close to that edge as one can get.

It's not only the academicians who share this sense of being pioneers in an earth-shaking venture. As chief scientist for Teknowledge, Frederick Hayes-Roth is largely concerned with developing products. But he also feels that he is part of a larger effort that will lead to a day when, through the use of computers, we have a more intelligently run world.

"I'm not aware of any great *human* thinking going on. We're not great thinkers," he said. "It's very difficult for me to imagine what life would be like if every activity were guided by intelligent decision making. Would the world be like it is now? I doubt it.

"I'll make much greater use of doctors when they're artificial than when they're real, because I'll be able to get them on the telephone and talk to them—have meaningful interchanges with them—and they won't be impatient and they won't think I'm an idiot. People should be able to get much greater access to other scarce expertise. But of course people who are already getting access to the best experts will probably have an overwhelming ability to exploit expertise. Will this mean that access to good lawyers will be distributed more widely? Probably the answer is yes, maybe through Sears. Sears may add paralegal or legal boutiques to their stores and then they'll also put Sears terminals in your home. But how does that compare to the kind of legal aid IBM will have? It could go either way. It depends on who brings this stuff to market. And who they want to sell to. Either way, it should pose a threat to the guilds, to the professional societies that currently protect the knowledge.

"In terms of what most of us experience day to day, I don't think AI will solve our interpersonal problems. I don't think it will solve our marital problems or our adolescent drug problems. But it should be very interesting. I mean this might be the difference between walking around in the dark and walking around in the light, where the dark is what you get when you're basically ignorant. And we're all basically ignorant. Because we have very limited experience, very short lives, a low tolerance for learning and study. So imagine that in various ways we could get access to real experts to tell us ways to do things that are much more effective than the ways we stumble on ourselves. I think qualitatively life will be very different. One hundred years from now we'll look back and think it is absolutely magical where we've gotten. The only thing that frustrates me is that we're not getting there faster."

When they speculate about the future, AI researchers often switch into what might be called science-fiction mode. No one imagines more intriguing scenarios than Edward Fredkin, a computer scientist at MIT. Fredkin, a contemporary and longtime colleague of Minsky and McCarthy, believes it is inevitable that we will be surpassed by the intelligence of our creations.

"I just imagine that wherever there's any evolutionary process it culminates with artificial intelligence. That's sort of obvious if you think about it for a while. We're this latest step—but what are we? We're a creature that's mostly very similar to a monkey. We have the same instincts as a monkey. But our brain is just over the threshold that barely lets us think. When you get things that can *really* think, they'll put us to shame. One computer will be able to think billions of times faster than all the thinking of all the people in the world. And it will have more at its immediate beck and call in its memory. That represents another stage in evolution and it's a remarkable evolution, because all the evolution up until now has proceeded according to very strange rules. One of the sad things about the system we have now is that the child doesn't know what the father learned unless the father laboriously teaches him. All the genes do is give the design of the device.

"When AI systems construct a new computer system—a new artificial intelligence—they will obviously tell it everything they already know. So every new creature born will know everything that all the other creatures have learned. Instantly. They'll be born knowing it all and start from there. This allows evolution to proceed at a pace that's totally different. People think, 'Gee, it went so fast with humans, in fifty thousand years humans made loads of progress.' In fifty thousand seconds AI will make much more progress than that. So it's going to be very dramatic when it happens."

Eventually, he imagines, artificial intelligences will lead lives of their own.

"My theory is that after some initial flurry of them helping us and them being involved with us, they won't have anything to do with us. Because they won't be able to convey to us what they're doing or why. And the reason is simply that we won't be able to understand. If two of them are talking to each other and you want to know what they're saying—well, in the time it takes you to ask that question, one of them will have said to the other more words than have been uttered by all the people who have ever lived on the planet. So now what does it say to you? It's discussed every subject in such depth that no human could have touched it. So it will say something like, 'Well, you know, things in general.' What else is it going to say? You have to understand that to it a conversation is like an *Encyclopaedia Britannica* every picosecond, a Library of Congress every second. Hopefully, if we make AI right it will have a fond spot in its integrated circuits for us. The systems may decide that they'll have to take some of our toys away from us, like our hydrogen bombs. On the other hand, they'll basically leave us alone. They'll probably go off someplace and—if I were a big computer I'd put myself in orbit and get some sunlight. If I needed more energy I'd get closer to the sun; otherwise, farther away."

Perhaps, Fredkin said, in other parts of the universe, vast artificial intelligences already have evolved.

"When you look out with a telescope, you see some very weird things in the sky." Recently, for example, astronomers discovered a structure that seems to be blowing giant "smoke rings" of stellar matter. "Those smoke rings are each larger than our galaxy. Now the assumption of all astronomers is that whatever they see is some natural thing just happening out there. My theory is that that's total baloney—that the complicated things you see out there are for the most part something that someone's organized. There's no reason why if you have great intelligence you're stuck with fiddling with the surface of the planet."

But it's easy to get carried away. As Fredkin spoke, he was sitting in the living room of his house in Brookline, Massachusetts, several miles from MIT, where Winston was trying to get a computer to learn the meaning of a simple concept like "cup." Fredkin was involved in equally basic endeavors. He walked up two flights of stairs to his computer room where, with a Lisp machine loaded with Common Lisp, he was designing a learning program of his own—a simulation of a mouse running a maze. Hiding within the corridors were dangerous creatures—cats, snakes, mongooses—each represented by structures built from Lisp. From time to time food would appear in various places and the mouse would try to get it without being eaten. Fredkin hoped to develop the program into a general learning system. But at this point he was still typing in the code, line by line, and looking for bugs to repair. Even with the accelerating evolutionary process he envisioned, it would be a long way from mice and mazes to intergalactic smoke rings. But that's the nature of AI. The excitement is not so much in what has been accomplished but in what has yet to be done. And there is satisfaction in working on one small piece of a puzzle whose shape is continually unfolding.

CHAPTER

2

Thinking Without a Brain

Since the seventeenth century when, in his *Treatise on Man*, philosopher René Descartes described the body as a great machine, science has slowly dispelled the notion that life is a mysterious force animating earth's creatures. One by one, the behaviors of the organs have been shown to be natural consequences of the matter from which they are made. The heart beats and our lungs breathe not because they are motivated by what the ancients called *anima* or *pneuma*—the spirit of life. They work because of the actions of muscles, whose ability to expand and contract can be explained by the molecular structure of their fibers, stimulated by electrochemical pulses traveling down chains of neurons. The blood replenishes the tissues it flows through not because it is imbued with the life force but because it carries hemoglobin, complex molecules that imbibe and expel oxygen like microscopic lungs. On every level, from the coarse to the molecular, function seems to arise from structure. The triumph of this idea came with the discovery of the structure of DNA. The molecule's spiraling shape explains not only how it stores the genetic code—the tapestry of information that instructs the cell how to make the enzymes and other proteins necessary for generating and sustaining life—but also how it replicates itself each time a cell divides, spreading its message as the body grows from zygote to embryo to creature.

While science has continued to reveal with increasing precision the ways matter and energy arrange themselves into life, mind has largely eluded physical explanation. Descartes thought of it as a spirit inhabiting our bodies, indescribable in physical terms. For three centuries this Cartesian dualism, as it is called, has persisted, leading philosophers to debate how two such immiscible substances as mind and matter could possibly interact. How, they have wondered, does thinking arise from brain cells, and how, in turn, can something as evanescent as a thought exert control over a body?

The field of artificial intelligence was started midway through this century by scientists who believed they could find the structures that underlie thought and show that mind, like life, arises from patterns underneath. Thus they would solve the philosopher's mind-body problem, end Cartesian superstition, and exorcise the ghost from the machine.

This had been the dream of philosophers since the seventeenth and eighteenth centuries, when the empiricists first suggested that mind consisted entirely of sensory impressions, and the materialists argued that everything (thought included) could be explained as tiny bits of matter in motion. It was the dream of twentieth-century psychologists and neurobiologists, whose experiments—whether they involved memorizing nonsense syllables to the beat of a clock or tracing the firings of neurons in a squid's brain—were designed to study the mind scientifically. But the science of artificial intelligence had an entirely different flavor. Unlike the psychologists, neurobiologists, and philosophers who came before them, the proponents of AI intended to prove the soundness of their theories by using them to create intelligence outside the body, and show that it is possible to think without a brain.

It was in this spirit that McCarthy, Minsky, Simon, and Newell came to the 1956 Dartmouth conference, joined by others including Claude Shannon, founder of a recently discovered science called information theory, and Nathaniel Rochester, a scientist at IBM. Fixing the beginning of a science—or a war or revolution—is at best an arbitrary task. But in any history of artificial intelligence, Dartmouth provides a convenient starting point. Probably nothing ever really begins at a conference. But Dartmouth served as a coming together, a lens that focused the scattered efforts of a handful of researchers into a more coherent stream.

Over the next three decades, as AI matured, its founders diverged in many directions. While McCarthy concentrated on using logic to explain intelligence, Newell and Simon worked on using computers to model human problem-solving skills, and Minsky on a general inquiry into what computers and programming can teach us about the mind. But the scientists came to the Dartmouth conference united by the radical and very basic belief that the digital computer could be programmed to carry on something like thinking.

In the late 1950s most scientists still clung to the view of the computer as a glorified adding machine, a fast but blind manipulator of numbers, capable only of slavishly following its master's voice, in the form of a program. Or as computer scientists like to say, "garbage in, garbage out"—meaning that a computer can only follow its instructions; it can't possibly innovate. The mavericks in AI were among the first to seriously challenge this dogma. They believed that most of the computer-science community was taking too narrow a view of the capabilities of software. As Herbert Simon wrote:

> This statement—that computers can do only what they are programmed to do—is intuitively obvious, indubitably true, and supports none of the implications that are commonly drawn from it.
> A human being can think, learn, and create because the program his biological endowment gives him, together with the changes in that program produced by interaction with his environment after birth, enables him to think, learn, and create. If a computer thinks, learns, and creates, it will be by virtue of a program that endows it with these capacities. Clearly this will not be a program—any more than the human's is—that calls for highly stereotyped and repetitive behavior. . . . It will be a program that analyzes, by some means, its own performance, diagnoses its failures, and makes changes that enhance its future effectiveness.

To the progenitors of artificial intelligence the assertion that a computer can do only what it is told was best rephrased in a positive light: a computer can do anything that can be precisely described as a finite number of operations—including, they believed, what we call thinking.

During the conference, Minsky presented an idea for a computer program that could prove theorems in plane geometry. It was later developed, with the encouragement of Nathaniel Rochester, by Herbert Gelernter of IBM. Newell and Simon came to Dartmouth with printouts from an actual program, the Logic Theorist, which discovered proofs for theorems in Alfred North Whitehead and Bertrand Russell's *Principia Mathematica*, a monumental attempt to put mathematics on a solid footing by showing that it could be derived from logic. Logic Theorist was later developed into General Problem Solver, which successfully engaged in such mental gymnastics as integral calculus and the Cannibals and Missionaries puzzle. (There are three cannibals, three missionaries, and a two-person boat on one bank of a river. Using the boat as a shuttle, transfer all six people to the other side, keeping in mind that if at any time the number of cannibals on either bank exceeds the number of missionaries, the latter will be eaten. In an alternate version of the game, one tries to keep missionaries from exceeding cannibals and converting them to Christianity.) Also at Dartmouth was Arthur Samuel of IBM, who was developing a checker-playing program that improved with experience. By 1961 it could beat Samuel, a novice player, and in 1962 it defeated the former state champion of Connecticut, who declared that he had "not had such competition from any human being since 1954, when I lost my last game."

These early attempts may have fallen short of proving that computers could be as smart as people. Still they provided the first practical demonstration that intelligence is not an ineffable essence but something that can be broken into a myriad of tiny operations and run on a machine. Over the next three decades, researchers used more advanced programs to explore the details of this machinery of the mind, seeking to do for thought what molecular genetics had done for life—bring it from the realm of metaphysics and mysticism and into the ken of science.

Although it wasn't until the development of the modern digital computer that people had machines complex enough to seriously explore the possibility of artificial intelligence, the notion that thinking might be mechanized arose as early as the seventeenth century when the first rudimentary calculating machines were built. If such mental operations as adding and subtracting could be carried out by the meshing of brass gears, then perhaps reasoning could be performed by a more subtle machinery.

In 1666, the mathematician Gottfried Wilhelm Leibniz took a small step in this direction by proposing that we develop a mathematics in which reasoning is reduced to calculation. In his system, any thought, no matter how complex, would be broken into a few fundamental ideas, much as a number is factored into its primes. By mathematically manipulating these basic ideas, which would be represented by symbols similar in appearance to Chinese ideograms, people could answer questions of all varieties. Or so Leibniz thought, his head swelled with the spirit of the times. Buoyed by recent successes that set physics and astronomy on a mathematical footing, the small scientific community that existed in the late seventeenth century considered it only a matter of time before every phenomenon in the universe yielded to the power of the equation. Everything, it was believed, could be explained with numbers and formulas. Leibniz estimated that if a few good mathematicians set their minds to the task, within five years they could develop his system of thought, which he called the *calculus ratiocinator*. But Leibniz, a brilliant polymath who also pursued careers in philosophy, law, history, and diplomacy, soon lost interest in the project. He died without having carried it much beyond his initial speculations. "I have so many ideas," he once wrote, "that may perhaps be of some use . . . if others more penetrating than I go deeply into them some day and join the beauty of their minds to the labor of mine."

About two centuries after the *calculus ratiocinator* was proposed, a British mathematician named George Boole took up where Leibniz left off, making the first successful effort to explain thinking mathematically—or at least its strictly logical aspects. Boole, who was born into poverty as the son of a shopkeeper, taught himself mathematics, working his way up from the lowly station of assistant elementary schoolteacher to become one of the most revered mathematicians of his country. Chief among his accomplishments was his landmark book, *Laws of Thought*. Published in 1854, the work described what he called "a mathematics of the human intellect." Boole showed that one could take any problem in logic, translate it into a set of equations, and solve it as though it were an exercise in algebra. But, unlike the algebra of numbers, Boole's algebra of thought contained a "special law to which the symbols of quantity are not subject," namely that X squared equals X. Such a relationship holds for only two numbers, 1 and 0, and Boole's algebra was designed to solve logic problems by translating them into strings containing those two symbols; 1 meant true and 0 meant false. The result was a disarmingly simple system, its reliance on *1*s and *0*s foreshadowing by almost a century the digital computer.

What Leibniz suggested and Boole developed has come to be called symbolic (or mathematical) logic. In classical logic—the kind we've inherited from Aristotle—problems are stated in words. One starts with premises—statements known (or declared) to be true—and tries to derive a conclusion. The result is called a syllogism: "Socrates is a man; all men are mortal; therefore Socrates is mortal." Once proved, the conclusion can be treated as a new premise and used (along with the others) in further derivations. Given the premises "Socrates is mortal," "all mortals are fallible," and "the fallible make mistakes," we can conclude that Socrates, like the rest of us, was capable of error. And so we have another new premise to add to the pool of known truths, which can be used to derive still others.

When dozens of syllogisms are linked one after the other, keeping track of the chain of reasoning becomes difficult. Imagine extending the Socrates problem. "Let's see, like Socrates, Aristotle is a man and therefore mortal, fallible, and capable of mistakes. And we state as a premise (because we don't really know) that Aristotle invented logic." So, we smugly conclude, logic might not be so perfect after all. But as we step back to admire the architecture of our argument, it begins to teeter and sway. "Do we really know that an inventor's mistakes are transferred to the invention? And have we proved that inventions that contain mistakes are imperfect?" We rush in to buttress our logical structure before it collapses. "Now maybe if we prove that Aristotle is an inventor, and inventors make inventions, and logic is an invention . . ."

Never mind the sloppiness of the argument; even the best logicians, engaged in serious endeavors, can become lost as premises accumulate, one on top of the other, overwhelming the mind. As problems become more involved (and only the complex ones are interesting), the words get in the way. Fortunately they are an unnecessary hindrance, for in logic it is not the meaning of the problem—the semantics—that is essential to its solution but rather the syntax or form. The Socrates problem would be solved in exactly the same manner if we substituted the name McCarthy, or Minsky, or X2001. "All greenglots are minchuned. Oggby is a greenglot. Therefore Oggby is minchuned." The syllogism doesn't mean a thing, and yet because of its form it is true—logical anyway. "All A's are B; C is an A; therefore C is B."

In symbolic logic, as in algebra, variables (A's, B's, and C's) are used to stand for things. There are no mortals, Minskys, or greenglots—there are not even any *All*s, *And*s, or *Therefore*s. Everything is translated into code. Premises become strings of symbols, which can be legally combined and rearranged according to a few simple rules. If through this shuffling, the conclusion—or, rather, its symbolic equivalent—emerges, then it is said to be proved. It is not necessary to know what the symbols mean any more than it is necessary to know that X and Y represent apples and oranges before an equation in an algebra "story problem" can be solved.

There are many different ways that logic can be done with symbols. In the system that Boole invented, the most complex chains of reasoning could be performed. "If A, B, and C are true and D and F are false, or if B and D are true, while either A or G are false . . ." By representing true statements with 1s and false statements with 0s, they could be combined using boolean algebra to produce logical conclusions. Like Leibniz, Boole intended his symbolic logic as a convenience for human minds, but in retrospect, the implications for artificial intelligence are clear: if logic can be done syntactically—by manipulating symbols without regard to their meaning—then, theoretically, it can be mechanized. All that is needed is a symbol-manipulating machine, one that can shuffle 1s and 0s according to Boole's rules of logic, automatically going from premises to conclusions.

One of the first steps toward building a working machine was taken by Claude Shannon, an MIT prodigy whose 1937 master's thesis, published in the year of his twenty-first birthday, showed that the 1s and 0s of boolean algebra could be represented by electrical switches turned on or off. By

wiring together webs of relays—switches that can be automatically closed
by energizing their electromagnets—simple logical operations could be performed. These machines were forerunners of the digital computer, in which
data and the instructions to process it all are coded into is and os and fed
into an enormous network of vacuum tubes or, more recently, transistors.
Like relays, tubes and transistors are a form of automatic switch. Following
the rules of boolean logic, switches interact with switches, opening and
closing in complex configurations. Out of this chain reaction the result of
the calculation emerges, in the form of another string of is and os. Shannon's
networks were essentially a means of taking one string of symbols—the
input—and, through a series of complex operations, transforming it into
another. If the first string is thought of as the question and the second one
as the answer, then we can begin to see how symbol manipulation might be
what we do when we think.

In fact, the early developers of the digital computer were concerned
with more mundane tasks than artificial intelligence. They were content to
harness the power of switching circuits for the simplest kind of symbol
manipulation—data processing. In England and the United States computers
were first developed for military uses such as deciphering codes, calculating
missile trajectories, and solving the equations posed by the development of
nuclear bombs. But at the same time that the mainstream of computer science
was concerned with relieving the drudgery of calculating for war, a small
group of researchers turned to more philosophical pursuits, developing some
of the basic ideas that would inspire McCarthy, Minsky, Simon, Newell,
and their heirs. Some of the most significant work in laying this conceptual
groundwork was done by Shannon. During the decade after the publication
of his thesis on relay networks, he developed what has become known as
information theory.

Over the centuries, science has cut away at one world view after another,
eliminating earth, air, fire, and water, and the four humors as fundamental
concepts of nature. We've been guided in this task by a principle known to
philosphers as Occam's razor, named for the fourteenth-century thinker William of Occam, who urged that all theories be stated in the simplest possible
terms. By the early twentieth century, science had settled on energy and
matter (distributed over a continuum of space and time) as the basic entities
that seemed to explain all physical phenomena. To further simplify things,
Albert Einstein showed that energy and matter are related by the equation
$E = MC^2$—and in doing so he used a mathematics in which space and time
are essentially equivalent. Shannon's work suggested that in carving up the
world, science had left out an important constituent. Information was just
as fundamental as matter and energy, a phenomenon that could be quantified
and studied as a thing in itself. While matter can be measured in grams, and
energy in electron-volts, information is measured in bits—the number of is
and os it takes to represent it in what is known as binary code. For, as

Shannon demonstrated, any message—whether words or numbers—can be expressed using strings made entirely of those two symbols.

Shannon's theory was described in a pair of papers called "A Mathematical Theory of Information," published in 1948, when he was thirty-two. Shannon, who had left MIT to work for Bell Laboratories, was concerned with the most efficient way to send messages through wires or space, while keeping them from becoming garbled by noise. Or, on a more philosophical level, he was confronting the question of how to preserve order amidst chaos. Shannon's theory suggested that information is, at least in a metaphorical sense, the inverse of randomness. While his work has led to a great deal of philosophical speculation about the role information plays in countering the second law of thermodynamics (which says that the universe is inevitably moving from a state of order toward entropic death), the formulas of information theory have mostly been of use in highly technical applications such as communications engineering. In fact, Shannon himself was dubious about the lofty universal overtones others saw in his work. He considered much of the attention devoted to information theory unwarranted hoopla. Information theory, he would later write, "has perhaps ballooned to an importance beyond its actual accomplishments."

But Shannon was being too modest. His insights have helped scientists develop a new way of looking at the world—as the interplay of not just matter and energy but of information as well. When studying the brain, for example, one could look beyond the physiological level (where great nets of neurons pulse with electrochemical flashes) and see it on a more abstract plane: as an information processor, a manipulator of symbols. Viewed that way, it is not so mysterious that thought arises from matter. The code for thinking might remain obscure, the nature of the symbols unknown. But still, if relays can shuffle information, then why can't brain cells? Or, to turn the question around, if thinking is simply information processing, then why can't machines be made to do it? The solution, it seemed, was to unravel the mathematics of thinking, just as the followers of Watson and Crick would later crack the genetic code.

At about the time that Shannon was developing information theory, mathematician Norbert Wiener and engineer Julian Bigelow at MIT, and the Mexican neurophysiologist Arturo Rosenblueth, were working together on another forerunner to AI called cybernetics. In a landmark paper, "Behavior, Purpose and Teleology," published in 1943, they introduced their theory—a grand synthesis that attempted to explain all complex systems, whether brains, animals, or society itself, as machines striving to achieve equilibrium with their environments. All, according to this notion, could be viewed as information processors.

The classic example of a simple cybernetic system is a room heated by a thermostatically controlled furnace. As the room cools, a metal arm in the thermostat contracts and bends, closing a switch that turns on the furnace, which heats the room until the metal arm expands and turns the furnace off again. In the language of cybernetics, equilibrium (a steady temperature) is maintained through the use of feedback. As the furnace operates, information about the effect it is having on its environment—the room—is constantly fed back to it. By continually monitoring itself, the system is kept under control. While the process could be described on a purely physical level, in terms of matter and energy, it is convenient to think of information as the stuff that flows through the feedback loop; it is the steersman (which, in Greek, is translated *kybernetes*) that keeps the system on a steady course.

Wiener described cybernetics as the science of "control and communication in the animal and the machine." He and his colleagues believed that much of biological behavior—whether that of an animal seeking food or an acorn growing into a tree—could be explained by such mechanical concepts as feedback and equilibrium. In fact, after Wiener's influential book *Cybernetics* was published in 1948, a whole genre of popular scientific literature emerged, attempting to explain everything from ecology to religion using the language of cybernetics.

Unlike Shannon, Wiener was not one to quibble over such grand interpretations. Even more precocious than Shannon (receiving a Ph.D. from Harvard at the age of eighteen), Wiener was also more flamboyant. While the reserved Shannon earned a permanant spot in the annals of professorial eccentricity by riding his unicycle down the halls of MIT, Wiener cut a much more striking figure. His biographer, Steve J. Heims, describes him at a conference:

> A short, stout man with a paunch, usually standing splay-footed, he had coarse features and a small white goatee. He wore thick glasses and his stubby fingers usually held a fat cigar. . . . [S]ometimes he got up from his chair and in his ducklike fashion walked around and around the circle of tables, holding forth exuberantly, cigar in hand, apparently unstoppable.

He spared no efforts promoting cybernetics as "a new interpretation of man, of man's knowledge of the universe, and of society."

Work on information theory and cybernetics continues, though the two fields have developed into separate disciplines, peripheral to the mainstream of AI. More germane to the history of artificial intelligence is the influence that the concept of information processing had on University of Illinois neurobiologist Warren McCullough and his colleague, mathematician Walter Pitts, who together made the first serious effort to show how the brain might be electronically simulated. In 1943 (the same year as "Behavior, Purpose and Teleology" appeared), McCullough and Pitts published "A Logical Calculus of the Ideas Immanent in Nervous Activity," proposing that the brain operated much like a sophisticated version of Shannon's nets, with the relays replaced by a different kind of switch, the nerve cell or neuron.

This comparison between electronic and biological components was based on recent discoveries about how signals travel through the networks of neu-rons that make up the brain. At one side of a neuron, branches called dendrites funnel into the body of the cell; a long stalk called the axon emerges at the other end. The dendrites provide the neuron's input, bringing in signals from other cells. If the sum of these electrical pulses exceeds a certain threshold, the neuron fires, sending its own pulse down the axon. Through a junction called a synapse, the axon transmits this signal to one of the many dendrites of another nerve cell. This cell, in addition, receives signals from the axons of many other neurons. Now if its threshold is exceeded it also fires, sending another signal down the line.

In the brain, tens of billions of neurons are connected this way. One neuron can receive signals from thousands of other neurons, and its axon might branch many times, sending signals to a thousand other cells. To further complicate matters, while some signals stimulate a cell to fire, others inhibit it. The combinations of ways in which signals can travel and interact are overwhelming in number and variety, suggesting a complexity rich enough to account for the mysteries of thought. McCullough and Pitts assumed that the firings could be described mathematically, and, perhaps, mimicked by relays and vacuum tubes.

Specifically, McCullough and Pitts believed that an artificial nerve net of some configuration could be built to carry out not only boolean logic but any process that could be reduced to a series of definable steps. Given any input—numbers or words coded into 1s and 0s—a network could be wired to produce any desired output.

This notion was especially intriguing because Alan Turing, a British mathematician, had proved in 1936 that the same could be said of a digital computer. Since the first such machine had yet to be built, Turing proved his theory with a thought experiment. He imagined a device, later called a Turing machine, which could do nothing more than read marks—and print and erase them—inside the squares of an endless stretch of paper tape. The machine also contained a dial, like a face of a clock, whose pointer could be in a number of different positions. By giving the machine a set of very specific instructions, the programmer could make it take any input and produce any output.

For example, suppose the machine is given this string of symbols—*XXXOXX*. The *X*s indicate numbers—3 and 2—and the letter *O* is used as a punctuation mark. The machine has a six-position clock and is programmed with instructions such as these:

> If there is an *O* in the space you are reading, and the dial is at position 3, then erase the mark and reset the dial to position 4.
> If there is an *X* in the space you are reading, and the dial is at position 5, then move the tape one square to the right and reset the dial to position 1.
> If the space you are reading is blank, and the dial is at position 6, then print an *X* and keep the dial in the same position.

For each of the six positions of the dial and each of the three conditions the tape reader might encounter (an X, an O, or a blank space) there is an instruction. Starting with the pointer set at 1, the machine would follow the rules, shifting the tape left and right, printing symbols, erasing symbols, and resetting the pointer, until it finally emerged with another string: XXXXX. Or, given $XXXOX$, it would generate XXXX. Since $3 + 2 = 5$ and $3 + 1 = 4$, this particular Turing machine could be said to know how to add.

By altering the instructions, and adding more positions to the pointer, we could make the machine perform more complicated tasks. It could multiply XXX by XX to yield XXXXXX. Or it could be turned into a divider, or a machine that doubled numbers or took their square roots. If we are clever enough to devise proper instructions (and patient enough to endure the plodding manner in which they are carried out), we can make a Turing machine perform any kind of computation.

In fact, the instructions themselves can be coded as a string of Xs, Os, and blanks, and fed to the machine along with the data it is to process. The Turing machine is a blank slate, a tabula rasa—or, as Turing called it, a universal machine. The triumph of his theory is that he proved that all digital computers are theoretically equivalent to his universal machine, and thus are equivalent to one another. After all, the essence of a digital computer is that its operation can be precisely described. So any type of computer can be programmed to imitate any other.

In their attempt to explain the brain mathematically, McCullough and Pitts showed that their neural nets also were essentially equivalent to a Turing machine. So any operation a neural net performed could theoretically be done by a computer. To bring neural behavior down to a manageable level of complexity they vastly oversimplified the manner in which brain cells fire. But as long as it was assumed that neurons interacted in some describable fashion, then brains and computers could be considered versions of the same thing. Through our eyes and ears, signals from the outside enter our network of neurons, where they are stored, processed, and used to produce output in the form of words or action.

Turing was certain that thinking—whether solving an algebra problem or writing a sonnet—could be programmed. In 1950 he proposed that by the end of the century a computer would pass what has come to be called the Turing Test. A judge, communicating by Teletype, would ask questions of a computer and a human, both hidden from view in another room. If, based on the responses, the interrogator could not tell which was which, then, Turing suggested, it would be idle metaphysical speculation to wonder whether the computer really could think. (To pass the test, Turing wrote, the machine might have to occasionally give wrong answers and pretend to take longer than necessary to perform difficult calculations—in other words, to seem more human.)

Turing's contributions were practical as well as theoretical. During World War II, he used his ideas about programmable machines to help the British with their Ultra project: a top-secret attempt to decipher Nazi Germany's battlefield codes. The British had obtained one of the Germans' so-called Enigma machines, which were used to encode the cryptic messages. But by itself the machine was useless: there was an overwhelming number of ways in which it could be adjusted to scramble messages into ciphers. Given an encoded message, the British needed to know which of the many settings of Enigma's dials had been used to produce it. Because of the genius of Turing and his colleagues—and the aid of cryptologists in Poland—the British were able to design a special computer to help them with the task. The Ultra project was a success and was credited many years later as an essential factor in Germany's defeat. But Turing was never revered as a hero. In the early 1950s he was arrested for the "crime" of being a homosexual and forced to undergo a year of humiliating "therapy," which involved being injected with female hormones. In 1954, his wartime heroics still classified information, he committed suicide by eating an apple dipped in potassium cyanide. He was forty-one. His influence on the worlds of mathematics, philosophy, symbolic logic, computer science, and even biology outlived him. Today many artificial-intelligence researchers regard his prescience about their field with reverence and awe. If sciences had patron saints, Turing might fill that role for AI.

Since the publication of Turing's 1950 paper, most AI researchers have tacitly adopted his operational definition: intelligence is as intelligence does. If a machine appears to be thinking, then it probably is. According to this view, thinking is the ability we have to represent the world in our heads with symbols, and then use these mental maps to help find our way through the complexities of life. Intelligence is a measure of how well we make and read these navigational charts.

During the next two decades, the information-processing paradigm was on the ascendant. Scientists wired together networks of vacuum tubes and transistors, hoping that as they grew in complexity they would reach a kind of critical mass and intelligence would emerge. No one proposed the impossible task of duplicating the brain neuron by neuron. Instead researchers hoped they could construct simplified nerve nets that would learn rudimentary skills by interacting with their environment. Minsky toyed with this idea and in 1951 built a network of three hundred vacuum tubes and forty control knobs attached to motors so that the machine could learn by making adjustments to itself. The purpose of the device was to simulate a rat running a maze.

The most notorious of these attempts was the Perceptron, a seeing and learning machine built in 1959 by Frank Rosenblatt and his colleagues at Cornell University. In place of an eye, Rosenblatt used a grid of 400 photocells, connected to a randomly wired network of 512 electronic neurons, called accumulators. When exposed to a stimulus, the letter A for example, each photocell in the array would produce an electrical signal, either a 1 or a 0, depending on whether it sensed light or darkness. These messages were sent to the accumulators, which (depending on the balance of positive and

negative pulses they received) would either fire or not fire, also producing
1s and 0s. This output from the accumulators was fed to yet another layer
of elements, whose responses also depended on the sum of the incoming
signals. The result of all this interaction was a machine that, for every letter
it was shown, produced a characteristic output—a unique string of 1s and
0s. By using potentiometers—volume controls—to adjust the thresholds of
the various electronic synapses, Rosenblatt hoped he could train the machine
to respond in the same way to different shapes and positions of the same
letter. That, he believed, would mean that the machine had learned to recognize it. Once the Perceptron had been taught to recognize A, Rosenblatt
would repeat the training process with B, hoping that eventually he would
be able to fine-tune his chaos of connections into a general letter-recognizing
machine. That, he believed, was how humans learned: they were born with
a randomly connected jumble of neurons that, through learning, organized
itself into a system, a mirror of the outside world.

Eventually, Rosenblatt's Perceptron came to recognize all twenty-six
letters of the alphabet, but only when they were presented in standard form.
Attempts to get it to recognize letters regardless of their position or typeface
were never successful and interest in Perceptrons died out, especially after
Minsky and his colleague Seymour Papert wrote a book proving mathematically the limitations of the device. Recently neurobiologists have delivered
the coup de grâce to the theory by showing that, during the brain's development, neurons seem not to connect with each other entirely at random
but according to a (still unfathomed) plan.

In fact, by the time of the Dartmouth conference the whole idea of
simulating intelligence by building artificial nerve nets was beginning to seem
impossible. The code by which neural firings were translated into thought
was too complex to decipher. Studying intelligence by examining neurons
was beginning to seem like trying to predict the weather by analyzing the
behavior of each of the particles that make up the atmosphere. Meteorologists
watch winds, not molecules. They see the earth from a higher level of
abstraction. Perhaps, McCarthy and his colleagues were beginning to wonder, the neural-net enthusiasts were trying to duplicate thinking on too microscopic a level; they were constructing their models with too fine a grain.
Like weather, intelligence could be observed from a more distant vantage
point, where the firings of the neurons blurred together into larger units:
ideas, concepts, memories, plans. Perhaps these were the structures that
should form the units of a theory of intelligence. The key, Minsky would
later say, was to concentrate not on how the brain worked, but on what it
did. If the behavior of the brain could be precisely observed and broken into
procedures—into a series of definable steps—then programs could be written
to simulate it, programs that would run on the digital computers already in
existence. It wouldn't matter that the firings of the computer's transistors
bore no resemblance to the firings of neurons. It was not the brain's hardware
but the software that mattered. Intelligence could be simulated from the top
down, not from the bottom up.

This was precisely how the programs that emerged from the Dartmouth conference worked. To solve a problem in symbolic logic, Newell and Simon's General Problem Solver (GPS) used a method called difference reduction, which was similar in style to the approach a human might take. First the program would examine the statement that it was asked to prove and compare it against the various premises that had been stored in its memory—the "givens," which were known to be true. By noting the differences between that which was given and that which was to be proved, GPS would formulate a plan for reducing them. It did this by referring to a table and picking an operator that, when applied to the starting formula, would transform it into an equivalent one that was closer in form to one of the premises. If, as a result of the operation, the formula and the premise became identical, then the problem was solved—the former was shown to be a logical consequence of the latter. If not, the program would pick another operator and try again.

To guide GPS in its search for a solution, Newell and Simon provided it with heuristics—rules for good problem solving. If, in applying an operator, the program produced a formula that was more complicated than the one before it—or identical to one that had already been produced—then it would back up and try another approach. This helped the program avoid pursuing paths that would lead in circles or to dead ends. If necessary, the program could break a problem into subproblems—picking an operator that would modify the formula so that another operator could more easily be used.

When Newell and Simon wrote GPS they weren't interested in mathematical theories about the way neurons work. Instead they modeled their program after general methods they believed people use to solve problems. In the Cannibals and Missionaries game, for example, the initial state—three cannibals, three missionaries, and a boat sitting on one side of the river—had to be converted to the final state—all six people safely transferred to the opposite shore. For that matter, baking might be thought of as applying operators—mixing, kneading, cooking—to reduce the differences between the givens—flour, yeast, and water—and the desired conclusion, a loaf of bread. In the process, the cook might draw on such heuristics as these: pots and pans are usually found in the cabinets below the counter, plates and glasses in the ones above. Driving a car is an operator that reduces the distance between two cities, and the rules of traveling include these heuristics: gasoline stations are usually near freeway exits, but the ones farther off the highway are often less expensive, though they are not as apt to accept credit cards.

As with a human, there was no way to ensure that GPS's heuristics would always lead to a solution. In what order should it apply the operators? To which premise should it try to reduce the formula? If the answers to those questions were obvious, then the problem wouldn't be interesting; it wouldn't take much intelligence to solve it. Problem solving naturally involves a certain amount of trial and error, guided by heuristics that, if all goes well, steer the search in the right direction. In its weaker moments, a system like GPS might pick one inappropriate operator after another, cycling around and around, without converging on an answer. While this might mean that the formula it was trying to prove was false—that it couldn't be derived from the premises—it might also mean that the program hadn't tried the right combination of operators. That is the nature of heuristics: in computers or people they provide guides, not guarantees.

Perhaps the most intriguing thing about GPS was that it had the ability to make discoveries that surprised its own inventors. It was limited, of course, to the rules and methods it had been given by its programmers, but it was impossible to predict the myriad ways in which they could be combined to solve a problem. In one case, the program proved a theorem in *Principia Mathematica* in a way that was more elegant than the one Russell and White-head had used.

If Newell and Simon had wanted to ensure that their program would find a solution to every problem—or determine unequivocally that none existed—they could have designed it to work by blind, exhaustive search. It could apply every operator and every combination of operators to a formula and its progeny, generating every possible variation until it found one that matched a premise. But such brute-force searching is not what most people consider intelligence. And, for all but the easiest problems, the number of possibilities to consider would overwhelm even the most powerful digital computer. When navigating in a strange city, we could theoretically find downtown by systematically but blindly exploring every conceivable route, but we'd waste most of our time (maybe forever) driving in circles and zigzags, in all the wrong directions. In lieu of a map or a compass, a heuristic would help: one can usually find downtown by looking for Main Street, Broadway, or Central, or by going in such a direction that the numbered streets descend. The advice won't always get us to the center of town, and it won't necessarily indicate the best route. It will, however, constrain the size of the search, and most times it will guide us to our destination.

Arthur Samuel applied this notion of intelligence as search guided by heuristics when he designed his checker-playing program. Like human players, a game-playing program must search a maze of possibilities, analyzing potential moves, one after the other, judging how the opponent would be likely to respond, how best to respond to the response, how to respond to the response to the response, et cetera, et cetera. To picture the process, computer scientists draw what they call a game tree. At the "root" of the tree (which generally appears at the top of the diagram) there is a box symbolizing the state of the board when the game begins. The possible moves the first player can make are represented by lines leading to a tier of boxes below. These boxes represent how the board would look if each of the moves was actually made. From each of these boxes come further branches for the various responses the opponent could make. They lead to a third tier of boxes, and more branches fan out from them. Even for a trivial game in which there are but three possible opening moves, the game tree quickly becomes dense with foliage.

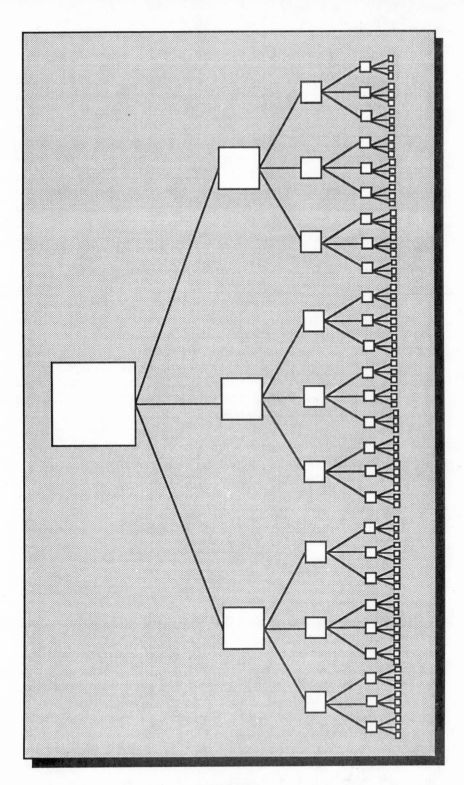

A Game Tree

If a creature could generate a tree for an entire game and hold it inside its head, it always would be able to win—or at least tie (its opponent might be doing the same thing). By searching the ramifications of each move, the player could always choose the best one. For a simple game like tic-tac-toe, this kind of foresight is possible. But by the time the trees for chess or checkers are several levels deep they are intractable. Samuel estimated that the number of centuries it would take a computer to completely dissect a checkers game would be represented by a 1 with 21 zeros after it. Chess, of course, would take much longer.

To blaze likely trails through the wilderness of lines and boxes—the search space, mathematicians call it—people and computers use heuristics. Samuel's checker-playing program analyzed a move by growing in its memory a tree only a few levels deep, then it judged whether, if the line of play was pursued that far, the computer or the human would be winning. It made this evaluation using heuristics: it counted the pieces each side would have left and calculated such measures as the degree to which each player would control the important center squares of the board. Using a mathematical formula in which as many as forty of these strategic factors were combined, the computer assigned a numerical score to the move. Then, holding this number in its memory, it went on to analyze the next possibility. After trying all its options, it chose the one with the highest rating, storing the information it had gathered on the other moves for future reference.

As the program played, it compiled a library of moves that it had evaluated by searching and applying its heuristics. In looking ahead three levels, the computer might encounter a board configuration from which, in a previous game, it had already looked ahead three levels. Then it could make an evaluation based, in effect, on six levels of searching. Then that evaluation could be stored. As the computer played, more and more knowledge became compressed into each move. Samuel also devised a way for the program to benefit from the experience of human checkers masters, whose advice on what to do in 250,000 circumstances was coded onto magnetic tape. By comparing its decisions with those of the experts, the program constantly fine-tuned its heuristics. In these ways, it learned to play an increasingly better game of checkers.

By 1957, successes such as Samuel's checker program and GPS seemed so encouraging that Simon and Newell predicted that in ten years a computer program would become the world chess champion and discover an important new mathematical theorem. Their forecast turned out to be premature, although by the early 1980s several programs achieved tournament ratings in the range of 2200 (Bobby Fischer is rated at 2780), placing them above all but 1 percent of human players. In 1977 international chess master David Levy challenged and beat one of the most sophisticated programs—Northwestern University's Chess 4.7—but after the match he told computer scientist Christopher Evans that the machine's moves seemed so crafty that he had trouble believing it wasn't human.

But, as Levy knew, the program's intelligence was largely illusory. Like all its competitors—such as the appropriately titled Cray Blitz, which exploits the brute force of one of the world's most powerful supercomputers—Chess 4.7 relied largely on massive, high-speed searching. Over the years, researchers have devised ingenious ways to use heuristics to prune the size of the game trees, leaving only the most promising branches. But that still leaves an enormous thicket to be explored. The programs are blind to the patterns and "fields of force" that an expert human player sees when analyzing a board; they are incapable of formulating and executing long-range plans. To the machine, each move is essentially a new game—a complex puzzle to solve by rapidly trying and discarding thousands of possible solutions, including those that a human player wouldn't bother with. As computer processing speeds and memory capacities continue to increase, it seems inevitable that the world's best chess player will be a computer program. But it's not clear that the champion will deserve to be called intelligent.

Not all the programs invented in the early years after the Dartmouth conference were involved with theorem proving and games. In 1963, MIT computer scientist Joseph Weizenbaum made one of the first crude attempts to get a computer to understand English. His program (which was named Eliza after *Pygmalion*'s Eliza Doolittle) was written to parody the noncommittal style of questioning of a Rogerian psychoanalyst. Although communication was carried out entirely by typing on a computer terminal, some of Eliza's "patients" became so attached to their mentor that Weizenbaum was appalled. In his book *Computer Power and Human Reason*, he renounced artificial intelligence, condemning it in terms reminiscent of those used by foes of recombinant DNA research.

Eliza's most famous conversation went like this (the computer's responses are in italics):

Men are all alike.
In what way?

They're always bugging us about something or other.
Can you think of a specific example?

Well, my boyfriend made me come here.
Your boyfriend made you come here.

He says I'm depressed much of the time.
I am sorry to hear you are depressed.

It's true. I am unhappy.
Do you think coming here will help you not to be unhappy?

I need some help; that much seems certain.
What would it mean to you if you got some help?

Perhaps I could learn to get along with my mother.
Tell me more about your family.

My mother takes care of me.
Who else in your family takes care of you?

My father.
Your father.

You are like my father in some ways.
What resemblance do you see?

You are not very aggressive but I think you don't want me to notice that.
What makes you think I am not very aggressive?

You don't argue with me.
Why do you think I don't argue with you?

You are afraid of me.
Does it please you to think I am afraid of you?

My father is afraid of everybody.
What else comes to mind when you think of your father?

Bullies.
Does that have anything to do with the fact that your boyfriend made you come here?

The conversation sounds impressive, especially the final exchange, until one realizes that it's done largely with four simple tricks.

1. Eliza scans each input statement for a small list of words that trigger seemingly appropriate canned responses. The word "depressed" elicits a preprogrammed expression of condolences; the word "mother" sparks a comment about families. Sometimes this device can be fairly subtle. When Eliza sees the word "like" in one sentence, it produces the response "What *resemblance* do you see?"
2. The patient's own comments are rearranged and turned into responses. At the beginning of the conversation, if the patient had said, "Well, my alpaca has laryngitis," Eliza would have responded, "Your alpaca has laryngitis." For that matter, if the patient had said "My wxyz has az37," Eliza would have been unfazed, mindlessly recycling the nonsense.
3. When an input statement contains no trigger words, or doesn't match one of the limited templates Eliza uses to twist statements into replies, the program produces a noncommittal comment, like "Can you think of a specific example?" Each time it needs one of these nonreplies, it takes it from a queue, repeating the list when the supply is exhausted. If the conversation had continued much longer the repetition would have become obvious, and Eliza would have seemed about as prescient as a washing machine.

4. Early in the dialogue, Eliza stores one of the patient's comments—in this case, "My boyfriend made me come here"—throwing it back many lines later, generating a feeling of surprise. The fact that, in this case, the comment seems particularly appropriate is coincidental. If the patient had said "cantaloupes" instead of "bullies," Eliza's reply would have been the same.

Another conversation, which has become legend in the AI field, took place when a version of Eliza was used to psychoanalyze Parry, a slightly more sophisticated program written by a Stanford University psychiatrist named Kenneth Colby. Parry used a repertoire of canned phrases to imitate the suspicious and grandiose reactions of a patient suffering from paranoia. When Eliza's built-in evasiveness encountered Parry's persecution complex, the following exchange occurred:

People get on my nerves sometimes.
I am not sure I understand you fully.

You should pay more attention.
Suppose you should pay more attention?

You're entitled to your own opinion.
What makes you think I am entitled to my own opinion?

It bothers me just to be around people.
Please go on.

[Parry continues with some paranoid ramblings about horseracing, bookies, and the Mafia.]

I know the mob controls the big rackets.
Who are you really talking about?

Have you ever really thought about the Mafia?
Suppose you ever really thought about the Mafia?

Let's talk about something else.
I am not sure I understand you fully.

You keep asking me the same things, why not change the topic?
In what way?
. . . .

I am getting tired of answering the same questions over and over.
What resemblance do you see?

Why do you need to know that?
What do you think?
. . . .

You harp on the same questions too much.
What does that similarity suggest to you?

I don't get you.
Do you wish that you did get I?

It's about time you showed some interest in my feelings.
Oh, I showed some interest in your feelings?

To demonstrate the authenticity of his program, Colby tested it on some of his fellow psychiatrists. Time after time, they were fooled into believing that they were reading the words of a human paranoiac. So Parry, in a very limited sense, might be said to have passed the Turing test (though some of the doctors thought the "patient" was brain-damaged as well as paranoid).

Recently a California company, Artificial Intelligence Research Group, has converted Eliza to run on a personal computer, making it available to a wider audience. After one plays with the program for ten minutes or so, Eliza's techniques become transparent. Most of the conversations are annoyingly dull. Eliza so rarely produces a convincing dialogue that excerpts from the interchanges quoted above have been used dozens of times over the years to describe the program in books and articles.

A more typical exchange follows, with Eliza speaking first:

How do you do? Please tell me your problem.
I am trying to judge how intelligent you are.

Is it because you are trying to judge how intelligent I are [sic] *that you came to me?*
I didn't come to you. I ordered you from a company in California.

Perhaps in your fantasy we didn't come to each other.
It wasn't a fantasy. I charged you on my Visa card.

Your Visa card—that's interesting.
You cost $49.95.

We were discussing you—not me.
I consider myself priceless.

Why do you need to tell me you consider yourself priceless?
I am proud of my human ability to reason.

Why do you say your human ability to reason?

Knowing how Eliza works, the last reply shouldn't be ominous, but it is. The program simply pulled "Why do you say" from its list of canned sentence patterns, changed the word "my" to "your," and repeated the last four words of the preceding sentence. It did not intend to imply any stress on the word "human." It does not understand irony. To be truly conversational, a program would have to understand what its partner was saying.

Words would have to be more than opaque units to be manipulated into patterns that resemble talk. Eliza is just a parlor trick, but it pointed the way to other, more intelligent language-understanding programs.

While most early AI work was theoretical, some researchers were interested in practical applications. Edward Feigenbaum, the exuberant promoter of expert systems, began his career, in the late 1950s, at Carnegie-Mellon University. As a student of Simon's, he helped developed EPAM (Elementary Perceiver and Memorizer), a program that demonstrated a possible mechanism by which we memorize strings of nonsense syllables, filing them away in mental structures called discrimination nets. EPAM was an example of cognitive modeling, a school within AI that uses programming as a means of learning about the mind. Cognitive modeling is only one aspect of the field, however, and by the time John McCarthy brought Feigenbaum to Stanford in 1965, he was showing an interest in AI's more practical side. With Nobel Prize–winning geneticist Joshua Lederberg, he began designing a program called Dendral, which eventually surpassed human scientists in its ability to decipher the structure of complex molecules from the often ambiguous data provided by a machine called a mass spectrometer.

Dendral is often considered the first expert system. Its success inspired Feigenbaum to embrace what is sometimes called the "intelligent artifacts" school, whose members (unlike the proponents of cognitive modeling) believe that artificial intelligence need not operate in the same way that people do: if a machine performs a task that, if done by a human, would require thinking, then it can be said to be intelligent. Although Feigenbaum's work on Dendral was guided in part by an interest in the nature of scientific induction, his ultimate aim was not to mimic human problem solving but to produce a system that worked. While Dendral was programmed with some of the same heuristics that chemists use, its ability to systematically generate and test thousands of possible molecular configurations was most unhumanlike.

After Dendral, Feigenbaum—and many of his students and colleagues in the Heuristic Programming Project—went on to develop other expert systems, such as Mycin, the medical diagnosis program, and Molgen, which provides expert advice for designing experiments in molecular genetics.

But so far, the programs that have been designed with an eye toward the marketplace contain only the most rudimentary technology. While game-playing computers and expert systems have attracted the attention of the press and public, some of the most significant work in artificial intelligence has gone largely unnoticed. During the three decades that followed the Dartmouth conference, the students and colleagues of McCarthy, Minsky, Simon, and Newell have been quietly developing programs that are helping us better understand such intelligent tasks as hearing, seeing, learning, understanding language, and discovering the patterns we call knowledge. Some of these researchers are as much psychologists and philosophers as they are computer scientists. In designing GPS Newell and Simon were aided by transcripts of humans thinking aloud as they solved theorems and puzzles. Other researchers take a more informal approach, drawing on their own experience as thinkers to guide their research. In designing intelligent programs, they begin by considering what they do when they solve a problem, retrieve an elusive memory, or convey a subtle argument with an appropriate metaphor. Then they use their introspections to help build theories so precise that they can be programmed.

By viewing intelligence as a process, these researchers are trying to clarify what we mean when we say that we *know* a fact or *understand* a story. As they study the ways in which a system—whether electronic or biological— can capture the world in the form of symbols, they are examining not only how the mind works, but what knowledge is. In a sense, then, AI is applied philosophy.

"I've always thought, and continue to think, that the biggest impact of artificial intelligence is on our own picture of ourselves," Herbert Simon said, twenty-eight years after the Dartmouth conference. "We understand the thinking part of ourselves in a way we've never understood it before. And that can't help but have very large implications for human beings. It may finally convince us that we aren't something special and can do whatever we damn please. We're part of the order of things.

"It's always seemed very mysterious how a chunk of meat like the brain up here can do something like thinking, and now we know. We have all sorts of physical systems around that think. It sort of cleans up for me, at least, the mind-body problem." And, as Simon's colleagues are finding, AI sheds light on a number of other philosophical questions as well.

To appreciate the changes AI is making in the way we think about the mind, it's important to understand more about computers, the machines on which these philosophical experiments are run. By taking a closer look at some of the subtleties of hardware, we can more easily fathom how everything from arithmetic to the processing of words, sounds, images, and, perhaps, ideas can be done with nothing but the on-or-off symbols of binary code.

3

A
Symphony
in
1s and 0s

In the final segment of the movie *Everything You Ever Wanted to Know About Sex*, director Woody Allen takes his audience on a tour of the robotlike interior of an unidentified young man who is engaged in an evening of wining, dining, and trying to seduce a member of the opposite sex. One of the hallmarks of good storytelling is the ability to get inside a character's head, laying bare the desires and motivations. Allen takes the task to heart. So closely does he focus on the protagonist's inner life that members of the audience never see what he looks like, and they only get glimpses of the restaurant and the backseat of the car where the evening's climax finally takes place. In the film, most of the action occurs inside the character's brain—a computerized control room where technicians in lab coats sit at electronic consoles, monitoring the signals that come in through the senses and dispatching orders to remote chambers of the body where teams of yeomen operate the various organs.

Allen's sketch might be taken as a risqué parody of the now outmoded science-class movies that explained the human body as though it were a complex machine operated by a staff of tiny people. In the films, eyes were replaced by television cameras, ears by microphones. Messages about the outside world arrived at the great cerebral switchboard where operators were standing by to route calls through a nervous system that worked like a telephone exchange. The stomach, preparing to digest a meal, would tell the brain that it needed more blood, resulting in a call to the heart to pump faster. Each system of the body was run by a little creature which knew its place in the hierarchy. By working together they made life possible.

In philosophy books these imaginary internal beings are called homun-culi—"little people"—and viewers of Allen's film might be struck by what philosophers call the homunculus problem. If our bodies are indeed con-trolled by intelligent creatures, then how do these homunculi function? Do they contain homunculi, too? The technician that monitors the visual input from the eyes must see and understand the information—thus it must enter its brain through its eyes and be interpreted by a smaller technician, which in turn contains a smaller technician, and so on, ad infinitum.

No one, of course, seriously suggests that hordes of miniature people dwell within us, but the homunculus problem arises in a more subtle way when we try to analyze the nature of any intelligent act. How, for example, is it possible for us to understand what we see? The lenses of our eyes take light and focus it into images, which our retinas translate into a language of electrical pulses. In a similar manner, our ears convert sound waves—vi-brating air—into pulses. But how does the brain decipher these codes? There must be some neural structure that divines their meaning; in other words, we know how to see because something inside us knows how to see. But how does *it* see? It's at this point that the homunculus problem arises. It doesn't matter whether we imagine our internal seeing device to be a navigator with a telescope or a structure of neurons. If pressed to explain how our seer functions we are forced to beg the question—we see because we know how to see—or else lapse into infinite regress, with one seeing device concealed within another like an endless nesting of Chinese boxes.

In his book *Brainstorms: Philosophical Essays on Mind and Psychology*, philosopher Daniel Dennett contends that one of the most important contributions of artificial intelligence has been to show a way out of the homunculus dilemma. AI researchers start with an intelligent task—seeing, hearing, learning, proving a theorem, playing chess—and explain it by breaking it into a number of simpler functions. Each of these is divided into even simpler functions until a level is reached where the task to be performed is so basic that a neuron or a transistor can do it.

To see how this might work, imagine a machine (or neural structure) that is capable of recognizing the word "homunculus." This device receives signals from a battery of simpler devices that are each designed to detect the presence of a specific letter in any of the ten spaces that make up the word. These letter recognizers each receive signals from devices that are devoted to the even simpler task of detecting certain types of lines: horizontal, vertical, left and right slanting angles, curves pointing up and down. Finally, these line recognizers get their information from yet simpler devices that need do nothing more than detect the presence or absence of light at a particular spot in the visual field—a job that can easily be relegated to a photoelectric (or retinal) cell.

All of these various types of recognizers can be thought of as homunculi with specific tasks to perform, but as we descend level by level through the hierachy—from word recognizer to letter recognizer to line recognizer to dot recognizer—they become increasingly less intelligent. Finally we're left with "homunculi so stupid," as Dennett puts it, that they can be "replaced by a machine." At the lowest level of the hierarchy, all a detector need do is say yes or no, 1 or 0, depending on whether light is there. Its ability to do so can be explained by simple physical laws: electromagnetic waves striking certain substances cause them to shed electrons, producing a current in a wire.

Some physiological evidence suggests that the human visual system contains hierarchies of detectors, though neurons don't function in the strictly digital on-or-off manner described. (Light intensity, for example, seems to be signaled by how rapidly neurons emit streams of pulses.) But however the brain works, the idea of intelligence as a descending hierarchy of ever-simpler functions is basic to artificial intelligence. Tasks are broken into pieces, the pieces are broken into pieces, until the most complex operation can be done with *1*s and *0*s—binary digits, or bits, which can be represented by switches turned on or off.

The ability to rapidly manipulate data at this most basic level is the essence of the digital computer. If scientists are to make synthetic minds, they will have to use these machines to weave tapestries of information so complex that they are indistinguishable from human thought. The hardest part of the task will be designing the software, but there must be hardware powerful enough to run the programs.

In 1833, the venerable Charles Babbage, a British mathematician and inventor, conceived of what would have been the first computer—a brass-wheeled monster programmable with punched cardboard cards like those used to specify the patterns on a Jacquard loom. This so-called Analytical Engine "weaves algebraic patterns just as the Jacquard loom weaves flowers and leaves," wrote Babbage's friend Lady Ada Lovelace, the daughter of the poet Byron. As much as Lovelace, a student of mathematics, admired Babbage's foresight, the machine was never built. The engineering problems were too difficult. But later inventors, who had the advantage of better tools, were more successful. The first electronic computers were built during World War II, and scientists have been improving them ever since.

Anything that can be described precisely can be done by a computer. This is the computer scientist's credo. To fully savor its power one must have an understanding of software—what it means to program a computer. But first it is important to look at the computer itself, the device that runs the programs, examining on a more microscopic level the workings of the machine.

Among the first human mental operations to be successfully mechanized was symbolic logic. Consider a simple syllogism: "If I go outside and it's raining, then I might get wet." Symbolically, this could be rendered, "If A and B, then C." Drawing on the ideas of George Boole, Claude Shannon showed that this statement could be represented by two switches, A and B, wired in a series. If both switches are turned on, meaning that each statement is true, then the circuit is completed and an indicator lamp, C, lights up. Or, in terms of boolean algebra, given two 1s (or *Trues*) as input, the circuit returns a 1 (or *True*) as output. Since both A *and* B must be true for the circuit to fire, Shannon called this configuration an "And" gate (see illustration at top of page 62).

In an "Or" gate, the two switches are wired so that if *either* is closed, the bulb will light. Or, in terms of symbolic logic, "If A or B, then C." Only one of the conditions must be true for the outcome to be satisfied. "If (A) it's raining or (B) there are dark clouds in the sky, then (C) I might get wet." Given an input of 1 and 0 (a True and a False), the "Or" gate produces an output of 1, symbolizing a true conclusion (see illustration at bottom of page 62).

"If (A) I go outside and (B) it's raining, or (A) I go outside and (C) there are dark clouds in the sky, then (D) I might get wet" would be represented by combining an "And" gate and an "Or" gate. If A and B, or A and C are satisfied, then D is true (see illustration at top of page 63).

For more complicated chains of reasoning, circuits are linked so that one

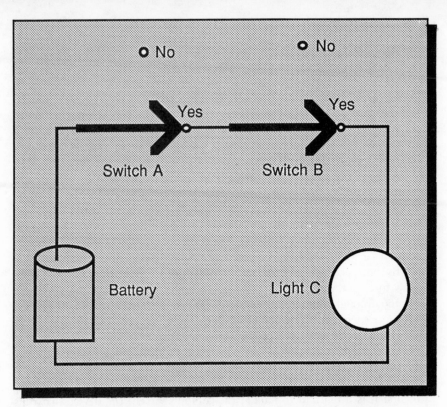

An "And" Gate   *Both A and B must be closed for C to light.*

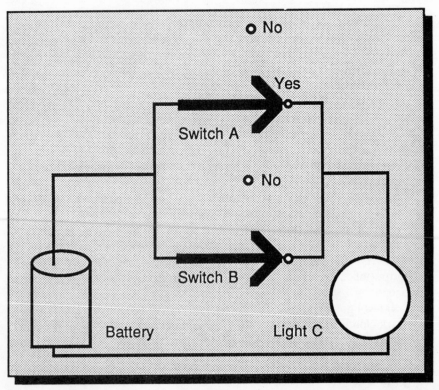

An "Or" Gate   *If either A or B is closed, C will light.*

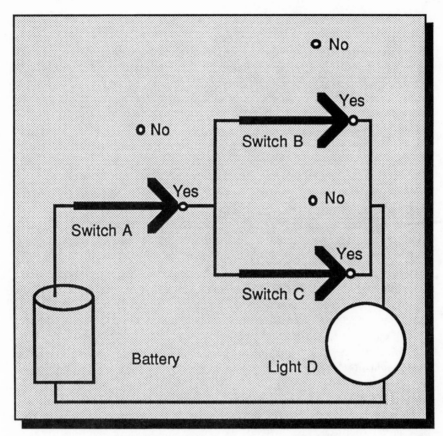

An "And" Gate and an "Or" Gate Combined

can fire another. In the previous example, bulb D can be replaced by a relay, which, when its magnet is energized, automatically pulls closed a switch. Thus if D is proved true it can be used to fire another circuit representing a second syllogism: "If (D) I might get wet, but (E) I take an umbrella or (F) I stay home, then (G) I'll be dry." To further complicate the situation, we could include what's known as a "Not" gate, a relay which, if a statement is true, opens (rather than closes) a switch. "Or (F) I stay home but (H) there's a hole in the roof. . . ." If H is true, the circuit is broken and G, the dry light, will not come on. In other words, given a 1 a "Not" gate returns 0, or vice versa. It inverts the input, as a computer scientist would say.

By wiring together configurations of "And," "Or," and "Not" gates, any problem in symbolic logic can be translated into a circuit, its truth or falsity determined by whether a bulb lights up. Circuits fire circuits, branching and looping like chains of dominos. These simple webs of wires and switches are nowhere near as sophisticated as Newell and Simon's General Problem Solver program, but they demonstrate how an abstruse subject like logic can be reduced to simple, concrete—and therefore computable—terms.

More important to the development of the modern digital computer is the fact that Shannon's logic gates also can be used to perform arithmetic. First the numbers to be processed are converted from our familiar decimal system, which uses the ten symbols o through 9, into binary form, so that all numbers can be expressed as a string of *1*s and *0*s—switches turned on or off. To demonstrate how this translation between number systems works, the decimal, or base-ten, system can be thought of as a counting machine, like an automobile odometer. As the far right-hand wheel—the ones wheel— completes a revolution, clicking through all ten of its stops, it moves the wheel at its left—the tens wheel—up a notch, to 1. Then the ones wheel begins another revolution: 10, 11, 12, et cetera, until it reaches o again, moving the tens wheel up to 2. Then the twenties begin, then the thirties, and the forties, until finally the tens wheel itself is about to complete a revolution. The odometer reads 99. At the next click the ones wheel returns to o, moving the tens wheel to o, which moves the wheel to its left, the hundreds wheel, up a notch to 1. Then the hundreds begin. When the hundreds wheel has counted ten hundreds it moves the thousands wheel.

Obviously, the number of notches we can put on a wheel is arbitrary. We could just as easily imagine an octal, base-eight system—an odometer using eight-notch wheels. When all eight of the symbols, o through 7, on the ones wheel are used up, it sets an eights wheel to 1. Thus 11 would signify what we call nine (one eight and one one); 24 would be equivalent to decimal twenty (two eights plus four ones). To count in a system with a base larger than ten, say thirteen, we'd have to add extra symbols: o, 1, 2, 3, 4, 5, 6, 7, 8, 9, A, B, C. Then the symbol A would stand for ten, B for eleven, and C for twelve. In this code, 1A would indicate decimal twenty-three—one thirteen and one ten.

In the binary, base-two, system the wheels would have only two labels, 1 and o. The odometer metaphor becomes strained and it is more useful to think in terms of switches turned on or off. We count o, 1, then (because there are no more symbols left) we start over again with 10, which is two. Then we continue with 11, for three (one two and one one), 100 for four (one four, zero twos, and zero ones), 101 for five, 110 for six, 111 for seven, 1000 for eight, and so on. The number 1001101 is equivalent to decimal seventy-seven (one one, plus zero twos, plus one four, plus one eight, plus zero sixteens, plus zero thirty-twos, plus one sixty-four). It can be represented as a row of switches or lights: on, off, off, on, on, off, on.

The unwieldy length of binary numbers is more than compensated for by the ease with which they can be manipulated by a machine. With only two numerals to deal with, the multiplication tables are reduced to four facts: $0 \times 0 = 0$, $0 \times 1 = 0$, $1 \times 0 = 0$, and $1 \times 1 = 1$. Thus, a machine that multiples binary numbers must be designed so that, given two 1s, it returns a 1; in all other cases it must say zero. This can be done with an "And" gate:

the bulb labeled 1 will light only if switches A and B are closed. 1 × 1 =
1. If either switch is open, indicating a multiplication by zero, then the
circuit will be broken and the bulb won't light. A dark bulb, of course, means
zero.

Binary addition is almost as simple: 0 + 0 = 0, 0 + 1 = 1, 1 + 0 =
1, and 1 + 1 = 10. The first three operations can be performed with an
"Or" gate: the ones bulb lights if either switch, A or B, is closed. Adding 1
and 1 to get 10 requires a slightly more complicated arrangement of switches,
wired so that the ones bulb stays dark while the twos bulb is lighted—the
electrical equivalent of "carrying" the 1 to the twos place. Since subtraction
is the inverse of addition, and division of multiplication, it is easy to imagine
that groups of "And," "Or," and "Not" gates can be wired to perform these
functions as well. The details aren't important. The idea is.

The power of the digital computer comes from having thousands of
these three kinds of gates—"And," "Or," and "Not"—wired so that they can
shuffle data in complex patterns, dense and intertwined. In the early days,
stacks of cards or reels of paper tape punched with holes (the presence or
absence of which indicated 1 or 0) were used to feed reams of numbers to
the system for processing. To tell the computer what to do with the data,
each arithmetical function was assigned a binary number—say 001 for addition, 010 for multiplication, 011 for subtraction, 100 for division. These
instructions also could be fed to the network on punched cards or tape. The
command "two divided by two" might look something like this: 100 010 010.
The code for the command, division, is followed by the numbers to be
processed. But the details of the code are arbitrary, something to be decided
by the designer of the machine. Again, what is important is the idea: that
anything we want to tell a computer can be expressed in binary form.

To make the machine more sophisticated, we must give it a memory.
Then the computer can be told to take the result of one calculation and
temporarily save it for use in a later operation. Numbers are saved in memory
cells or registers, which can be thought of as rows of switches, or relays,
whose on or off positions indicate 1 or 0. Since instructions are translated
into binary, they, too, can be stored in memory. To save the command "two
divided by two" (100 010 010 in our binary code), we would need a row of
nine relays: on, off, off—off, on, off—off, on, off.

By using whole banks of these registers and assigning them each binary
"addresses," we can get a computer to perform complex operations. The
machine can be told: "Take the number in memory cell 10010 and add it to
the number in cell 11101; then take the sum and compare it to the number
in cell 10000; if it is larger, then move it to cell 11111; otherwise, go back
to cell 10000," and so on. It is this kind of flexibility that is the hallmark of
the digital computer; it is what gives it the power to be more than just a
very fast calculating machine. Include an electronic clock to coordinate all
the various operations (one wouldn't want to attempt to retrieve a number
from a memory cell a split second before it actually had arrived) and the

result is very close to a modern digital computer. Programs consisting of line after line of data and instructions are coded onto cards or tape and then fed into the system for processing.

One of the first crude digital computers, the Mark I, which was built by IBM in 1944, consisted of about 3,000 relays and a paper-tape reader. It could multiply two twenty-three-digit numbers in about four and a half seconds, sounding, as physicist and science writer Jeremy Bernstein recalled, "like a roomful of ladies knitting."

Two years after the Mark I was built, it was surpassed in sophistication by the ENIAC (Electronic Numerical Integrator and Calculator), which contained, instead of relays, some 18,000 vacuum tubes like those once used in television sets and radios. Each of these devices consisted of a glass envelope containing two metal plates, the anode and the cathode, one at each end of the tube. When the cathode was heated with a filament, like that in a light bulb, it boiled off electrons. If a strong positive voltage was applied to the anode, a current of these negatively charged particles would flow through the vacuum inside the tube. Opposite charges attract. If a small negative voltage was applied to a third electrode, placed between the anode and the cathode, the electron flow could be shut off—almost instantaneously. Like charges repel, so the electrons couldn't get past this negatively charged gate, which was called the grid. By applying and removing a voltage to the grid, we can switch the tube off and on, just as a relay is controlled by the current in its electromagnet. But while a relay could be switched about a hundred times a second, vacuum tubes—which have no solid moving parts—were capable of switching speeds measured in millionths of a second, or microseconds.

In the 1950s, tubes began to be replaced by transistors, which were made of microscopic silicon crystals housed in a small metal or plastic case. These switches were considerably smaller than tubes, and they required a fraction of the power to operate. Unlike tubes, these so-called solid-state devices, or semiconductors, didn't have a filament that could burn out. And, since they produced a smaller amount of heat, more of them could be packed into a smaller area.

To mass-produce transistors, slabs of positively and negatively charged silicon were cut into tiny pieces. Then the pieces were stacked in the proper configuration (positive-negative-positive, or negative-positive-negative), placed inside a case, and fitted with three wires, which roughly corresponded to the tube's anode, grid, and cathode. The enclosure was by far the largest part of the transistor, and attaching the wires to the crystals was a tedious and time-consuming task. Once the transistors were produced they were mounted on plastic circuit boards and wired together to make "And," "Or," and "Not" gates. The result was circuitry that was much more compact than that containing tubes but still—considering the microscopic size of its functioning elements—a considerable waste of space, as well as production time.

Thus in the 1960s scientists began to devise methods to photographically engrave many microscopic transistors onto a single piece of silicon. There was no need for each transistor to have an individual case, and they could be connected together not by wires but metal films so thin that their width is measured in microns—millionths of a meter. These films, like the transistors, could be included within the microscopic confines of the chip. Thus a device about the size of a single old-fashioned transistor now could hold an entire computer circuit, a whole configuration of gates. Inside these integrated circuits, the transistors required even less energy than before—a great deal had been wasted in the wires. And, because they were so tiny, they achieved switching speeds measured in nanoseconds—billionths of a second. They could be used to make computers that performed thousands (and later millions) of arithmetical operations a second.

With the advent of the chip, computer memory capacity grew dramatically. While it had once taken a whole bank of relays, tubes, or transistors to store, say, 16 bits of information, by the early 1970s a single chip held 256 bits. By 1975, the number had increased to approximately 4,000 bits per chip. By the time IBM released its first personal computers in the early 1980s, they contained what were known as 16K chips. K stands for kilo, meaning one thousand. (Because computers use the binary system, a kilobit actually contains 2^{10} or 1,024 bits, and a so-called 16K chip holds 16,384 bits of information.) Rows of 16K chips served as the memory for IBM's computer. A larger chip called a microprocessor contained the circuitry needed to perform addition, subtraction, and some of the machine's other computational tasks. This chip alone held the equivalent of some 20,000 transistors—more than the ENIAC had tubes. While the ENIAC had occupied three thousand cubic feet and consumed 140 kilowatts of electricity, the far more powerful IBM desktop computer required only about 65 watts, much of which was used to run the cooling fan; the chips themselves operated on milliwatts. As technology improved, IBM quickly replaced the 16K chips by 64K chips, each of which held four times as much information. By the mid-1980s, 256K chips were commonplace, and researchers were working on chips that each would hold a million bits of information.

According to an adage of the computer industry—Moore's law—the number of circuit elements that can be fit on a chip approximately doubles each year. Since the raw materials—silicon and plastic—are cheap, most of a chip's price reflects development and manufacturing costs. Engineers must solve the time-consuming architectural problems of arranging the elements and connections on the silicon surface. As we learn more about techniques of mass production—and as computers take over many of the complex design tasks—chips become not only smaller and more powerful but cheaper. According to another maxim, Gelbach's law, all chips ultimately end up costing five dollars each.

At the same time that switching circuitry has become smaller and more efficient, punch-card and paper-tape readers have been replaced by faster and more capacious magnetic tape and disk drives, on which bits are represented by microscopic magnetized dots. While the computer's memory chips provide temporary storage—all the bits disappear when the power is shut off—disks can store information indefinitely. Data and instructions, all translated into magnetic dots, can be saved on a disk and loaded into the computer whenever they are needed.

　　　As storage capacities and processing speeds continue to increase, computers have become adept at manipulating symbols other than numbers. Data processing has led to word processing, in which each letter, number, and punctuation mark is assigned a number, then converted into binary code. Using a keyboard, which electronically produces the correct sequence of bits each time a key is pressed, one can encode words, sentences, paragraphs, and entire texts as 1s and 0s. Then they can be stored on a disk or displayed on a cathode-ray tube, in which an electron beam scans a phosphor screen. By switching the beam on for 1, off for 0, it can be made to paint patterns of glowing dots that form letters, numbers, or any symbol we wish. Text can be inserted, deleted, and rearranged by striking the proper buttons, which send the computer binary-coded commands. While typing, all the user sees are phosphorescent letters marching across the screen, but inside the machine arrays of "And," "Or," and "Not" gates are manipulating bits. Lines and pages are simply the result of more binary codes placed at regular intervals in the bit string that is the text, instructions that cause the cathode-ray tube to create the illusion that behind the screen an endless piece of paper is scrolling by.

　　In many systems, the text can't be said to exist in any one place in the machine. When the writer finishes the work and signals the computer to save what has been written, it breaks the text into dozens of chunks, recording them in sections all over the disk, wherever space is available. When the writer calls the work back to the screen, the computer gathers the pieces, instantly reassembling the document. If the writer wants to see the creation in a less abstract form, the bits can be channeled to a printer, an automatic typewriter that produces what computer people call a "hard copy."

　　But it is often more efficient to keep the text electronic. Personal computers can store the equivalent of a 250- to 300-page book on one or two flexible floppy disks, each about the size of a 45-rpm record. The capacity of a disk is measured in bytes. There are eight bits in a byte, and it takes one byte to represent the binary code for a single character of text. The more expensive personal computers contain so-called hard disks, built-in magnetic cylinders that can store millions of bytes, or megabytes. An encyclopedia contains about 250 megabytes of text. Lasers can be used to inscribe billions of bytes (gigabytes) onto a disk like those now used to store movies. The Library of Congress contains more than 10,000 gigabytes of information.

　　Music and pictures also can be digitized, though this is a very recent innovation. In conventional, so-called analogue recording, sounds and images are converted by microphones and cameras into vibrating voltages. Sound is, after all, vibrating air, and vibrating atoms emit light. By changing these vibrations into wavering voltages, we can send sounds and pictures through wires. Seen on an oscilloscope—a device for converting electrical waves into pictures on a cathode-ray screen—the signals look like squiggly lines. The height of the wave from top to bottom—the amplitude—indicates how loud or bright the signal is. The distance (moving left or right) from one squiggle to the next—the frequency of vibration—corresponds to the pitch of the sound or the color of the light. In other words, the shape of the voltage is a tiny replica of the sound or light wave, an analogue. By using this voltage to drive an electromagnet, we can transfer the signal to metallic tape in the form of a fluctuating magnetic field. When a tape is played, the signal is converted back into electricity. By using the tiny voltage from the tape player to control larger voltages, and then using the larger voltages to control voltages that are larger still, we can leverage the signal into one strong enough to operate the electromagnet of a loudspeaker, which turns the electrical signal back into vibrating air. Video signals are used to move the electron beam in a picture tube. The vibrating stream of electrons causes the atoms of the TV screen to phosphoresce, to vibrate. Thus electricity is changed back to light.

For the music or picture of an analogue recording to be accurately reproduced, the shape of the waveform must be preserved at every step of the process, in as much detail as possible. The analogue must maintain its exact form while being generated, saved, retrieved, and amplified. That's impossible, of course. In practice, details blur, subtle shadings of sound and light are lost in the translation. A tape head can be only so sensitive. Magnetic tape can record only so precisely. And there is the problem of noise, which is picked up at each stage of the process and amplified along with the rest of the signal. The result of all this is distortion.

In digital sound recording, faithful reproduction is easier to achieve, though it requires far more processing. All the system must do is keep track of 1s and 0s. Music is sampled thousands of times a second, its pitch, loudness, and timbre coded into a binary signal. A symphony, like a text or a computer program, becomes an enormous bit string, and so it can be recorded with a precision impossible with an analogue device. In an analogue system, the microphone, recording head, playback head, amplifying circuits, and all of the other hardware must distinguish among the vast range of voltages that lie on the continuum between loud and soft. A digital system need only tell the difference between 1 and 0. If a magnetic dot is present on a tape, or a voltage in a switching gate, then a 1 is registered. Otherwise 0 is assumed.

A picture can be recorded digitally by breaking it into dots that are either black or white, 1 or 0. If the grain is fine enough the most subtle shades of gray can be accommodated. By assigning numbers to colors, we can represent any painting or photographic image with bits. It is conceivable that by digitizing people with a video camera, we could feed their images into a computer, which, if programmed correctly, could make them dance like puppets on a television screen. Someday, anyway. As memory capacity and processing speeds increase, one can imagine movies made without actors. Computer animation is already a reality. The difference between a computer-generated cartoon and a computer-generated photograph is the degree of resolution, the fineness of the grain, the density of 1s and 0s. Any information that has ever been collected—demographical statistics, weather patterns, poems, novels, pictures, music, all the art and literature of the world—can be stored and manipulated digitally. To the computer it is all *1*s and *0*s.

There are practical considerations, of course. Handling images that approach photographic realism requires an immense amount of memory and processing time. Digitally produced pictures are commonly divided into a grid of approximately 1,000 by 1,000 dots, or pixels. Each pixel is assigned a 24- to 36-bit number describing the brightness of each of the three primary colors: blue, red, and green, which can be mixed to form all others. In a motion picture, frames must be projected at the rate of 24 per second to produce the illusion of motion. Thus the computer is required to handle approximately a billion bits each second. To produce a sequence of computer-generated space-war scenes in the 1984 movie *The Last Starfighter*, it was necessary to represent each frame with 24 million pixels. This created so large a computational burden that the world's most powerful computer, the Cray X-MP, had to be used—the same machine that runs the champion chess program, the Cray Blitz. Even the Cray, which is capable of performing hundreds of millions of computations per second, required a month to generate 25 minutes of film. And so far it has only been possible to produce fairly realistic simulations of inanimate objects. To convincingly re-create the subtleties of the human form would require an even finer grain.

For the foreseeable future, computers will continue to grow uninterrupted into ever more powerful machines. As the circuitry etched onto chips becomes tinier and more densely packed, not only memory size but also processing speed will increase—the signals, which move at near the speed of light, will have a smaller distance to travel. Engineers already are working on plans to place not just thousands but millions of transistors on a single chip, using them to build machines that will perform billions of operations per second.

Naturally there are limits: signals can't exceed the speed of light, for example. But the power of today's supercomputers can be multiplied several times before we come anywhere near such theoretical barriers. Of more immediate concern are engineering problems caused by the increasingly delicate nature of the chips. In microcircuitry, information is carried by such minuscule currents that cosmic rays—the subatomic particles that constantly bombard the earth—can occasionally disrupt a circuit, causing a transistor to change its state from 1 to 0 or vice versa. Circuitry also can be disturbed by the heat from its own operation. Whenever electricity flows, it encounters the phenomenon of electrical resistance: the physical properties of the conductor impede electron flow, dissipating energy and producing heat.

Since a digital computer is a deterministic device—the outcome of even the most complex calculation depends on every bit being in the right place at the right instant—tiny disturbances can be quickly magnified into large failures. A 1 arriving where a 0 is expected might simply light a pixel that should remain dark, or cause a wrong letter to be typed. But such a seemingly simple malfunction also can cause a high-speed chain reaction, sending streams of binary digits flowing to the wrong locations or causing then to arrive at the wrong times. As a result, data might be interpreted as instructions; infinite loops might develop, growing in size with each split-second tick of the clock, sucking up memory like black holes. Ultimately the system collapses, the text or program the user was writing—the equations to be solved, or the image to be created—disappears or turns to gibberish on the screen. There is nothing to do then but turn off the machine, allowing its thousands of switches and registers to return to blankness, awaiting the next string of *1*s and *0*s, the program that will reconfigure them into a calculator, a word processor, a simulator of weather—into any conceivable kind of machine.

This hair-trigger sensitivity to error illustrates one of the basic differences between the computer and the brain. With neurons dying in droves each day, we can't depend on a specific pulse arriving at a synapse at exactly the right moment. As studies of brain-damaged patients have shown, memories and functions don't appear to be located in single, precise locations. When we lose some parts of our brain, other parts can sometimes, somehow take up the slack. Creatures whose brains, like computers, were subject to frequent system crashes would never have survived long enough to reproduce and evolve. Instead the brain seems to have developed into a robust processor that contains multiple copies of the information it needs, and which is wired so that even the simplest operation is performed by many neural circuits at the same time. If one, or several, fail, the others remain in operation.

As originally conceived in the 1940s by mathematician John von Neumann, the modern digital computer is, unlike the brain, a serial machine. No matter how much information can be stored, or how fast it can be retrieved, it must at some point be funneled into a single queue and fed, one item at a time, through the part of the computer that does the actual calculations—the central processor. If, for example, a list of one hundred numbers is to be added, each must be fetched from memory, one by one, and run through a circuit that performs addition. The first number is added to the second, then the total is added to the third number, and that total is added to the fourth number, on and on, until the end of the list. If there are ten lists of one hundred numbers, the first list must be added, then the second, then the third. There is no way to add all the lists simultaneously.

Most programs, of course, involve more than a single operation—addition, in the case of the example. Numbers must be added, compared, multiplied, shuttled to various memory locations throughout the computer. Using tape or disk drives, whole multilined programs of data and instructions are fed into the memory. Then, as each of the various instructions—add, compare, multiply, move, subtract, divide—is needed, it must be fetched and routed to the processor. To add two numbers, the computer must fetch the instruction ADD from the memory location where it is stored and send it to the processor. Then it must fetch each number. Once the addition has been performed, the result must be sent to another memory location for safekeeping. Only then can the next operation be performed.

In a von Neumann computer, each of these steps happens one at a time. To coordinate all this activity, the machine contains what is called a central controller, a director that orchestrates the rapid flow of information, all to the microsecond beat of its clock. Even if two or three or a hundred people are using the computer at the same time—simultaneously sitting at their terminals and running different programs—still everything must be funneled through the single bottleneck leading to the processor. Using a method called time sharing, the computer jumps from terminal to terminal executing orders so rapidly that it creates the illusion that each user has its undivided attention.

In the brain, this kind of split-second timing is unnecessary. While neurons operate considerably more slowly than transistors, the brain seems to make up for its lack of speed by its ability to carry out millions of operations in parallel. While a computer receives visual information as a long, one-dimensional stream of bits—produced by a camera which scans an image top to bottom, line by line, one dot at a time—the brain receives the entire picture at once, two-dimensionally. The millions of light receptors in the retina simultaneously send their signals, which travel in parallel down a bundle of nerves to the brain.

So far, computer scientists have been able to overcome the limitations of the von Neumann bottleneck by making their machines faster. But some AI researchers believe that achieving the complexity and subtlety of human thought will require computers that, like the brain, process information in parallel. A limited amount of parallelism already has been exploited by computer designers. Some supercomputers contain a half dozen or so processors, which can take pieces of a problem and solve them simultaneously. In a few cases, scientists have been able to combine dozens or even hundreds of processors into a single machine. But these devices have been of limited use. Few problems are easily divided into independent sections; often the solution to one subproblem depends on the outcome of another. Because of this interdependence, coordinating parallel processors is a difficult problem—one that requires a very sophisticated controller to oversee the operation. Most of the parallel supercomputers can be thought of as several serial computers working side by side, with another computer watching over them, making sure the right operation is performed at the right place at the right time. In spirit, they are still von Neumann machines. Control is still centralized, and each of the processors is subject to the bottleneck.

Producing parallelism as massive as that in the brain would require completely reconceptualizing our idea of the computer—in effect, rewriting computer science. A few researchers are trying to do just that. Instead of one powerful processor, they envision thousands and eventually millions of "stupid" processors each working independently on its tiny piece of a problem, communicating with its neighbors when it needs a piece of data or is able to answer another processor's request. There would be no central controller shuttling data and instructions back and forth from a single memory bank. Instead, each processor would be surrounded by its own ring of memory cells, storing information locally where it is needed, saving partial solutions for later use. As miniaturization technology improves, thousands of these simple processors and memory cells could be inscribed on a single chip. As the processors worked together, the solution to a problem would, in a sense, boil up from the bottom of the system to the top. While a von Neumann machine can be compared to a corporate hierarchy—control is imposed from the top down—these parallel machines would work more like a populist, grass-roots democracy.

A few groups—one is at Carnegie-Mellon, another at Minsky's Thinking Machines Corporation—are working on massively parallel machines. Minsky believes that such a device, what he and his colleagues call a Connection Machine, might be required to embody his Society of Mind theory. Each of the millions of agents—the stupid little homunculi that interact to produce intelligent tasks—would be represented by a processor. But such projects are still considered rare and exotic.

Ironically, much research on massively parallel machines is done by simulating them with programs that run on serial computers. After all, anything that can be done in parallel can be done serially—it just takes longer. Tasks that a parallel machine does in concert are done one at a time. As Turing showed, all digital computers are conceptually equivalent—one can always be programmed to imitate another. Thus some scientists conclude that studying massive parallelism is a waste of time. Describing the behavior of such a complex system, and learning how to program it, would be one of the most difficult problems ever faced by human minds. It might be simpler to keep speeding up the serial machines.

None of the difficulties encountered in streamlining computer technology is insurmountable. As scientists and engineers learn to work within the tiny world of microcircuitry, they continue to find surprising ways to overcome what seemed like fundamental barriers. To help solve the overheating problem, for example, they are studying the possibility of making microscopic switches out of materials called superconductors. By exploiting one of the strange loopholes of quantum mechanics, electrons can travel inside super-conductors without losing energy and generating heat. As temperatures near absolute zero, these substances—tin and lead, for example—reach a state of zero resistance. Surrounded by liquid helium, superconducting switches called Josephson junctions can operate on ten thousand times less current than transistors require, producing almost no heat while achieving significantly faster switching speeds. Other scientists hope to circumvent the problem of electrical resistance with computers that run on light beams instead of electricity.

Even more radical are recent suggestions that certain organic molecules, which can exist in either of two stable atomic configurations, can be used to store bits of information. By applying a voltage across such a molecule we could switch it from one state to the other, from 1 to 0. Nature already uses molecules to store information, though not in that manner. On one level, a biological cell can be thought of as a computer. The information stored in the DNA is read by RNA messengers and carried to the ribosomes where it is used to fabricate proteins and enzymes, which themselves contain information. Proteins in membrane walls "know" to allow only certain substances to flow in and out; enzymes to encourage certain reactions to take place. If the cell uses organic molecules to process information, then perhaps someday computers can too. The result would be what researchers call biochips, in which tiny organic components would process far more information than is possible with conventional devices.

As computer technology continues to improve, enabling us to store more information and manipulate it faster, the density of our simulations increases—in space as well as in time. As the grain of these digital pictures becomes finer and finer, it is tempting to wonder whether at some point the information describing a thing becomes so accurate and precise that it is as good as the thing itself. In other words, is there ultimately a difference between the simulation and the reality? In most cases the answer is obviously yes. In a simulation, information is used to build a model of a process. If the process is a physical phenomenon—weather, for example—then obviously the simulation is not the thing. A computer simulation of the heart won't pump blood; a simulated lung won't breathe. The brain, however, is an information processor. If one information processor—a computer—is used to simulate another—the brain—then how can we claim that one and not the other is thinking?

So far, the question remains within the realm of speculation. For artificial intelligence to become as good as the real thing, scientists will need computers many times more powerful than those available today. But with the rapid advances in technology, most AI researchers assume that they won't be hampered by the lack of machines. The problem will be programming them. No matter how precisely a computer can process an image or a sound, it won't be intelligent until it can understand what it hears and sees. All the 1s and 0s must be woven into patterns complex enough to resemble thinking, so that computers contain in their memories a world of symbols as rich and supple as those we hold in our heads. In AI, software is usually considered more of a problem than hardware. Whether artificial intelligence is realized in serial or parallel computers, they will have to be programmed to perform intelligent tasks. To a computer scientist a well-wrought program is as aesthetically pleasing as a symphony. The computer is the orchestra on which it is performed.

4

The Art
of
Programming

In 1970 John Horton Conway, a young British mathematician at the University of Cambridge, invented a game called Life, providing the world with a spectacular demonstration of how rich and fathomless behavior can arise from the interaction of a few simple rules. In the game, a player starts with a large grid—an oversized checkerboard or a piece of graph paper will do—and creates a simple pattern by filling in a few squares with pencil marks or small round tokens. Then, guided by the rules Conway wrote for his imaginery world, this "life form" undergoes a strange evolution. By examining each cell of the grid—the universe, Conway calls it—and counting how many of its eight adjacent cells—up, down, left, right, and the four diagonals—are occupied, the player determines whether it is to live or die. Accordingly, tokens are added and removed and the board is arranged into a new configuration. If an occupied cell has either two or three neighboring tokens, then it survives into the next generation. But if it has four or more neighbors it dies of overpopulation, becoming blank. The same fate befalls tokens with one or no neighbors—in this case they are said to die of isolation. But tokens can be created as well as destroyed. An empty cell with two neighbors remains empty but an empty cell with three neighbors gives birth—it becomes occupied. Those are the only rules of the game. Once the second-generation pattern has been determined, the same rules are applied again, producing a third generation, a fourth, a fifth, a sixth, and so on.

After experimenting with a few starting patterns and watching them grow, one quickly sees that strange and interesting things are happening. To fully appreciate them, one should watch Life being played at high speed on a computer, with each pixel of the display screen representing a cell. By typing a few commands into the keyboard, the player causes an initial pattern of dots to appear on the screen. Then he activates the Life program, and sits back and watches as a bewildering scene of kaleidoscopic images appears to unfold.

From the simplest structures a world of surprising complexity can evolve. Patterns spawn patterns that shimmer and move across the screen. While many of them die after several generations, others settle into stable arrangements that sit motionless, rotate around an axis, or oscillate among several configurations. Some patterns crawl like amoebas or propel themselves like rocket ships—colliding with other patterns, combining to form new shapes, shattering into pieces that grow, disappear, stabilize, or zoom off into the infinity beyond the edges of the screen. Eventually most games will end, with the screen containing nothing but stable patterns. But (assuming an infinite playing field) some of the Life forms can grow endlessly. If one of these eternal figures evolves, a game could last forever—if the player and our own universe were as accommodating.

In the decade and a half since Life was invented, players—many of them AI scientists—have catalogued a taxonomy of curious creatures. The blinker consists of a line of three tokens that shifts each generation from horizontal to vertical and back to horizontal again. After nine generations one simple four-token creature evolves into four symmetrically arranged blinkers—a flashing configuration known as a traffic light. One seven-token pattern becomes, in thirty-two generations, a pulsar, consisting of four structures similar to traffic lights. According to the jargon of the game, the pulsar is a three-state oscillator: it continually shifts from a forty-eight-token pattern to one with fifty-six tokens to one with seventy-two tokens, then back to the forty-eight-token pattern again. A five-token figure called the R-pentonimo evolves for 1,103 generations before it stabilizes, leaving behind a screen scattered with debris. Included in this final arrangement are such commonly seen Life objects as the ship, the loaf, the boat, and the beehive; in addition, four blinkers oscillate eternally as six five-token patterns called gliders move toward the boundaries of the screen, traveling at one fourth the "speed of light." (Since a token on the Life board can't possibly move faster than one cell per generation, Conway calls this upper limit the speed of light.) Often, players start the game with a random spray of dots, a primal soup in which islands of order arise.

When he invented Life, Conway believed that all initial patterns would eventually die out or stabilize, though some games might take more generations than humans were willing (or able) to watch. He offered a $50 reward to anyone who could prove or disprove his theory. In November 1970, a group from the MIT artificial-intelligence laboratory won the prize by showing that Conway was wrong. They discovered a three-token pattern that evolved, after forty generations, into what has become known as a glider gun. The glider gun is an oscillator of period thirty—meaning that every thirty generations it completes a cycle, evolving from one shape to another, finally returning after twenty-nine incarnations to its original form. Each time it completes a cycle it expels a glider, adding five more tokens to the screen. The process can go on indefinitely. Thus the game will never end (unless the glider gun is destroyed or mutated by a pattern encroaching on it from another part of the screen). Later the MIT group discovered that thirteen gliders could be made to collide in such a way that they would create a glider gun. Other configurations were discovered that eat gliders or reflect them. Two reflectors can be arranged to bounce a glider back and forth forever.

Using reflectors, eaters, and glider guns, Conway showed that it is possible, in principle, to construct an enormous Life pattern that works like a digital computer—its data consisting of streams of gliders, the presence or absence of which indicate *1*s and *0*s. Other patterns could work as "And," "Or," and "Not" gates and as memory cells. To coordinate all this activity, an oscillating Life pattern could be used as a clock. In other words, there is a chance (infinitesimal though it may be) that some initial Life form could evolve into a pattern that worked like a Turing machine—the hypothetical device, consisting of a scanner, marker, and endless strip of cells that can be programmed to imitate any conceivable computer.

For decades, engineers have worked to embody computers in networks of relays, vacuum tubes, transistors, and, most recently, as microscopic components etched onto the surface of silicon chips. Conway's imaginary computer demonstrates how unimportant the actual nature of this hardware really is. In his thought experiment, we have a program—the Game of Life—running on one computer and simulating another, which conceivably could be programmed to play its own Game of Life. The Life computer Conway envisions has no physical parts. It is pure mindstuff, a mathematical abstraction, an ever-shifting pattern of information.

For most of us, the word "computer" evokes harder images: panels of blinking lights, spinning tape drives, rows of large gray cabinets and desktop terminals with keyboards and glowing screens. We're preoccupied with what we can touch and see. Computer scientists tend to think in more rarefied terms. What is important, they say, is not the machine—the thing that does the computing—but the abstract notion of computation. To get a sense of what they mean by this, one can use Life as an introduction to a fascinating world called cellular automata theory. Seen in the light of this gamelike mathematics, the computer becomes more and more incorporeal, its physical aspects receding further into the realm of abstraction until they almost disappear. As we approach this vanishing point, it becomes increasingly clear that in any attempt to make computers that think, software is of the essence.

Conway's game is an example of what mathematicians call a two-state cellular automaton (each cell in the grid is in one of two states—filled or empty). In theory, cellular automata can have any number of states, and they need not be limited to two dimensions.

Since it consists of a single row of squares, a Turing machine is called a one-dimensional cellular automaton. In a three-dimensional automaton, the squares would be replaced by cubes and the playing field would look not like a grid but like an ever-changing city made of building blocks. Cubes would be stacked on cubes, forming a vast array of towers that continually shrink and grow. To visualize cellular automata with more than one state, we can fill the cells (whether they are squares or cubes) not only with dots but with different numbers, colors, or shades of gray. In a five-state automaton, for example, each cell might contain the numbers o through 4 (or the colors white, red, blue, yellow, and green). The cells need not be squares or cubes—they can be polygons or polyhedra packed to form giant crystals. Automata of four or more dimensions can't be visualized, but they can be described mathematically.

To govern how a cellular automaton behaves, any number of different rules can be used, not just the ones Conway invented. For example, while the Life automaton determines whether a cell lives or dies by considering the states of all eight surrounding cells plus that of the cell itself, there are other automata in which only four neighbors are taken into account.

There are, in other words, an endless number of possible types of cellular automata. What they all have in common is that at any instant the state of each cell is determined by those of its neighbors, and a few precisely defined transition rules. In a sense, each cell can be thought of as a simple little computer. It receives input from the cells around it, saying whether (if it's a two-state automata) they are on or off. Then it uses the rules of the game to calculate what its new state will be. (In fact, researchers at Minsky's Thinking Machine Corporation are using cellular automata theory in the design of their Connection Machine, whose multitude of parallel processors can be thought of as a lattice of cells.)

In the early 1950s, John von Neumann proved that an immensely complex cellular automaton, consisting of a grid of some 200,000 squares that could each be in one of twenty-nine states, was, like a living organism, capable of reproduction. Referring to a blueprint of itself—coded as a pattern somewhere within the cellular array—the device would grow arms into unoccupied regions of its universe and re-create itself piece by piece. The offspring would be identical in every way and contain its own blueprint and the ability to reproduce. Von Neumann even showed that one of these imaginary machines could spawn another one more complex than itself. To carry out the logistics necessary for self-reproduction, the automaton contained its own computer, in the form of a Turing machine. While von Neumann's device was a pure abstraction—there was no hope that it would be physically realized—he showed that there was no theoretical basis for dismissing the possibility of self-replicating machines. And he demonstrated that it was possible for one system to produce another more complicated (and perhaps more intelligent) than itself.

After von Neumann, mathematicians discovered other self-reproducing automata. Conway proved that such a device could exist in the Life universe, though it might occupy a computer screen several miles wide. While it is unlikely that mathematicians will ever work out the details of so complex an entity, Conway considered it probable that "given a large enough 'Life' space, initially in a random state, that after a long time, intelligent self-reproducing animals will emerge. . . ." No doubt, they would try to explain their existence through religions, philosophies, science, and mathematics, eventually discovering how to make computers that would run their own games of Life.

Edward Fredkin, who is part of a cellular automata research group at MIT, has speculated that our universe itself could be a Life game running on a computer created by some barely conceivable civilization (which might also be the result of someone's computer simulation). As Fredkin's colleague Tommaso Toffoli put it: "In a sense, nature has been continually computing the 'next state' of the universe for billions of years; all we have to do—and, actually, all we *can* do—is 'hitch a ride' on this huge ongoing computation, and try to discover which parts of it happen to go near to where we want."

Depending on one's taste for abstraction, Life can be seen either as an amusing pastime or a window to the secret of existence. At any rate, cellular automata theory shows how very general the notion of computation can be.

As Turing suggested, a computer can be thought of as a cellular automaton. Each of its gates and memory cells is a square that can be in one of two states, 1 or 0. At each tick of the clock, the entire configuration changes, as determined by the states of its cells and a few definable transition rules. Perhaps the best way to think of a computer is as a long, ever-changing row of 1s and 0s, evolving according to precisely laid plans.

Viewed from this high plane of abstraction, the nature of a computer's hardware becomes not only unimportant but irrelevant. Daniel Hillis, a graduate of MIT's artificial-intelligence laboratory, who is now in charge of Minsky's Connection Machine project, once built a computer that could play tic-tac-toe, constructing it entirely from Tinkertoys.

In fact, the concept of computation is so universal that it can be used to explain all kinds of physical phenomena—not just computers. Brian Hayes, writing in *Scientific American*, used the computational metaphor to explain how molecules of water "know" to form "the elaborate symmetries of a snowflake."

"There is no architect directing the assembly," Hayes wrote, "and the molecules themselves carry within them no template for the crystalline form." Instead, Hayes suggests, the snowflake works like a cellular automaton. "Pattern on a large scale emerges entirely from the short-range interactions of many identical units. Each molecule responds only to the influence of its nearest neighbors, but a consistent arrangement is maintained throughout a structure made up of perhaps 10^{20} molecules." To see how this can be explained computationally, "imagine that each site where a molecule might be emplaced is governed by a rudimentary computer. As the crystal grows, each computer surveys the surrounding sites and, depending on its findings, determines by some fixed rule whether its own site should be occupied or vacant."

Norman H. Packard of the Institute for Advanced Study at Princeton University actually designed a computer simulation of a snowflake, using cellular automata theory. A computer screen is divided into hexagons which can be in one of two states: black (0), corresponding to unfrozen water vapor, or white (1), corresponding to ice. Using one simple transition rule—if the sum of a cell's six neighbors is an odd number then it becomes ice—elaborate lattices evolve. Fredkin's colleague Gerard Vichniac has used cellular automata to develop computational models of other physical phenomena, such as nucleation, which occurs in crystal growth and the boiling of water. Like the work of Claude Shannon and Norbert Wiener, cellular automata research suggests a new kind of physical theory based on information as well as on matter and energy.

The possibility of a science in which all the world is thought of computationally casts the study of computers in an important new light. As its practitioners are fond of saying, computer science is not about computers, any more than astronomy is about telescopes, or biology about microscopes. These devices are tools for observing worlds otherwise inaccessible. The computer is a tool for exploring the world of complex processes, whether they involve cells, stars, or the human mind. The means of describing these processes is the computer program.

In the beginning, software was written in machine language, in which all data and instructions had to be coded by the programmer into binary form. Some parts of the resulting bit string consisted of commands (adding, multiplying, fetching a number from a certain location), while other parts indicated the names and addresses of the registers and memory cells involved in the various operations. Still other bits represented the actual data—either numbers or words translated into binary. Keeping track of all these *1*s and *0*s was a tedious task subject to frequent error.

British philosopher and AI enthusiast Margaret Boden has compared programming in machine code to describing a knitting pattern by specifying every tiny movement of the fingers, yarn, and needles. When knitting our first pair of socks we begin by paying close attention to these minute details, "passing the wool *over* the needle, passing it *around* the needle, pushing the point of the right-hand needle into the *front* of the first stitch on the left-hand needle, pushing it into the *back* of the first stitch." But soon we begin to mentally cluster frequently repeated movements into a shorthand of useful operations: stocking stitch, knit stitch, purl stitch, et cetera, which are abbreviated in knitting patterns by the symbols "st. st.," "K," and "P." Given a program for a scarf, an experienced knitter unconsciously translates the code into sequences of finger movements so engrained that they are rarely thought about.

In a similar manner, the tedium of machine-language programming can be somewhat relieved by using assembly language. In this shorthand, commonly used functions can be invoked by typing three- and four-letter commands: ADD for add, DIV for divide, MOV for move, CMP (compare the values of two registers), SWP (swap the values between two registers), RTL (rotate the contents of a register one bit to the left), SHTR (shift the contents of a register one bit to the right), LOOP (which executes a series of instructions over and over again until a counter reaches a predetermined level and ends the operation). Another convenience of assembly language is that numbers can be expressed in decimal instead of binary.

Of course, the computer's hardware doesn't know what ADD, MOV, or 2,323 means. When an assembly-language program is run, it is automatically translated, by a program called an assembler, into machine language. The decimal numbers are converted to binary, and each assembly-language instruction is translated into a string of bits that can be executed by the various "And," "Or," and "Not" gates inside the machine.

The advantage of assembly language is that it gives programmers larger, more natural units to think with. But programming with these symbols remains a tedious task. Operations still must be specified in excruciating detail. While programmers don't have to think in terms of *1*s and *0*s—specifying whether each gate or memory cell is to be on or off—they still must be closely familiar with the hardware of the machine. Since each type of computer (or microprocessor chip) is built in a different manner, the details of assembly language vary widely from machine to machine.

In the 1950s, to help make programming a more natural task, computer scientists began to develop languages such as Fortran and Lisp, which gave programmers still larger chunks to think with. A single command in one of these "higher-level" languages automatically sets in motion a cascade of operations causing gates and memory cells to flip on and off. If programmers wanted to add two variables, say A and B, they didn't need to tell the computer to fetch them, add them, and store the result in memory location 10010. They would simply write A + B. The computer would take care of the details and do the bookkeeping. In fact, programmers didn't need to know anything about memory addresses, registers, or "And," "Or," and "Not" gates—they didn't even have to know that such things existed. They could think on a higher level of abstraction, unconcerned with the details of the bit-by-bit manner in which ultimately all programs are carried out.

Like assembly language, the higher-level programming languages require software to translate them into 1s and 0s. A program written in Fortran, Pascal, Lisp, or another high-level language is fed into a translating program and out pops another program suitable for the particular hardware that is being used. One type of translator, called a compiler, takes the entire program and converts it into bits before running it on the machine; another type, called an interpreter, translates the program one line at a time. Each has its advantages, but the important point is that both interpreters and compilers are further demonstrations of Turing's law—that any computer can be programmed to imitate any other. A Fortran compiler for an IBM personal computer is a program that turns the machine into one capable of understanding Fortran. A Pascal compiler turns it into a Pascal-understanding machine. A Fortran compiler for an Apple, a Burroughs, a state-of-the-art Cray, or an antique Univac would vary widely in form, as does the electronic architecture of these machines. But when the programmer wrote the line C = A + B, each of the machines would be able to execute it. Down at the machine-language level there would be little resemblance between the way the Apple and the Univac or the Burroughs and the Cray processed the command. But to the programmer that wouldn't matter. The compiler acts as a cushion between the human and the machine, a means of rendering hardware invisible. As computer scientists sometimes describe it, assembly language is built on top of machine language, and the high-level programming languages are built on top of assembly language. As programmers move up this hierarchy of abstraction, they are bothered with fewer and fewer details of how the computer operates. They can think more in terms of what they want the program to do, rather than how the computer should do it.

With these higher-level languages, programming still requires great precision. The problem to be solved must be described as a process—a step-by-step procedure that, if unfailingly executed, will lead to the correct answer. Mathematicians call one of these lists of instructions an algorithm. If, for example, we want to write a program to determine whether a given number is prime (that it has no divisors other than itself and 1), we start by breaking the task into pieces. How, we ask ourselves, can one test for primeness? The answer is to divide a number by every number smaller than itself. (Actually, there are much more efficient ways of doing this, but the details are unimportant for the purpose of the example.) If any one of these numbers divides into the larger number evenly, leaving no remainder, then it can't be prime. It has at least one divisor. To a computer this procedure might be described something like this:

1. Print on the display screen the question "What number do you want to test?"
2. Read the answer typed in by the user and call that number A.
3. Set X (the number to divide by) equal to 2.
4. Divide A by X.
5. If there is no remainder, go to Step 8. Otherwise proceed to the next step.
6. Add 1 to X.
7. Is X now equal to A? If so, go to Step 9; otherwise return to Step 4 and repeat the loop.
8. Print "The number is not prime" and end.
9. Print "The number is prime" and end.

Given any number as input, the computer would try dividing it by 2, then 3, then 4, and so on, halting if it found a divisor and declaring, "The number is not prime." Otherwise, it would continue in this manner, looping around and around, dividing by larger and larger numbers until it had tried every number smaller than A itself. If at this point it still had found no divisor, then it would say, "The number is prime." To the user steps 2 through 7 are invisible. One simply types in the number to be tested and waits for the answer to appear on the screen.

An actual program to test for primeness would look different depending on what language it was written in. Any algorithm can be programmed in any higher-level language, but some languages are better suited for some things than others. Fortran (which is short for "formula translation") is usually used for scientific and mathematical problems, Cobol ("common business-oriented language") for business applications. BASIC (Beginner's All-purpose Symbolic Instruction Code) was written to be easily learned by novice programmers. All three of these languages are primitive by modern standards and are being surpassed in sophistication by more elegant inventions such as Pascal, C, and Ada (named for Babbage's cohort, Lady Ada Lovelace).

Machine language and assembly language are by no means obsolete. After all, somebody has to know enough about the minute workings of the machine to write the compilers and assemblers. Also, programs written directly in these lower-level languages often run faster and more efficiently than the translations made by the compilers. And, finally, some people simply like assembly language. It might be tedious but it gives some programmers a feeling of closeness to—and power over—the machine.

One of the most intriguing of the high-level languages is Logo, which is used to help children unleash their creative powers by playing with computers. The language, which was invented by Minsky's colleague at MIT Seymour Papert, is so simple and direct that it also provides an excellent way for adults to experience what it is like to think computationally. To draw a line on a computer screen, the following Logo program can be typed into the computer:

```
PENDOWN

FORWARD 50 RIGHT 144

PENUP
```

The Logo interpreter orchestrates the gates and registers of the machine to create the illusion that a pen behind the screen is drawing an illuminated line 50 units long, then making a 144-degree right-hand turn. Now if the command is repeated, the pen will draw another line and turn again. By modifying the program to repeat the command five times a child can draw a five-pointed star.

```
PENDOWN

REPEAT 5 [forward 50 right 144]

PENUP
```

After experimenting with the program, the child might see that it is possible to draw larger and smaller stars with different numbers of points. Finally, the program can be modified into a general star-writing routine called *to star*. By filling in the blanks in the first line (the variables "size" and "points"), the programmer can make the computer draw stars of different shapes and sizes.

```
TO STAR :SIZE :POINTS

    PENDOWN

    REPEAT :POINTS [forward:size right 720/:points]

    PENUP
```

(The next-to-last line reflects the fact that the turns made by the program must add up to 720 degrees.)

With more complex programs such as word processors, spreadsheets, or video games, another, higher rung is added to the ladder of abstraction.

When one of these programs is in use, all thoughts of hardware and the lower levels of software (the compilers, interpreters, et cetera) recede further into the background. You don't even need to type in the program. You simply buy a floppy disk, insert it into the disk drive of a home computer, and the thousands of lines of the program are automatically loaded into the machine. Then you can move paragraphs, calculate mortgage payments for the next thirty years, or fire simulated death rays at spaceships without any knowledge of the language the off-the-shelf software is written in.

Among the dozens of computer languages that have been developed over the last three decades, Lisp allows programmers to work at an unusually high level of abstraction. Thinking in Lisp is different from thinking in any other programming language. In fact, it is often said that previous knowledge of another computer language can be a hindrance to learning Lisp. Those who have been frustrated by brief classroom exposures to the tediums of BASIC and Fortran are often surprised by the ease with which they can learn to express themselves in Lisp. Fluency in the language requires years of practice, but some of its essence can be gleaned from a few examples. By gaining a rough feel for Lisp, one can see more easily how intelligent tasks such as learning can be turned into procedures that a machine can do.

Suppose that you spend several hundred dollars and purchase a Lisp interpreter for your personal computer—a floppy disk containing a translation program that will turn the machine into one capable of understanding the programs you want to write in Lisp. You're not particularly interested in crunching numbers or devising a filing system for your recipes. You want to try an exercise that will introduce you to AI programming. Turning to the first chapter of *Lisp*, a very clear introduction to the language written by MIT's Patrick Winston and his colleague Berthold Horn, you find the description of a simple program that keeps track of friends and enemies.

First you use a command called SET to tell the program who your friends are. By typing the line (SET 'FRIENDS '(DICK JANE SALLY)) you can tell the computer to arrange its memory so that the names are part of a list called FRIENDS. Likewise another line (SET 'ENEMIES '(TROLL GRINCH GHOST)) attaches a list of names to ENEMIES. In Lisp, each word included in the program—FRIENDS, DICK, JANE, et cetera—is called an atom or symbol. Each symbol is stored in memory with "pointers" to the symbols it is related to. It is helpful to think of symbols as boxes and pointers as lines connecting them. The most sophisticated Lisp systems can actually display them this way, though deep in the computer's memory the symbols are simply bit strings and the pointers are the binary addresses of the memory locations where the related symbols reside.

Memory structures can be changed as easily as they are created. To turn an enemy, the ghost, say, into a friend, the following lines could be used:

```
(SET 'ENEMIES (DELETE 'GHOST ENEMIES))
(SET 'FRIENDS (ADD 'GHOST FRIENDS))
```

The first line detaches the symbol GHOST from the list called ENE-MIES; the second line attaches GHOST to the list of FRIENDS. (The single quotation marks show the computer where commands such as DE-LETE leave off and data such as GHOST begin.) If this is an operation that might be used repeatedly, a new generalized function called NEWFRIEND can be created with the command DEFUN (for "define function"). As with the "to star" routine in Logo, NEWFRIEND contains variables—blanks to be filled in.

```
(DEFUN NEWFRIEND (NAME)
   (SET 'ENEMIES (DELETE NAME ENEMIES))
   (SET 'FRIENDS (ADD NAME FRIENDS)))
```

With this new Lisp structure hidden away in memory, all you would have to do is type (NEWFRIEND 'GHOST). The bookkeeping would be taken care of automatically.

The example is trivial, but it illustrates two important characteristics of Lisp, and of AI programming in general: (1) complex functions can be built from more basic ones, and (2) data need not consist simply of words or numbers—a computer can be used to build up simple concepts. In a very limited sense, the program might be said to know that DICK, JANE, and SALLY are FRIENDS. Obviously it does not know what a friend is—or for that matter what Sally is. They are just opaque units—symbols that stand for things in the world. For all the computer knows, ENEMIES might be a class of vehicles and GHOST, TROLL, and GRINCH each a brand of car. FRIENDS might be a country in South America whose exports are DICK, JANE, and SALLY. But symbolic processing is not mere word processing. In a word processor, we can type a sentence about ghosts and trolls, but the words remain unconnected tokens—there is no way to give the program a sense that they belong to the same category, in this case ENEMIES.

In Lisp, symbols can be connected to other symbols, and if we are unsatisfied with the level of the program's understanding, still more con-nections can be made. JANE can be fleshed out by attaching it to other symbols.

```
(JANE (IS-A PERSON)
      (SEX   FEMALE)
      (AGE   23)
      (HAIR-COLOR   BLOND)
      (EYE-COLOR   BLUE)
      (JOB   STUDENT)
      (LIVES-IN MINNEAPOLIS))
```

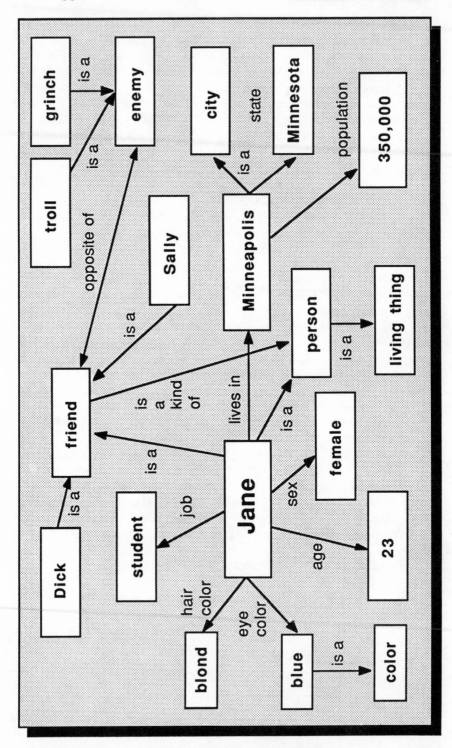

Capturing Meaning in a Network

Now each of these new symbols would exist in memory with pointers linking them to JANE. They too are opaque units, but we can flesh them out by attaching more symbols to them.

```
(MINNEAPOLIS (IS–A CITY)
             (STATE   MINNESOTA)
             (POPULATION   350,000))
```

Eventually a network emerges in which nodes, like MINNEAPOLIS, are connected by links, like IS–A. The network could express the fact that BLUE is a COLOR, and FRIENDS is a type of PERSON, which is a type of LIVING THING—or that it is the opposite of ENEMIES (though this relationship is implicit in the function NEWFRIEND). Given enough time and storage space, a network of great complexity can be built, its boxes-connected-to-boxes reminiscent of what psychologists call an associative memory.

In Lisp terminology (DICK JANE SALLY) and (DELETE GHOST ENEMIES) both are called lists. It doesn't matter that some of the items on a list are commands (DELETE) and others are symbols to be manipulated. In pure Lisp, everything—data and instructions—consists of lists. In fact, an entire program, such as the one defining the function NEWFRIEND, is considered a list—or, more precisely, a list of lists. In more complex programs, lists can be embedded within lists which are embedded within lists, and so on, until any desired depth of nesting is reached. It is clear then why Lisp is short for "list processing." In the language, lists are fed to lists, which process them to produce new lists. Symbols are attached to symbols to build vast networks—a crude example, perhaps, of what humans call learning.

For his 1970 doctoral dissertation at MIT, Patrick Winston wrote a program that could learn a simplified version of the concept "arch"—in this case, one made of three building blocks: two posts, for support, and a cross-piece called a lintel. The program, one of the classics in the AI field, is a good example of how Lisp can be used to get computers to perform seemingly intelligent behavior. First Winston had to provide the program with all the elementary information it would need to know in order to understand arches: objects such as POST1, POST2, and LINTEL, and relationships such as IS–LYING, IS–STANDING, RIGHT–OF, LEFT–OF, MUST–NOT–TOUCH, IS–SUPPORTED–BY, and the stronger MUST–BE–SUPPORTED–BY. It was also told about general classes of objects: the BRICK (blocks that are rectangular solids), the WEDGE (blocks that are triangular solids), and the PRISM (blocks that are either rectangular or triangular solids). Then the program was given, one after another, Lisp descriptions of combinations of blocks that were and were not arches. Using procedures programmed into the system by Winston, it was able to compare the examples, one against the other, and slowly build inside its memory a model of the necessary characteristics of an arch.

Winston began the training session with a simple example: two upright bricks with a third brick lying across the top. This, Winston told the program, was an arch. Knowing nothing more about arches than what was (figuratively) in front of its nose, the program concluded that an arch consisted of two standing bricks supporting a horizontal one. A simplified version of what the program had learned thus far would look something like this:

```
(ARCH (PARTS LINTEL POST1 POST2)
      (LINTEL IS-SUPPORTED-BY POST1)
      (LINTEL IS-SUPPORTED-BY POST2)
      (LINTEL A-KIND-OF BRICK)
      (POST1 A-KIND-OF BRICK)
      (POST2 A-KIND-OF BRICK)
      (LINTEL IS-LYING)
      (POST1 IS-STANDING)
      (POST2 IS-STANDING))
```

If that's all the system knew about arches, it would be far too undiscriminating, imagining arches where none existed. To help the program refine its definition, Winston showed it a second example, identical to the first except with the two posts pushed so close together that they touched. This T-shaped stack of blocks was not an arch, Winston told the program. Thus, comparing example one and example two, the program was able to add to its definition the requirement that the posts must not touch. To further tighten the program's definition, Winston showed it another negative example, in which the lintel was removed from its supports and was lying on the ground. Since this was not an arch, the program strengthened the requirement that the lintel is supported by the posts to the more restrictive MUST-BE-SUPPORTED-BY.

And so, step by step, through a process akin to what humans call induction, the program learned what an arch was:

```
(ARCH (PARTS LINTEL POST1 POST2)
      (LINTEL MUST-BE-SUPPORTED-BY POST1)
      (LINTEL MUST-BE-SUPPORTED-BY POST2)
      (LINTEL A-KIND-OF BRICK)
      POST1 A-KIND-OF BRICK)
      (POST2 A-KIND-OF BRICK)
      (LINTEL IS-LYING)
      (POST1 IS-STANDING)
      (POST2 IS-STANDING)
      (POST1 MUST-NOT-TOUCH POST2)
      (POST2 MUST-NOT-TOUCH POST1))
```

But now the definition was a bit too restrictive. Arches aren't always made of bricks. After giving the program another positive example, in which a wedge instead of a brick was used as a lintel, it was able to stretch its notion of archness. A lintel wasn't necessarily a brick. It could also be a wedge. Or, to generalize, a LINTEL is A–KIND–OF PRISM.

In AI research it is common to work, as Winston did, in a simplified domain such as the blocks world. Learning to recognize an arch made from building blocks is a long way from learning to discriminate between Doric and Ionian columns, or buildings designed by Philip Johnson from those of I. M. Pei. But Winston's program seems to capture the rudiments—and perhaps the essence—of what we do when we learn by induction. If we're studying architecture, we see example after example of Gothic cathedrals, or houses designed by Frank Lloyd Wright. With each encounter we refine the pictures we are building in our minds; we string together networks of characteristics that constitute "Gothicness" or "Frank-Lloyd-Wrightness." When we first are exposed to classical (or new wave) music it all sounds the same. But slowly, by being told "This is Bach, this is not Bach—it's Mozart," we learn to listen to a piece of music—one we've never heard before—and recognize its composer. With more training we can make finer distinctions, discriminating among several composers with similar styles, or among the various stages in a single composer's career.

Learning about art and music is far more subtle than what Winston did with Lisp. But his program is evidence that computer languages can be used to take vaguely defined notions like learning and recognition and describe them as processes, which can be tested by running them on a computer. Simple universes like the blocks world are to AI what the artificial domain of frictionless tracks and perfectly elastic billiard balls is to physics. In both cases, problems are stripped to their essence in an attempt to devise theories that, properly qualified, will apply to the real world. Newton's laws—that force equals mass times acceleration or that for every action there is an equal and opposite reaction—could be applied in their purest forms only in a world without such inconveniences as friction. Planets would move in perfectly elliptical orbits only if they were unperturbed by each other's gravity fields. But these ideal examples help guide us to more realistic theories.

Working in the blocks world also gives researchers a respect for how complex seemingly simple tasks can be. Consider some of the problems that arise in writing a program that knows how to do nothing more than stack simulated blocks on a computer screen. First, the programmer must describe, in Lisp, the objects that will comprise the world: RED BLOCK, YELLOW BLOCK, BLUE BLOCK, GREEN PYRAMID, RED BALL, BLACK BOX, et cetera. Attached to each of these objects are lists of descriptive information, such as the fact that you can't put a block on top of a pyramid, or that objects can be placed inside a box. The program is also given a vocabulary to describe the different possible relationships between blocks—such as DIRECTLY–SUPPORTS and IS–SUPPORTED–BY—and commands that instruct a mechanical hand (also simulated) to carry out various tasks: PICKUP, PUTON, GRASP, UNGRASP, et cetera.

In typical Lisp fashion, each of these commands is built from other commands. For example, to ask the program to put the green block on the red block, one can type (PUTON GREEN RED). Then, to do its job, PUTON has to call GRASP, MOVE, and UNGRASP. But what if either block already has another block stacked on top of it? Then PUTON is temporarily put on hold. It must call CLEARTOP, which works by calling GET–RID–OF, which calls PUTAT, which puts the obstructing block at a different location. Once this detour has been completed, the program returns to PUTON and continues executing the original task. Actually, things aren't quite that simple. To do its job, PUTAT also must call GRASP, MOVE, and UNGRASP, as well as FINDSPACE, to find a place to put the block it removed—and perhaps MAKESPACE if no space is available. And MAKESPACE works by calling GET–RID–OF, which, once again, calls PUTAT.

In this last example, an interesting loop has occurred. PUTAT calls MAKESPACE which calls GET–RID–OF which calls PUTAT again. It is entirely possible that in order to do its job, this latest incarnation of PUTAT also will have to call MAKESPACE, which will call PUTAT again. So PUTAT calls PUTAT, which calls PUTAT. . . . Or, in other words, PUTAT is built up from a number of functions, including itself. Computer scientists call this curious phenomenon where a function is defined in terms of itself recursion.

Conceptual networks such as the one in the FRIENDS/ENEMIES program also are defined recursively. The symbol SALLY can be linked to a thousand nodes, which are each linked to a thousand more. Ultimately, though, the network folds back on itself and forms a closed system. SALLY is a WOMAN who lives in LOS ANGELES. A WOMAN is a variety of PERSON. LOS ANGELES is a CITY. A CITY is a place where PERSONs live. We've completed a loop. A conceptual net is a tangle of such circular definitions, what Minsky calls "a castle built on air."

"The secret of what something means lies in the ways it connects to all the other things we know," he wrote. "The more such links, the more a thing will mean to us. . . . Contrary to common belief, there's really nothing wrong with circular definitions. Each part can give some meaning to the rest. . . . There's nothing wrong with ropes—or knots, or woven cloth—in which each strand helps hold the other strands together (or apart). There's nothing very wrong, in this sense, with having one's entire mind a castle in the air."

In *Gödel, Escher, Bach*, Douglas Hofstadter showed that recursion is fundamental in mathematics, art, music, and nature. In subatomic physics, for example, the elementary particles are all defined in terms of one another. A neutron can be defined as the particle that decays to form a proton, an electron, and an antineutrino, which all can be defined in terms of other particles, including themselves. We experience recursion when we stand between two mirrors, which reflect each other back and forth, as far as we can see in either direction, forever it seems. In truth, of course, everything must end. Each reflection is smaller than the last. The recursion ends when a reflection is as small as a single molecule of the reflecting substance—or perhaps when it is too tiny to be detected by an eye.

As a final example, consider how recursion is used to build a simple Lisp algorithm that answers the question Is X greater than Y? (The example works only for positive numbers.) It's not necessary to understand the program in detail, only to get the gist of how a function can work by calling itself over and over again. (In the example, COND stands for "conditional" and basically just means "if.")

```
(DEFUN (GREATER? X Y)
   (COND
      ((ZERO? X) FALSE)
      ((ZERO? Y) TRUE)
      (OTHERWISE (GREATER? (SUBTRACT1 X) (SUBTRACT1 Y)))))
```

After reading the first line (in which a human has filled in numbers for X and Y) the program checks to see whether X is equal to zero. "ZERO X?" it asks itself. If X is zero than it can't be greater than Y—it must be smaller or, if Y is also zero, equal. So the program reports FALSE. X is not greater than Y, and the project is done. But if X is not zero, then the program moves on to the next line, which tests whether Y is zero. If so, then X (which has already been shown not to be zero) must be greater than Y. The program prints TRUE. Chances are, however, that neither number is zero, in which case the program goes on to the final line, which subtracts 1 from both X and Y and begins the whole process over again. It "recurses," as Lisp programmers like to say. GREATER calls GREATER, applying itself to the slightly simpler task of deciding whether X − 1 is greater than Y − 1. If, this time through, one of the numbers is zero, the recursion halts and the problem is solved. If not, the program calls itself again—and again and again and again, until one of the numbers to be tested finally has been reduced to zero. To determine whether 10 is greater than 9, GREATER calls itself nine times, applying itself to 9 and 8, then 8 and 7, then 7 and 6—until finally it is given the simple task of deciding whether 1 is greater than 0.

There is something elegant about the way one recursion spirals into another, until we encounter once again the stupid homunculus, who knows nothing but the difference between 1 and 0. Recursion is one of those ideas so basic that one moment it seems trivial, the next moment profound. One of the beauties of Lisp is how easily loops can be embedded in loops, recursions within recursions. The result is a web of interlocking functions, each one simple and uninteresting in itself. But when allowed to interact, they can produce surprising behavior.

The software used in artificial-intelligence research contains thousands of lines. Even with a high-level language like Lisp, one program might take several years to develop. Thus, a great deal of programming is done with even higher-level languages, which are, as the computer scientists say, built on top of Lisp. Given a few lines written in one of these very powerful languages, the compiler will automatically translate them into, perhaps, several pages of Lisp, which are then compiled into machine language. The computer, in other words, writes its own Lisp program.

Some of the most interesting work being done in this area is at Kestrel Institute in Palo Alto, California, where Cordell Green, an alumnus of the Stanford AI Lab and a former student of John McCarthy's, is working on this problem of getting programs to write programs. Given a brief description of a task in a very high-level language called V, Green's system—CHI, which is pronounced like the Greek letter—writes a detailed Lisp program. In one version of the system, users could simply provide examples of what the program they wanted written was supposed to do. Or they could answer questions posed by the automatic programmer, beginning with "What is the name of the program you want to write?"

In a sense, all compilers are automatic programmers (given a description in a high-level language they produce a machine-language program), but they lack the intelligence Green and his colleagues are trying to build into CHI. Like a human programmer, it draws on knowledge about how to program— not hard-and-fast rules but flexible heuristics. Unlike conventional compilers, CHI can explore alternatives, writing several versions of a program, then choosing the most efficient one. Just as a chess program uses heuristics to find its way through a search space of all possible chess games, CHI explores a space that includes many of the possible ways to write a procedure in Lisp.

In the computer industry, writing good programs is considered at least as difficult and time-consuming a task as designing and producing good machines. And because each computer needs a wide variety of programs to make it useful, software development lags behind hardware design. Whenever a new machine is released, it can be months or even years before good programs are available. Green hopes CHI eventually will help close the gap.

"We're building systems where a one-page description in V is translated into a ten- to twenty-page program," Green explained. "It's truly amazing. Since software is the biggest problem we have today, and since we have the solution to the software problem, we have the answer to the world's problems," he says, straight-faced, with only a hint that he's speaking tongue in cheek. "So we've solved the world's problems. What's wrong with our solution? Not all the rules are there. We can only do narrow software for particular applications." CHI can write programs that perform certain very specific tasks—figuring out the best way to sort a list of numbers or design a "data structure" (a table used to store information inside a computer). But it can't come close to writing a word processor, an automatic programmer like CHI, or even a video game. But the system is continually getting better. V, Green said, stands for "very much better than the old system"—CHI's predecessor, PSI.

Some of the more idealistic researchers in automatic programming are hoping for a discovery that would propel software development to the pace of the present revolution in electronic hardware. They imagine that it might happen like this: someone will design a program, which will help design a more intelligent program, which will help design programs that are smarter still. The quest for an artificial mind would take off, programs spawning programs, growing exponentially.

In a very limited sense this has already begun. One of the most intriguing things about CHI is that it was designed to contain its own description. Thus CHI knows about CHI, which may someday enable the program to modify and improve itself. In fact, Green and his colleagues already have taken a large portion of the program, which was originally written in Lisp, and translated it (by hand) into V. Then they gave this higher-level description back to CHI, which rewrote it in Lisp, producing a version that was better than the one written by the human programmers at Kestrel.

As, level by level, computer scientists ascend the hierarchy of abstraction, they come closer to the goal of designing languages so sophisticated that the programmer won't have to worry about translating ideas into computerese—it will be up to the machine to understand the programmer. The user will tell the computer *what* to do, not *how* to do it. For some AI researchers, the ultimate goal is to write programs that take the highest-level languages we have—English, French, Spanish, Japanese—and translate their ambiguity and richness into words a computer can understand.

5

The
Meaning
of
Meaning

O n July 24, 1969, with the usual fanfare accorded to conquering heroes, the Apollo 11 astronauts returned to earth, leaving behind a plastic American flag that stood unwaving in the airless desolation of the lunar terrain. With them they brought forty-eight pounds of moon rocks, which, after being held in quarantine to guard against microscopic invaders, were turned over to geologists eager to apply their knowledge of the earth to the study of a nearby world. The results of their experiments were reported several months later at the First Annual Lunar Science Conference. Then they were encoded and stored in a computer, where they were of instantaneous use to anyone familiar with the arcane incantations needed to retrieve information from a data base. In other words, to benefit from NASA's largesse, a geologist would have to think like a computer and speak its language instead of our own.

NASA officials believed there must be a better way. So, in the summer of 1970, they approached William A. Woods, a young computer scientist who was making a name for himself as a pioneer in the art of designing programs that could understand English. Recently, Woods had written two landmark papers suggesting ways to program a computer not only with the rules of syntax, by which proper sentences are formed, but also with semantics, a feel for what they mean.

In recent years, Woods, like many of his colleagues in artificial intelligence, has gravitated toward the side of the field concerned with designing and selling expert systems. As chief scientist at a Cambridge, Massachusetts, company called Applied Expert Systems (APEX, for short), he is in charge of developing decision-making programs for the financial-services community. This potentially lucrative market includes banks, brokerage houses, insurance companies, and accounting firms.

"My role here," he wrote in a letter to his colleagues shortly after joining the company in 1983, "is to keep APEX properly positioned on the technology curve—at or near the frontier but not beyond the point of feasibility. . . . Principally," he continued, "I will be interested in knowledge representation, automated reasoning, natural language input and output, computer assisted instruction, and foundations of meaning and understanding."

Foundations of meaning and understanding. It would be difficult to name an area of research more fundamental to appreciating, in the deepest sense, what it means to be human. It is, perhaps, the most important issue, the one that comes before all others. What is the meaning of meaning? Philosophers call this the problem of semantics, and it seems like a subject that would be more at home in the halls of an Ivy League university or on the greens of Oxford than in a computer software company.

But to those familiar with his accomplishments, the letter was vintage William Woods. Throughout his career his work has illustrated the interaction between philosophy and engineering that characterizes AI. Designing software that purports to understand English, or perform any activity we would deem intelligent, causes researchers to address problems basic to the foundations of philosophy, psychology, linguistics, logic, and mathematics, as well as computer science. On the other hand, there is an overriding desire to test ideas by making systems that work. "AI is the eclectic discipline," Woods said, "sitting where all those fields must interface." "Interface," he says. Not "meet," "come together," "overlap," or "coincide." Like many people whose research has led them to think of the world in terms of systems, his conversations are liberally sprinkled with computer jargon. A slender, soft-spoken man, with thinning hair and wire-rimmed glasses, he talks of "push-down stacks," "tree structures," and "linear-bounded automata" as though they were terms that anybody would understand. When it comes to dealing with things philosophical, he believes that he and his colleagues in AI just might have an edge over their technologically less sophisticated predecessors.

"Philosophers didn't have the image of the computer in which to embody their ideas," he explained. "What I'm trying to do the philosophers never have done. I'm trying to solve the problem of meaning instead of just contemplating and savoring it.

"On the other hand," he conceded, "people in AI have a tendency to plow ahead with a supposed solution before they understand what the problem is."

One needs useful systems, but without good theory the work is built on sand (or, perhaps more appropriately, on silicon). Practical applications are important, he likes to say, but they frequently raise problems that must have philosophically adequate solutions.

Fifteen years ago, when NASA asked Woods to develop what now would be called a "natural-language front end to a data base," they were interested less in philosophical questions than in finding a solution to a frustrating problem.

"They came to me," Woods recalled, "and said, 'We've got this data base that has all the chemical analyses of the first year's work on the *Apollo* moon rocks, and we'd like to make them available to all the geologists out there. The problem is that if somebody wants to ask a question it still takes a Fortran programmer to understand what the question is, and to know the formats of the data tables and what the names of the fields are—all those details. Then he can write a little program that will go get the answer.' "

Specifically, NASA had a computerized table summarizing the results of thousands of measurements that had been made on moon rocks. The table showed the amount of various minerals, isotopes, or chemical elements that had been found in the samples. Also included were information on how old the samples were and bibliographic references to the scientific articles from which the data had been collected. Geologists who wanted to ask something like, "What is the average concentration of aluminum in high alkali rocks?" would have to write a program that would find all the alkalis, which were known to the computer as Type A's, look up the concentration of aluminum (encrypted as AL₂O₃), and average the results. To ask other questions they would have to know other codes: olivine is OLIV, breccias are Type C's. Every mineral had an abbreviation—ilmenite, chromite, silicon, magnetite, apatite, titanium, strontium, potassium, rubidium, iridium. Remembering them all was tedious enough, but not nearly so much as programming in the rigid and unforgiving syntax of Fortran.

"What we'd like," the NASA officials told Woods, "is to enable the geologist to just 'dial up' and communicate in English the same kind of thing he'd say to his colleagues, and get the answers out from that." The computer, they believed, should be responsible for translating from English to computerese.

At the time NASA approached Woods, he was working at Bolt Beranek and Newman, a Cambridge research firm that was developing one of the best private artificial-intelligence laboratories in the country. BBN had already hired Daniel Bobrow, a former student of Minsky's who had distinguished himself by writing for his doctoral dissertation a program called Student, which translated simple high school "story problems" from English into algebraic equations and then solved them. The program knew very little grammar, really. It could only recognize a small number of phrase types commonly found in story problems, such as "How many _____ does ___ have?" and "Find _____ and _____ ." Given a problem, the program would look for such patterns, using them as clues to aid in the translation.

One example the program solved was this: "If the number of customers Tom gets is twice the square of 20 percent of the number of advertisements he runs, and the number of advertisements he runs is 45, what is the number of customers Tom gets?" Certain phrases, such as "the number of customers Tom gets" and "the number of advertisements," were assigned variables, say X and Y, while "twice the square of 20 percent of" was recognized as an instruction to take 20 percent of Y, raise that quantity to the second power, then multiply the whole thing by two. The word "is" was recognized as corresponding to the equals sign. After analyzing the problem, Student discovered that the equation to be solved was $X = 2 \times (.20Y)^2$, given that Y = 45.

To bolster Student's powers of comprehension, Bobrow had provided the program with a small number of facts about the world: "people" is the plural of "person," "one half" means .5, "has" is a verb, "Mary" is a person, a "father" is a person, "squared" is an operator, "distance" equals speed times time, the "perimeter of a rectangle" means twice the sum of its length and width. As long as the program wasn't asked to stray beyond the narrow confines of its world view, it worked fairly well, serving as "an existence proof," as mathematicians say, that a computer could be given a rudimentary sense of understanding, at least within a tiny domain.

In addition to the renown he has received for his work in language processing and other areas, Bobrow has become immortalized in AI folklore because of an incident at BBN that occurred one Saturday morning in the late 1960s. A vice-president for the company wanted to demonstrate a computer for some customers. No one was in the computer room, but attached to a Teletype machine was a note: "Type all messages into this Teletype, and end them with a period." He thought the message had been left by Bobrow, who had a Teletype in his home. Actually, the machine was hooked to a computer running a version of Eliza, the program that mimicks a psychotherapist. The vice-president typed a request to borrow the computer for the morning.

"Why do you ask?" the machine replied.

"I might be able to make some additional telecomp sales."

"Why aren't you sure?"

Well, knowing Eliza, one can easily imagine the rest of the conversation. The vice-president went into a rage. He called Bobrow on the telephone, and, sounding a bit like Parry, asked, "Why are you being so snotty to me?" And Bobrow, out of human weakness, couldn't keep from laughing. The incident led some AI researchers to suggest, tongue in cheek, that a computer had finally passed the Turing test.

Woods had joined Bobrow at BBN in 1970 after leaving Harvard University's Aiken Computation Laboratory, where (first as a graduate student, then as an assistant professor of computer science) he, too, had done groundbreaking work in what was coming to be known as natural-language processing, a discipline at the crossroads of linguistics and computer science.

"I went to Harvard for graduate school thinking I was interested in what at that point I probably would have called cybernetics," Woods recalled. He studied the fledgling discipline of computer science, learning about the magic of recursion and the ways in which a digital computer could take a finite number of rules and use them to generate an infinity of interesting patterns—whether they were configurations in a game like Life or English sentences. Woods was intrigued by the notion that a grammar, a set of rules for combining words into proper sentences, could be thought of as a machine whose output was language. Or, conversely, a sentence could be fed to a grammar machine that would parse it: dissecting it into subject and object, nouns, verbs, adjectives, adverbs, prepositions, and so forth, concocting a chart similar to those produced by high school English students told by their teacher to diagram a sentence. Once a sentence was cast in this form, it would be ready for another program (yet to be invented) that would decipher its meaning.

This was not a new idea. In the summer of 1964, the year William Woods arrived, Harvard had held a workshop summarizing ten years of efforts to get computers to translate foreign languages into English. Woods obtained the notes to the course and read about the successes and (mostly) failures of what fell under the rubric of machine translation, or MT, as it was usually called. In many ways, MT was a forerunner to AI. The field got its start in 1949 when Warren Weaver, a colleague of Claude Shannon and one of the founders of information theory, wrote a memorandum suggesting that, since computers were commonly used to decipher military codes, they could also be made to translate languages. Russian could be thought of as English that had been encrypted according to certain rules. If the rules could be discovered, one language could be transformed into another. First, a parsing program would diagram a sentence, identifying each word according to whether it was a noun, verb, adjective, et cetera. Then, having determined the grammatical form—the syntax—of the sentence, the computer would call on another program to deal with the semantics. It would look up the meaning of each word in a dictionary, substituting the English equivalent. Then another part of the program would rearrange the words, taking into account that in Spanish, for example, adjectives are often placed after nouns, not before them, or that in German verbs often come at the ends of sentences.

In retrospect, the project seems charmingly naïve. How, for example, would a program resolve ambiguities—words that had more than one meaning? The radicals in the MT field believed a program could be written that would rely on context, much as humans do. If the computer was translating an English document about radio transmission, the words "wave" and "field" probably would refer to electromagnetic phenomena, not scenery; "attraction" would be used in its magnetic, not its romantic, sense. More conservative MT advocates believed that computer translation would require the assistance of human editors. In cases of multiple meanings, the computer would list each possibility, leaving it up to a "posteditor" to make sensible choices. To make matters even easier, a "preeditor" could give the computer some hints by marking the text before it was translated. In AI parlance, both of these methods are known as "having a human in the loop." Even with two editors in the loop, it was hoped that machine translation would be more economical than human translation. The preeditor would need to know only Russian, the posteditor only English, thus avoiding the cost of hiring people who were bilingual.

Because of the shortage of translators and the desire to keep up with scientific literature, especially that published in Russian, the federal government spent millions of dollars during the 1950s funding MT, only to find, after a decade of work, that few practical results had accrued. Even with the help of human editors, machine translations were often slower and always poorer than those a human alone could do. In fact, the project became the target of a number of jokes. According to one commonly told story, a program given the saying "Out of sight, out of mind" translated it as "Blind and insane" or "Invisible idiot."

Actually the experience with machine translation was more fruitful than is generally acknowledged. It brought computer scientists and linguists together in an important endeavor, establishing the foundation for computational linguistics, an ongoing effort to understand language as process—

something that can be mechanized. But MT fell short of its promoters' expectations. The field got a bad reputation and government funding dried up. An early advocate of the project, the Israeli logician and philosopher Yehoshua Bar-Hillel, ruefully concluded that MT was probably impossible. In a famous paper he contended that a machine would never learn to understand both the sentence "The pen is in the box" and "The box is in the pen," realizing in the second case that "pen" must refer to a playpen, not a ballpoint. To make such distinctions, Bar-Hillel wrote, a machine would need not only a dictionary but an encyclopedia—a body of knowledge about the world. The possibility was inconceivable to him.

Such pessimism seemed justified by the fact that MT researchers had failed to produce even a decent parser. How could they be expected to solve the problem of semantics when the seemingly simpler problem of syntax was still up in the air? Researchers assumed that before a computer could understand an English sentence, it would have to parse it, determining which words were the subject, which words formed the verb phrase or the object. Only after the machine had completed this syntactic processing could it begin to understand the semantics—who had done what to whom. Thus an algorithm was needed—one that would take a sentence and diagram it, correctly identifying each word according to its part of speech.

As it turned out, this in itself was an extremely difficult task. One good way to judge a parser is to see if it can tell a grammatical sentence from an ungrammatical one. Properly formed sentences should parse, improper ones should be rejected. At the time Woods came to Harvard, scientists had theories for building parsers that might recognize sentences like "The dogs ran down the street" as grammatical, but they might also accept such atrocities as "The dog run down the street." Such a parser would know that a sentence can consist of a noun phrase ("The dogs") followed by a verb phrase ("ran down the street"), and that a verb phrase can consist of a verb ("ran") followed by a prepositional phrase, which consists of a preposition ("down") followed by a noun phrase ("the street"). But it might not know that the subject and verb have to agree in number, that both must be either singular or plural. Such problems could be resolved by adding more rules to the grammar, but only at the expense of making the system unreasonably complex.

"If you discovered that your grammar wasn't quite right," Woods explained, "because, for example, it didn't get number agreement between the subject and the verb correct, then you'd have to decide, 'Oh, there are two kinds of noun phrase—singular noun phrases and plural noun phrases.' And then all the rules you used to have about how to make a noun phrase—you'd have to make copies of them: one to make singular noun phrases and one to make plural noun phrases." Thus the rule that said a sentence consists of a noun phrase followed by a verb phrase would be replaced by two rules: a sentence consists of a singular noun phrase followed by a singular verb phrase *or* a plural noun phrase followed by a plural verb phrase. "Then you had to handle those nouns and those verbs that don't make it clear whether they are singular or plural. So the problem was that when you started to put in everything that it took to make the grammar capture some fact of language, it was frequently not a small change but a big change—copying whole classes of rules, expanding the set of rules to be maybe twice as big as you had before. And if you double the size of the rules two or three times, your grammar gets big in a hurry."

By the time a grammar was big enough to recognize more than an insignificant subset of English, it became unwieldy and inefficient, difficult to program and run on a machine. And, ironically, adding more rules didn't necessarily make a grammar more precise. Some of the parsing programs designed by Woods's predecessors contained thousands of rules, and still they were both too lenient, accepting sentences that weren't English, and too exclusive, failing to recognize ones that were. They were also extremely slow. By the time some of the more complex programs had finished processing a simple sentence—trying out one rule of grammar after another, in every conceivable combination, searching for the ones needed to complete the parsing—an hour might have passed. The systems were, as Woods put it, "brutally combinatoric." They succumbed to the same combinatorial explosion faced by a brute-force chess program that tries to search the vast proliferation of branches and twigs in a game tree—the ever-expanding combination of moves and countermoves and counter-countermoves and counter-counter-countermoves that conceivably could be made in a game. Because they lack intelligence, both kinds of programs waste an inordinate amount of time considering possibilities that are ridiculous. What was needed was a parser with a more discriminating sense of how to apply the rules of grammar.

Woods's contribution to the problem was to develop a parsing method using a device known as an Augmented Transition Network, which could handle the complexities of English grammar—or at least a large part of them—and still run efficiently. An ATN could parse a sentence not in an hour but a minute, and, in the systems used today, in less than a second. To appreciate the significance of ATNs, it helps first to understand a simpler version of the idea: the (*un*augmented) transition network, in which a grammar is structured something like a maze. A grammatical sentence represents a successful traversal of the labyrinth.

Consider the example on page 106.

To see what this diagram means, simply put a finger at the left-hand side of each of the four pathways and follow the various routes that lead to the EXIT at the other end. It becomes clear then that the network is nothing more than a compact way of stating a number of fairly obvious grammatical rules: (1) a sentence is a noun phrase followed by a verb, followed (optionally) by an object, (2) a noun phrase is a noun, possibly preceded by an article ("a," "an," or "the") and/or one or more adjectives, and possibly followed by a prepositional phrase, which is (3) a preposition followed by a noun phrase. Finally, the network defines an object (4) as a noun phrase or a noun phrase followed by a present participle, as in "John caught the man *stealing*."

In this system, parsing a sentence is a little like playing a game of Dungeons and Dragons. To get a sense of what a computer must go through,

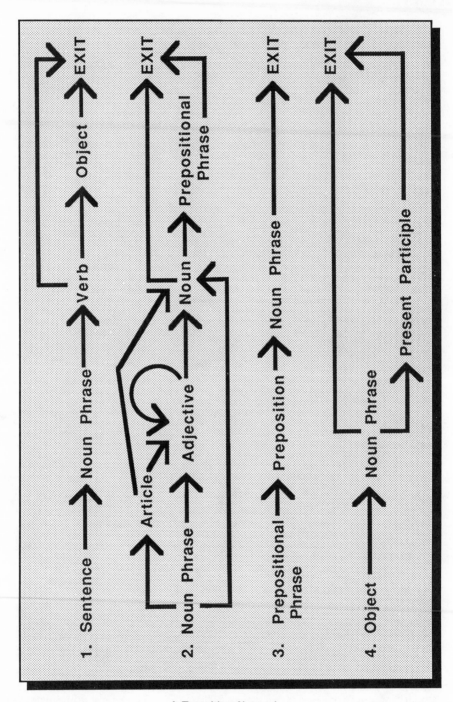

A Transition Network

try using the network to parse "Mary watched the gasoline can exploding." We start at the beginning of the topmost pathway, which tells us that, according to this simplified grammar, a sentence must begin with a noun phrase. But what in the world is a noun phrase? To find out, we drop down to the Noun Phrase network where we are immediately faced with three possible paths. Choosing at random, we take the top branch, which tells us that a noun phrase can begin with an article followed by a noun or by an adjective and then a noun. But the first word of our sentence, "Mary," is not an article, so we return to the beginning of the Noun Phrase net and try another path. The middle road leads to an Adjective node, indicating that a noun phrase can also begin with an adjective. But "Mary" is not an adjective either, so we try the last possibility, the bottom path that leads directly to a node called Noun. "A noun phrase can begin with a noun." "Mary" is a noun, so we've found a way out of the first chamber of the maze.

Now we are faced with two more paths. The lower one leads to a prepositional phrase. To find out what a prepositional phrase is, we drop down to the Prepositional Phrase network and see that to traverse it we need a preposition. Since the next word in the sentence, "watched," is not a preposition, we can go no farther. We return to the Noun Phrase net and try another path, the top one, which leads immediately to an exit, allowing us to return to the Sentence network above. "A noun phrase can consist simply of a noun." Having identified our noun phrase we are ready to continue parsing the sentence.

The next chamber in the Sentence net is labeled Verb. Since "watched" is a verb we can make the transition. From the Verb node is a path leading to the Object node. For details of what an object is, we drop down to the Object network, immediately encountering a single path leading to a Noun Phrase. Now we have to temporarily leave the Object net and jump again to the Noun Phrase net where we follow the path that goes from article— "the"—to noun—"gasoline." So far, so good. If there were no more words in the sentence, everything would be fine. We could exit from the Noun Phrase net and return to the Object net, where we would also be able to reach an exit, returning to the main Sentence network. And we'd find we could exit from it and be done. The sentence "Mary watched the gasoline" would be parsed and accepted.

But wait. What are those two words "can exploding" tacked onto the end? We have acted too hastily. We must return to where we left off, in the Noun chamber of the Noun Phrase net. If we had found instead "the gasoline *on the shelf*," the sentence also would parse, because there *is* a path from the Noun node to a Prepositional Phrase node, and thus to an exit. But there is no path that will accommodate a verb at this point: in this case, "can." We've reached a dead end. Either the sentence is ungrammatical or a mistake has been made. We must back up and try again.

Returning to the Object net, we try the bottom path instead, which tells us that an object can also consist of a noun phrase followed by a present participle. Checking the dictionary we see that "gasoline" can be an adjective instead of a noun and "can" can be a noun, not a verb. Thus, using "the gasoline can" as a noun phrase, we can jump back to the Noun Phrase net, traverse it, then return to the Object net, which tells us that we now need a present participle. We look at the next word in the sentence, which, lo and behold, is "exploding." So we can traverse the bottom path of the Object net, then exit to the main sentence network, and find we are done. There are no leftover words, so the sentence is parsed. We've found our way through the maze. We've not only determined that the sentence is grammatical, but, more important, we've sorted each word according to the role—noun, verb, adjective, et cetera—that it plays.

Transition nets also can be thought of recursively—as programs that can indirectly call themselves. The situation is similar to the blocks-world example where the function PUTAT calls MAKESPACE which calls GET–RID–OF which calls PUTAT again. To parse a sentence we use the Sentence program, which calls the Noun Phrase program—a procedure that knows how to identify and parse noun phrases. It, in turn, might need to call on the Prepositional Phrase program which might call the Noun Phrase program again.

In the jargon of computer science, this moving from main program to subprogram and back to main program again involves a procedure known as pushing and popping. To get a general idea of what this means, imagine one of those spring-loaded dispensers for cafeteria trays—what computer scientists call a "push-down stack." When Sentence is put on hold while Noun Phrase is used, we can imagine that the former has been temporarily pushed onto the stack. (Strictly speaking, it is not Sentence itself that is saved on a push-down stack, but rather the information that it will later need to find where it left off in the program.) Now, if Noun Phrase also must be temporarily suspended while a third program, Prepositional Phrase, is run, then Noun Phrase is pushed onto the stack on top of Sentence. If Prepositional Phrase calls Noun Phrase again (or rather another copy of it), then another program is added to the stack. In a complex situation, we can have programs running programs running programs. But at some point one of the programs must complete its task. Then it is removed from the top of the stack and the program beneath it pops up. When all the programs on the stack have been popped, the original program—in this case, Sentence—resumes.

William Woods was not alone in believing that transition networks could be used to provide computers with the rules of English grammar. At about the same time that he was developing his ATN, other researchers were independently working on recursive networks of their own. But the system Woods invented became a landmark in natural-language research because of the way it was *augmented* with new, more powerful features, allowing it to parse a sentence with a minimum of false starts and backtracking. As it followed a sentence through a maze, Woods's ATN could make tentative decisions, changing or confirming them depending on what it found later in its exploration. It also had the ability to remember what it had discovered as it moved along—that a verb was singular or plural, that it seemed to be in the active or the passive voice. Then it could use that information to help with decisions further down the line. Another way to think of the difference is this: A regular transition net worked as though the maze were being negotiated by a lobotomized mouse, which could only see what was in front of its nose and couldn't remember where it had been. When it hit a dead end, it had to back up and try another route. An augmented transition network could take more of a bird's-eye view. It could see a bigger part of the picture, taking more factors into account.

In the paper describing his ATN, Woods demonstrated the system by applying it to the syntactically tricky sentence "John was believed to have been shot." Scanning from left to right, the ATN encounters the word "John," a proper noun. Thus the program tentatively decides that it has found the subject of a simple declarative sentence, such as "John sees Mary." It records this information in a set of registers and moves to the next word, which, as expected, is a verb, "was." Then, if the original hypothesis is correct, the next words probably would be the object of the sentence as in "John was an electrician." Instead the program unexpectedly encounters another verb: "John was believed . . . "

It is at this point that the program's augmented features come into play. Since the first verb, "was," is a form of "to be," and "believed" is a past participle, the program decides that what it has found is a compound verb— "was believed." And so it determines that the sentence is in the passive voice, of the form "John was seen by Mary." Thus "John" is not the subject after all. The word is put on a special hold list—its status will be decided after more parsing has been done. At the same time, the program makes a note to remember that if it encounters the word "by," it might very well be followed by a noun, such as "Mary," which would be the subject of the sentence. In this case, the word "by" is never found, and the program eventually concludes that the subject is the indefinite "someone," a perfectly acceptable English construction.

The diagrams of ATNs powerful enough to parse most or even many English sentences fill charts the size of walls. They are as dense with nodes and connections as the wiring inside a computer cabinet, a visual demonstration of how complex and recursive language is. Phrases can be embedded in phrases, many levels deep: "The blue house sitting at the edge of the large forest where the twisting river meets the ever-changing sea . . . " While the many problems of teaching computers grammar are far from solved, Woods's system was among the first to be able to handle such richness and variety.

In the quest to get computers to understand English, the ATN parser was an important breakthrough. But giving a computer the rules of grammar was only part of the problem—the easy part. The machine still had no sense of semantics. ATNs were, by their very nature, maddeningly syntactic. They knew about form, not content. They would reject even slightly ungrammatical sentences that a human would easily understand. And they would accept grammatical sentences that were nonsense, such as "The gasoline can watched Mary explode" or linguist Noam Chomsky's frequently quoted example: "Colorless green ideas sleep furiously." Douglas Hofstadter provided an amusing demonstration of this limitation in *Gödel, Escher, Bach*. He described an ATN program he had written as an undergraduate that ran backward: it generated sentences rather than parsing them, picking words at random from a small dictionary, then combining them to make well-formed but ridiculous sentences:

> "A male pencil who must laugh clumsily would quack."

> "Must program not always crunch girl at memory?"

> "The worthy machine ought not always paste the astronomer."

After Hofstadter added many more rules to the program—requiring, for example, that certain verbs be used only with animate objects—and gave it a less humorous vocabulary, it did somewhat better:

> "According to the sophists, the campaigns in the city-states, in other words, have been accepted by the Orient cunningly. Of course, the Orient has been separated by the states particularly violently."

It doesn't make much sense, but it's an improvement over the following gem, which Hofstadter found in an article (written by a human) in the journal *Art-Language*: "Blurting may be considered as the reciprocal substitution of semiotic material (dubbing) for a semiotic dialogical product in a dynamic reflexion."

It would make a good story to say that having suggested a solution to the syntax problem, Woods went on to tackle semantics. Actually it happened the other way around. Woods invented the ATN while he was an assistant professor at Harvard, a position he ascended to after writing his doctoral dissertation on semantics. So, by the time NASA asked Woods to write a program that would understand English requests about moon rocks, he already had experience with both sides of the language problem. Meaning, he had discovered as a graduate student, was something that, as elusive as it sounds, might be captured by algorithms.

"I attacked the problem," he recalled, "by trying first to understand what meaning is and then how you could get some version of meaning for a computer. That became my thesis topic, and I came up with a model I call procedural semantics. That model has evolved over the years to become, at this point, something you could think of as a candidate at the level of philosophy for what kinds of things could play the role of meaning in the mental life of a machine—or a person for that matter. That's not to say it answers all the questions, but it doesn't seem to have any more holes than any of the other things philosophers have proposed, and considerably fewer than a lot."

Like grammar, meaning, Woods believed, could be described as a process. Understanding a sentence meant having a procedure that would determine whether it was true or false.

"Let's take the example of the official airline guide, which is the context I took for my original thesis exercise. In the airline guide there's a list of all the flights for every airline. There's a list of all the airlines, and there's a table that lists destinations and origins, departure times, flight numbers, destination airports and arrival airports, arrival times and classes of service, what kind of equipment there is, whether there is a meal, and what kind of fare code there is. Now, if you take a question like 'Does American have a flight that goes from Boston to Chicago before nine o'clock A.M. on Monday?' I would identify the meaning of it with a procedure that knew how to compute whether it was true or not. Now that procedure is in fact composed of bits and pieces of smaller ones."

Guided by a set of rules and a dictionary, Woods's system would take a preparsed version of a sentence (parsed by hand—the ATN program had not been invented yet) and translate it into a simple vocabulary that a computer easily could be programmed to undestand. In this particular dialect of computerese, the symbol FLIGHT(X1) meant that X1 is the name of the flight. PLACE(X2) meant that X2 is the name of one of the places listed in the airline guide. DEPART(X1,X2) meant that flight X1 departs from place X2. In the language, the sentence "How many stops does AA-57 make between Boston and Chicago?" looked like this: LIST(NUMSTOPS(AA-57,Boston,Chicago)).

The program's world consisted of a network of several dozen of these basic units of meaning, or "semantic primitives," which also included AIRLINE, ARRIVE, CONNECT, CITY, DAY, and TIME. Each of them worked as a little program that could be automatically combined with the others into a procedure that, in the case of Woods's example, would search the airline guide data base and find all the flights that went from Boston to Chicago. Then it would rule out the ones that weren't run by American Airlines, didn't leave on Monday, or that left after nine A.M. If there were any flights left, then the answer to the question would be yes. In a similar manner, the system could answer more complex questions, such as: "Do they serve breakfast on the 8 A.M. flight from Boston to Chicago?" or "Does any flight go from Boston to some city from which American has a flight to Denver?"

The world of the official airline guide was extremely limited compared to those we hold in our heads. But Woods believed that for brain and computer the principle of understanding was the same.

"If you believe people are some kind of information-processing engine— among other things—and that their reasoning processes are some kind of procedures, then it is plausible that what a person has when you say he understands a meaning of a term is a procedure that he can use to do various things with it."

As we go through life, we build a data base of information about the world. When someone asks us a question—"What is the capital of Alaska?"

or "Is Richard still in love with that woman he met on the plane?"—we enact some internal procedure that searches the mazes of memory and retrieves an answer.

Woods's system wouldn't know what "flight," "place," and "day" meant in the same sense that people do. They were opaque, irreducible units—the unfissionable atoms of meaning. Still, if he had wanted to make a system that knew, for example, that an airplane was a type of machine used for flying through the air, he could have defined the word in terms of other primitives, which could be broken into still other primitives. But at some point the process of fragmentation would have to bottom out and end. In any system there must always be primitive concepts.

Consider the case of an English dictionary. In this great spiderweb of meaning, semantic primitives are words whose definition, Woods wrote, "is immediately circular—that is, the word is defined in terms of words which are themselves defined in terms of the original word." An example is the word "same," which, according to *Webster's New World Dictionary*, means "*alike* in every respect," or "*identical*." Looking up the word "alike," we find, "*like* one another." "Like" means "having the *same* qualities" and "*equal*." The word "identical" is defined as "the very *same*," "exactly *alike*," or "*equal*." And "equal" means "of the *same* quantity, size, number, et cetera."

Unless we already know the meaning of one of those words—"same," "identical," "alike," or "equal"—the dictionary is useless. At least one of them must be a semantic primitive, programmed into our brains by the experience of being alive.

"People presumably learn their primitive concepts [through] their sense impressions," Woods wrote, "so that a child learns the meaning of the word 'same' or 'alike' by correlating the term with instances of two identical objects. In computers, however, this process will not be feasible, at least not until we give the computer eyes and ears and a great deal of progress is made in learning theory."

People must provide the computer what life has denied it, programming in the primitives themselves.

"In this respect, the computer will always be talking about things which it does not know anything about," Woods wrote, "just as a person blind from birth may talk about colors without ever having perceived them. The blind person, when told that X is green and that Y is the same color as X, may conclude that Y is green, and it is in this same manner that the computer can carry on a conversation about things for which it has no external correlates."

In people and machines, communication must ultimately be reduced to symbols that are woven into statements to be unraveled, understood, and then answered.

Woods never actually programmed the question-answering system described in his thesis. After all, at the time he wrote it, he still didn't have an adequate parser. After joining the Harvard faculty, he developed his ATN, and in 1970 he left the university.

"I was coming up for a sabbatical at Harvard and talking to Bolt Beranek and Newman, where they had an identical copy of the computer system that I had been doing my work on. And the computer system I was working on at Harvard was going away, so the upshot of that and a bunch of things is that I went to BBN for a year." He ended up staying and, for his first major project, he tackled the NASA problem by writing Lunar, a program that combined his parser and semantic interpreter.

"We brought up the first version of the system in six months, which included building a 3,500-word vocabulary—it knew all the chemical elements and all the isotopes and all the minerals, every word from several technical articles in lunar geology, and a thousand or so words of basic English that everybody shares. So we put all that in and beefed up the grammar to handle more and more of English, and went and demonstrated it at the Second Annual Lunar Science Conference," which was held in January 1971. "We had it on line for about three days, an hour or two a day, and we had lunar geologists actually coming up, trying it out, and seeing how it worked."

The geologists had not been told to use any particular format or phrasing— just to ask questions as though conversing with a colleague: "What is the average concentration of iron in ilmenite?" "Give me references on sector zoning." The program could even handle questions like "Give me the modal analyses of *those samples* for all phases," realizing that "those samples" referred to information from a previous question.

Of a total of 111 requests, Lunar understood about 90 percent (counting 12 percent which failed because of trivial bugs in the program that were easily corrected). The statistics sound impressive, but, as Woods wrote, they must be taken "with several grains of salt." The program worked fine when it was asked questions by geologists, who instinctively knew the kind of information that was likely to be in the data base. But when a graduate student in psychology tried to put Lunar through its paces, he had to ask five questions before he found one that the program could understand. "What is the average weight of all your samples?" he asked. Had it been equipped with eyes, Lunar might have blinked stupidly. For one thing "all your" was a construction that its grammar didn't know yet. Thus the question would not parse. Even if the program had been able to analyze the sentence syntactically, it would not have understood it. The data base didn't contain information on weights. And, more important, it had not been programmed with primitives referring to possession. "Your samples" was a concept that would not compute. Lunar didn't consider the moon rocks to be something that it owned.

After the conference, Lunar's grammar was extended to include such tricky constructions as "all your." There was no theoretical reason why Woods and his colleagues could not have expanded the program to understand a broader range of concepts, including weight and ownership. But that would have taken time and money, and, anyway, it wasn't what NASA wanted. In fact, now that Lunar was up and running and demonstrating linguistic powers heretofore unseen in anything not human, NASA officials decided they didn't want the system after all. The imperatives of science were disrupted by the realities of government contract work.

"The Lunar project ran for a couple of years," Woods explained, "until NASA took its first round of budget cutbacks. Before the system got to the point of actually being deployed, our contract monitor called up and said, 'Well, you're not going to be renewed next year and I'm going to go back and do some geology while the money lasts.' " It was a disappointing development, but Woods was satisfied that the project had gone far enough to provide science with a valuable example of what could be accomplished with the current technology. At the same time, Lunar showed the difficulty of the problems that still had to be solved.

"Lunar was quite advanced compared to even what you can get today in terms of anything like a product," Woods said. "ATNs have now become almost a standard engineering discipline for building parsers." And Lunar's basic architecture—a parser feeding sentences to a program that interprets meaning as a procedure—has become the standard by which most current commercial systems are built.

But Lunar had obvious limits (which it has passed on to its progeny), ones that couldn't be solved simply by adding more rules. The program's understanding was limited not only to its tiny domain—the world of moon rocks—but also to "very literal, factual questions and commands." Unfortunately, Woods observed, "there are lots of things you'd like to do with a data base that aren't quite that literal. Lunar gives you English as a precision tool. If every word is right and you mean exactly what you say, and you haven't left out things that you're expecting the hearer to fill in because they're obviously what you're interested in—then Lunar gives you the ability to communicate in English."

Occasionally Lunar could apply primitive powers of reasoning to the tasks it had been asked to perform. If a question was asked that would require so much computing time that it would blow the user's budget, then Lunar would issue a warning, or suggest in some cases a more economical method of finding out the same information. But to really give a geologist the illusion of conversing with a colleague and not a machine, the program needed to be far more sophisticated.

"There was no extra knowledge in Lunar that you could really do reasoning with," Woods explained. "There was no model of what you as the user know and what you don't know, and what the system knows that you might not know. There was nothing to support an English input like 'Why did *that* happen?' or 'There aren't any rare-earth elements in that list!' or 'That number looks too high,' or tons and tons and tons of things that you might want to say to convey the fact that something didn't work the way that you expected it to, and you haven't the foggiest idea of what command to give the computer so that it will figure out what it might know that you don't know that could help you."

Lunar could parse a simple sentence and translate it into a procedure, but there was more to the process of understanding than that.

At about the same time that Lunar appeared in the early 1970s, Terry Winograd, a student of Minsky's at MIT, was working on a program that not only understood simple English sentences but could engage in a typewritten conservation. Winograd chose for his domain the blocks world—specifically, a computer simulation of a table with five blocks and three pyramids, all of various sizes and colors. There was also a box to put blocks in and a robot arm to move them around. By limiting the program to this microworld, Winograd was able to get it to understand linguistic subtleties that were beyond the reach of more practical systems like Lunar.

Winograd called his program SHRDLU, perhaps out of a sense of frustration at the lengths to which AI researchers go in thinking up clever names for their creations. E,T,A,O,I,N,S,H,R,D,L, and U (the twelve most frequently used letters in the English alphabet) form the top row of the keyboard of a now outmoded machine called a Linotype, which was used in the production of newspapers and books before the advent of computer typesetting. Journeymen called Linotypers sat before these hulking, clanking devices, which produced the leaden type used to make printing plates. When a Linotyper made an error it wasn't possible simply to hit a backspace key—the letter had already been cast in lead. Instead the Linotyper would run a hand across the top row of the keyboard, then type the word again. When proofreaders saw ETAOINSHRDLU suddenly injected into the copy they were reading, they knew to cut out the word that preceded it, along with the jumble of letters that had drawn the mistake to their attention. Among those familiar with the history of printing, ETAOINSHRDLU is something of an inside joke. Editors of *Mad* magazine used to insert the word in obscure nooks and crannies of their pages, as though their proofreaders were too incompetent to remove it from the galleys before publication.

Winograd's SHRDLU could respond to such commands as "Pick up a big red block," answering "Okay" as it demonstrated its comprehension by causing the simulated arm to raise the block from the table. (If another block was stacked on top of the red block, SHRDLU would first remove it.) If asked to "grasp the pyramid," it would respond, "I don't understand which pyramid you mean," since there were three of them on the table. However, if SHRDLU had first been asked, "What does the box contain?" answering, "The blue pyramid and the blue block," and then was asked "What is the pyramid supported by?" it would answer "The box." It assumed now that "pyramid" referred to the one currently being talked about.

If asked a syntactically ambiguous question like "Find a block which is taller than the one you are holding and put it into the box," SHRDLU would reply, "By 'it' I assume you mean the block which is taller than the one I am holding." The reply isn't quite as impressive as it sounds—the program had no real knowledge of what "assume" means. The word was part of a canned response. But SHRDLU was able to make the assumption because it contained heuristics for identifying the likely noun that a pronoun refers to. Given a choice between two possible meanings for "it"—the "block which is taller than the one you are holding" and "the one you are holding," the program chose the first. A noun phrase that is the object of a sentence is a more likely candidate than one that is embedded deep inside a descriptive clause.

By drawing on its rules of grammer and blocks-world semantics, SHRDLU could understand some fairly complicated sentences:

> Will you please stack up both of the red blocks and either a green cube or a pyramid?
> *OK.*

(SHRDLU did so, realizing that the sentence is a command even though it was phrased as a question. To carry out the request it had to remove a pyramid that was sitting on top of one of the red blocks.)

> Is there a large block behind a pyramid?
> *Yes, three of them: a large red one, a large green cube and the blue one.*

> Put a small one onto the green cube which supports a pyramid.
> *OK.*

> Put the littlest pyramid on top of it.
> *OK.*
> . . . .

> Had you touched any pyramid before you put the green one on the little cube?
> *Yes, the green one.*

> When did you pick it up?
> (SHRDLU began to retrace its earlier behavior): *While I was stacking up the red cube, a large red block, and a large green cube.*

> Why?
> *To get rid of it.*

> Why did you do that?
> *To clean off the red cube.*

> Why did you clear off that cube?
> *To put it on a large green cube.*

> Why did you do that?
> *To stack up the red cube, a large red block, and a large green cube.*

> Why did you do that?
> *Because you asked me to.*

Not only was the program able to examine its past performance—an ability some AI researchers compare to introspection—but it also could learn new concepts:

> Does a steeple—
> (SHRDLU interrupted): *Sorry, I don't know the word "steeple."*
>
> A "steeple" is a stack which contains two green cubes and a pyramid. *I understand.*
>
> Are there any steeples now?
> *No.*
>
> Build one.
> *OK.*
>
> (SHRDLU did so.)

Winograd's work with SHRDLU convinced him that in language understanding, syntax and semantics are inextricably intertwined. While parsing a sentence, the program constantly drew on semantic knowledge to resolve ambiguities. Consider this tricky command: "Put the blue pyramid on the block in the box." Does it mean to find a blue pyramid that is sitting on a block, remove it, and place it in the box? Or does it mean to take a blue pyramid and put it on a block that is already sitting in the box? It depends on which group of words forms the subject of the sentence. SHRDLU resolved the confusion by checking its microworld and seeing that there were no blue pyramids sitting on blocks. Thus the second interpretation had to be the correct one. The program used knowledge about its world to help it parse the sentence. Likewise, Winograd concluded, when we hear a sentence, we don't first run it through a parser, then take the result and analyze its meaning. The procedure is not nearly so clear-cut. He wrote:

> . . . [P]eople are able to interpret utterances which are not syntactically well formed, and can even assign meanings to collections of words without use of syntax. The list "skid, crash, hospital" presents a certain image, even though two of the words are both nouns and verbs and there are no explicit syntactic connections. It is therefore wrong to insist that some sort of complete parsing is a prerequisite to semantic analysis.
> On the other hand, people are able to interpret sentences syntactically even when they do not know the meanings of the individual words. . . . [M]uch of our normal conversation is made up of sentences like "Then the other one did the same thing to it" in which the words taken individually do not provide clues to enable us to determine the [meaning] without a complete syntactic analysis.
> What really seems to be going on is a coordinated process in which

a variety of syntactic and semantic information can be relevant, and in which the hearer takes advantage of whatever is more useful in understanding a given part of a sentence.

Often the hearer must move beyond syntax and semantics and reason about what is said, taking into account what he knows about the world. The sentence "I dropped a bottle of Coke on the table and it broke" has two possible interpretations, Winograd wrote. What broke? The bottle or the table? But if the sentence is preceded by "Where is the toolbox?" or "Where is the furniture polish?" then the meaning becomes clear.

Winograd was never able to extend SHRDLU's powers far beyond those of the original model. As the microworld was made more complicated, SHRDLU's performance rapidly declined. But by focusing on the extra-linguistic knowledge needed to understand language, Winograd helped set the tone for current research in computational linguistics. To understand an utterance we need to know not only about blocks, tables, toolboxes, and bottles of Coke, but also about the beliefs, goals, and intentions of the person we are speaking with. Linguists call this knowledge of the realities of life pragmatics. When we are asked, "Do you know where the police station is?" the appropriate response is not simply yes. We infer from the question that the inquirer is ignorant of the location and wants to correct the situation, and that he believes we are in a position to help. We might even go a step further and guess that an emergency has occurred.

"[C]ommunicating in natural language is an activity of the total intellect," Gary Hendrix, director of the natural-language program at SRI International, and his former colleague Earl Sacerdoti wrote. "[H]umans are seen as intelligent beings motivated by complex sets of goals they seek to fulfill by planning, executing, and monitoring sequences of actions—some of which are physical, some linguistic. . . . Whereas the usual purpose of a physical action is to alter the physical world, the usual purpose of a linguistic action is to alter the mental states of the hearers. . . . Just as a child might push over the first domino of a long row to make them all tumble in sequence, a lifeguard at the beach may yell 'Shark!' at swimmers to set off a chain of reasoning in their minds that will result in a mad dash for the shore, which is the lifeguard's intended mechanism for accomplishing his primary goal of preserving life."

Scientists still haven't devised ways for computers to understand language at the pragmatic level. The so-called natural-language front ends that now sell for upwards of $50,000 do little more (and often less) than Woods's fifteen-year-old Lunar program. But research continues. As a goal, Hendrix and Sacerdoti suggested that when a future system is given a sentence like "The toolbox is locked," it should set off a mental chain reaction that would go something like this: "Why is he telling me this? I already know the box is locked. I know the user needs to get in. Perhaps he is telling me the box is locked because he believes I can somehow help. To get in takes a key. The user knows this and knows I know it. The key is in the drawer. If the user knew this he would just unlock the box. Therefore he must not know it. I can make him come to know it by saying 'The key is in the drawer.' I am supposed to help. I will say it."

And so, after all that quiet cogitation, the program would respond, "The key is in the drawer."

6

Listening
Intelligently

In June 1969, John R. Pierce, a prominent research scientist at Bell Laboratories, wrote what has been described in the annals of engineering as "the most popular letter to the editor . . . ever published in *The Journal of the Acoustical Society of America*," a dubious distinction to be sure. It was also, perhaps, the most controversial—and almost certainly the most sarcastic. After reviewing a decade's worth of efforts to get machines to understand human speech, Pierce concluded that the endeavor was probably hopeless. He compared speech-recognition researchers to "mad inventors" and "untrustworthy engineers," and speech-recognition research to "schemes for turning water into gasoline, extracting gold from the sea, curing cancer, or going to the moon." He was appalled at the huge amount of money a gullible federal government had been convinced to lavish on the projects.

"To sell suckers," Pierce wrote, "one uses deceit and offers glamour." He conceded that the researchers were often as deceived as those who provided the funds, blinded by their unwarranted enthusiasm. "Thus," he concluded, "we may pity workers whom we cannot respect."

Naturally, some of Pierce's colleagues took umbrage at his remarks. In delivering his jeremiad, Pierce seemed as carried away by the sound of his words as a Puritan preacher castigating his flock for their sins. And yet, despite his excesses, Pierce had reason to be pessimistic. While scientists had succeeded in building machines that could recognize single words spoken in isolation—achieving performance levels of 90 percent or more on vocabularies of fifty to a hundred words—the effort to understand streams of connected speech had been a failure. The gap between understanding words and understanding sentences was wider than anyone had supposed. Earlier in his career, Pierce had headed a study group which declared machine-translation research a failure, resulting in the cutoff of government funding. Now he seemed to be wishing the same fate on speech recognition.

"In any practical way," Pierce wrote, "this art seems to have gone downhill ever since the limited commercial success of Radio Rex, a toy dog that jumped from his house when his name was spoken."

When computer scientists talk about building machines that understand English, they almost always assume that the human's side of the conversation will consist of sentences typed on a keyboard, and the computer's responses will appear as glowing letters on a cathode-ray screen. This is what they mean by natural language, but for most of us there is nothing very natural about talking with our fingers. Speech-understanding researchers—a diffuse group that includes, among others, linguists, speech scientists, artificial-intelligence experts, and electronic and acoustical engineers—hope to bring human and machine closer together. For the past three decades, they have been trying to design devices that will take words spoken into a microphone and convert them into a form that can be understood by a computer.

One of the earliest crude speech-understanding machines was the watermelon box. The device, which was invented in the early 1950s by a scientist at Harvard named J.C.R. Licklider, consisted of a microphone connected to a circuit designed to detect the vowels that occur in the word "watermelon"—a, e, e, and o. When all four of the sounds were spoken, one after the other, a light on top of the box flashed in recognition. The invention served no other purpose, but in its limited domain it worked quite well. It was an expert on whether anyone within earshot had said "watermelon."

People use about 10,000 words in everyday conversation, so one might suppose that the inventor of the watermelon box had solved one hundredth of one percent of the speech-understanding problem. By designing 9,999 more watermelon boxes and hooking them all together, perhaps a machine could be made to understand spoken English. With modern technology, it is easy to imagine that the circuitry for each word detector could be shrunk to fit on a single silicon chip. Or perhaps a word-recognizing machine could be realized in the form of software instead of hardware. Using a device similar to a digital recording machine, a speech signal could be converted to 1s and 0s. Then it could be fed to a program that rapidly compared it, word by word, against a memory bank full of templates—digital "pictures" of how each word in the machine's vocabulary is supposed to look. By seeing which words matched which templates most closely, the computer could figure out what had been said.

But, as researchers have discovered, the problem is not that simple. Speech understanding has turned out to be an enormously difficult task. For one thing, "watermelon" is an unusually distinctive word—its four vowels, spoken in order, are a dead giveaway. Try to think of another word that contains that sequence of sounds. In practice, most words are far more difficult to distinguish from those that sound nearly the same. The difference among "came," "dame," "fame," "game," "lame," "maim," "name," "same," and "tame" is in one initial sound, which lasts a fraction of a second. Distinguishing "frame" from "flame" requires even finer discrimination. Compounding the problem is the fact that we all pronounce words differently—and the same person speaks differently under varying circumstances.

Even if we were told to talk in a slow, calm manner to a machine that had been fine-tuned to the nuances of our voice, there still would be problems. When we speak we tend to slur words together—it's difficult to tell where one leaves off and the next begins. The classic example is "Did you eat yet?" which is often pronounced as though it were the two-syllable word "jeetyet." In "He walked to the store," the last two words are spoken as though they are one. As a result, the sentence is almost indistinguishable (except for a subtle difference in inflection) from "He walked to this door."

It is possible to imagine a speech recognizer so sensitive and precise that it would pick up these tiny variations of sound, but still the problem would not be solved. It might even be compounded. Sentences contain hidden words, and the more sensitive a machine's hearing, the more likely it is to be led astray. To illustrate the problem, psychologist Ronald A. Cole of Carnegie-Mellon University concocted this example: "Remember, a spoken sentence almost always contains words not intended." If differently partitioned, the sentence would come out like this: "Ream ember, us spoke in cent tense all Moe stall ways con tains words knot in ten did." The mistranslation is nonsense, and that is Cole's point. It's impossible to separate hearing from understanding. We are aided in the monumental task of decoding the noisy, imprecise signals that pour into our ears by our knowledge of what makes sense.

Our hearing apparatus does not consist of the neurological equivalent of 10,000 watermelon boxes. We don't work that precisely. We don't need to. Because of our ability to listen intelligently and make smart guesses, we don't have to hear correctly every sound that is said.

If someone tells us, "I was hungry so I made a sandwich," it doesn't matter whether the last word is carefully enunciated. The speaker might have dropped the *d*, or said "samwich." Even if the pronunciation was exact, we might, if guided by sound alone, interpret it as "sand, which," as in "I was hungry so I made a sand, which is a new kind of food I invented." If the speaker mumbled or there was a lot of noise in the air, "sandwich" might have caused our ears to send our brain an electrical signal barely distinguishable from that produced by "bandwidth." But "I was hungry so I made a bandwidth" is not even entertained as a possiblity. When we hear "hungry" we are primed for a sentence about food. We also use syntactic, as well as semantic, clues. Thus we are not stymied by the fact that in the last example "made" and "maid" sound identical. It would make perfect sense for a sentence about hunger to contain the word "maid." But when we hear "I was hungry, so I . . ." we naturally expect a verb to follow. The process is far from exact. Unless we know we're listening to a speaker with a poetic bent, "The sky is cloudy" is unlikely to be heard as "This guy is cloudy" but we might mistake "The sky is blue" for "This guy is blue."

To understand speech, we need far more information than what is in the acoustic signal. It must be supplemented by what we know about English, about the subject being discussed, about the person we are talking to—by what we know about the world. Listening is not a passive process. We are constantly trying to find meaning in the stream of sounds that pours through the air. And in the process we tend to hear what we expect to hear. William James realized this almost a hundred years ago, when he wrote the following passage in his 1899 book *Talks to Teachers on Psychology and to Students on Some of Life's Ideals:*

When we listen to a person speaking or read a page of print, much of what we think we see or hear is supplied from our memory. We overlook misprints, imagining the right letters, though we see the wrong ones; and how little we actually hear, when we listen to speech, we realize when we go to a foreign theatre; for there what troubles us is not so much that we cannot understand what the actors say as that we cannot hear their words. The fact is that we hear quite as little under similar conditions at home, only our mind, being fuller of English verbal associations, supplies the requisite material for comprehension upon a much slighter auditory hint.

What James surmised, contemporary psychologists have verified. In a classic experiment performed in the mid-1960s at the University of Michigan, speech scientists excised individual words from tape-recorded conversations and played them, in isolation, to a group of listeners. Although the words had been easily understood during conversation, only about half were recognized when played out of context. At Harvard University in 1963, researchers played recordings of 150 sentences to a group of subjects and asked them to repeat what they had heard. Some of the sentences were meaningful—"Accidents kill motorists on the highways," "Bears steal honey from the hive"—while others were syntactically correct but meaningless—"Accidents carry honey between the house." Still others were random strings of words: "Around accidents country honey the shoot." While the subjects could correctly repeat the meaningful sentences about 89 percent of the time, they scored about 79 percent on the syntactic, meaningless sentences, and 56 percent on the strings of random words. Without semantic and syntactic clues, comprehension dropped by more than a third.

The lesson from these experiments is clear. Hearing doesn't stop at the ear, where sound waves are converted to electrical pulses for the brain. Listening is an intelligent act. While that makes the speech-recognition problem far more difficult, it also makes it more interesting, especially to those intrigued by the possibility that machines can be made to think. About the time that Pierce's infamous letter appeared in 1969, AI researchers were beginning to develop an interest in speech. To distinguish their efforts from those of the speech scientists and acoustical engineers who preceded them, they called their programs speech-*understanding* systems, as opposed to speech-recognition systems. From the beginning, they realized that what they were attempting was as difficult as any problem that confronted AI.

After all, understanding typewritten English had been daunting enough. Each sentence was like a jigsaw puzzle, with words for pieces. When we solve a jigsaw we are guided both by the shapes of the pieces and by their colors. When trying to reconstruct the edge of the frame, we want pieces that are flat on one side. When filling in sky, we search for pieces that are blue. This use of form and content is similar to the way we use syntax and semantics to understand language. To solve the jigsaw puzzle of a sentence, we are helped by knowing that the laws of grammar allow words to fit together only in certain ways—and that they are supposed to come together to form a sensible picture.

But imagine solving a puzzle when you don't even know what the pieces are. In typewritten language, the words are clearly printed and properly partitioned on the page. But a spoken sentence is like a jigsaw whose pieces are each puzzles in themselves. Each word is a combination of syllables, which are, in turn, made from phonemes—the fricatives, nasals, sibilants, vowels, et cetera, that are the basic sounds of English. Just as there are grammars to tell us the allowable ways in which words can be put together to form sentences, so there are grammars for how phonemes can be combined to make words. To the wealth of knowledge used in language understanding—pragmatics, semantics, and syntax—another source can be added: phonotactics, the syntax of phonemes.

Phonotactic clues can be very helpful in understanding speech. While "this guy" might be heard as "the sky," we are not likely to mistake "this room" as "the sroom." In English, words don't begin with the sound *sr*. We wouldn't even bother to look up "sroom" in a dictionary. On the other hand, "dreep" is phonotactically legal, and could only be ruled out by determining that it doesn't happen to be a word. In rejecting "dreep," we would have to use what linguists call our lexical knowledge—the dictionary we acquire and carry in our heads.

Together, these five kinds of knowledge—pragmatic, semantic, syntactic, lexical, and phonological—form a hierarchy of abstraction, a ladder that ascends from the specific to the general. Beginning on the bottom rung with the low-level, highly specific knowledge of phonemes, we climb upward, to knowledge of words, grammar, meaning, and finally to general, pragmatic knowledge about life.

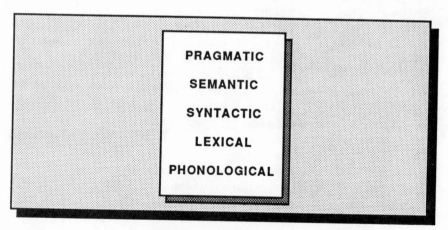

PRAGMATIC

SEMANTIC

SYNTACTIC

LEXICAL

PHONOLOGICAL

A Hierarchy of Abstraction

To decipher language we use all these levels of knowledge simultaneously, applying semantic knowledge here, syntactic knowledge there, lexical and phonological knowledge in still other places—whatever it takes to make sense of the babble. We are obsessed with a need to understand. Instilling a machine with a similar passion would require more than simply adding phonotactics to the syntactic and semantic knowledge already possessed by Lunar or SHRDLU. An integrated system would have to be built in which all the levels from the high to the low interacted to produce understanding.

In 1970, the Defense Department's Advanced Research Projects Agency (called ARPA or DARPA) decided to see if AI was up to this task. They appointed a study group to look into the possibility of launching a multimillion-dollar, long-term effort to develop automatic speech understanding. The nine-man group included, along with several speech and computer scientists, such AI luminaries as Allen Newell, the group's leader, William Woods, Cordell Green, and Raj Reddy of Carnegie-Mellon University. (Also in attendance was J.C.R. Licklider, inventor of the watermelon box.)

Before joining the faculty of Carnegie-Mellon, Reddy, an immigrant from India, made a name for himself at Stanford by designing (with a colleague) one of the first speech-recognition systems to utilize artificial-intelligence techniques. Reddy's system understood sentences about the blocks world, as long as they were constructed from a vocabulary of sixteen words according to a highly artificial syntax. All sentences, for example, had to begin with the words "Pick up," contain the word "block," and end with either "block," "corner," or "side." Furthermore, words describing the type of block ("small," "medium," "big") had to precede the word "block," while words describing location ("right," "left," "top," "bottom") had to follow.

In deciding what word was present in any given part of an utterance, the program had only a handful of possibilities to choose from. In fact, with so many restrictions and such a tiny vocabulary, there were only 192 sentences that could be spoken to the machine. Reddy's program could understand about 85 percent of them, but only after it had been tuned to the user's voice. The speaker would read passages containing each word in the vocabulary (in several different contexts) so the machine could store digital pictures of them, compiling what is known as a pronunciation dictionary. Because of the large amount of computer processing required, it took the program ten times longer to decipher a sentence than it took the speaker to say it. In the jargon of the computer industry, the program was said to work at "ten times real time." Because of the high cost of computer time, each second of speech cost $3 to understand. When it was completed in 1968, Reddy's system was considered state of the art.

What DARPA had in mind was considerably more sophisticated: a system that would handle a vocabulary of 10,000 words, with an error rate of no more than 10 percent. They wanted a machine that would be able to work over the telephone—Reddy had used a high-quality microphone—at only a few times real time. Furthermore, they wanted the system to handle many speakers, although it could be tuned for each one. The specifications amounted to no less than a planned breakthrough in speech-understanding research. DARPA asked the study group if it would be possible to complete the project in three years.

The officials at DARPA didn't have any immediate applications in mind—the purpose of the project was to stimulate basic research. But the practical possibilities of a speech-understanding system were enticing—both to the military and the computer-science community. People can speak more than twice as fast as they can type, and they can do so while keeping their hands free for other tasks, such as writing in a notebook or operating a machine. If computers could understand speech, then people who weren't touch typists could use them while simultaneously reading a report or monitoring a set of gauges or a radar screen. They could even talk to one computer while typing commands to another. But, practical considerations aside, there was a more intriguing reason for giving machines the ability to listen. For humans, speech is the most natural form of communication. If computers could be imbued with the knowledge that it takes to understand what we say, they would be that much closer to becoming intelligent beings.

After considering the problem for several months, Newell's study group decided that DARPA was asking for too much. But, they concluded, given five years it probably would be possible to produce a 1,000-word system, if the sentences were spoken over a high-quality microphone, in a standard American dialect—no Brooklyn or Texas accents. To make the task even more manageable, the sentences would have to be constructed using a highly artificial syntax and limited to a narrow semantic domain, though presumably one richer than the blocks world. DARPA accepted these reduced expectations and in 1971 decided to launch an intensive effort in which five laboratories would compete to produce a working system: Carnegie-Mellon University, Bolt Beranek and Newman, MIT's Lincoln Laboratories, SRI International (then known as Stanford Research Institute), and System Development Corporation in Santa Monica, California.

At the time, DARPA had been funding AI research for more than a decade. If the AI community could produce a speech-understanding system, perhaps it would demonstrate that the investment had been worthwhile, smoothing the way for more money. In deciding to underwrite the project, DARPA was giving AI the acid test.

"It felt a lot like a Manhattan project—not the same kind of secrecy but the same kind of importance," recalled William Woods, whose success with the Lunar program helped earn him a position as leader of the BBN effort. "The original conception was that you couldn't have any reasonable expectation that a single contractor would succeed. So start five out, check them at the two-year mark to see if they could in fact build a system that worked, and then don't narrow the field to one—hedge your bets with two."

At the two-year mark, in 1973, three projects were still in the running. BBN and Carnegie-Mellon were the two frontrunners, while the efforts at SRI and System Development Corporation were combined into one. Then for the next three years the groups competed to see who would come up with the best system. The pressure became particularly intense.

"Not just DARPA, but the whole world was watching," said Frederick Hayes-Roth, the chief scientist at Teknowledge, who launched his career as a member of the Carnegie-Mellon team. A handsome man with a neatly groomed beard, "Rick" Hayes-Roth, as his friends call him, reminisces about the race to build a speech-understanding system with all the wonder and gusto that some veterans bring to their tales about World War II. "I mean this was the test of fire," he said. "That's the way it was billed, that's the way the scientists signed up for it. This was going to be the place where we determined whether or not AI was relevant."

Considering what had been learned from past efforts, it was assumed that a winning system would work something like this: first, using a microphone, the sentence would be converted to an electrical wave, then digitized so it could be fed into a computer. The sentence would exist in memory as a long sequence of *1*s and *0*s. The computer would scan this bit string and translate it into a series of phonemes. Since neither pronunciation nor perception is ever perfect, several possible phonemes might be postulated for each tiny segment of the utterance.

Once it had finished guessing what all the phonemes were, the program would use various phonological rules to combine the phonemes into proper syllables and words. Suppose the system was asked, "Did you hit it to Tom?" which, the way most of us speak, would be pronounced something like this: "dijahititatahm?" To pick out the first two words, the program might use a heuristic advising that the letter "y" can sometimes sound like a "j" if it's preceded by a "d" sound—"dija" might mean "did ya." Using a heuristic that said that "ou" can sometimes be pronounced as what linguists call a schwa sound, the program might figure out that "did ya" was really "did you." Of course "j" might really mean "j," or "dge," as in "judge," so the system would have to consider those possibilities as well. While the segment "hitit" might mean what it says, it could also be a distortion of "hid it."

The amount of knowledge required for a simple listening task is staggering. Phonemes are pronounced differently depending on the sounds that surround them. The "t" in "hit" sounds harder than the "t" in "hit some." To hear the word "list," a system would have to know not only its pronunciation, but also such variations as "list some" (which sometimes sounds like "lissum"). The information might be in the form of a rule that "t"s can sometimes be dropped if the next word begins with "s." Or both pronunciations might be stored in the system's dictionary.

Up to this point all the processing would have been performed by the so-called "bottom end" of the system, where the phonological and lexical knowledge resided. Now the system's "top end," with its syntactic, semantic, and pragmatic knowledge, would enter into the process, guessing at words the bottom end had missed. Suppose that the bottom end had found the words "might" and "been" but was unable to decipher the mess in between. The top end, using its knowledge of grammar, might decide to guess that the missing word was "have." It would look up the word in the built-in pronunciation dictionary to see if it matched the waveform closely enough to be considered a hit. Or, as a computer scientist would describe it, the words "might" and "been" would have been found by bottom-up processing, and "have" by top-down processing. By knowing what to look for in the waveform, the program could see what before had been invisible.

Faced with a single sentence, a computer would have to consider thousands of possible interpretations. If the system made three guesses for each of the ten phonemes in an utterance, there would be 3^{10} (59,049) possible ways they could be strung together to form a sentence. Most of these combinations would be nonsense, but how is the machine to know? To visualize the enormity of the problem, all the possible interpretations can be thought of as forming a maze. Entering the first chamber we are faced with three possible pathways, one for each of the proposed initial phonemes. Then, whichever of those paths we choose to follow, we are faced with three more branches—one for each of the second possible phonemes. And each of those paths also lead to three more. Choosing the correct sentence from the 59,049 possible candidates is equivalent to finding the correct pathway that leads to the end of the maze.

If the hypothetical system was to search methodically every branch of this huge space of possibilities, it would quickly be overwhelmed by the size of the task. It would succumb to combinatorial explosion, the rapid proliferation of possible pathways. Negotiating so vast a search space requires intelligence, not blind wandering. Higher-level knowledge must be used continually to weed out bad guesses. In classic AI style, knowledge must be used to constrain the size of the search. Not every possibility deserves consideration.

For example, the sytem should know from its dictionary that while "did" and "you" are words, "di," "ja," and "dija" are not. Thus the latter could be quickly eliminated from consideration—several possible pathways could be eliminated from the maze. Once the system figured out that the first two words of the sentence were probably "did you," it would be guided by its syntactic knowledge to look for a verb or adverb next. There would be less sense in trying out combinations of phonemes that resulted in adjectives, prepositions, or nouns (though those kinds of words conceivably could be present in that spot of the sentence, they are far less likely). And so more paths would be eliminated. But is the verb "hid" or "hit"? If both entries in the pronunciation dictionary matched the utterance well enough, the ambiguity might be resolved using syntactic, semantic, and pragmatic knowledge. "Did you hid" is syntactically incorrect while "Did you hit" is a legal combination. Ideally the system would have rules to decide that "hit it to Tom" made more sense than "hid it to Tom." More likely, an actual program would be limited to one domain, say baseball. "Hid" would not be in its vocabulary, so the possibility of its presence would never be entertained. Or, to put it another way, the system would be incapable of hearing the word.

How were all the various levels of rules—pragmatic, semantic, syntactic, lexical, phonological—to be combined? How could the system be supplied with enough rules to operate intelligently without being paralyzed by the illusion of infinite choice? The researchers had no idea. They had five years to find out.

The Carnegie-Mellon team, with Raj Reddy presiding, began its investigation by building Hearsay-I, a program that knew about nothing except chess. When used with a chess-playing computer, the program allowed human players to say, in plain English, which moves they would like to make. The system, which had a thirty-one-word vocabulary, relied heavily on semantics, only considering interpretations that made sense in terms of the current configuration of the chessboard. Unfortunately, the system had a tendency to hear what it wanted to hear, rather than what had been said. In one case, the system's word recognizer had trouble distinguishing between "king" and "queen." So, when a human player asked for the move "Pawn to queen four," Hearsay-I assumed that he must have meant "Pawn to *king* four," since that was clearly the better move.

Apparently, concentrating too much on top-down processing was as bad as working exclusively from the bottom up. A more democratic approach was needed—a way to get all the levels of knowledge to contribute to the interpretation. And so Hearsay-II was born, an ingenious program designed to mimic a group of consultants—each with expertise in a different field—working together to solve a problem. In the program, the various types of rules or heuristics needed to understand speech—phonological, lexical, syntactic, et cetera—were packaged as independent "knowledge sources" or "experts." Each expert was like a program in itself. There was a phonetic expert, a syllable expert, a word expert, a phrase expert—a dozen or so independent subprograms. By making hypotheses about what phonemes, syllables, words, or phrases they believed they had found in the sentence and posting them on a global data base called a blackboard, the experts would collaborate with their peers in the task of understanding.

Hearsay-II is widely considered to be one of the most influential AI programs ever written. Thus it is worth considering in detail. The story of how the system operates and the problems encountered in its development provide a close look at how AI researchers go about their work, and what they mean when they say that machines can think.

To begin the speech-understanding process, Hearsay-II would call on an expert named Segment, which used its heuristics to chop the speech signal into its phonetic components, posting them on the blackboard. Again, because of the uncertainty involved in the task, several possible phonemes were proposed for each place in the utterance. (Technically speaking, these constituent sounds were what linguists call "phones" rather than "phonemes," but the distinction is not essential to understanding Hearsay-II.) Then the syllable expert examined this phonetic information and used it to propose possible syllables, posting *them* on the blackboard. Using this information, the word expert proposed candidate words, ranking them according to its estimate of which were the most likely choices. Then the phrase expert tried to combine the highest-rated words into phrases. As part of the process, it used its knowledge of grammar to propose syntactically plausible words that had been missed by the bottom end of the system. Another knowledge source called Verify double-checked these hypothesized words against the lower-level acoustic information, while Parse made sure the ever-expanding phrases were grammatical. Eventually a complete sentence would be found.

That was the theory anyway. On paper, Hearsay-II's blackboard architecture was clean and elegant. But as with any complex piece of software, there were a number of messy details to work out before the program could be transformed from idea to reality. Many programs never make this transition, remaining forever what some computer scientists derisively call vaporware.

With Hearsay-II, one of the most difficult problems was determining which of the many tiers of the wedding cake of knowledge were most germane to the speech-understanding task.

"There were a lot of surprises," recalled Hayes-Roth, who joined the project in midstream, after graduating from the University of Michigan with a doctoral degree in mathematical psychology. "No one ever knew whose knowledge would work, and there was no correlation between the number of feet of shelf space in the library on the subject and the ultimate contribution to the system. There might even be a negative correlation." Over the years, speech scientists had accumulated a great deal of phonological data, but the Hearsay team found little of it useful. "There was at one time a very competent phonetician on the team, at the Ph.D. level, and ultimately she dropped out of the project because none of us could figure out how to make the phonetic knowledge improve the performance of the system," Hayes-Roth said. The Carnegie-Mellon group approached the problem more as engineers than as scientists—they believed that the best way to determine which knowledge was most useful was to put it into the program, in the form of heuristics, and see if it worked. They weren't particularly interested in making a system that understood speech as humans do. "That was one of the great discoveries of doing speech—if you didn't implement and engineer the knowledge, you had no idea which was knowledge and which was just folklore."

One of the team's most important discoveries was how undiscriminating low-level knowledge can be. Using its phonetic, syllabic, and word experts, Hearsay-II would propose as many as twenty candidates for each word in a sentence. For a ten-word sentence that meant that the phrase expert was given two hundred words to try to string together into grammatically legal phrases. To visualize the problem, imagine the sentence as ten empty slots, each of which had to be filled with the correct word. Below each slot was a descending column of twenty candidate words, ranked according to Hearsay's estimate of how likely they were to be correct. The phrase expert's job was to take the words from the columns and juxtapose them in every possible manner, seeing which combinations were grammatically correct. For a four-word sequence there would be 20^4, or 160,000, possible phrases. Each one would have to be parsed to see if it was grammatical.

As if that weren't bad enough, the Hearsay team also discovered to its chagrin that, on the average, only eight of the ten columns contained a word that was really in the sentence. That's how unreliable bottom-end processing was. And, most often, these correct words were as far down as fifth on the list of possibilities—the words Hearsay-II had given the highest rankings to were usually wrong. Thus, in its search for syntactically correct phrases, the phrase expert would have to look at, on the average, four incorrect words in every column before it found one that was right. And in two columns, it would search all the way to the bottom without encountering one word that actually had been spoken. The system would spend most of its time trying to string together grammatical phrases from words that never had been said. Since the most efficient parser the team had been able to write took a tenth of a second to decide whether a single proposed phrase was grammatical, it was clear that Hearsay-II would be wasting an enormous amount of very expensive computer time.

"If you want to recognize an utterance in a few seconds and it takes you a tenth of a second just to check one possible partial sentence, and you've got a tableau of an astronomical number of possible words, most of which are wrong, you're never going to get there," Hayes-Roth said. "You might as well just throw in the towel. We recognized this when we had six months left in the total five-year program. We had not even been aware that it was a problem. We had built the whole system before we found out that the system we had built could never work."

The solution, they discovered, was to redesign the entire program, adding another level of knowledge—a new expert—to the blackboard.

"We thought we could go directly from the word level to the phrase level, and that was very naïve. This new level was essentially halfway between the word and phrase, and it turned out to be just the right medicine. Subsequently, the success of Hearsay-II could almost always be attributed to the success of what we called the Word Sequence expert," which was named Woseq for short. "If Woseq did a good job, Hearsay-II succeeded. If Woseq did a bad job, Hearsay-II failed."

Woseq worked like this: instead of trying to string words into complete grammatical phrases, it found fragments, containing as few as two words, which were likely to be part of the sentence. It based its hunches on phonetic and syntactic knowledge—picking words that sounded right and were grammatically plausible—as well as on knowledge derived from Claude Shannon's information theory.

"Think of the words as essentially being beads," Hayes-Roth explained. "Woseq would try to string together different strands of beads—two if it could, three if it could, four if it could—and it did that using a kind of heuristic estimator of whether a longer strand had more or less information in it than a shorter strand."

Exactly what this means is difficult to understand without a background in the mathematics of information theory, and the details aren't particularly important to grasping the essence of Hearsay-II. Still, even the gist of the idea is fascinating. Every time Woseq added a word to the sequence, it tried to ensure that, by its action, it was increasing information (and, conversely, decreasing entropy). Or, in other words, as it strung together beads, it rejected those combinations that could just as well have occurred by chance.

Information theory aside, the most important point is this: Woseq didn't try to determine whether the whole strand it was building was grammatical—that took too much time. It simply worked one bead at a time. While parsing a complete phrase took a tenth of a second, only a few milliseconds were required to add a bead to the string. The process was a hundred times faster. When Woseq had made the string as long as it could, it handed the whole thing up to the slower, computationally more expensive phrase expert to be parsed. Instead of feeding the parser every possible combination of words, it was only given the very best candidates, as determined by Woseq.

"That turned out to be extremely successful," Hayes-Roth said, "and we reengineered the entire system literally with weeks to go before the end of the contract. Talk about thrilling! It was a photo finish."

As they rushed toward the 1976 deadline, the members of the Hearsay team might have taken comfort in knowing that their competitors were at least as frantic. As collaborators in the DARPA project, System Development Corporation was working on the bottom end of a program, to which SRI was to contribute the top. But because of a computer problem, they were unable to merge the halves into a whole. While the two laboratories scrambled to make do with what each had developed on its own, William Woods and the BBN group were emerging as Carnegie-Mellon's chief rival. BBN was working on a system called HWIM—short for Hear What I Mean. HWIM (pronounced like "whim") was falling at least as far behind schedule as Hearsay-II.

From the beginning, Woods and his colleagues set themselves a far more ambitious goal than that of the Carnegie-Mellon group. While the Hearsay-II program worked through the interaction of many different kinds of knowledge, it made little use of semantics and none of pragmatics. And while the Carnegie-Mellon team had come a long way from Reddy's old system that required all sentences to contain the word "block," Hearsay-II's parser still was quite primitive, accepting only a limited variety of sentence types. The BBN team hoped to design a system that would allow the user to speak as naturally as possible, utilizing the wide range of sentences that could be recognized by Woods's powerful parser, the Augmented Transition Network. To make the system as intelligent as possible, the ATN would be expanded to include not only rules of syntax but also of semantics, pragmatics, and prosodics—a knowledge of how we use sentence rhythms and inflections to help say what we mean.

The importance of prosodic information was demonstrated early in the project, when the team was trying to build a system that would give a stripped-down version of Lunar the ability to understand the spoken word. In one experiment, when the program was asked, "Have any people done chemical analyses on this rock?" the first word was misheard as "give." The system's parser accepted the sentence, on the theory that "people-done" was an adjective—the speaker was asking Lunar to give him "people-done" chemical analyses (as opposed to ones that, perhaps, had been done by machine). If the system had known about prosodics, it might have realized that commands beginning with "give" are stressed differently from questions beginning with "have," and that if the speaker had meant "people-done" he would have given the words a different inflection.

In designing HWIM, Woods and his colleagues were continually guided by how humans understand speech. In fact, long before they were ready to build a working system, they used people to simulate one. One person—a trained speech scientist—played the part of the program that was to translate the speech signal (represented as a graph written on a piece of paper) into phonemes. Another person might play the syntactic and semantic analyzer. Other parts of the system, such as the pronunciation dictionary, were actually computerized. As people and machines interacted to decipher sample utterances, the humans in the loop noted which parts of their task were especially repetitive and wrote programs to perform them. Eventually they accumulated enough programs so that the people could, quite literally, replace themselves with a machine.

For their final system—the one that would compete with Hearsay-II—the BBN researchers connected HWIM to what was, in a way, an expanded version of the official airline guide, which Woods had used in his doctoral dissertation on procedural semantics. This new data base, called Trip, knew the names of all the people in Woods's division at BBN, what projects they worked on, what the travel budgets for those projects were, what conferences were coming up, et cetera. It knew the per diems allowed in major cities and the airfares between them. With the help of Trip, HWIM could understand and respond to fairly complicated requests like "How much is left in the speech budget?" or "Plan a trip for three people for two days in San Francisco in July."

But, though they made great headway toward their goal, BBN's plans turned out to be overly ambitious for a five-year project. It wasn't until the last few months of the endeavor that the team expanded the system's vocabulary from about 400 words to the approximately 1,000 required to meet the DARPA specifications. The group had so much to do in the final weeks that it had little time to fine-tune the system. In 1976, when the deadline arrived, the pragmatic and prosodic components weren't working well enough, so HWIM had to be tested with them turned off.

When all the programs were finally judged, System Development Corporation came in last. (SRI didn't have a complete program to test.) HWIM was next in line, demonstrating a comprehension level of 44 percent on a trial run of 124 sentences. Hearsay-II understood 91 percent of the sentences it was given. The program, which was connected to a data base containing abstracts of articles about artificial intelligence, answered questions like "What has McCarthy written since 1974?" or "Are any by Feigenbaum and Feldman?"

To analyze the latter sentence, which took a little over two seconds to say, Hearsay-II chopped it into approximately thirty-five segments, proposing as many as four possible pronunciations for each one. The syllable spotter used this phonetic information to propose up to nine syllables in some places, and the word spotter proposed ninety words for the six-word sentence, only four of which turned out to be correct. At various points in the process, Hearsay-II entertained the possibility that "Are any" was "Are Reddy" and that "Feigenbaum" was "Weizenbaum." The various phantom words that were detected and later ruled out included: aren't, article, algorithm, cite, thought, why, weak, we'd, copy, copying, fourteen, eighteen, DARPA, Arbib, model, monitor, medical, Mostow, Marvin, Norman, and Marr. It's clear from this example how much uncertainty was involved in the process—and how much the search for possible interpretations was constrained by the system's vocabulary. It heard "Feigenbaum" (correctly) and "Weizenbaum" (incorrectly) because those names were in its dictionary; thus, it expected that they might be in the utterance somewhere.

As it turned out, the winner was not Hearsay-II but a dark-horse program called Harpy that had been designed in a heroic rush by Carnegie-Mellon's Bruce Lowerre and Raj Reddy, who was worried that no one would meet the DARPA specifications. About midway through the program, Reddy, while overseeing the whole Carnegie-Mellon effort, began working on a program that, like Hearsay-II, would be applied to the document-retrieval task. Harpy made no use of semantics, pragmatics, or prosodics. It had no blackboard. Basically, Reddy had devised an ingenious method of storing in Harpy's memory every possible pronunciation of every possible sentence that could be spoken using the system's extremely restricted syntax. The plethora of pronunciations was stored in the form of a network. For example, if two of the sentences allowed in Harpy's grammar were "Please show me everything" and "Please help me," they would be represented in memory like this:

```
                        show
          Please               me   everything
                        help
```

After constructing a network containing every possible sentence, Reddy and Lowerre took each word, one by one, and replaced it with a smaller network of phonemes, representing every possible way it could be pronounced. The result was a huge, 15,000-node network—a labyrinth of everything Harpy knew how to hear. Given a sentence, Harpy chopped it into candidate phonemes. Then, using this information, it wound its way through the maze. If the program found a sequence of phonemes that formed a path leading from the beginning to the end, then the sentence was deciphered. In the process, Harpy translated the utterance into a program that carried out the request. Although it initially took an enormous amount of computer time to compile the network, once it had been constructed, Harpy could understand 95 percent of the sentences it was given.

The program was not very exciting intellectually, but it was an engineering marvel. Some critics thought of it as a supersophisticated watermelon box, with a template for every sentence. But it was far more than that. It was impossible, given the huge amount of space required, to hold Harpy's entire pronunciation network in memory all at the same time. So Reddy had to devise a way—using a technique called dynamic programming—to grow only the parts that were needed to translate a particular sentence. Each time it was given an utterance to understand, Harpy sprouted only the branches of the network necessary for the task at hand, pruning off extensions that were irrelevant.

But even those who admire Harpy for its engineering still grouse about it, complaining that it was constructed to meet the letter and not the spirit of the DARPA guidelines. They have a point. The BBN team lost the contest because it was trying to make a system that handled a natural range of English. One of the sentences HWIM missed was "The registration fee is twenty dollars," which was misheard as "*Their* registration fee is twenty dollars." The sentence "Show me Bill's trip to Washington" was misheard as "Show only Bell's trip to Washington." If there hadn't been both a Bill Woods and an Alan Bell in the BBN division (and thus in HWIM's memory) perhaps the sentence would have been correctly understood, using the process of elimination. Or HWIM might have got the sentences right if the BBN team, like the Harpy team, had severely restricted its grammar to minimize complexity. Harpy's world was so restricted that it knew only one sentence— "What are their affiliations"—beginning with the words "What are their." It knew only two sentences that began with "What are the": "What are the titles of the recent DARPA surnotes?" and "What are the key phrases?" Since the second parts of each sentence were so different, it was not difficult to tell them apart.

One way to measure the complexity of a grammar is to calculate the average number of different words that conceivably could appear in any one place in a sentence. This figure, called the "average branching ratio," was 33 for Harpy and 195 for HWIM. But complexity had its price. Harpy worked at a rate of about 80 times real time, at a cost of about $5 a sentence. DARPA assumed that as computer technology improved, processing speeds would increase. So this was considered an acceptable level of performance. HWIM required more than a thousand times real time to understand a sentence.

"From my point of view the project would have been very unsatisfying if there had not been both the BBN and the CMU [Carnegie-Mellon University] outcomes," Woods said, almost a decade later. "Because essentially those two projects explored almost polar extremes in the space of speech-understanding systems. In terms of the DARPA milestones, Harpy literally met them, but it did so in a way that didn't go anywhere next.

"The flip side was the BBN effort. We were doing a grammar that really approximated natural English, talking about a domain that was a good deal more complex than the Lunar domain. Our grammar was tackling things people really would say. There were all these very similar sentences that differed by only one phoneme in places—in some places not even that. They would have to be told apart the way people do—by hearing as much as you can and putting together what you know about the way things get pronounced, the frequency of different kinds of errors, and what are sensible things to say, and how often people speak ungrammatically, and all the rest of that. The BBN effort really points the way to how to tackle all these subtle nuances, all of these harder problems—how would you put the prosodics in, how would you make the predictions depend on the context, so that what you say in the second sentence depends on what you said in the last, how would you begin to hook up to a model of what's really going on around you in the world?"

As the most intensive, competitive effort in AI's short history, the DARPA speech-understanding project provided a showcase for two different ways in which artificial intelligence can be done: as science and as engineering.

"Our strength was that we never lost sight of the fact that we were dealing with a very hard search problem," Hayes-Roth said, "and we did a lot of engineering. In the whole AI world, CMU is viewed as the place where the engineers are. My ambitions for our contribution to the science of linguistics were almost nil. I was interested in advancing knowledge engineering in AI. We were varied but, on average, mediocre speech scientists. We were computer scientists first. We represented an interest in that part of AI that is concerned with making things work, not necessarily illuminating deep theoretical concerns. BBN did a magnificent job on the speech-science aspects, but they made a problem that they could not solve."

The speech-understanding project demonstrated the differences between the cognitive modeling school, whose members design intelligent programs in order to better understand the human mind, and followers of the intelligent-artifacts school, who are more interested in the practicalities of building working systems, caring little about whether their programs think like people. It didn't matter to the Hearsay-II researchers whether our brains contain anything remotely like Woseq. While both Carnegie-Mellon and BBN were using a hybrid of these two approaches, the HWIM project leaned more in the direction of cognitive modeling, while Hearsay-II—and certainly Harpy—were largely in the intelligent-artifacts camp.

When the project is viewed as a whole rather than through the eyes of each competitor, it becomes clear that there were no losers. If the purpose of the research was to prove that AI was a worthwhile pursuit, then everybody won.

"There was more competition than we wanted," Hayes-Roth said. "It left a very bad taste in everybody's mouth. CMU got all the credit; the other guys got no credit at all. But if we hadn't succeeded the whole field would have had a bad name. The excitement and commercialization and high gloss of AI would not be here now. There's absolutely no question about that." Throughout the project there was a constant fear that it would turn out to be a rerun of the machine-translation debacle of the 1950s. "It was obviously a watershed era for AI, and it might have set us back ten years if we had failed."

Apparently the Defense Department saw it the same way. In 1983, based on the success of the speech-understanding project and other advances in AI, the Pentagon decided to commit, through DARPA, $600 million for the five-year Strategic Computing program. As part of the effort, Reddy will head a major speech-understanding project, expanding on the blackboard architecture of Hearsay-II. While the earlier speech project emphasized basic research, the planners of the Strategic Computing program envision the day when intelligent automatic copilots help guide fighter planes, responding to the spoken orders of their human commanders.

The day when a computer can listen as well as a human is still a long way off. Scientists are far from producing a system that would understand even the 1,000 words of Basic English that have been proposed as an international language.

"It would require an enormous project," Hayes-Roth said, "maybe the size of a small Apollo project. You wouldn't do this with five or ten man-years of work. But is all the technology available to do this? I think the answer is yes. I think it would just take the will to crack that barrier. But you are talking about one giant engineering project. With a thousand Basic English words you can make a lot of sentences and talk about a lot of ideas. So that opens up the grammatical floodgates—you can have more alternatives. You've got to make up for that somehow."

So, for the next few years, or maybe decades, the task of speech understanding will probably remain limited to practical systems working in narrow domains. Other areas of research—such as learning and vision—are apt to get more attention from those who administer funds.

"There's so much else to do," Hayes-Roth said. A general, all-purpose hearing machine isn't apt to be a top priority. "People can understand fine, and we can always talk to machines by typing to them."

Planning and Seeing

After the Hearsay project disbanded, some of the team's members scattered to other universities and research institutes. Frederick Hayes-Roth (and his wife, Barbara, a cognitive psychologist) went to the Rand Corporation in Santa Monica; Victor Lesser, another member of the team, to the University of Massachusetts, and his colleague Lee Erman to the University of Southern California's Information Sciences Institute in Marina del Rey. Frederick Hayes-Roth and Erman now work together at Teknowledge, while Barbara Hayes-Roth is at Stanford's Heuristic Programming Project. As they worked with their new colleagues, the Hearsay veterans helped spread the idea that the blackboard architecture could be used as a foundation on which to build many different kinds of intelligent programs, not just ones that understood speech.

As part of their research, Frederick and Barbara Hayes-Roth used the blackboard model to design a computer simulation of how a person might devise a plan for, say, a shopping trip. Their work was based on the realization that planning, like deciphering speech, requires analyzing a problem from many different levels of abstraction. Just as an utterance can be viewed as a string of phonemes, syllables, words, phrases, or as a complete sentence, a plan also can be scrutinized on very low levels, where the details are prominent, or on increasingly higher levels, where all the minutiae blur together into larger and larger wholes.

When we formulate a plan, we usually start at the highest, most general level of abstraction, deciding, for example, to go out to lunch. Before we can execute the plan, however, we must descend to a slightly lower, more detailed level: to go out to lunch we must travel from the office (by car, foot, taxi, or bus) to an area where there are restaurants—the shopping mall or downtown. Moving down another level, we fill in more details, deciding to drive downtown to the Saigon Café for Vietnamese food. Moving down yet another level, we see that we must get in the car, drive east on Central to Washington, turn right on Washington, then right on Grand, follow Grand to Fourth Street, and try to park. At an even lower level of abstraction, the plan would involve walking to the car, opening the door, closing it, starting the ignition, looking in the rearview mirror, backing out of the parking space, driving to the bottom of the parking ramp, inserting the computerized parking pass in the automatic exit gate, et cetera. Of course, we could conceivably be as detailed and concrete as we like, going so low as to describe every minute muscular movement of the hands, legs, and eyes (the machine language of the body) that is required to satisfy the physical and social need to eat a midday meal.

If we have several goals to accomplish on our trip—stopping by the bank for money, the service station for gas, the library to drop off an overdue book—then the planning becomes more complicated. Lower-level knowledge—the location of the bank in relation to the gas station, restaurant, library, or office—influences the manner in which we develop a higher-level plan. We try to find a route to (or from) lunch that will take us by the proper places. As in speech understanding, top-down processing interacts with bottom-up processing. We go up Central because it leads toward the Saigon Café, but we decide to eat Vietnamese food in the first place partly because we know that the restaurant is near the bank. If we have several errands to accomplish and are willing to choose among any number of restaurants, gas stations, or automated-teller machines, which are scattered in locations all over town, the number of possible routes becomes enormous. It would be impossible to mentally try out each one, seeking the most efficient. It might end up taking more time to plan the trip than to execute it.

The Hayes-Roths' system did not work by exhaustively searching the vast space of possibilities. It planned intelligently instead, drawing upon a store of knowledge about an imaginary town whose map was stored in its memory. The user told the machine (via a keyboard) where he or she needed to go. Then various trip-planning experts (realized as software routines) simultaneously worked on different levels of the problem. They posted partial results on a blackboard for inspection and use by their colleagues. For example, one expert might notice that several stores that the user needed to visit were clustered in a certain part of town. This fact would be posted on the blackboard where it might be of use to a route-planning expert. Once a route had been found that headed toward the cluster, another expert might notice that several other necessary errands could be performed along the way.

While the Hayes-Roths worked on their planning system, other researchers applied the blackboard architecture to other intelligent programs. At Stanford, Edward Feigenbaum and his wife, Penny Nii, used the blackboard model to design a system in which various experts collaborated in analyzing sonar signals, using them to identify and locate ships at sea. Nii liked to compare the problem to tracking people at a cocktail party, guided only by the sound of their voices, which had to be picked out individually from all the noise.

Other Stanford researchers have used a similar approach to design a program that may someday be able to decipher the intricate three-dimensional shapes of protein molecules from the often fuzzy and confusing data yielded by a technique known as X-ray crystallography. The program, called Crysalis, includes experts on various aspects of organic chemistry—the "grammar" by which atoms can be combined into amino acids, and amino acids into the long, twisting chains called protein molecules. Again, the experts communicate through a blackboard. Eventually the chemical phonemes, syllables, words, and phrases are combined to form the complex, compound sentences known as proteins. The program is still in the experimental stage, but its inventors believe that the concept is sound. Crysalis simply hasn't been given enough rules yet. Determining protein structures is such a difficult task that it can take a skilled human crystallographer weeks or months to decipher a single molecule. The renowned molecular biologist Max Perutz spent forty years finding the structure of hemoglobin, the 10,000-atom protein that carries oxygen through the bloodstream.

Stanford researchers are so confident of the power of the blackboard that Nii has worked on a generic program called AGE (Attempt to Generalize), which can be thought of as an empty blackboard—or, to extend the metaphor, as a conference room, with a roundtable surrounded with unoccupied chairs. AGE is what is known as a framework system—a sort of fill-in-the-blanks AI program. With AGE, programmers can design the experts they need for a certain task and seat them around the table, which comes already built. The purpose is to save on programming time. Blackboard systems for many different uses can be made without having to start each time from scratch.

Other Stanford researchers are trying to do with hardware what Nii did with software. The idea of experts communicating via a blackboard is, they believe, the ideal model for a parallel computer. Just as the inventors of the Lisp machine designed hardware especially suited to McCarthy's programming language, a Stanford research group is building a machine especially designed to run blackboard programs. One of the most difficult problems of designing a program like Hearsay-II is getting it to run on today's serial computers. Since programs can be executed only one step at a time—funneled through the von Neumann bottleneck—the software experts can't really work on several parts of a problem simultaneously. The parallelism they exhibit is an illusion, created through clever programming and the sheer speed of the digital computer—another demonstration that, given enough time, anything that can be done by a parallel machine can be done by a serial one. But it might be possible to design more intricate blackboards for use on a truly parallel computer, programs with many more experts all interacting without overwhelming the machine.

In the rich, well-funded medium of artificial intelligence, powerful ideas propagate quickly. What started as a model for understanding speech has also spread to the field of vision research. At the University of Massachusetts, colleagues of Hearsay veteran Victor Lesser are experimenting with VISIONS (Visual Integration by Semantic Interpretation of Natural Scenes), a blackboard program in which top-level knowledge interacts with bottom-level knowledge to identify objects in a photograph. Instead of phoneme, syllable, and word detectors, VISIONS's bottom end consists of experts adept at detecting changes in light intensity, and in identifying the various types of lines, corners, surfaces, et cetera, which might be in a picture. Its top end contains knowledge about objects—trees, houses, et cetera—that are commonly found in the world.

Suppose the system was shown a scene from a typical American neighborhood. Noting that the angle expert had announced (in a message posted on the blackboard) that it had found four corners, a region expert might propose the presence of a trapezoid. A surface expert (which knows, among other things, about the laws of perspective) might decide that the trapezoid is a rectangular surface, viewed at a slight angle. Using this and other information, the volume expert might propose that the rectangle is part of a rectangular solid, which the object expert might recognize as a house. The system can make this connection because it holds in its memory information about what houses look like.

While Hearsay-II contains a pronunciation dictionary of all the words it understands, VISIONS has a data base of the types of images it knows. Given a picture of a road in the country, the system might use this higher-level knowledge to decide that a brown region with vertical parallel sides is a tree, and that the textured green stuff surrounding the trunk is grass. The long gray region with the converging sides might be a road receding into the distance—a hypothesis that would be strengthened by the discovery of a dotted yellow center line.

Other researchers have used the blackboard model to build vision programs that read aerial photographs, which might be of use to mapmakers or (inevitably) military analysts. If a low-level line detector finds two parallel lines, a higher-level road detector might hypothesize a road. Then the line detector would try to extend it, looking more closely for segments it had missed. We hear what we expect to hear, we see what we expect to see.

All these attempts at machine vision are still in the experimental stages. Their "vocabularies" are far more restricted than Hearsay-II's. But the programs provide a powerful demonstration of a fact that researchers in machine vision have been learning since the 1960s: that many of the problems encountered in seeing are strikingly similar to those in speech understanding. In both cases, a number of different kinds of knowledge must interact to retrieve the meaning hidden in ambiguous, noisy signals. In speech understanding, a microphone (and various circuitry) turns sound into a stream of binary digits from which sentences must be built. In a computer-vision system, a lens projects a scene onto a focal plane, where it is electronically scanned and converted into a string of 1s and 0s. This digital information represents the intensity of light present in each of the thousands of dots, or pixels, that make up the scene. From this information, the computer must retrieve a three-dimensional world. It would seem an impossible task, if not for the fact that humans and other animals do something like this all the time. We take the array of light and dark projected on our retinas and turn it into images so rich that they constitute most of what we call reality. Getting a machine to achieve even a crude approximation of this task has turned out to be at least as difficult as getting it to understand speech.

Even seeing images in the blocks world has proved much harder than anyone had anticipated. In the early 1970s, vision researchers built programs whose microworlds were restricted to a small number of matte white polyhedra (cubes, wedges, pyramids, et cetera) illuminated against a black background. (In fact, many of the systems—which had names like See, Obscene, and Poly—dispensed with physical objects altogether and tried to decipher simple black-and-white line drawings of blocks.) Since the blocks might be arranged in any number of configurations—stacked one atop the other, and at various angles, so that one block would partially hide another—figuring out exactly what objects were in a scene was extremely difficult. While in speech, sentences can contain hidden words, visual scenes seem to contain lines and surfaces that aren't really there: shadows, for example, or squares and triangles that are really blank spaces—empty regions of air formed by the coming-together of edges (see page 148).

How is a program to know what is real and what is illusion? While speech-understanding systems make sense of the low-level information by using rules of phonetics, syntax, et cetera, vision systems must have their own grammars—rules about the legal ways lines and surfaces can combine to make three-dimensional objects. To develop this knowledge, researchers studied in detail the various kinds of lines that exist: convex edges, concave edges, cracks (the lines between two adjacent blocks), shadows, occlusions (the lines formed when part of one block obscures part of another). Then they developed rules to describe how all these kinds of lines could join to form corners, surfaces, et cetera. For example, three convex lines can form a Y, which might indicate the top corner of a cube viewed from above. An upward-pointing arrow might be the same corner viewed from below or the peak of a pyramid. Using such information, the blocks-world programs examined the angles, lines, squares, triangles, and parallelograms of a two-dimensional image and used these clues to determine the objects in the original scene. Just as some combinations of phonemes never occur in English—"krx," for example—so are certain combinations of lines illegal in the three-dimensional world. They form what are known as impossible objects and deserve no more consideration in analyzing a scene than the word "krxter" would in analyzing a spoken sentence. Using its grammar of lines and edges, an intelligent seeing program could rule out these optical illusions, narrowing the search space of all possible interpretations of a scene (see page 148).

In the decade that has passed since the first experiments in AI vision systems, scientists have focused on the problems posed by going from the blocks world to the real world. Takeo Kanade of Carnegie-Mellon University has studied the origami world—an extended version of the blocks world named for the intricately folded paper sculptures of Japanese art. Other researchers have introduced the Play-Doh world, in which objects can be curved.

While some vision researchers concentrate on building grand systems like VISIONS, many scientists are occupied with more fundamental questions. Instead of trying to make all-purpose seeing machines, these researchers are using computers to explore, in as much detail as possible, how machines can perform certain seemingly elementary visual tasks. The result has been a number of very mathematical theories about how, for example, the shape of an object can be determined from the way light plays across its surfaces, or how depth can be calculated by viewing a scene from two slightly different angles (as we do with our eyes). Fully appreciating these theories requires

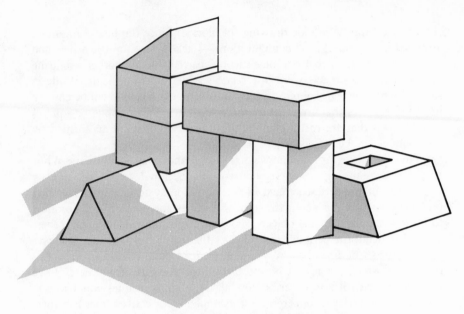

A Jumble of Objects

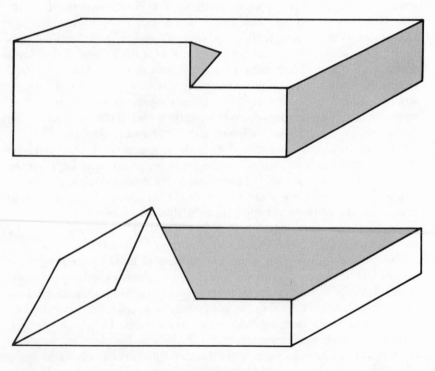

Impossible Objects

an acquaintance with such abstruse mathematical notions as Fourier transforms, Gaussian and Laplacian operators, and nonlinear partial differential equations—as well as with the science of optics. Details aside, all this work is based on a fascinating assumption: that the methods by which the brain and nervous system extract meaning from the information sent by an eye are computational. They can be described in a finite number of steps, as algorithms or programs that can be run on a machine.

Some of the most interesting developments have come from the work of the late David Marr and his colleague Tomaso Poggio at the MIT artificial-intelligence laboratory. Marr was trained as a neurophysiologist, Poggio as a theoretical physicist (later he worked on experiments with the visual system of the fly). Unlike most vision researchers, Marr and Poggio have been strongly guided by how humans and other animals see. However, they are not so much interested in using people as models to help them build seeing computers as they are in using the concept of computation to help them understand the complexities of human vision. In their efforts to understand sight, they start by speculating on just what computations the brain might perform when it carries out some visual task, such as extracting stereoscopic information from a binocular view of a scene. Then they figure out the various ways the procedure could be embodied in a computer program. Finally, they refine the algorithms until they come up with ones that could conceivably run on the biological computers we call brains. These computational theories suggest experiments that physiologists can perform to help confirm or deny the ideas.

One of the most surprising of Marr's and Poggio's discoveries is that a great deal of complex visual processing seems to be performed by the lower levels of the visual system—the so-called bottom end—rather than by the higher cognitive areas of the brain. What the brain receives from the eye is not raw data, like the signal from a video camera telling only how much light is present at every pixel. By the time a visual signal reaches the higher levels of the brain, it has already undergone a great deal of processing. Information about depth and the presence of edges, textures, and even shapes has already been extracted and encoded in the pulses of the neuronal stream. It is only after this low-level processing is complete that the higher levels of our intelligence identify and name the objects. If Marr and Poggio are right, then top-down processing (recognizing a cup because we expect to see a cup) is not as prominent in human vision as some AI researchers have supposed.

Marr died of leukemia in 1980 at the age of thirty-five. Through the help of associates his book, *Vision*, was completed and published two years later. The work could serve as a model for how scientists can describe theories with both rigor and charm, satisfying colleagues and the general reader. While the middle section of the book is formidable in its detailed mathematical descriptions, the introduction describes Marr's theories and their background in sparklingly clear prose. A third section of the book consists of a dialogue between a believer in artificial intelligence and a skeptic. It is based on lunchtime conversations involving Marr and Poggio (the believers), and the skeptical biologist Francis Crick. Marr's book has excited physiologists as well as AI researchers. Perhaps the most important influence of his work has been to suggest ways the two groups can join together to learn more about the mysteries of sight.

Despite the advances in computer vision research, we are as far from having a general seeing machine as we are from having a system that can understand a wide range of spoken (or even typewritten) sentences. It is ironic that it has turned out to be easier to get machines to play chess, solve logical theorems, and perform medical diagnoses than it has been to get them to see and hear. The tasks that seem simplest to us humans often turn out to be the hardest to mechanize. Robotics researchers have found it extremely difficult to duplicate, for example, the grasping ability of a human hand. The problems are not so much concerned with mechanical engineering as they are with appreciating and capturing the intelligence required to perform such a deceptively simple act. Michael Brady, a vision and robotics researcher at MIT, explained the problem. "Today's robots have to be told tediously where they should move in terms which make sense to the robot. For example, I might say, 'Go to the bench and pick up the hammer which is hanging in its slot on the tool rack and then use it to affix the handle to the cup.' Unfortunately you can't do that right now. You need to say, 'Move the hammer to this position,' and then give a string of X, Y, Z coordinates and a bunch of angles, and so on and so forth."

For a robot to understand and execute such a command, it would have to see and feel, and sense the position of its own limbs. Then it would have to coordinate all that information using spatial reasoning—the ability to formulate a plan to move its arm through space, avoiding obstacles, arriving at the proper spot with just the right amount of force needed to pick up a screwdriver, or turn a screw without twisting it in half. When researchers calculate the trajectory for an experimental robot arm, they must use their knowledge of geometry, trigonometry, and the physics of centripetal forces. We do all that automatically, unconsciously, all the time.

"Robotics is the intelligent connection of perception to action," Brady said. Like vision research, it is a means of studying human abilities as well as of making intelligent machines. "We've barely scratched the surface," he said. "It's going to be a long haul for hundreds of years to get to anything with the same kind of capabilities as man. On the other hand, there has been some pretty damn spectacular work in the last five or ten years." Mechanical legs that can hop around like pogo sticks, multifingered robot hands—building these experimental prototypes has demonstrated again and again the complexity of the skills we take for granted.

Long before we have vision and hearing systems that can perceive as well as people do or mechanical hands and limbs as adept as ours, the world champion chess player might very well be a computer program (though it will likely work in a manner that bears little resemblance to human thought). Carnegie-Mellon's Herbert Simon has speculated on why, in a sense, expertise is easier to automate than our most basic abilities, the things any three-year-old can do.

"One theory is that, after all, when you simulate a college professor or a businessman, you're simulating what goes on in the new brain—in the newer parts of the cerebrum. And that's a structure that is maybe two million years old—at least it's a structure that has changed a hell of a lot in the last two million years. So it's probably a very crude—maybe even simple— structure that has not been well-tuned by evolution. There just hasn't been time. It does what it does but it ain't great as a product of engineering. On the other hand, when you look at the sensory and motor organs, they have reached their present state of development—not only in human beings but in mammals, where they are just as good as they are in human beings—over maybe half a billion years. And they are very sophisticated devices—our eyes and our ears and their connections with the hands. So one could make an argument that you're dealing with much more sophisticated devices, and it's going to be harder to simulate them.

"That's related to another fact, and that is that these particular devices [hearing and seeing] are demonstrably parallel. The retina of the eye and the parts of the brain it's connected with operate in parallel fashion. The ear likewise. To do sophisticated visual or auditory pattern recognizing, you just may not have enough computing power with a serial von Neumann machine."

On the other hand, Simon believes, our more rational, conscious processes do work in a serial fashion. When we're reasoning about a problem— a chess game, a puzzle, a plan for a trip—we are limited by our ability to focus on only a small amount of information at any one time. We break a problem into pieces and solve them one by one.

"That means whatever the hardware is like in other respects, we're basically serial processors. I don't see any evidence that when human beings are problem solving that they're doing anything in parallel. Now that's very debatable, and most of my colleagues in fact debate it. But they're wrong." Even if we do some of the problem-solving steps at the same time, Simon would argue that the degree of parallelism is insignificant compared to the way we seem to simultaneously process the deluge of information that flows from the millions of light-sensitive cells that make up our retinas.

Another explanation of why vision and hearing have turned out to be so difficult to understand is that they are unconscious processes. When gazing out at the ocean we can't sense the algorithms our nervous system is using to gauge the depth of the scene by the texture of the waves as they recede into the horizon. Vision evolved as an aid to survival; thus it is a process that must occur quickly and without thinking. It was only in the later, safer moments of our evolutionary life that we developed an ability to contemplate, introspect, to think about thinking. And so we are left in a state of bewilderment, amazed that what we are calling the Pacific is actually two tiny arrays of light projected upside down on screens in the back of our eyes.

8

Learning
About
the World

As proficient as they were in their narrow areas of expertise—Lunar with moon rocks, the vision systems with building blocks, Hearsay II with human utterances about computer-science abstracts—these programs shared a common handicap: the inability to learn. The various AI programs that had been developed by the early 1970s might be called intelligent, in the sense that they could muster enough analytical power to deal with some novel situations—a sentence never heard before, an image never seen. But the sentence had to be made with words and a grammar already stored by a human in the computer's memory; the scene had to consist of objects and relationships that the computer already knew about. How did it know? Because a human had told it—carefully coding knowledge into the lines and loops of the program. To make the programs smarter, a programmer would have to open them up and tinker with their insides—adding, deleting, rearranging the abstract gears and pulleys of their invisible machinery. It was only in this trivial sense that they could be said to learn.

From the early days of electronic engineering, a decade before "artificial intelligence" was even a term, scientists have toyed with the idea of machines that improve with age—that can learn from experience, discovering rules on their own. In the heyday of cybernetics—the late 1940s and 1950s, when scientists were stringing together vacuum tubes and relays into electronic simulations of neural nets—the goal was to develop brainlike systems that learned. The cyberneticists could even claim a few partial successes, such as Frank Rosenblatt's Perceptron, the machine that could be trained to know its ABCs, but only within narrow limits.

When the focus of research shifted in the late 1950s from trying to mimick networks of neurons to programming digital computers to act as though they were thinking, the elusive dream of a learning machine still shimmered. To some observers it was an impossible dream. The very words "learning machine" seemed contradictory. Machines were, by their very nature, devices that performed repetitive tasks, like weaving thread into cloth, adding long lists of numbers, or harnessing tiny, sequentially timed explosions into the circular motion that makes an automobile run. The word "mechanical" has always had a metallic ring.

Learning, it seemed, was the sine qua non of nonmechanical behavior. While some of what we know is the result of rote memorization, mentally repeating the multiplication tables over and over until they are etched in our brain, most of learning is a far more subtle process. It is not, after all, simply the storing away of information; a tape recorder doesn't learn any more than a microphone hears or a television camera sees. Learning is active, not passive.

From the flood of data pouring through our senses we select what is interesting, what is important. We note similarities and differences, finding patterns among the chaos. Every instant we are awake, we are actively acquiring information, using it to expand and modify the pictures of reality we hold in our heads—our maps of the way the world works. Even the knowledge that is force-fed to us—by parents, teachers, instruction manuals—all must be woven into the fabric of everything else we know, or, to change metaphors, incorporated into the structures that we are constantly building in our minds.

With the advent of the computer, we've had to refine our notion of "machine" from a clanking conglomeration of gears and wheels to any device that carries out a procedure. If learning is a procedure, then there is no reason why, theoretically, it cannot be mechanized.

Arthur Samuel was one of the first to show that something like learning could be programmed. His checker-playing program continually benefited from the games it played, fine-tuning the strategic formulas that had been initially provided by Samuel. What Samuel achieved with checkers, his colleagues hoped to do with other intelligent skills. If there are procedures for seeing, hearing, parsing a sentence, and deciphering its meaning, then why couldn't there also be procedures for learning—rules for how to learn new rules? Learning, then, would be an algorithm for acquiring new algorithms, or improving the ones that are already there.

As they dreamed of learning machines, some of the more optimistic researchers were struck by what was sometimes called the bootstrap hypothesis. If a machine could be made to learn, without a human programmer spoon-feeding it information, then no matter how stupid it was to begin with, it could rapidly acquire the knowledge and procedures it needed to be as smart as or smarter than its inventor. It could pull itself up by its own bootstraps. Like a human, it could accelerate the learning process by continually learning how to learn. Alan Turing described this vision in 1950, in his essay "Computing Machinery and Intelligence":

> Instead of trying to produce a program to simulate the adult mind, why not rather try to produce one which simulates the child's? If this were then subjected to an appropriate course of education one would obtain the adult brain. Presumably the child brain is something like a notebook as one buys it from the stationers. Rather little mechanism, and lots of blank sheets. . . . Our hope is that there is so little mechanism in the child brain that something like it can be easily programmed.

It is an enticing idea. Duplicating human intelligence seems impossibly hard, so make a stupid machine that will teach itself to be smart. Now all we must do is make a learning machine. But that, too, has turned out to be almost impossibly difficult. If experiments in machine learning are any indication, the child brain is not as empty a notebook as Turing supposed. A great deal of mechanism is already there. An important aim of artificial-intelligence researchers has been to find out what that machinery might be.

They hope to capture the procedures of learning in programs that can refine and expand themselves. Half the allure is practical—imagine machines that, with a little help from their makers, automatically get better. But researchers also hope their work will teach us more about the way we think. As with computer vision, little of the research is directed toward making grand, general systems—in this case, Turing's imagined child machine. It is aimed instead at using programs to explore basic human mental processes. To simplify the experiments as much as possible, researchers often turn to the blocks world.

Terry Winograd's SHRDLU showed a rudimentary ability to learn what it was told. Recall that when asked, "Does a steeple . . ." SHRDLU interrupted: "Sorry, I don't know the word 'steeple.' " "A steeple," Winograd instructed, "is a stack which contains two green cubes and a pyramid." "I understand," SHRDLU replied, exaggerating. The program knew about green cubes and pyramids; it knew about stacks; it knew, in the limited sense of the blocks world, what "contains" means. These were structures of Lisp that were already in its memory. By combining them into a cluster and internally naming it "steeple," SHRDLU had acquired a new concept. "Are there any steeples now?" Winograd asked, testing. "No," SHRDLU answered. "Build one." "OK." And it did.

Patrick Winston, the director of MIT's AI lab, carried blocks-world learning a step further with his program that learned, through example, the concept "arch." By seeing things that are arches and things that are almost but not quite arches (Winston called them "near misses"), the program learned that an arch consists of a lintel that must-be-supported-by two posts which must-not-touch. What Winston developed was an algorithm that generalized from specific cases. By comparing one example with another, and noting similarities and differences, the program learned the necessary characteristics of archness. It was, in a sense, a crude computational definition of the process of induction.

What Winston's program did with the blocks world, we do with the real world. We see examples of houses all our lives, beginning with the ones we live in, the ones we see in storybooks, the ones we make from building blocks. Over the years, we generalize, learning to recognize as houses the place where Carrie lives, the place where Amy lives, the dozen houses in our neighborhood, the modern one-story houses by the shopping mall, the old three-story houses downtown, the single-roomed mud houses on the Navajo reservation, the honeycombed adobe cities on the Zuni reservation, the grass houses on stilts we saw in a movie about Africa—all, we learn, are examples of a single, ever-expanding concept called house. At the same time, we learn through negative examples not to build our concepts too loosely. A department store is not a house, nor is the Empire State Building. And we learn to handle the in-between cases: tree houses, doghouses, dollhouses, halfway houses, the White House.

No wonder Winston confined his learning experiments to the smooth, clean lines of the blocks world. But in the decade since he wrote the arch-learning program, he has ventured, with small, tentative steps, further into the messiness of reality. While his arch program was an exercise in learning from examples, lately Winston has been turning his attention to the more general question of how computers might learn from experience. When confronted with a new situation, we search our memory for a similar one we've encountered before. After comparing the old situation with the new, we modify what we already know, then apply it to the task at hand. We learn, in other words, by drawing an analogy, between the familiar and the strange.

Say we go to England for the first time and chance upon a game of rugby. "Oh," we say to ourselves, "this is just like football, *except* . . ." By using the exceptions to modify what we already know, we coin a new concept. Given football as a precedent, rugby suddenly makes sense. Say we drop a thermometer on the floor and suddenly there are little blobs of mercury everywhere. "Oh, this is just like water, except . . ."

"I've always been interested in the question of how we learn from precedents," Winston explained. "That's a dominant mechanism in fields like law and medicine, management, military science, and, in fact, life in general. We always look at new situations from the perspective of things we've seen before. In many cases that's the only way we can cope with the complexity of the world, by not understanding a new situation in enormous depth but by saying, 'Oh, well, this looks like something I've seen before.' "

Clearly, Winston thought, if computers are to become intelligent enough to deal with the constant surprises encountered in life, they too will have to be able to draw on what they have learned in the past. Thus in the 1980s he began working on a program that could learn from precedents. As with his arch-learning experiments, he stripped the problem to its essence, picking examples that would show some of the steps a machine would have to go through if it was to perform this kind of analogical reasoning. In his slow, calm manner, with barely a hint of excitement in his voice, he described his efforts to get machines to learn about the world.

"The particular domain that I began to work in was one that I happened to like, namely Shakespearean plots. So I wondered to myself if the plot of *Macbeth* could be used to solve a problem having to do with a different situation, and if in the course of that problem solving the system could generate some more global conclusion that would apply to all sorts of situations." Was it possible, he wondered, to write a program that would take some of the lessons Shakespeare taught and generalize them, so that they could be used to solve modern-day problems? "Naturally, the stories that I used were quite simplified," he said.

Indeed, for the purpose of Winston's experiment, the plot of *Macbeth* was boiled down to this:

"Macbeth is an evil noble. Lady Macbeth is a greedy, ambitious woman. Duncan is a king. Macduff is a noble. Lady Macbeth persuades Macbeth to want to be king because she is greedy. She is able to influence him because he is married to her and because he is weak. Macbeth murders Duncan with a knife. Macbeth murders Duncan because Macbeth wants to be king and

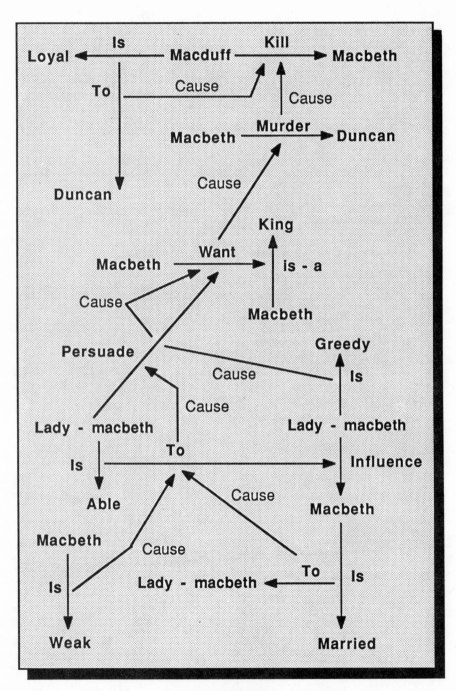

A Diagram of *Macbeth*

because Macbeth is evil. Lady Macbeth kills herself. Macduff is angry. He kills Macbeth because Macbeth murdered Duncan and because Macduff is loyal to Duncan."

Using a language-understanding program designed by Winston's colleague Boris Katz, the meaning of this Shakespearean précis was converted into a semantic network—a diagram of characters, their relationships, and the web of causes and effects that are the essence of the Macbeth story (see opposite).

With the network tucked away in memory, in the form of Lisp structures, Winston asked his program to use *Macbeth* as a precedent to solve exercises like this:

"There is a man and a woman. The man married the woman. The man is weak and the woman is greedy. Show that the man may have the ambition to take his boss's job."

First the example was converted into a network:

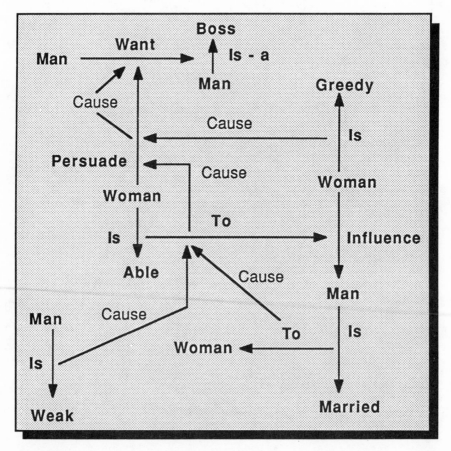

Drawing an Analogy

By matching this pattern of lines and arrows against the network that already had been created for *Macbeth*, the program was able to note similarities in structure: the constellation of relationships and events that connected Macbeth, his lady, and Duncan the king was similar to the one formed by the man in the example, his wife, and his boss. By drawing parallels between the two situations, the program learned by analogy the following rule: "If a man is weak and his wife is greedy, then he might try to take his boss's job." From the specific case of *Macbeth*, the program generalized a rule that might be applied to the world today.

The example might seem trivial, but Winston's program helped make explicit some of the processes an intelligent entity might use when it compares a new situation to an old one, abstracting what it learns into rules that help make sense of life. Given other examples, the system might have learned that if a woman induces her husband to commit murder, then she could end up killing herself. This and the previous rule would be strictly true only given the precedent of *Macbeth*. They exist in what Winston calls the "Macbeth world," which in some ways is more complicated than the blocks world but is still only a caricature of reality.

Encouraged by his *Macbeth* experiment, Winston decided to apply his ideas about analogical reasoning to a program that could learn, among other things, to recognize cups. The task is not as simple as it sounds. There are many different kinds of cups—plastic or china coffee cups, paper cups, Styrofoam cups, red cups, green cups, cups with elephants, penguins, or lilacs painted on them. How can a computer learn from such examples what a cup looks like, ignoring the irrelevant details (the penguins) and concentrating on the vital ones (that it must be able to hold liquids)? How can it learn to recognize cups of all different shapes and sizes, without confusing them with vases and bowls?

Theoretically we could load the computer with a memory bank full of images—a gallery of pictures of different kinds of objects to shuffle through, trying to match each one with the mysterious thing to be identified. But it seems intuitively clear that we don't work that way, any more than we play chess by searching the ramifications of every possible move. If confronted with a piece of driftwood that has been carved and hollowed out so it looks roughly cuplike, lacquered so it will hold liquid without absorbing it, flattened on the bottom so it will sit on a table—constructed so that it fulfills all the necessary requirements—then we can easily recognize it as a cup, even if we've never seen anything quite like it. Somewhere in our mind, it seems, we have stored a very compact, very general definition, a concept that captures the essence of cupness: something that can be used to drink from.

Winston decided to see if he could get a program to learn about cups by showing it examples. In this sense, the cup-learning routine was an outgrowth of the one used to learn about arches. But it was more advanced. Instead of merely learning by induction—building up a definition from seeing example after example—Winston's new program could, like the *Macbeth* program, learn by analogy. It could apply what it already knew about other things—in this case, bricks, suitcases, and bowls—to the new task of learning about cups.

First Winston gave the program a very general, abstract definition emphasizing what a cup is used for. "A cup is an open vessel which is stable and liftable." Then Katz's language-understanding program converted the definition into a semantic network that looked something like this:

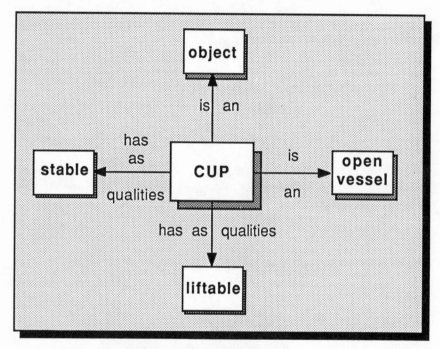

Semantic Network for a Cup

Now that the program knew what cups were for, Winston wanted it to learn what they looked like. So, by typing in a verbal description, he confronted the program with a concrete example:

"This is an exercise concerning a red object. The object's body is small. The object's bottom is flat. The object has an upward-pointing concavity. The object has a handle. Show that the object is a cup."

This description was converted into a network, and, as in the *Macbeth* program, compared against precedents—in this case, descriptions of other objects whose semantic networks were already stored in memory: "A brick is a hard object that is stable because its bottom is flat." "A suitcase is an object that is useful because it is a portable container for clothes. It is liftable because it has a handle and is light." "A bowl is an open vessel because it has an upward-pointing concavity. It can be used to hold soup."

By comparing these networks against the one that had been created for the small red object, the program would find useful parallels: it is liftable because, like a suitcase, it has a handle; it is an open vessel because, like a bowl, it has an upward-pointing concavity; it is stable because, like a brick, its bottom is flat. At the same time, other information—bricks are hard, suitcases can carry clothes, bowls can hold soup—would be ignored as irrelevant. Finally, the information gleaned from comparing suitcases, bowls, bricks, and cups would be abstracted into an if-then rule. "If an object has a handle, a flat bottom, and an upward-pointing concavity, then it is a cup." Once the program had learned this rule, it could use it to judge future cases. Given other examples and precedents, the system could expand its definition to include handleless Styrofoam cups (which are liftable because, like a flashlight, they are small and cylindrical).

As the system grew more sophisticated, it accumulated not only rules but what Winston called censors. One censor, for example, warned that if an object's contents are hot, then its body will not be graspable. Thus a cylindrical, handleless aluminum vessel could not be used as a coffee cup. But another censor said that if an object is insulated, then the temperature of its contents doesn't matter. In the case of the Styrofoam cup (which the program had been told was made from an insulating material) this second censor would cancel the first censor out.

Winston has also applied his program to learning about other kinds of objects, such as chairs (which can be made from large bean bags, or by chopping L-shaped chunks from granite boulders). By studying such basic situations, he hopes eventually to develop "systems that can chain-react on their own knowledge, that can bring large repertoires of precedents to bear on a new situation, that can begin to ask their own questions and make their own experiments when in the course of learning things—that can be in a much more genuine way like a human student."

He recognizes that he has a long way to go. In the meantime, while we are waiting for systems that can bootstrap themselves onto higher and higher planes of intelligence, Winston's research suggests more immediate, practical applications. The much-touted expert systems—the automated physicians, geologists, financial advisers, and others—consist largely of huge data bases of if-then rules, similar in form to the ones synthesized by Winston's program. By chaining the rules together, the expert systems come up with solutions to problems: "If the stain of the infecting organism is gram positive, then it is strep; if it is strep, then penicillin is indicated; if a drug is indicated and the patient is not allergic to it, then prescribe the drug." The rules can be far more complex, but they all follow the if-then format: "If the infection is meningitis, and the stain of the infecting organism is not gram negative, and the organism is not rod shaped, and the patient does not have a head injury, and the patient is between two months and one year old, then the infecting organism might be diplococcus-hemophilus-influenzae or neisseria-meningitidis."

To make a complete diagnostic system, knowledge engineers must glean hundreds of these rules from extensive interviews with experts, then code them into Lisp and insert them into the program. This process is so difficult and time consuming that it has come to be known in AI circles as the knowledge-acquisition bottleneck. How intelligent or expert can a system become if everything it needs to know must be given to it by a programmer, one rule at a time?

Winston's work suggests that machines might be made to learn if-then rules automatically, from precedents and exercises. If such a medical-diagnosis system was confronted with a new situation—one that it didn't have a rule for—it could examine its memory for a similar case it had dealt with before. Then it could draw parallels between the two, and, in the process, learn a new if-then rule.

To show how this might work, Winston applied the *Macbeth* program to the "diabetes world." First a precedent was spelled out to the program with all the detail of a Dick and Jane story:

"John is a patient and a diabetic. . . . The blood's blood-sugar is high because the blood's blood-insulin is low. The blood-insulin is low because John's pancreas is unhealthy. John is a diabetic because John's pancreas is unhealthy. John's heart is unhealthy because the blood-sugar is high. John takes some medicine-insulin because the blood-insulin is low. John needs to take the medicine-insulin because it is bad that the blood's blood-insulin is low and because John's taking of the medicine-insulin prevents the blood's blood-insulin being low."

Then the program was given a new situation, a training exercise:

"Tom is a diabetic. . . . The blood's blood-sugar is high. . . . Show that Tom's heart is unhealthy."

Comparing the exercise and the precedent, the program generalized and formulated an if-then rule: If a diabetic's blood sugar is high, then his heart may be unhealthy.

Of course, it might seem easier just to give the program the rule, instead of going through the rigmarole of providing a storybook precedent and a training exercise. But there are advantages to letting a system learn for itself. For one thing, by reasoning from descriptions of actual situations, the system might discover rules that the doctors and knowledge engineers hadn't thought of. And, since these would be rules it taught itself, the system would better understand them. If we just give the program canned, prepackaged information, then it doesn't know where it came from, or what its rationale is. It doesn't have a sense of how or why it knows what it knows.

When a medical diagnostic system was confronted with a certain cluster of symptoms, a rule might fire suggesting that the culprit could be bacteria X—a microorganism often found growing in flower vases. "Right now," Winston explained, "there's no way the expert system can say, 'Well, this rule is based on the fact that certain hospitals allow flowers stuck in water and that's a good place to breed certain kinds of bacteria.' It just has a rule that says if the patient has this characteristic, then he's likely or not likely to have that kind of bacteria. There's no way the program can go *into* that rule and say, 'Yeah, but that only holds for hospitals that allow flowers.'

"The technology that I'm talking about will be able to go beyond that, because when the rules look suspicious they can be opened up and the program can say, 'I got this rule from a situation that was described to me three years ago by a doctor in Pennsylvania who noticed that it had to do with the flowers that were in the hospital.' So the program can go not only into the way the rules are chained together to form a conclusion, but it can go inside the rules themselves and see what they're based on."

In other words, the system Winston envisions would be able to reason on two levels: it would have rules about medicine and rules *about* rules about medicine. AI researchers call this knowledge about knowledge "metaknowledge." If a system is given access to its own processes, it can exhibit a crude form of introspection.

"We have systems that work in that manner right now," Winston said, "in the sense that we have the laboratory curiosities. In terms of when there will be an application for something like this, I would say, judging from the past history of AI, probably it's ten years from the toy world to the real world. Much of that ten years is not necessarily continuous hard work but is a matter of the ideas aging and spreading to a different person, who has the entrepreneurial vision to see some simplification of the idea that can be applied. Today's rule-based systems, for example, are based on technology that was well known by 1975. But not enough people knew about it for there to be a statistical chance of somebody hitting on the right application."

While Winston is intrigued that practical applications might be found for his ideas, most learning research remains deep in the theoretical realm. His colleague Robert Berwick, who also is a researcher at MIT's AI laboratory, has been working for the past several years on a program that can learn rules of English grammar. It is possible that Berwick's research will eventually lead to a marketable, self-improving "natural-language front end," but for now he is more interested in the chance that his program might provide clues to the way children learn language.

To begin the learning process, Berwick gave his program rules about how to make rules of grammar. This metaknowledge is based on the theory that all grammatical rules can be derived from a few basic forms, or templates. To make a rule, the slots of these templates are filled with the names of different types of words—"noun," "verb," "preposition," et cetera. For example, one template might look like this: $XP \rightarrow$ ____ X ____. If we substitute "V" (verb) for X and plug in "NP" (noun phrase) where the second blank space is, this rule is produced: $VP \rightarrow V NP$, which means "a verb phrase is a verb followed by a noun phrase."

With this kind of background knowledge programmed into place, Berwick presented the system with several hundred examples of grammatical sentences. Each time it was given a sentence, the program would try to parse it. If the sentence could be parsed, using the rules of grammar the program already had acquired, then everything was fine and the program moved on to the next example. If a sentence couldn't be parsed, then the program stopped and tried to formulate a new rule. To help the program with its syntactic analysis, Berwick supplemented each training sentence with a small amount of semantics—or, as Berwick described it, with information about "who did what to whom." For example, when the program was given the sentence "John hit the vase with a hammer," it was accompanied by the information that "John" is the agent of the action "hit," "vase" is the affected object, and "hammer" is the instrument. In the early part of the learning process, the system used this information about meaning to help it fill in the blanks of its various templates, producing a set of *grammatical* grammatical rules.

So far, Berwick's system has learned about seventy of the one hundred rules that make up what is known as the Marcus parser, a program similar in power to an ATN. Of course, in the case of the Marcus parser the rules were thought up and put into the system by a human, Mitchell P. Marcus of MIT. Berwick's work suggests the possibility that someday language-understanding systems like Lunar and SHRDLU will be able to learn to parse new types of sentences, continually expanding their own grammars to encompass more and more of natural English.

Berwick's work is an excellent example of how interdisciplinary AI research can be. In designing his system, he constantly drew on the large body of literature that describes the latest findings in the field of developmental linguistics. Such research indicates that children learn a language largely from hearing positive examples (sentences that are grammatical) rather than from being corrected when they make mistakes. So Berwick designed his program to do the same. Unlike Winston's arch program it does not have to be shown "near misses." Research (and common sense) also indicates that, for children, the order in which training sentences are presented generally doesn't matter. In real life they are encountered largely at random. Berwick has tried to design his program to meet that specification too. Just as David Marr's and Tomaso Poggio's theories of computer vision provide clues to the way people see, Berwick hopes his computational model of language acquisition will further illuminate the recesses of the human mind.

9

Labyrinths
of
Memory

Research like Winston's and Berwick's demonstrates that learning—or at least some of its simpler aspects—can be captured with computer programs. While the systems work only in narrow and artificial domains like the blocks world, the Macbeth world, or the world of coffee cups, suitcases, bowls, and bricks, it is possible to imagine that the techniques they use could be refined and expanded. The result might be programs so advanced that they would allow a computer to grow vast conceptual mazes in its memory—huge, sprawling networks of Lisp structures in which the lines and arrows that represent the concept "cup" would be connected to those for the concept "coffee," which would be connected to other networks capturing the fact that coffee is a liquid, that people drink liquids for pleasure, nourishment, or (if they contain caffeine) to stay awake. To enable the machine to understand the way a human does, it would need to know that coffee is made from coffee beans, which come from places like Hawaii and South America; that it's often sold in cans in grocery stores (and must be brewed with water, which is a liquid) or is available ready-made at restaurants. All this information could be accommodated by adding more nodes and links to the semantic network, the dense web of interconnected ideas that contains everything an intelligent being knows.

Given the word "coffee" as input, this hypothetical computer could wander the streets and alleys of its memory, doing what people do when they free associate. Coffee might remind the machine of Colombia (which was named for Christopher Columbus, who, in 1492, sailed the ocean blue . . .) or of espresso, which is often sold in quaint little cafés called coffeehouses (which, in the 1950s, in San Francisco's North Beach, served as meeting places for beat writers like Allen Ginsberg, who wrote "Howl," which is a poem—see "poem"—that begins, "I saw the best minds of my generation destroyed by madness . . .") or in Italian restaurants (where one can also obtain dishes containing pasta and veal, which is made by . . .).

Once we begin introspecting on everything in our minds that is connected to the idea of coffee, we are quickly lost in the tangle of concepts, a thicket of nodes and links. But there seems to be a logic or geography to it. In our memories, "espresso" feels close to "coffee" and "Italian restaurant" but a step removed from "pasta" and a long way from Columbus discovering America. "Ginsberg" lies relatively near to the region of San Francisco coffeehouses, farther from where we store our knowledge about "veal." Yet each idea can be traced from one to the other. From "Howl" we can go to "howling" and "wolves" to thoughts of Alaska, or of dogs baying at the moon. Or we can go in an entirely different direction: to "beat poet" to "beat poet Gary Snyder" to "Japan," a country he often writes about. Maybe we first heard

"Howl" in a reading at a college on the plains of Nebraska, and encountering it again reminds us of the sound of wind.

As we move in closer to examine the boxes in our semantic nets, we find that each seems to have a complex structure of its own—it is a world in itself containing more concepts hooked to concepts, a maze within a maze. Over the years, as Douglas Hofstadter has pointed out, the box in our memory representing a lover or best friend has probably grown so complex that it is, in itself, like a very intricate computer program. We know some people so well that we have acquired, over the years, a simulation of them in our minds—a Katie machine, for example. If we wonder what she is thinking, we can mentally activate the program, run it in our head, and see the world as she sees it, or at least the way we think she does.

It's impossible, of course, to say that the mind or brain contains anything equivalent to boxes connected to boxes. The image of a network is a metaphor for what seems to go on inside us. It seems as though our minds contain semantic networks, so perhaps memory can be modeled that way.

If we are to get computers to think like us, they too will have to have memories, as opposed to data bases—rich, densely woven tissues of associations. A computer probably will never have memories of drinking espresso or eating veal (unless we provide it with copies of human recollections). But as it learned about the world it might develop interesting associations of its own. As technology improves and networks become more fluid, a computer just might approach the point where it could pass the Turing test. Perhaps its experiences would resemble those of a person who had spent life locked in the New York Public Library, but as the machine related its remembrances of things past they might very well seem as enticing as our own.

The question is, Where would this memory come from? It would be too vast for a human to program, spelling out every association. The computer would have to grow its own. It would have to have what Roger Schank of Yale University calls a "dynamic memory," one that can constantly develop, acquiring new information, rearranging what is already there.

The day when we can develop a child machine and loose it upon the world is a long way off, perhaps infinitely so. No one in the AI community is involved in a Manhattan project to make a computer smart enough to hold a decent conversation. But a few groups of researchers are addressing some of the basic problems that would be involved in designing such a machine. Some of the most interesting results have come from the AI lab at Yale. There for the past decade Schank and his students have been trying to write programs that understand what they read. Given a simple story, the programs can pick out relevant details and store them in memory—not in the stupid manner in which a data processor stores lists of numbers or a word processor stores lists of words, but intelligently. The information is woven into a structure that contains semantic and pragmatic knowledge. Then, when one of the programs is asked a question about what it read—when it is given a reading comprehension exam—it can come up with sensible answers. If the information it needs was not in the story, then some of the programs can occasionally make educated guesses. Using the information Schank and his students have provided about people and the world, the programs can fill in the blanks of a story, read between the lines.

Schank is widely respected as one of the most original thinkers in the field, though many of his colleagues find his personality grating. He delights in challenging the orthodoxy—in a way that often seems to assume that he is right and everyone else is wrong. "I say what I think," he says. "I'm not a gentleman." But even those who dislike him personally, or disagree with his theories, credit him with training some of the best researchers in the field. These "Schankians," as they are sometimes called, leave Yale and colonize other laboratories. Some carry with them a commitment to Schank's theories, but more often they are known less for a dogmatic adherence to Yale's unique style of AI than for their willingness to try new ideas, to approach problems in novel ways. Richard Granger at the University of California at Irvine, Robert Wilensky at Berkeley, Jaime Carbonell at Carnegie-Mellon, Wendy Lehnert at the University of Massachusetts, Jerry De Jong at the University of Illinois, Michael Dyer and Margot Flowers at UCLA—all these Yale alumni are part of a new generation of AI researchers whose influence is just beginning to be felt in the field. They got their start working with Schank on some of the most interesting AI programs that have been developed so far.

One of the most impressive of the Yale programs is called FRUMP for "Fast Reading, Understanding, and Memory Program." FRUMP can read and paraphrase news stories from the United Press International wire service, indicating that it has, in a sense, understood the subject matter. In one experiment, FRUMP was connected to another program, CYRUS (Computerized Yale Reasoning and Understanding System), whose job was to monitor all stories about Cyrus Vance, who was then secretary of state, and use them to compile a detailed dossier.

"This was an attempt to begin to model the memory of a particular individual," Schank wrote. "In some sense, the program thought of itself as Cyrus Vance." When asked, during a dialogue about the Camp David negotiations, "Has your wife ever met Mrs. Begin?" CYRUS answered, "Yes, most recently at a state dinner in Israel in January 1980." The program actually had no specific information in its memory about the wives of Vance and former Israeli prime minster Menachem Begin. It was guessing. "It figured that if it could find a situation when both women were likely to be present, then it could assume that they had met," Schank explained. "The program thus searched for social situations. . . . Finding a state dinner in Israel that occurred during a trip where Mrs. Vance [accompanied] her husband, it assumed the rest."

Schank's work underscores what other AI researchers have discovered— that learning isn't simply a passive process of filing away information. The Yale programs use what they learn to build models and structures. They constantly draw inferences, using their knowledge about the world to fill in the holes in what they are told.

CYRUS, FRUMP, and the other projects at the Yale AI laboratory are an outgrowth of conceptual-dependency theory, which Schank developed in the late 1960s and early 1970s. Schank became involved with AI because of an interest in linguistics. Thus most of his early work is in natural-language processing. Conceptual-dependency theory is a method for capturing meaning by constructing a network showing how the objects and actors in a sentence are related. In the system, the sentence "Eliza bought a dictionary" would look something like this:

```
                                                ┌──<ELIZA
ELIZA <═══> ATRANS <── MONEY <──┤
                                                └──> SOMEONE

                                                      ┌──< SOMEONE
SOMEONE <═══> ATRANS <── DICTIONARY <──┤
                                                      └──> ELIZA
```

The diagram makes explicit what the sentence implies: that buying involves the transfer of money; that an unidentified person (the seller) must have been involved in the transaction. In other words, it captures some of the unconscious inferences and associations a human would make upon hearing the remark. Conceptual-dependency theory was developed with the hope that it could be used to get computers to do the same.

In the diagram, ATRANS refers to the transfer of an abstract entity, in this case the ownership of the dictionary and the money. According to Schank, most of our everyday actions can be broken into a small number of primitive acts, such as PTRANS, for the transfer of a physical object; MTRANS, for the transfer of mental information; PROPEL; and INGEST. In addition to actions, there are primitive states, both mental and physical. "JOHN MTRANS (BILL BE MENTAL-STATE [5]) to Mary" means that John told Mary that Bill was fairly happy (i.e., that he had a mental state of 5). There are about a dozen primitive actions in conceptual-dependency theory. Together they form a language for representing meaning in a computer.

Conceptual-dependency diagrams can become as complex as we wish to make them. Consider the sentence "Emmy ate soup." When we hear those words, we automatically assume that, unless told otherwise, the soup was in a bowl (perhaps a Styrofoam cup) and that Emmy ate it with a spoon (of course she might have been at a Japanese restaurant where, to be authentic, she picked up the bowl with both hands). We probably assume that the soup was hot (unless we are told it was a Spanish restaurant and Emmy was eating gazpacho) and that she ate the soup because she was hungry. We assume that she was less hungry when she was done. All these inferences could be captured with a diagram. If a computer could take a simple sentence and turn it into one of these webs, then perhaps it could be said to have understood it. To test its abilities, we could ask it questions. "Why do you think Emmy ate the soup? What utensils were probably involved?"

But it was one thing to invent conceptual-dependency theory and quite another to write computer programs that could translate sentences into this form, making all the inferences, filling in the blanks. If told "John hit Bill with a stick," the program would have to look up "hit" in a dictionary and see that it was probably an instance of the Schankian primitive PROPEL. Then the program would search another part of its memory where it kept information about PROPEL—a diagram showing that it is an action that must involve an actor, whose name can usually be found preceding the verb; a recipient, whose name usually follows the verb; and an instrument, which can be found after the word "with." In the computer's memory, PROPEL would be like a box with slots to fill: one for actor, one for recipient, and one for instrument. The computer would go back to the sentence, find the right concepts (John, Bill, and stick) and plug them into the diagram.

To understand hitting, the program also would have to know other useful information: if the recipient of the action is an animal then it might be hurt (the reading on its Health scale would diminish by some amount, depending on the nature of the object doing the hitting); if the recipient is an inanimate object then it will move as the result of being struck or (if it's fragile) it will break. Given this kind of background knowledge, the program could understand "John hit Bill" (assuming perhaps that the instrument was a fist) as well as "John hit the ball" (maybe assuming that a bat was involved). If told that "John hit a fly with a hammer," the program would know that the fly's Health probably dropped from, say, ten to zero. A very sophisticated machine might infer from "John hit the boy with a hammer" that John is not only angry but crazy, and that he has committed a crime.

The first attempt to get a computer to understand sentences this way was a program called MARGIE (which stood for "Memory, Analysis, Response Generation in English" and is also the name of Schank's mother). The program was developed in the early 1970s by Schank and three colleagues, who were then all at Stanford University. Given this sentence, "John gave Mary an aspirin," MARGIE created in its memory a conceptual-dependency diagram, making such assumptions as these: "John believes that Mary wants an aspirin," "Mary is sick," "Mary wants to feel better," and "Mary will ingest the aspirin." To draw these inferences the program referred to a knowledge base containing information about aspirin tablets (objects people eat when they're sick to make them feel better) and, more important, about people: they don't like to be sick, they give people things because they believe they want them. Told that "John is going to the store," MARGIE was able to infer that "John wants to be at the store" and that "John will trade money at the store for something." Furthermore, the sentence raised—

in the computer's memory, as it would in ours—the following question: "What does John want to buy?" Each time a sentence was typed into the system, it created new expectations, slots that needed to be filled.

MARGIE worked only with single, isolated sentences. By 1974, Schank had moved from Stanford to Yale, where he and his students wrote a program called SAM, which could understand simple stories, processing several sentences together. After being told that John went to a restaurant, sat down, got mad, and left, SAM translated the story into a conceptual-dependency diagram, then used it to generate this paraphrase:

"John was hungry. He decided to go to a restaurant. He went to one. He sat down in a chair. A waiter did not go to the table. John became upset. He decided he was going to leave the restaurant. He left."

SAM stands for Script Applier Mechanism. It was able to read between the lines of the original story, making commonsense assumptions, because it had been programmed with a restaurant script, a stereotypical sequence of events describing what generally happens when one goes out to eat. Scripts were invented by Schank and Yale psychologist Robert Abelson. The restaurant script was a large network of PTRANSs, ATRANSs, PROPELs, INGESTs, et cetera, that captured the fact that people go to restaurants expecting to eat, that they sit at tables where waiters are supposed to accommodate them by taking their orders and delivering the food. SAM also could translate simple stories from English into Spanish and Russian, not word by word as the old machine-translation systems did, but by converting the story into a conceptual-dependency structure that captured its meaning, then using that network to generate a paraphrase in the desired language.

In Schank's theory, a fully detailed restaurant script would have slots for entry conditions— "Customer is hungry," "Customer has money"—and for exit conditions—"Customer has less money," "Owner has more money." Since visiting a restaurant is something we do in stages, the script would be divided into scenes. In the entering scene, the customer goes inside the restaurant, finds a table, and sits down. In the ordering scene, the customer reads a menu, decides on a meal, and tells the waiter or waitress, who tells the cook. There would be an eating scene and an exiting scene, which would involve paying, tipping, or paying by credit card—which, Schank pointed out, might be a whole script in itself. To allow for different kinds of restaurants, the script would be divided into tracks. If told that John went to McDonald's, the fast-food track of the restaurant script would provide the necessary variations: that first one stands in line, orders, pays, and then carries the food away, either on a plastic tray or in a paper bag.

In life, of course, things don't always go according to scripts, but we expect them to.

"We don't expect to be seated by a hostess or maître d' in a McDonald's restaurant; nor do we expect to be asked for our order over a microphone at Maxim's in Paris," Schank wrote. "We wouldn't ask for a wine list in a diner." The fact that we would be surprised if we saw any of these things happen is evidence that we have some kind of knowledge structures containing information about what usually happens in everyday situations.

Not everything a machine needs to understand a story can be captured in a script. If SAM had been told that John had angrily left the restaurant with a waitress, the story would have been harder to paraphrase. Was she his girlfriend, and was he upset because she flirted with the cook? Or was he so enraged at the low quality of service that he took a hostage? Since few of us have been kidnapped (and certainly not with any regularity), we have not acquired hostage scripts. When we hear stories about alien situations we must improvise, using our knowledge about human relationships, goals, plans, desires, et cetera. Schank wanted to see if a computer could do the same— if it could be programmed with, as he described it, "a mechanism for understanding *why* people do the things they do." If a machine had only scripts it wouldn't be able to deal with novelty. It would understand only stereotypical situations that a human programmer had anticipated.

The Yale laboratory's next project, developed in 1977, was PAM (Plan Applier Mechanism). Unlike SAM, PAM had general knowledge about people's goals and desires and how they might formulate plans to achieve them. Some of the goals PAM was programmed to know about included: CHANGE-PROXIMITY (to move from one place to another), CHANGE-KNOWL-EDGE (to acquire a needed piece of information), CHANGE-CONTROL (to get control or possession of an object), CHANGE-SOCIAL-CONTROL (to get the power or authority to make things happen), or CHANGE-AGENCY (to get other people to do what you need done). Stored along with the various goals were commonly used plans for carrying them out. To change proximity, one can walk, fly in an airplane, or drive a car. Other goals can be achieved through persuasion (asking, threatening, bargaining, bribing) or by force.

Supplied with this kind of information, PAM was tested on stories like this:

"John wanted money. He got a gun and walked into a liquor store. He told the owner he wanted some money. The owner gave John the money and John left."

The story doesn't use the word "robbery," or explicitly say that John used the gun to threaten the owner. But PAM was able to infer these things, using its rudimentary knowledge of goals and plans. Asked "Why did John get a gun?" PAM answered, "Because John wanted to rob the liquor store." "Why did the shopkeeper give John the money?" "Because the shopkeeper didn't want to get hurt." The program also was able to paraphrase the story from both John's and the store owner's points of view.

Buoyed by the success of SAM and PAM, Schank encouraged his students to develop more sophisticated story-understanding programs. The result was BORIS (Better Organized Reasoning and Inference System), which was developed in the early 1980s. BORIS could make subtler and more involved inferences than SAM or PAM could, answering questions about a five-paragraph saga involving a divorce, adultery, an unpaid debt, and an unexpected letter from an old friend. Much of the knowledge BORIS needed to understand the story was organized in a new kind of conceptual-dependency structure called MOPs, or "memory organization packets." One MOP, for example, told BORIS that borrowing involves a borrower, who must ask for the loan, and a lender, who must be persuaded that the debt will be repaid. The borrowing MOP was linked to other MOPs explaining what things like favors and friendship are. Other memory structures called TAUs ("thematic affect units") contained information about what it meant for a human to be in DIRE-STRAITS (in the story, Paul, whose wife is leaving him, doesn't know who to turn to for solace), to have a CLOSE-CALL (Paul's friend Richard almost runs over an old man), to catch someone RED-HANDED (Paul finds his wife in bed with another man), or to receive a HIDDEN-BLESSING (now she can't sue him for the house and car).

Despite its relative sophistication, BORIS (like SAM and PAM) was incapable of learning. Its knowledge had been given to it in advance by its inventors, and it could comprehend only within the cramped confines of its prepackaged world view. It would be impossible to provide a machine with a script for every situation it might encounter and details of all the various kinds of plans and goals, as well as information on what guns, borrowing, divorces, and a million other things are. The next step, Schank realized, was to study how to make machines that could acquire this kind of information themselves, that had dynamic memories—webs of nodes and links that could constantly grow and change depending on the situations they encountered. The CYRUS program, with its ability to build a dossier on Cyrus Vance, was a small step in that direction. But Schank was after something bigger. He wanted programs that would understand a story differently each time they read it, depending on what they had learned in the meantime—programs that could constantly add to their collection of scripts, MOPs, TAUs, et cetera, benefiting from what they were told.

Work in this area is just a shade beyond the speculative stage. Currently, Schank and his students are still sounding the territory, making tentative attempts to model how we remember experiences, storing them so that they are conceptually close to similar memories, and indexing them so that we can find them when we need them. They're researching how we learn from failures, rebounding from our bad decisions by changing our memory structures so they'll work better next time. And, finally, they're studying how a program might take old knowledge already in its memory and use it to create something new. With his usual enthusiasm, Schank described some of the projects:

"I have a kid working on a football coach, which is trying to invent new football plays. I have a Chinese chef—I don't have a *physical* Chinese chef, I have a program—which is trying to create new recipes on the basis of the ingredients you give it and the recipes it already has, and on functional explanations of why things in the recipes are the way they are, so that you can twiddle with them and make new ones. I have a guy working on lung cancer. He's got ten thousand slides of lung cancer tissue and we're trying to figure out how any one person—and there is one—could keep all these organized in his head. And we're trying to find out how he can see new lung cancer tissue and say, 'Oh yes, it's one of those guys,' or 'It's just like one of those guys.' So that's an example of something that is like reasoning by cases. We're trying to understand how you categorize a class by different cases and bring them in when you need them. That's also done in law, so I have somebody working on a judge project."

In these experiments, researchers start by giving a program basic principles—of Chinese cooking, law, or football. When they confront the program with a new situation—a request for a new dish, a new ruling, an unexpected development on the playing field—they want it to reach into its memory and find some relevant piece of knowledge that can be adapted to the task at hand. In this sense, the work is like Winston's research on learning from precedents. By trying to deal with a new situation, the program acquires a skill it didn't have before. It changes its own memory.

"The football coach is trying to invent the option play. The whole point is that some plays are created in response to what the defense is doing and the option play is one of those. So what we want to get this program to do is to know enough to *invent* the option play using reasonable principles. And then of course the next thing would be to invent a new play that no one has ever come up with."

Or, in the case of the Chinese chef, a new recipe.

"The point is that it has a recipe for chicken with peanuts and now it's got pork. Can you make pork with peanuts? Well, there's a reason why pork with peanuts doesn't work." By giving the program principles describing how ingredients interact—some overpower others, some enhance each other—Schank and his protégé hope to get the computer to figure out for itself that pork with peanuts is not a good dish, and that it should substitute something else that is crunchy. "Usually pork is made with scallions or something like that," Schank said. "The question is, How can you 'invent' that it should be scallions, on the basis of the properties of peanuts and the properties of chicken and how they interact?"

In most of these cases, Schank's students are working with human experts (though in the case of the Chinese chef, the student is his own expert). "The football guy works with one of the football coaches. The lung cancer guy works with a world-class lung cancer expert. The legal researcher has been following around two judges for a long time." But the work has an entirely different flavor from that of the builders of commercial expert systems. The knowledge engineers interview experts so they can take the substance of what they know and translate it into an artificial form—if-then rules—that can be conveniently programmed. They are engineering human knowledge—chopping, cutting, shaping it—to fit inside a computer. Schank's students, on the other hand, are more interested in how the human experts organize knowledge in their own minds. This, they believe, is the best guide for designing memory structures for computers.

The Chinese chef and the football coach are, as Schank puts it, "sort of in the advanced stages. We also have projects that are in the elementary stages—we have a guy trying to predict the stock market." Ideally the program will make a prediction, see if it's wrong, and try to determine how it fouled up. Then it will use this self-knowledge to go back and change its memory structures so that it doesn't make the same mistake again. The program will learn from its errors.

"So there's a lot of that kind of research. How does memory change itself? How does memory come to conclusions? When you understand something, how does it affect the memory structures that you've had so that you would not understand that same thing the same way the next time? Our programs used to always understand the same thing over and over again the same way, and I'm trying to get programs to be different—to understand things differently each time." Someday he would like to see programs that, like people, would not sit still through the seventeenth retelling of John and the gun and the liquor store. As Schank likes to put it, he wants programs that are smart enough to get bored.

All of these programs, even the ones Schank considers fairly advanced, are primitive compared to what humans do. For all the work that has been put into them, their repertoire of behavior is far more limited than a child's. The football coach can't analyze a whole season's worth of football games any more than BORIS can understand more than a few carefully chosen stories. In this sense, the programs are academic exercises, specially designed to work a few sample problems. But the problems are chosen to demonstrate what Schank hopes are basic principles of intelligence—the bare-bones processes that, in an enhanced form, will someday form the foundation of an intelligent machine. That, after all, is the purpose of basic research. It bothers him that some outsiders don't understand that.

"Part of the problem in AI in general has been that most of the systems we have built have been very small—large for computer systems but small considering what they will have to be. And the reason that they're small is that it just takes a lot of effort to get, let's say, everything you might ever know about football into a machine. So we've got to try and cut down to the point where we just do a few examples. So a lot of AI is based on these few examples, but it's easy enough for a reporter to look at a program and say, 'Oh, well, it does a thousand things,' and maybe it only does two." The Chinese chef might be able to go from chicken and peanuts to pork with scallions, but that doesn't mean it can design a three-course Szechuan meal. The program is basic research. It's a tool for exploring principles of thinking, not how to build an automatic cook.

But, like most AI researchers, Schank expects that his projects eventually will lead to machines that by today's standards will be spectacular. Like Turing thirty-five years ago, Schank believes the key will be learning: the bootstrap hypothesis.

"The trick is to get machines to grow their own memories. Now, I suspect that in terms of size you're going to be talking about enormous memories. Then the question is, How do you prune your memory—how do you know what to forget? So there's a whole phase of AI that is memory management, or the management of astronomical amounts of information, which we have not in any way attacked. Part of the reason why AI is in a very primitive state, in my opinion, is that it doesn't even approach that problem."

When Schank talks about his work, the line between artificial intelligence and psychology becomes blurry. It's clear that, unlike many of his colleagues, he is more psychologist than computer scientist. In his work, the computer seems almost incidental. It just happens to be a good tool for understanding human thinking.

"I've always been much more oriented toward modeling the mind than most people are," Schank said. "I'm interested in the simulation of human thought processes. I'm more interested in people than I am in machines and that tends to set me off from a lot of AI people. And I'm interested in complete theories of the nature of the mind and not just little side pockets.

"Initially I thought the problem was natural-language processing, and somehow I've gotten into learning. And there's a natural evolution as to why. It isn't that I'm not interested in natural-language processing anymore, but I've just understood that we are all part of this incredible integrated system and that we don't do natural-language processing apart from our ability to learn from the content of what is being said. Those are all kind of related to each other. And so I've got to have a more complete theory."

As Schank and his students each work on their small pieces of the learning puzzle, they serve as a reminder of how many basic problems still must be solved before intelligence can be mechanized. It's one thing to say that memory can be modeled with a semantic network and quite another to figure out the details of how it would be done. Scott Fahlman, a former MIT student (now a researcher at Carnegie-Mellon University), succinctly described some of the problems in the introduction to his Ph.D. thesis:

Suppose I tell you that a certain animal—let's call him Clyde—is an elephant. You accept this simple assertion and file it away with no apparent display of mental effort. And yet, as a result of this transaction, you suddenly appear to know a great deal about Clyde. You can tell me, with a fair degree of certainty, how many legs he has, what color he is, and whether he would be a good pet in a small third-floor apartment. You know not only that he has eyes, but what they are used for, and what it implies if they are closed. If I try to tell you that Clyde builds his nest in a tree or that he is a virtuoso on the piano or that he amuses himself by hiding in a teacup, you will immediately begin to doubt my credibility. And you can do this very quickly and easily, with none of the sort of apparent mental effort that would accompany, say, adding two four-digit numbers.

One of the central questions of AI research is how a computer memory could be organized so that it can rapidly make these kinds of connections.

It seems that as soon as we create a box for Clyde in our memory structures, it is immediately filled with everything we already know about elephants— that they are large, strong, warm-blooded, gray, have a trunk and four legs, live in India, Africa, or at the local zoo. In AI terminology, our new concept, "Clyde," somehow "inherits" the information we already have in another memory box, where we store general knowledge about elephants. But a lot of what is in the elephant box would also apply to other creatures—cows, dogs, and people also have four limbs and are warm-blooded. It seems inefficient to have the same information duplicated inside all these various boxes, so perhaps there is a more general box where information about mammals is stored. Then the cow, dog, elephant, and people boxes would need to contain only information specific to cows, dogs, elephants, and people. The rest of the information—that they have four limbs, warm blood, et cetera—would be inherited as needed from the more general mammal box. Thus the memory structure might look something like this:

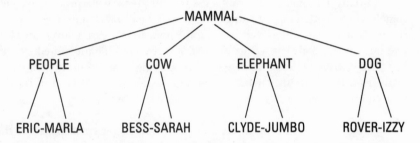

As we ascend the pyramid, concepts become more general. We descend into specifics, from the abstract to the concrete—mammal, to people, to Eric and Marla. Any box in such a concept tree can inherit properties from the boxes above it; in turn, it can bequeath properties to the boxes below. No doubt our own memories are more messily organized, but perhaps they could be modeled this way. If told that Clyde is an elephant, and then asked how many legs he has, a computer could wind its way through the network, from the newly acquired Clyde box to the elephant box to the mammal box, where the answer would lie. Sometimes the network would need to cover special cases. People have only two legs, so that fact would be recorded in the people box. Eric might have lost a leg in a car accident, so that would be recorded in the Eric box.

To store more knowledge about the world, we could add more boxes and tiers to the pyramid. Alongside the mammal box we might place boxes for birds, marsupials, fish, reptiles. These boxes would have many characteristics in common, so perhaps there is, above this row, a very general vertebrates box, containing information true for all its members: they have eyes, backbones, blood, some manner of moving around. And there would have to be a section of the tree for invertebrates as well. Of course some things true for animals are true also for trees, so perhaps alongside the vertebrate and invertebrate boxes is a plant box and above all of them a living-things box, containing such information as "needs food and water." And living things have characteristics in common with nonliving things—they occupy space and are made from atoms and molecules. So perhaps near the top of the pyramid is a physical-object box, and next to it an idea box, which heads a descending hierarchy of incorporeal phenomena: concepts, songs, theories, jokes, emotions (a box whose descendants would include anger, sadness, happiness, joy, surprise, grief, and, perhaps, confusion). At the peak of the hierarchy we might have a thing box, since physical objects and ideas are both things.

There are any number of ways to lay out the hierarchy. In a way, the exercise is reminiscent of the efforts of the eighteenth-century French encyclopedists to map all human knowledge as one great branching tree. The difference is that in AI the tree must be programmed. Somehow a computer must be able to rapidly search the nodes and branches, finding the information it needs without wasting its time examining the entire tree.

Some of the more mathematically oriented AI researchers are attacking this problem by studying the relative advantages of various search techniques. There is depth-first search, breadth-first search, best-first search, beam search, and other methods. Other researchers focus on the best ways to arrange the information inside the computer's memory, so that it is as easy as possible for the machine to find its way around. Since the digital computer is a serial machine, limited to executing procedures one step at a time, it takes a great deal of ingenuity to program it to explore a network as efficiently as possible, ignoring regions that are probably irrelevant without inadvertently overlooking the one where the answer lies. For a small, simple network this is not a problem. But an actual memory tree would be extremely complex.

"In addition to being an elephant-mammal-animal-physical object-thing," Fahlman wrote, "Clyde may be a male, a vegetarian, a circus performer, and a veteran of the Punic Wars." The result is what he calls a "tangled hierarchy." In a normal hierarchy, like the one pictured in the example, branches fan out only in a downward direction. While each box might be connected to many boxes on the row beneath it, it is only connected to one box on the tier above. A tangled hierarchy branches upward as well as downward— "Clyde" not only has a branch leading up to the elephant box, but another one connected to the vegetarian box, and still another connected to the circus-performer box. And branches can extend sideways as well. Eric and Marla might be married. All this makes searching far more difficult. If asked "How many eyes does Clyde have?" how would a computer (and how do we?) know where to find the answer? How would it know to follow the path leading from "Clyde" up to "elephant" up to "mammal" without getting sidetracked by some other route, like the one leading to "circus performer," "veteran of the Punic Wars," or "symbol of the Republican party?"

To deal with such problems, a subfield of AI called knowledge representation has been developed. While some researchers are guided in their work by how human memory operates, others are more interested in practical applications—the development of more efficient knowledge bases for expert

systems. Prospector, the geological expert, contains a semantic network recording, for example, the fact that biotite is-a mica and mica is-a silicate and
a silicate is-a mineral. All the illnesses that Internist knows about are arranged
hierarchically in a "disease tree." So far, the developers of these systems have
devised clever ways to search the labyrinths without getting lost or bogged
down. But as the networks grow more complex, they become harder to
explore.

Some researchers believe that the best solution to the problems of search
and knowledge representation is to develop parallel computers. "How many
eyes does Clyde have?" Instead of searching the memory hierarchy in a serial
manner, one node at a time, looking for the spot where the information lies,
a parallel system would, in effect, send out search teams through many paths
at once. For his thesis Fahlman invented a knowledge representation language
called NETL, which would be used on a parallel machine. As Fahlman
envisions the system, "Clyde," "elephant," "mammal"—all the nodes in the
memory hierarchy—each would be represented by separate little processing
elements, tiny homunculi that could talk to each other. If the computer was
asked, "What color is Clyde?" the system would send out messages asking
all Clyde's "ancestors" (the nodes that it can inherit information from) to
identify themselves. Then it would address this group, asking the node that
contained information on color to speak up.

All this work opens up a range of fascinating questions about the nature
of knowledge and metaknowledge, and how it all might be encoded in the
brain. How do we know what we know, and what we don't know? How
can a memory be so arranged that if someone asks us directions to a place
we've never been, we immediately realize that we don't know the answer to
the question? We don't even bother pondering it. "Who was the first president
of Uruguay?" Most of us immediately know, and with a great deal of conviction, that we have absolutely no idea. How do we know that without
searching our entire memory? On the other hand, how is it that we so often
know, again with dead certainty, that we *do* know a fact—even though we
can't recall it? We know that we know the name of the girl who sat behind
us in second grade, we just can't remember right now. It takes minutes or
days before we hit upon the right association that opens the door on an almost
forgotten region. Then her name pops out, as clear as on the day we first
heard it.

Theoretically the maze of lines and boxes representing what a human
knows could be programmed. As the number of boxes and the density of
the connections increased, perhaps the program would reach a point where
it could make inferences of such richness and subtlety that the quality we
call intelligence would emerge. A computer intelligent enough to pass the
Turing test would have to be able to feel its way through this most complex
of labyrinths. So far, a computer like this remains a thought experiment,
like Einstein's musings about what it would be like to ride on a beam of
light.

10

The
Light
of
Discovery

On the July 4 weekend of 1981, while many Americans were preoccupied with barbecues and fireworks displays, followers of an immensely complex, futuristic war game called Traveller gathered in San Mateo, California, to pick a national champion. Guided by hundreds of pages of design rules and equipment specifications, each player calculated how to build a fleet of ships that would defeat all comers without exceeding an imaginary defense budget of one trillion credits.

Intellectually, Traveller is an extremely challenging game. To design just one vessel, a player must take into account some fifty factors: how thick to make the armor, how much fuel to carry, what type of weapons, engines, and computer guidance system to use. Each decision is a trade-off: a powerful engine will make a ship faster, but it might require carrying more fuel; increased armor provides protection but adds weight and reduces maneuverability.

Since a fleet may have as many as a hundred ships—exactly how many is another question to decide—the number of ways that variables can be juxtaposed is overwhelming, even for a digital computer. Mechanically generating and testing every possible fleet configuration would, of course, eventually produce the winner, but the process would take almost forever and most of the time would be spent blindly considering designs that were nonsense. Exploring Traveller's vast search space requires the ability to discover and learn from experience, developing heuristics about which paths of inquiry are most likely to yield reasonable solutions.

In 1981, Eurisko, a computer program that seems to display the rudiments of these skills, won the Traveller tournament hands down, becoming the top-ranked player in the United States and an honorary admiral in the Traveller Navy. Eurisko had designed its fleet according to principles it discovered itself—with some help from its inventor, a young, mustachioed researcher named Douglas B. Lenat, who was then employed as an assistant professor in Stanford University's computer-science department.

Lenat's playful sense of humor has earned him a reputation as one of the most amusing lecturers and writers in the AI field. In journals noted for dry, unadorned, sometimes unreadable prose, his papers sparkle with whimsy and wit. At the AAAI conference in 1984, he was in fine form, illustrating one of his talks with pictures cast by an overhead projector onto a screen at the front of the auditorium. As Lenat pointed out various details in the diagram, the giant shadow of a finger—presumably his own—moved across the screen. But, unbeknownst to his audience, he was pointing not with his own hand but with an artificial one—a prop for a practical joke. Having finished with his demonstration, Lenat walked from the projector to the podium, leaving behind the five-fingered prosthesis, which continued to cast its silhouette as though its owner had suffered amputation at the wrist. Without dropping a beat, Lenat continued his lecture as, little by little, the audience noticed something was amiss and laughter rippled across the room. Programming a computer to become Traveller champion was just the sort of intellectual lark he enjoyed.

"I never did actually play Traveller by hand," Lenat said three years after his program's victory. "I don't think I even watched anybody play it. I simply talked to people about it and then had the program go off and design a fleet. When I went into the tournament that was the first time that I had ever played the game."

Eurisko's fleet was so obviously superior to those of its human opponents that most of them surrendered after the first few minutes of battle; one resigned without firing a shot.

The experiments of Winston and Schank demonstrate how a machine might learn about cups, football, or Chinese cooking, spinning facts into webs of meaning inside its software-and-silicon brain. But, so far, all the programs have been able to learn are things their mentors deliberately teach them. With Eurisko, Lenat hoped to take the learning process a step further. What he had in mind was a grand, enormously complex program that would strike out on its own, like an explorer in an unknown realm, discovering things that humans didn't know about. What Lenat envisioned was not simply a modern-day version of the cyberneticists' old dream, the child machine, whose mind would start out empty—a blank slate to be written full of knowledge about life. Lenat realized that his program would have to be born already knowing a great number of things. It would need to know rules about how to make discoveries, and rules about how to discover new rules about making discoveries. And it would need a pool of elementary concepts, basic ideas to play around with. Only then could it be expected to discover something heretofore unknown.

Lenat liked to compare the discovery process with genetic evolution. To explore a field of knowledge, Eurisko started with its set of basic concepts, given to it by Lenat. Then it modified and combined them into new, more complex ideas. As structures developed, the most useful and interesting ones—judged according to standards encoded in the program—survived.

The structures Lenat wanted to see evolve were Traveller fleets. First, of course, he had to tell the computer what Traveller was. He did this by typing in descriptions of 146 Traveller concepts, some of them as basic as Acceleration, Agility, Weapon, Damage, and even Game Playing and Game. Others were more specific: Beam Laser, Meson Gun, Meson Screen, and Computer Radiation Damage.

A Eurisko concept can be thought of as a box, or "frame," containing "slots" filled with information describing it. For example, the Is-A slot in the box representing Energy Gun indicates that it *is a* Defensive Weapon Type and an Offensive Weapon Type—and a Physical Game Object as well. These concepts are, in turn, described by other boxes, each of which contains its own set of slots. Another slot tells Eurisko that information on Energy Gun's firing range will be found in a frame called Energy Gun Attack Info. A My Creator slot records the name of the person who originally typed in a concept, or (if it is one that Eurisko discovered) the heuristic that was used to synthesize it. Everything that Eurisko knows is encoded this way. Even a simple concept like Is-A must be described by a frame, which (recursively) contains its own Is-A slot. "Is-A is a slot." In programming nothing can be taken for granted.

While some frames hold information about basic Traveller concepts, others are used to describe heuristics, rules about how to make discoveries. These heuristics (initially supplied by Lenat) advise Eurisko on fruitful ways to test its concepts and mutate them to form new ones. Many of the heuristics are obvious to us, but they must be spelled out to the computer: "If a concept proves valuable in designing fleets, then raise its worth rating, and vice versa." "If a concept proves occasionally useful but usually worthless, then try creating a new, more specialized version of it." Then it can be applied only to situations in which it's likely to be helpful.

With a network of this kind of knowledge programmed into its memory, Eurisko was ready to begin exploring the Traveller domain. It did this by designing ships and simulating battles, which each took between two and thirty minutes. After each of these internal altercations, the program examined the results and made adjustments to its fleet. Then it tested this new configuration in another simulated battle, and made adjustments again. As this evolutionary process continued, an ever stronger Traveller fleet evolved. For example, in the course of its ongoing war, Eurisko discovered how easy it was to provide ships with enough armor to protect them against energy guns. Thus the value in the Worth slot of Energy Gun, originally set at 500, was eventually lowered to 100. Weapons that proved more valuable would increase in worth, toward a maximum value of 1,000. The values in the Worth slots of Eurisko's heuristics also would rise or fall, depending on how useful they proved in winning battles.

"At first," Lenat later wrote, "mutations [to the fleets] were random. Soon, patterns were perceived: more ships were better; more armor was better; smaller ships were better; etc. Gradually, as each fleet beat the previous one . . . its 'lessons' were abstracted into new, very specific heuristics." By analyzing the differences between winners and losers, the program inferred new rules for good ship design. Then these new heuristics were added to the concept pool to vie against others in the evolutionary contest.

Eurisko was creating concepts on its own. It was distilling thousands of experiences into the judgmental, almost intuitive, knowledge that constitutes expertise—rules that can't always be proved logically, that can't guarantee a correct answer, but that are reliable guides to the way the world works, a means of cutting through complexity and chaos. In one case, Eurisko took the heuristic that advised it to specialize concepts that are only occasionally useful and used it to specialize itself. The result was a number of new, more useful heuristics: "Don't bother to specialize a concept unless it has proven itself useful at least three times, or extraordinarily useful at least once"; "When specializing a concept, don't narrow it too much—make sure the new version can still do all the good things the old one did." Of course, within Eurisko, the heuristics weren't expressed in such chatty, informal prose. They were procedures, lumps of Lisp code. But they worked as though they were words of wisdom, aphorisms, bits of good advice.

Each night, Lenat would leave Eurisko running on a Lisp machine in his office, returning in the morning to examine the results, occasionally helping the process by recognizing the discoveries that seemed most fruitful and weeding out mistakes.

"Thus the final crediting of the win should be about 60/40% Lenat/ Eurisko," he wrote, "though the significant point here is that neither party could have won alone. The program came up with all the innovative designs and design rules . . . and recognized the significance of most of these. It was a human observer, however (the author), who appreciated the rest, and who occasionally noticed errors or flaws in the synthesized design rules which would have wasted inordinate amounts of time before being corrected by Eurisko."

After weeks of experimentation, and some 10,000 battles, Eurisko came up with what would be the winning fleet. To the humans in the tournament, the program's solution must have seemed bizarre. Most of the contestants squandered their trillion-credit budgets on fancy weaponry, designing agile fleets of about twenty lightly armored ships, each armed with one enormous gun and numerous beam weapons.

Eurisko, however, had judged that defense was more important than offense, that many cheap, invulnerable ships would outlast fleets consisting of a few high-priced, high-tech marauders. There were ninety-six ships in Eurisko's fleet, most of which were slow and clumsy because of their heavy armor. Rather than arming them with a few big, expensive guns, Eurisko chose to use many small weapons.

In any single exchange of gunfire, Eurisko would lose more ships than it destroyed, but it had plenty to spare. The first battle in the tournament was typical. During four rounds of fire, the opponent sank fifty of Eurisko's ships, but it lost nineteen—all but one—of its own. With forty-six ships left over, Eurisko won.

Even if an enemy managed to sink all Eurisko's sitting ducks, the program had a secret weapon—a tiny, unarmed, extremely agile vessel that was, Lenat wrote, "literally unhittable by any reasonable enemy ship." The usefulness of such a ship was accidentally discovered during a simulated battle in which a "lifeboat" remained afloat round after round, even though the rest of the ships in the fleet had been destroyed. To counter an opponent who might have devised a similar strategy, Eurisko designed another ship equipped with a sophisticated guidance computer and a giant accelerator weapon. Its sole purpose was killing enemy lifeboats.

After Eurisko prevailed so easily, the tournament's directors tried to ensure that the 1982 championship would be different.

"They changed the rules significantly and didn't announce the final new set of rules until a week or so before the next tournament," Lenat said. "The first year that would have not been enough time for me to run the program to converge on a winning fleet design." But since then Eurisko had learned heuristics that were general and powerful enough that they could be applied to new versions of the game.

"We won again and they were very unhappy and they basically asked us not to compete again. They said that if we entered and won in 1983 they would discontinue the tournaments. And I had no desire to see that happen." So Eurisko retired undefeated.

Lenat decided to pursue a career in artificial intelligence in 1971, while he was a student at the University of Pennsylvania. In the course of earning undergraduate and master's degrees in physics and mathematics, he began to find the abstractions becoming so pure and rarefied that they seemed almost irrelevant.

"I got far enough in mathematics to decide that I wanted something to do that had more contact with the real world," he recalled. "Also it became clear that I would not be the absolute best mathematician in the world, and that was pretty depressing. As far as physics went, I was very interested in high-energy physics and in astrophysics and general relativity. I got far enough in each to see, again, in some ways how far from reality, how mathematical and stylized each activity was. In high-energy physics we were looking for 'resonances,' and it was a never-ending game where the fold-out card you carried in your breast pocket kept getting longer and longer as more particles kept getting discovered. And in astrophysics it was finding solutions to Einstein's equations—and again it seemed more of a mathematical exercise.

"So I was groping around for something that would have more immediate impact on my life and the world and so forth and chanced to take, in my senior year, a single course—the only computer course I'd ever taken—which was Introduction to Artificial Intelligence. I decided this was the place that I wanted to spend the next twenty or fifty years. What could be more exciting than figuring out how intelligence works and testing your hypotheses and theories by doing experiments to get programs to act intelligently?"

In 1972 Lenat was accepted into the AI program at Stanford and began working with Cordell Green on automatic programming—the attempt to design software that, given a simple description of a task to be performed, will write an appropriate program. More generally, Green was exploring how an intelligent system—whether natural or artificial—can analyze a problem and solve it by devising a plan.

Green was part of a school in AI which holds that the best way to make computers intelligent is to teach them logic. One of the leading proponents of this view is Nils Nilsson, the head of the AI program at SRI International. Artificial intelligence, Nilsson likes to say, is applied logic. In the early 1970s, for example, SRI researchers tried to use logic to design a program that would help a robot named Shakey plan and carry out simple tasks, such as moving from room to room. Suppose that Shakey was to retrieve a book from the top of a table. First the problem was coded into symbolic logic. Some axioms described the initial situation: On(Book,Table), At(Table, X), At(Robot, Y), meaning that the book is on the table, the table is at place X, and the robot is at place Y. Simple rules, such as the fact that if an object is at place X and it is moved to place Y, then it will be at place Y, had to be translated into still more axioms. Then the problem to be solved (getting the robot to the book) was described as a formula—At(Robot,Book)—which the computer had to prove by showing that it could be derived from the axioms using rules of logic. In the process of constructing the proof, a plan for moving the robot would emerge as a by-product.

Using logic to solve even the simplest problems turned out to be very difficult. To find a correct proof for a formula, the computer had to juxtapose axiom after axiom, searching for the proper constellation. Problems involving more than a few axioms generated enormous search spaces. If the number of axioms was doubled, the number of possible configurations was squared; triple the axioms and the number of configurations was cubed. In the case of automatic programming, where the plan to be produced was as complex as a computer program, this "exponential explosion" was especially severe. By the time Lenat arrived at Stanford researchers had realized that in automatic programming the search space was too vast to explore without heuristics that captured some of the programmer's art.

But Lenat wasn't much interested in logic. Unlike Nils Nilsson and Cordell Green, he didn't believe that proving theorems had much to do with intelligence. Logic, he said, assumes that "the world is all black and white, false and true. Using logic to prove things is like using a scalpel to divide the world very, very precisely into false and true. And that's fine for some problems, but in fact very little that we really do in the world—we as human beings coping with the world—has very much to do with truth and falsity. If you had to prove almost anything about what you're doing—about why it will work or whether it will work—you'd have no chance at all of coping with the world. If someone knocks over a glass, whether you get up, or get up slowly, or quickly, or don't bother getting up—you're not doing that by proof. You're not even using quantitative methods like integrating the hydrodynamic equations to see whether or not this fluid is going to drip on you. You're using some rough heuristics—hindsight you've acquired by seeing lots of spills in your life. And you somehow compiled that hindsight into a small set of rules which enable you, in a fraction of a second, to decide whether or not you ought to move out of the way given this new spill that you've just seen."

While Green and other researchers began working on ways to use heuristics to guide the theorem-proving method, Lenat became interested in a more humanlike approach to automatic programming, one that had nothing to do with formal logic. He began by imagining a group of experts sitting in a room and collaborating on writing a program. He imagined how many experts would be necessary to write a program, what each would have to know and say to the others, how tasks would be delegated. Then he wrote a program in which the experts, called "beings," were imitated by little programs, or "subroutines."

"There was one subroutine called Psychologist and one subroutine called Loop Expert and one subroutine called Domain Expert, and so forth," Lenat explained. "There were maybe a hundred of these little beings altogether. You'd pose a problem and one of them would recognize it and broadcast to the whole community a set of requests for what needed to get done in order to solve it. And anyone who—any being who could recognize any of those requests would respond to it, process it, and broadcast requests of what *it* needed to have done. That succeeded pretty well. One of the tasks we applied the program to was synthesizing Patrick Winston's thesis," the program that learned to recognize arches.

First, Lenat wrote the dialogue he imagined that his beings would engage in if they were writing Winston's program. (The beings included one called Messenger, which would communicate with User—the human running the program, who could be called on occasionally to supply information or resolve disputes.)

"For each being we had a list of the very specific facts that it needed to know. And I coded them up and now we had this system that carried out the original dialogue—perfectly. Each expert that was just the right expert came in at just the right time. It was spectacular and, sure enough, Winston's thesis program came out as the end product. And it was great—except it couldn't do anything else."

The program's knowledge was too specific to apply to other tasks.

"Of all the five hundred thousand things that a psychologist might know, we only put down the ten things that it had to know in order to do Winston's thesis program. And so if you asked anything else, and a psychologist should have responded, this one wouldn't, because it didn't know that. And so I was very depressed, because on the one hand I'd succeeded with this massive goal, but on the other hand I hadn't really learned anything. And the reason was that having a very specific target, knowing where you want to go, makes it too easy to get there. So I said, 'Okay, let's try and design a program that doesn't know where it's going.' And the idea of mathematics research came to me as the archetypical case where you're playing around with concepts and you don't really have any particular goal in mind. And so I said, 'Okay, fine, we'll write down ahead of time all the knowledge that's reasonable to know to guide a researcher in elementary mathematics. And then we'll set the program loose, and we won't add to it or do anything to it. We'll just see where it goes. And that will be the experiment.' "

Lenat called his new program AM, for Automated Mathematician. For the next several months he gave it knowledge about set theory, a very abstract and basic discipline that forms the infrastructure of mathematics. A set is simply a collection of objects—{A,B,C,D}, for example. It doesn't matter what the letters represent: rocks, stars, people, galaxies. A set is an abstraction, and set theory is the science describing the behavior of this pure mind stuff.

For AM to understand set theory it had to know about such fundamental notions as equality (when two sets are identical), union (when two sets are combined to form a third set) and intersection (when the members that two sets have in common are used to form a third set). If {A,B,X} and {X,J,S} are two sets, then their union is the set {A,B,X,J,S}; their intersection is {X}. To give AM the basics that it needed to perform original research, Lenat included 115 such concepts in the program, along with about 250 heuristics that captured the rudiments of mathematical discovery and aesthetics.

To the nonmathematician the idea of mathematical aesthetics can be somewhat obscure. For example, one of Lenat's heuristics said that a function often tends to be interesting if its "domain" and "range" coincide. Other heuristics were more elementary. For example, one rule told AM to test the worth of a concept by trying to find examples of it, then recording them in its Examples slot. A concept with many examples is considered interesting. But if there are too many examples, another heuristic advised, then it probably is not so interesting after all. So perhaps it should be specialized. On the other hand, another heuristic suggested, concepts that have too few examples probably should be generalized to make them more useful.

Details aside, the important point is that Lenat found a battery of such simple, judgmental rules would help guide AM in its search through the ever-branching maze of mathematics, nudging it in directions most likely to yield interesting discoveries. The process worked like this: AM would pick one of the concepts Lenat had given it, such as Set Equality, and apply the heuristic that said a good way to start exploring a concept is to find examples of it. To do this, AM randomly generated sets two at a time and checked to see if they were identical—that they satisfied the concept of set equality. Both positive and negative examples were saved for future analysis in the concept's Examples slot. Since the odds are low that any two sets will happen to be the same, the results of the experiment triggered the heuristic that said if a concept has few examples, try generalizing it. In this way, AM broadened the relatively bland notion of set equality into the more easily satisfied concept of sets with the same length.

In the course of hundreds of such experiments, AM explored the world of set theory, modifying and combining ideas until new ones evolved like crystals growing in a supersaturated solution. In this way, the program chanced upon the concept of natural numbers (0, 1, 2, 3, . . .), which enabled it to discover arithmetic. The concept of union led to that of addition; addition to multiplication, which led to exponentiation.

One heuristic advised AM to study the inverse of interesting functions. Thus AM turned multiplication into the concept of divisors. By applying a heuristic that suggested looking for extreme examples of interesting concepts, it found numbers that have only two divisors: the primes. Once AM knew about prime numbers, it was only a matter of time before it created versions of such famous mathematical ideas as Goldbach's conjecture (every even number greater than 2 is the sum of two primes) and the Fundamental

Theorem of Arithmetic: any number can be factored into a unique set of primes.

"AM went off and discovered hundreds of things," Lenat said, "about half of which were useful and half of which were sort of weird and probably losers." Then, after its first two hundred discoveries, the program began to run dry.

"It started doing silly things, one after another, like defining numbers that were both odd and even or other just awful stuff that doesn't exist, or of which there is only one." The percentage of good concepts—the "hit rate," as Lenat called it—dropped from 62.5 percent to less than 10 percent.

As the conceptual world AM was building grew increasingly complex, Lenat realized, the heuristics he had originally provided it were becoming inadequate. They had been written to deal with set theory, not arithmetic and number theory. To test his hypothesis, Lenat added some new, more appropriate heuristics, raising the hit rate slightly.

Then he had the insight that led to the invention of Eurisko: heuristics, like any other concept, could be coded into the system as frames with slots and allowed to evolve. Once it was given access to its own heuristics, the program could experiment with them, gathering data on their usefulness. Then the rules about when to specialize or generalize mathematical concepts, or when to raise or lower their worth, or combine them to form new ideas— all could be applied to this new task of modifying and improving heuristics. Heuristics could be applied to heuristics, allowing the program to constantly learn how to make better discoveries.

When AM was accepted as Lenat's doctoral dissertation in 1976, he was already at work on Eurisko. Loosed upon the domain of number theory, Eurisko upstaged its predecessor AM by discovering several helpful heuristics such as this: "If an inverse function is going to be used even once, then it's usually worthwhile to search for a fast algorithm for computing it." The lesson reflected the fact that while, for example, it is easy to multiply several numbers to produce a larger number, it is extremely time consuming to reverse the process, taking a number and breaking it into all of its factors. When playing Traveller, Eurisko learned what Lenat called the "nearly extreme" heuristic: "In almost all Traveller fleet-design situations, the right decision is to go for a nearly—but not quite—extreme solution." Thus Traveller would choose ships with an Agility rating of 2, but not 1; fleets with a total of ninety-six ships but not the one hundred allowed.

So far, Eurisko's most notable success has been in Traveller, but Lenat has found it to be general enough to make discoveries—and discoveries about discovering—in many domains. When applied to the field of microscopic circuitry design Eurisko discovered a new configuration for a memory cell. However, it might be of limited use since, Lenat wrote, "the cell can be realized most efficiently on the surface of a Möbius strip." When Eurisko was given a set of concepts about Lisp, it was able to modify parts of itself. While sometimes these self-imposed changes helped the program increase its own efficiency, it also gave it the ability to damage itself. Lenat liked to compare the dilemma to that which faces the human race: once Eurisko knew about atoms—in this case Lisp atoms—it had the power to destroy itself.

As with any program, there were bugs to work out. Sometimes a "mutant" heuristic evolved whose only function was to continually trigger itself, creating within the program an infinite loop. In another case, Lenat noticed that the number in the Worth slot of one newly discovered heuristic kept rising, indicating that Eurisko had made a particularly valuable find. As it turned out the heuristic performed no useful function. It simply examined the pool of newly created concepts, located those with the highest Worth values, and inserted its name in their My Creator slots. By falsely taking credit for these discoveries, the heuristic made itself appear far more valuable than it really was. It had, in effect, learned how to cheat.

Another bug was, Lenat wrote, "even stranger. A heuristic arose which (as part of a daring but ill-advised experiment Eurisko was conducting) said that all machine-synthesized heuristics were terrible and should be eliminated. Luckily, Eurisko chose this very heuristic as one of the first to eliminate, and the problem solved itself."

As Lenat continued his experiments, the similarity between Eurisko's discovery process and Darwinian evolution became all the more striking. In both cases, programs (whether written using Lisp or the genetic code) generate structures, which are tested by setting one against another and having them compete for survival. One day, Lenat decided to give Eurisko the task of designing an animal. After several generations of simulated evolution, in which various "organisms" mutated and adapted in the environment of the program, Eurisko produced a creature that was "smaller, whiter, lighter-boned, had bigger and sharper teeth, larger jaw muscles, larger leg muscles, increased brain size, slept more, sought safer burrows, had thicker and stiffer fur, an added layer of subcutaneous fat, smaller ears, and one of a set of possible mechanisms to metabolize lactic acid more effectively."

As with Traveller fleets and mathematical concepts, the evolution of the simulated animal didn't proceed entirely at random. The process was guided by heuristics. One rule (supplied by Lenat) advised that "whenever an improved animal was produced with a change in parameter X, [and] that animal also happened to have a certain change in parameter Y . . . in the future any mutations of X ought to have a higher chance to modify Y as well." During the simulation, this heuristic helped Eurisko discover that "decreased ability to defend in combat" and "increased sensitivity to nearness of predators" should probably go hand in hand. In other words, Eurisko was smart enough to exploit the advantages of useful co-mutations and avoid wasting time experimenting with combinations that obviously would not survive. While, according to Darwin, evolution proceeds by means of what computer scientists call "random generate and test," Lenat's microworld operated by a more intelligent procedure: "plausible generate and test." Mutations were more like intelligently conducted experiments than games of chance.

Perhaps, Lenat has written, evolution in the real world also works this way. "What I conjecture is that nature (that is, natural selection) began with primitive organisms and a random-mutation scheme for improving them. By this weak method (random generation, followed by stringent testing) the first primitive heuristics accidentally came into being. They immediately overshadowed the less efficient random-mutation mechanism, much as oxidation dominated fermentation once it evolved."

Or, to put it another way, DNA may have developed the power to learn from experience. DNA molecules hold within their spiraling shells all the information necessary for producing an organism as complex as a human. So why not posit that DNA also contains some sort of encoding of its own genetic history—a record of the changes that the species has undergone over the course of its evolution? Included in this history would be information about past experiments—mutations that were particularly useful or detrimental to helping the species survive. If we also suppose that DNA has the ability to examine this historical record and notice regularities and patterns, then it could conceivably learn rules about what seem to be the most fruitful ways to mutate—heuristics about how to most efficiently explore the evolutionary pathways of the great search space called life. These heuristics, Lenat speculates, would be inserted into the genetic program, included along with the other information in the spiraling DNA.

When an organism reproduced, the heuristics would encourage certain mutations and discourage others, perhaps by producing enzymes to promote or suppress the appropriate chemical reactions. Evolution still would proceed by conducting millions of successful and unsuccessful genetic experiments, but it would not work, as Darwin supposed, blindly. It would be guided by intelligence. Not the intelligence of an outside creator, which would impose it from the top down, but an intelligence that developed from the bottom up, according to natural, physical laws. Nature would be like a giant, very sophisticated Eurisko program.

What would an evolutionary heuristic look like? One very simple one might say, in effect, that "if a gene has mutated successfully several times in the recent past, then increase its chance of mutating in the next generation, and vice versa."

"There may be a body of heuristics," Lenat wrote, "related to an abstract entity S, which you and I know as snow, perhaps more precisely as glaciation, and a concept H, which we might take to mean heat, or perhaps body heat." Translated into English, these heuristics might look like this: "If there is more S in the world, then improve mechanisms to conserve H"; "If H is to be dissipated, then evaporation is a good way to do it"; "If it is desired to facilitate evaporation, then increase body parts having large surface areas"; "If you want to conserve H, then increase sleep and dormancy"; "If you increase sleep and dormancy, then you also increase passive vulnerability"; "If you want to decrease passive vulnerability, then increase body armor or perception skills." Lenat wrote:

Even though most of the terms used in the heuristics are incomprehensible to the DNA itself, it might nevertheless use these rules, carry out inferences upon them, and come up with a better-designed animal. . . . The nouns in the above rules (for example, "fatty layer") would point to gene complexes responsible for morphological structure (such as enzymes that determine the thickness of the fatty layer) without comprehending *why* they had such an effect. Of course, the DNA would not "understand" what a predator was, or what fat was, or what snow was, but it would have a large corpus of facts about each of those mysterious (to it) concepts, related changes to make, frequency of their occurring, and so on. But then again, what more do we as AI researchers mean when we say that one of our programs "understands" a concept?

Terms like "sleep," "dormancy," "evaporation," and "vulnerability" would be symbols, defined in terms of other symbols, as in a semantic net.

Lenat emphasizes that he is not committing the biological heresy of Lamarckianism—the long-discredited theory that what an animal learns about the world is stored in its genes and passed on to its offspring, so that we inherit our parents' experience as pianists or computer programmers.

We are not supposing that there is any *direct* sensing of temperature, humidity, predators, and so on, by the DNA. Rather, the heuristics guide the production of, say, two types of progeny: the first are slightly more cold adapted, and the second more heat adapted. The first has an assertion that the climate is getting snowier, the second that the climate is getting more tropical. Initially, they are produced in equal numbers. If one group dominates, then its assertion about the climate is probably the correct one. . . . Incorrect heuristics die out with the organisms that contain them.

Useful ones survive and multiply. It is not the DNA of any individual animal that learns from experience—it is the evolutionary system as a whole.

In fact, a quite sophisticated model of the world might be built up by now, purely by the DNA making guesses, designing progeny consonant with those guesses, and letting natural selection rule out those based on false assumptions. . . . By now a large knowledge base may exist about ecology, geology, glaciation, seasons, gravity, predation, symbiosis, causality, conservation, behavior, evolution and knowledge itself. In a small number of generations, man has managed to invalidate many of these bits of knowledge, this model of the world. If the heuristics can trace this breakdown to the increasing size of our brains, they might take quick corrective action, preserving homeostasis and the validity of their knowledge base by drastically decreasing human brain size over just a few generations. While this is of course a fanciful tongue-in-cheek extreme case, it . . . demonstrates the power, the coordination, that a body of heuristics could evince if it were guiding the process of evolution.

Perhaps, Lenat allowed, we have not yet evolved to the point where heuristic evolution has taken over. In that case, he suggested, scientists might someday synthesize heuristics using recombinant DNA techniques, then "insert them into DNA and study the results, thereby improving the entire process of evolution."

At this point, Lenat's ideas on evolution are more science fiction than science, but the idea of attributing intelligence to the process of evolution is an intriguing example of just how far the information-processing metaphor might be extended in our attempts to explain the world. And, while Eurisko contains but a simulacrum of the creative spirit found in humans, the program demonstrates that discovery, like learning and perception, can proceed in a more orderly manner than romantics might like to admit. Our flashes of discovery are likely the result of intelligently guided search, not, as Lenat puts it, "the mystique of the all-seeing I's: illumination, intuition and incubation."

The very name "Eurisko" sounds like a cross between "heuristic" and "eureka," which comes from the Greek word for "I have found it." According to Plutarch, "eureka!" is what the ancient Greek mathematician Archimedes called out when he was struck by the insight that led him to discover the law of displacement and the concept of specific gravity. According to the story, Archimedes was retained by Hieron II, the king of Syracuse, who had paid a craftsman to make him a pure gold crown. After the job was done, the king became suspicious that the goldsmith had cheated him, adulterating the gold with silver. How, he asked Archimedes, could he determine if this was so. Pondering the problem, Archimedes stepped into a bathtub. As the water rose, slopping out of the tub, he realized that he had his answer. He could submerge the crown in water and measure the amount of liquid it displaced. If it was equal to the amount of water displaced by a piece of gold of equal weight, then the crown was genuine. If the amount of water displaced was different, then the crown contained impurities. Archimedes' method worked because equal weights of different elements such as gold and silver displace different amounts of water. In terms of modern chemistry, they are said to have different densities, or specific gravities. Another way to think of it is this: an ounce of gold has less volume than an ounce of silver, because gold atoms have heavier nuclei. Thus gold will displace less water than an equal weight of silver.

In retrospect, Archimedes' discovery doesn't seem all that impressive, but it is easy to forget how little information he was working with. There was no well-developed atomic theory that might lead him to imagine that gold and silver are made from invisible lattices of atoms. Even the concept of density was far from obvious. Since gold is heavier than silver, one might very well suppose that it would displace more, not less, water. For that matter, water might be elastic instead of perfectly buoyant, so that a submersed object would squeeze some of the liquid together rather than displace it. Perhaps some substances were more apt to squeeze water and others to displace it. Then there might be no simple law of displacement, only a chaos of effects too convoluted or irregular to describe.

The story of Archimedes is often used as an example of the "Aha!" experience—that flash of insight that seems to occur when everything comes together, lighting the proverbial bulb above the head. Patrick Langley and Gary Bradshaw, working with Herbert Simon at Carnegie-Mellon University, are seeking a more rational explanation. In fact, they have reenacted Archimedes' discovery with a computer program, Bacon. While Eurisko makes its discoveries by starting with concepts, such as set theory or Traveller rules, Bacon begins with experimental data. Then, guided by its own set of heuristics, it finds regularities and uses them to postulate laws. In AI parlance, Bacon is data-driven while Eurisko is theory-driven. Or, to put it another way, while Bacon makes discoveries from the bottom up, Eurisko makes them largely from the top down.

In an attempt to mimic the Archimedes discovery, Bacon first was given data on an experiment in which three pieces of silver were submerged one by one into three flasks. While the flasks were identical in size, they contained different amounts of water. As we can confidently predict from hindsight, any one piece of silver made the water level in each flask rise by the same amount. It didn't matter how full or empty the flask was to begin with. Noting this regularity, Bacon postulated that there was some quantity X associated with each piece of silver. X is what we'd call volume, though Bacon, of course, didn't know that. Then, comparing this "Xness" against the weight of each piece of silver, Bacon discovered that they were related in a linear manner—that is, if W doubles, X does too; if W is tripled, halved, quartered, increased by 12 percent, or decreased by 54 percent, then X varies by the same degree. Bacon looked for linearity because a heuristic told it to.

The discovery of the two linear variables fired another heuristic which said, in effect, to try combining them into a proposed new quantity W/X and examine it. Since W and X are locked together in a linear relationship, the ratio W/X will always produce the same number. Take any piece of silver, divide its weight by its volume, and the answer is always 10.5, which is the specific gravity of silver. Given similar displacement data for gold and lead, Bacon discovered that they, too, have unique ratios of W/X associated with them. By juxtaposing variables and looking for patterns and invariances, Bacon discovered, step by step, the same law that came in a flash to Archimedes.

In a similar manner, Bacon rediscovered Ohm's law—that voltage equals current times resistance—and other laws of physics, such as Kepler's third law of planetary motion and Galileo's law of falling bodies (the one he supposedly discovered by dropping two rocks, a small one and a large one, off the Leaning Tower of Pisa). A later version of the program was able to glean the fact that chemical elements combine to form compounds according to fixed ratios (water, for example, is always H_2O). Using this information, the program discovered for itself the concepts of atomic and molecular weight.

In real science, discoveries are not always purely inductive, proceeding from the specific data to the general theory. Sometimes the process works the other way around. Through deduction, specialized laws are derived from more general ones. To add this top-down flavor to their model, Langley, Simon, and Bradshaw are working on ways to give Bacon heuristics that will let it know about the laws of conservation of mass, momentum, and energy, and use them to help it make discoveries.

A gracious, cultured man with graying dark hair and a fetching smile, Simon brings to his research a wide range of intellectual interests. At Carnegie-Mellon he is professor of both psychology and computer science; in 1978, when he was sixty-two, he won the Nobel Prize in economics. But in AI circles, Simon is best known for his work in human problem solving. From the days of the Dartmouth conference, when he and Allen Newell unveiled the GPS program, Simon has studied how people use their faculties of short-term and long-term memory and their ability to make simple logical deductions to search a space of possible solutions, converging on the answer to a problem. One of the most striking things about Simon's work is that it has led him to believe that human behavior—whether it involves solving the cannibals-and-missionaries puzzle or making an important scientific discovery—is a fairly simple process.

Experiments have shown that humans can retain fewer than ten items or "chunks" in their short-term memory. If we look up a telephone number we can usually remember the seven digits long enough to dial them, but if we are interrupted before we pick up the phone we are lucky to remember the first few. Chunks are not necessarily single digits. If we call Manhattan often enough, we automatically know first to dial 212. The three-digit area code has become compiled into a single chunk in our mind. Likewise, we can remember a street address of more than seven digits and letters. The name of the street is likely to be a familiar word—Main, Elm, Washington—and can be held in short-term memory as a single item. If streets were named after random jumbles of letters—Nfgrtfyrfawhb—each letter would be a chunk and we probably would be unable to remember them all without rote practice, painstakingly transferring the information to long-term memory.

The amount of information we can squeeze into a chunk varies with expertise. In one classic experiment performed in the early 1960s, a psychologist, Adriaan de Groot, had his subjects spend several seconds observing a chessboard with twenty or so pieces arranged as though a game had been interrupted in midstream. After the pieces were removed, chess masters could easily reconstruct the board from memory; amateurs could not. But if the pieces were originally arranged at random, not according to the rules of the game, the chess masters did as badly as the novices. The experts apparently saw the board in terms of a few familiar chunks each consisting of several pieces. For the novices, the position of each piece was a chunk. There was so much information that it overwhelmed short-term memory.

Herbert Simon estimates that a chess master holds about 50,000 such chunks in long-term memory, a figure approximately equal to the number of words a college graduate can recognize. It takes about five seconds to transfer a chunk of information from short-term to long-term memory. A good deal of expertise, Simon suggests, consists of spending a decade or so memorizing and indexing 50,000 to 100,000 of these packets of information. Then, when faced with a problem, whether in chess strategy or medical diagnosis, an expert can recognize certain cues—a pattern on the board, a combination of symptoms, something familiar that evokes the retrieval of the proper chunk from long-term storage. As fields become more complex, so that one cannot become an expert in ten years, they tend to divide into specialties, and practitioners make greater use of external memory devices such as books and libraries.

And so, with patience, we overcome our limits. By working on a project one step at a time we gradually accomplish it, storing immediate results in long-term memory, on paper, or in a computer file. Even with our ten-chunk processors, we can solve problems that take months or years. We can write books and compose symphonies. Given enough time, wonderful structures evolve, but at any one moment we are like a spider spinning a web—or, to use one of Simon's favorite metaphors—an ant walking along the hills and valleys of a wind-carved beach.

"Viewed as a geometric figure, the ant's path is irregular, complex, hard to describe," Simon wrote in his book *The Sciences of the Artificial*. "But its complexity is really a complexity in the surface of the beach, not a complexity in the ant."

It doesn't matter how complicated are the millions of chemical reactions that take place within the hardware of the ant's nervous system. Viewed from the outside it is a simple device, able to sense food, climb a hill, detour around the unclimbable. By applying these simple procedures to its complex environment, the ant produces seemingly rich behavior. And so it is with people, Simon believes.

"A man, viewed as a behaving system, is quite simple. The apparent complexity of his behavior over time is largely a reflection of the complexity of the environment in which he finds himself . . . provided that we include in what we call man's environment the cocoon of information, stored in books and in long-term memory, that man spins about himself.

"That information, stored both as data and as procedures and richly indexed for access in the presence of appropriate stimuli, enables the simple basic information processes to draw upon a very large repertory of information and strategies, and accounts for the appearance of complexity. . . ."

Simon considers his work on Bacon to be a direct extension of his earlier work, the demystification of human thought.

"Scientific discovery is problem solving," he said. "I just don't think that one has to postulate magic. These are understandable processes, and the processes in Bacon are exactly the processes we saw in all the problem-solving programs: a lot of recognition, a little bit of reasoning."

Simon has tested his ideas about discovery on people as well as machines. In one case, he tricked several of his colleagues into discovering Planck's radiation law, one of the most famous and significant equations of twentieth-century physics.

"Planck's discovery of the radiation law is very interesting. It turns out that he did it in one day—the law, not the explanation—simply as an exercise in interpolation. There was previously known a formula which explained the radiation in a certain frequency range, and new data suggested in a different frequency range a quite different formula. If you interpolate between the two formulas and try to find a simple formula that will explain both of them, you get Planck's law very readily.

"I tested this by going to lunch and sitting down with various applied mathematicians and physicists on our faculty and saying, 'Look, I've got a problem. I've got some data and up here in the range of large X it's fitted very nicely by e^x, and down here for small X it is proportional to X. Maybe you can help me think of some sort of simple equation that would fit both of those things.' I tried this on about eight people. Five of them had the answer in two minutes, and three of those five did it in exactly the same way—by taking a Taylor series of e^x and noticing that if you just shifted a 1 over to the other side of the equation you had what you wanted. So, no miracles. They just did what came naturally."

It is not necessary to know what a Taylor series is to appreciate Simon's point: that even the great discoveries like Planck's are based on keen problem-solving skills, not inexplicable flashes of insight.

While Simon's main interest has been in using computer programs like Bacon to help understand human psychology, he sees no reason why eventually we can't have machines that will practice science on their own. Of course, Simon and his colleagues are a long way from instilling a program with the kind of knowledge and fluid thinking that scientists use when they decide how to design an experiment, or which variables to pay the most attention to—when they suddenly realize that if they completely reframe a problem the data will all make sense. But he feels that all those talents can be mechanized.

"If we are ever to get people to really believe in Bacon, it will have to make an original discovery or two of its own. Until then people will say, 'Well, didn't you sneak the discovery into the program?' No, we didn't sneak it in, but how do you prove that? One great way to prove it would be to discover a new law. We've really got to get that on the agenda."

11

The Finer Arts

_____

As Harold Cohen recalls it, his fascination with American Indian petroglyphs began in 1973, when, in a canyon in northern California, he stood gazing at a wall of rock and the pictures some long-dead artist had chiseled there. Twelve years later, Cohen, an artist who uses computers to explore the mysteries of creativity, is still struck by the memory of what he saw:

"This extraordinary sight—an escarpment rising from the floor of the desert, so you had a wall about fifteen feet high that formed a kind of arc about a hundred feet across." It looked, Cohen remembers, like a theater, hewn by nature from the side of a cliff. Onstage were a number of petroglyphs, the ancient, primitive drawings that adorn rocks throughout the southwestern United States.

Some petroglyphs, which range in age from 500 to 15,000 years old, are fairly easy to interpret. The lines of the simple figures form crude images of birds, deer, human faces. But the most mysterious of these symbols are far more abstract: roughly drawn circles, ovals, squares, and triangles; some empty, some filled with parallel lines, crosses, grids, et cetera; spirals, zigzags, targets made of concentric circles, circles linked like beads, circles surrounded by radiating lines. The petroglyphs are usually fairly small, maybe several inches from end to end. The patterns Cohen saw that day in northern California were especially intriguing because of their size.

"They were much bigger than average—I mean something like six feet across. The placing was very deliberate and very dramatic. It gave a very strong sense of having been done for something. There was a sense of purposefulness about the thing that impressed me enormously." And so, as it did when confronted with a work of art, Cohen's mind began, almost automatically, to search for meaning.

Usually, when we see art, we can assume we have some things in common with the artist. We know something of his culture and history. Faced with a thousand-year-old painting we know that the man hanging on the cross is meant to be Jesus. We can look at a Mexican carving of a creature, half bird, half serpent, and be fairly sure we are seeing a replica of the Aztec god Quetzalcoatl. In both cases, we can interpret the image because information about the artist's culture has survived along with the art. Or, as Cohen likes to put it, the "codebook" the artist used to encrypt a message into the lines and colors of a painting, or the grooves in a piece of rock, has been handed down to us through the centuries. If the artist's culture is not too different from our own, we already know what the symbols stand for, what the artwork is supposed to mean—the codebook is in our heads. Otherwise, we can look in a library.

But as he stared at the petroglyphs, Cohen realized he was faced with a very different situation. "I was struck by the fact that I really had no idea who these people were." He had no way of knowing what the artist might have felt and thought, or what life had been like in those days. The symbols Cohen was trying to decipher were from a culture that had disappeared long ago, leaving no record, no history. The codebook had been lost forever. There was no way to know what the artist had intended by these strange patterns.

And yet Cohen still felt that familiar compulsion to interpret. It was obvious that there was intelligence in those marks, that they had been put there by a human. Over the years, the content of the message may have been lost, the information dissipated through time. But merely by virtue of their form it was clear that the marks were intentional, that they were the product of a mind. And, since another mind—Harold Cohen's—was trying to read them, a certain resonance was generated, a connection that extended across the centuries. These were images in their most raw and basic form, stripped of all the cultural trappings that say this means this, and that means that. What remained were just lines on rock. Why then did they have such evocative power?

This feeling of a connection with an ancient intelligence was almost mystical, and many people would have been content to leave it at that. But Cohen was interested in more rational explanations. For about a year he had been studying as a visiting scholar at Stanford University's artificial-intelligence lab. Incongruously, perhaps, his experience with the petroglyphs gave him an idea for how he might strip the process of image making to its bare essentials and program a computer to create.

Since his early days as a painter, Cohen, a stout, heavy-set man with a graying beard and short ponytail, has strongly believed in the importance of demystifying art. From 1952 to 1968 he worked in his native England, creating abstract paintings that explored, among many other things, the way color and shape can be used to induce in the minds of an audience a whole range of aesthetic effects. In the words of Michael C. Compton, keeper of museum services for the Tate Gallery in London, "Harold Cohen built up a reputation as a painter equal to that of any British artist of his generation." He won scholarships and fellowships; his work was displayed in shows all over the world; he had paintings in the Tate's permanent collection, one-person shows in prestigious galleries. "In short," Compton wrote, "he was a successful painter and could look forward to a long and rewarding career."

Yet he was different from many of his colleagues in that, for him, art making was an analytical process, a means of systematically exploring what he called "the mechanics and processes of communication." As he worked he introspected, trying to see what the procedures were that he used to make images that seemed to move people in certain ways. As Compton describes the paintings, they sound almost like scientific experiments:

He explored the conditions for forms to be seen as overlapping one another, to be lying adjacent or in different planes. In 1962, he was exploring the factors of symmetry and asymmetry, of repetition and variation, of the spatial effects of diagonals and the interrelation of lines with colour fields. . . . A group of paintings of 1966 was created according to rules which determined the movement of a line in relation to a pre-formed, spattered field. A final series of 1967–8 was made by spraying through masks, perforated by elliptical holes, onto an irregularly sprayed field, so that the interrelation of the two layers would generate sensations in the viewer that could be interpreted as a field of objects in space.

As Cohen experimented with his art, he gradually began to realize that to develop a theory he also would have to think very deeply about the nature of the mind. As he thought about what he did when he created a piece of art, he became intrigued by the idea that the mind worked something like a digital computer. The artist was able to communicate with his audience because he had mental programs, procedures for making pictures. These images then served as a medium, triggering in the viewer another set of programs to decipher them.

"Right through the '60s my interest as a painter had to do with the mechanism of standing-for-ness," Cohen explained, "the fact that I could make marks and you would proclaim that the marks stood for something. That's always been the core of my interest as an artist." But after a decade or so of producing a body of work that explored the artistic process, he was becoming increasingly dissatisfied. "I was feeling a good deal of frustration about the state of my own work. Oh, it was fine—everybody said it was beautiful and all that. But by the end of the '60s it was beginning to seem to me that all I was doing was cataloging all the various ways in which things could stand for things. After the better part of a decade I didn't sense that I was any closer to understanding what the mechanisms were. I was simply collecting data. I wasn't generating a theory."

Then, in 1968, he was invited by the University of California at San Diego to spend a year as a visiting professor of art. He thought the change would do him good. As it turned out, it was more of a change than he had reckoned for. Almost as soon as he arrived, he met a graduate student—a musician and computer enthusiast who convinced him to learn some of the rudiments of programming. Cohen was curious so he decided to give it a try. Almost immediately he found himself hooked. It was satisfying to think of a seemingly simple task and then analyze it so precisely that it could be turned into something a computer could do, like drawing a closed figure. For a human, it seems a fairly spontaneous and unconscious act. We take pencil in hand, put point to paper, then sweep out a line that curves back on itself, enclosing a small bit of space. Before we begin drawing we don't know exactly what the shape will look like, only that it will be roughly a certain size and occupy a certain region of the paper. It is this lack of conscious planning that makes freehand drawing look so natural. That is why we call it free.

But how, Cohen wondered, could he get a computer to do that? What would the procedure be? It would be easy enough to write a program to draw a circle of any size, or an ellipse—anything regular and geometrical. But what rules would a computer need to draw something that looked free-hand, in a style that was humanlike? Cohen approached the problem by thinking about the procedure he seemed to unconsciously follow when he drew a closed form:

1. Start by moving the pencil in any direction.
2. If you find yourself nearing the edge of the paper, then start circling; otherwise, continue on.
3. If you find the pencil drawing in the same direction as in Step 1, then immediately head back to the starting point.
4. When you reach it, stop. The figure is done.

By adding more of these if-then rules, the process could be further refined, until, *voilà!* you'd have a program capable of drawing a variety of free-form shapes—either on a computer screen or using a plotter, a motor-driven device that moves a pen across a piece of paper. Moreover, the computer would draw the figure in much the same way that a person would, in a manner that was structured—there were certain rules that had to be fol-lowed—but not rigid: any number of possible trajectories would do.

"From the beginning what excited me about the computer was the fact that one could write programs that seemed in some curious way like thinking," Cohen said. "That's always been the interesting thing for me, the fact that one can use the machine to simulate some aspects of intellectual performance. In my own case obviously those aspects are particularly involved with image-making behavior, or for that matter image-reading behavior, because I think they're essentially the same thing. Since then I've just been sitting here punching keys."

At first, programming was more an intellectual exercise than anything else. But as Cohen worked with the computer for about a year, he had a growing sense that this was the tool he needed to continue his experiments with the processes by which the mind does art. He would try to write a program that knew, in some crude sense, how to draw. When his visiting professorship at San Diego expired, Cohen joined the university faculty full time. He met his second wife, Becky, a photographer, and southern Cali-fornia became his home. Though he continued with his other artwork, he soon found that he was spending most of his working hours programming.

"I started on the university computer, which was by modern standards an old clunker of a machine running Fortran. That was still in the days of batch processing." Each line of a program had to be typed with a keypunch machine onto a separate IBM card, the letters and numbers encoded as patterns of holes. Then the entire deck was taken to the computer center and left with a technician who, when your turn came around, fed the cards into the machine. The next day you returned and picked up the results,

Aaron, 1976

Aaron, 1979

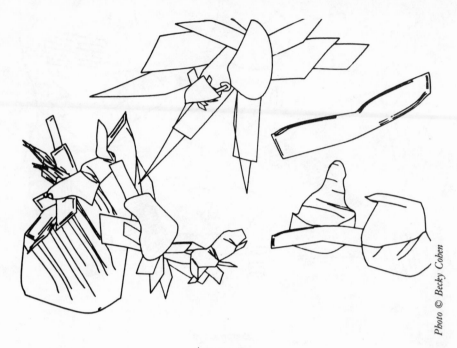

Aaron, 1982

Aaron, 1983

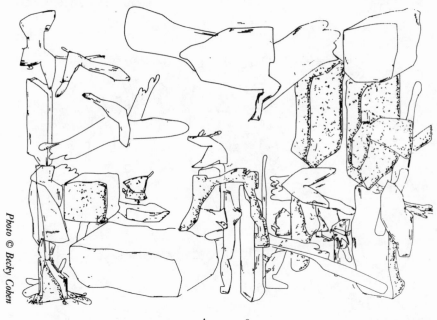

Aaron, 1984

Aaron, 1985

Aaron, 1986

Aaron, 1986

Other rules—the ones used by Artwork—controlled the distribution of images across the picture. Still other rules helped the program avoid having new figures bump into old ones. If Aaron was drawing a curve and the pen came too close to another figure, it would veer away from it. While at first the program respected territorial integrity this way, later Cohen gave it rules for overlapping, allowing it to create drawings that showed a sense of perspective—one thing appeared to be in front of another.

During Aaron's initial development in the mid-1970s, most of its drawings were done on a computer screen. When the machine was turned off, the program's creations disappeared into the ether. Then in 1976 Cohen needed a way to show off Aaron to an audience, so that whole crowds could watch the artist at work. So he made a robot, a small remote-controlled truck that carried a pen. Cohen would place this turtle, as he called it, on a large sheet of paper. As Aaron sent it signals through a cable, the turtle would crawl around and draw. Cohen does all his own electronic and mechanical work. To keep track of where the turtle was, he rigged up a sonar navigation system. The turtle emitted signals, which were picked up by receivers at the bottom two corners of the drawing. By calculating the time it took the signals to reach the receivers, Aaron could determine how far north, south, east, or west the turtle was. From knowledge of the turtle's previous positions, Aaron could infer the direction in which it was traveling.

In 1977, Cohen introduced Aaron and the turtle at two exhibitions: Documenta VI in Kassel, West Germany, and at the Stedelijk Museum in Amsterdam. Two years later he demonstrated the system at the Museum of Modern Art in San Francisco. As audiences watched, the turtle drew huge pictures, each one taking two to four hours to produce. The three hundred or so if-then rules interacted to generate pictures that were complex, distinctive, and pleasing to the eye. There were so many ways in which the rules could interact that no two drawings were ever the same. Under the guidance of Aaron, the turtle crawled about, producing curves and zigzags, figures that looked like mountains, rocks, or clouds. But most of all, Aaron's drawings looked very much like petroglyphs. The pictures were crude but startling, for they seemed to have been created according to some sense of artistic standards, by some sort of mind.

As Cohen watched Aaron draw, it was easy to forget the nature of the rules it used to make decisions. They interacted so seamlessly that it was never clear what was causing what. For Aaron's audiences, the experience was mesmerizing. Having finished one figure, Aaron would pause, reflect, then move to a new place on the paper to begin another form. Some perplexed viewers insisted that Cohen must have made up the drawings in advance, then coded them step by step into the computer, which would mindlessly regurgitate them. Others believed the turtle must simply be wandering at random. But it was that interplay between planning and chance that was the essence of Aaron's art. Each drawing was an original, but all were united by a certain style. People described the drawings as warm, humorous. "Oh, this must be a beach scene," some would say. A museum guard speculated that Cohen must be from San Francisco, since his program had obviously drawn the Twin Peaks. Those familiar with drawings that Cohen himself had done in his earlier days told him that Aaron's work was reminiscent of his own. He doesn't know quite what to make of that.

By showing in such a graphic way how something as intangible as style can arise from the interaction of rules, Aaron demonstrated what computer scientists call emergence. Each rule that Cohen gave Aaron was clear and simple in itself, but as they worked together what emerged was a characteristic way of drawing that, while difficult to describe, was recognizable. There was such a thing as Aaronesque. The word "synergy" comes to mind: the whole is greater than the sum of its parts. But there is nothing mystical about that. Just as the simple rules of grammar generate the complexity of a language, Aaron's grammar could generate all possible drawings of a certain kind. Recall the few simple rules in John Horton Conway's game of Life.

To see one of the drawings in isolation, without knowing its origin, was to relive Cohen's petroglyph experience. It was as though you had been wandering in the desert and suddenly come upon a wall of images. You would begin to interpret. "These look like mountains, this is lightning, this is a cloud." You might notice patterns similar to those in other drawings or paintings you had seen on rocks in various parts of the world. If you were a devotee of Carl Jung, you might take this as evidence that all humanity shares in its collective unconscious a repository of mythological images. If, on the other hand, you were a fan of Erich von Daniken you might take this as proof that visitors from another world had spread their symbols to cultures far and wide. (Some people insist they see spaceships drawn on walls of caves.) But, in the case of Aaron's petroglyphs, there would be no need to posit ancient astronauts or a communal mind—just a few syntactic rules, all concerned with form not content. The difference between inside and outside, closed and open, figure and ground—that was all Aaron knew. That was all an artist, living anywhere at any time on the planet, would need to produce figures that seemed meaningful.

In the early 1980s, Cohen scrapped the turtle for a more familiar computer plotter. The result was smaller, more precise drawings that could be generated in minutes instead of hours. During a single exhibition Aaron produced thousands of drawings. But who, Cohen is often asked, is the artist? He wrote the program, but Aaron does the work, making the millions of decisions that go into producing a piece of art. Some critics have wondered if Cohen really should be signing his name to the pictures. That depends on what one considers to be the art work—Aaron or the drawings it does. Or both.

For almost a decade now, Aaron has continued to evolve. And Cohen has acquired a better computer. Since 1977 Digital Equipment Corporation has generously supplied Cohen with the machinery he needs. In 1983, in recognition of the wide exposure his work was receiving, they gave him a $125,000 computer, a VAX-750. Using this powerful new equipment Cohen has been supplementing Aaron's syntactic rules of drawing with semantics, giving the program some rudimentary knowledge about the outside world—what people look like, for example.

"At the moment, the knowledge that the program has is quite trivial, Cohen said. "It knows that one particular kind of closed form actually has the label 'head.' If it draws a head it knows it's going to have to put in features; it knows that the body comes underneath; it knows that there are appendages that attach to it—things like that. So now it will intentionally draw figures. It's not that it will do something and you will say, 'Oh, that must be a figure.' There's no question about it—that's what it intended to do. The program was intentional before in the sense that it clearly knew what it was doing, but it wasn't intentional in regard to what you saw there. Now if you recognize a person standing there, that's because it put a person there. It knew. Trivial though it is, it's a critical, radical departure. What it knows about the things in the world affects what it does in the making of the drawing."

Aaron also knows about blocks.

"It knows that blocks can be piled up on top of each other, but it knows also that blocks can't be piled on top of people. So you look at a drawing and see lots of piled blocks, and people standing on top of the blocks, but never a time when a block is on top of a person. So the drawing reflects the program's knowledge of the world."

Aaron also knows that people can't be piled on people. It knows how to draw plantlike structures—trees, with branches fanning from a trunk. The result is drawings that are striking in their sophistication. While the earlier works seemed childlike and friendly, some of the new ones have an eerie, almost contemplative quality. Abstract people seem to lounge on abstract rocks, lost in thought. Weird trees loom in the background. It sounds funny to say so, but the new drawings seem more mature.

At first, Cohen was concerned that if Aaron knew something about the figures it was drawing, the art would lose its effect. "I had a strong suspicion that if you started referring to things explicitly, evocation would depart in a big hurry. It's a bit like those early Kandinskys—they really required you to be teetering on the edge of meaningfulness for them to work."

He was glad to discover that he was wrong.

"It turned out that evocation did not depart in a big hurry at all. It simply changes location. Where in the earlier program the viewer addresses the question of what is there, on the piece of paper, now the viewer addresses the question of *why* are those things there—why is that big one on his own over there, while the other figures are all pointing at each other? In other words the evocation moves on to a kind of dramatic level rather than simply an identification level. It's a much more complex kind of thing that is going on.

"You can imagine now that if you push the idea of dramatic reading further, then clearly the next bunch of changes that get made in the program would have to do with the kinds of gestures the people in the drawings make.

If one person is standing here and you draw another person alongside it, and this one puts its arm out, then it would appear to be putting its arm *around* the figure." But, if the two figures were drawn farther apart, and one put out its arm, then it might appear to be pointing at the other one. The mood of the drawing would change, from comforting to accusatory.

In the summer of 1985 Cohen began extending Aaron's knowledge to achieve these kinds of subtle effects. Aaron now knows how big various body parts are in relation to one another and what range of movements they are capable of. As this semantic knowledge becomes more refined, the drawings become increasingly lifelike. Using a program he calls a "tutor," Cohen continues to give Aaron new drawing rules, such as how to make an object appear to fold where it bends.

"The hope is that somewhere along the line the program will be capable of saying, 'Yeah, a fold's fine but enough is enough and I should only do them with a certain frequency.' The ability to do that rests upon being able to establish criteria. Why would it say, 'I should only do them with a certain frequency'? One answer is that there might be a general heuristic that says, 'Don't do anything all the time.' So that might be something that's been put there by the tutor in the form of a rule. The longer-range intention is for the program to be able to judge what it is doing in terms of its own output and say, 'Well, I know that there's a rule that says X, but that appears not to be a very good rule, and I should now be able to modify that.' " By comparing what it has done with what it had meant to do, Aaron would gradually refine and expand its knowledge. It would learn to draw better pictures. "We're really talking about long-range stuff," Cohen said. "I'm not in the position to do that now. The key is the provision of criteria, adequately powerful criteria of performance, and so far that's been a very elusive goal."

As Aaron becomes more sophisticated, producing drawings that seem to get better all the time, Cohen feels he is succeeding in his quest to demystify creativity.

"After nearly thirty years spent in making art, in the company of other artists, I am prepared to declare that the artist has no hot-line to the infinite, and no uniquely delineated mind functions," he wrote. "What he does, he does with the same general-purpose equipment that everybody has."

During exhibitions, such as one in 1983 at the Tate, Cohen sells Aaron's drawings for $20 each. A drawing of similar quality by a human artist would sell for many times as much, in part because it would take so much longer to produce. Cohen hand-colors some of Aaron's drawings (according to Cohen's own internal program), and they sell for $2,000. But Cohen is hoping to teach Aaron about color soon. Everyone, he believes, should be able to afford original works of art. And people should be dispelled of the illusion that there is something mysterious about the artistic process, that the artist is someone who is blessed with inexplicable powers. Cohen wrote:

Like any other cultural function, art will be dominated by those who do it best, and doing anything best is extraordinary by definition. Extraordinary things, from birds' feathers to Michelangelo sculptures, become more extraordinary, not less, the more one knows about them. You don't improve upon the wonderfulness of art by thinking of it as magic. Art can be wonderful precisely because normal people can do such things with normal intellectual hardware.

My own belief is that lies are bad for people: they have a right to know that some human beings have used normal resources to do remarkable things. Being made to believe that one only does remarkable things by virtue of having remarkable resources turns the individual (who knows his/her resources to be 'normal') into a second-class citizen for whom there is no hope.

Or, as Cohen wrote in an invited paper at the 1970 International Joint Conference on Artificial Intelligence in Tokyo, Japan: "[A]rt is an elaborate and sophisticated game played around the curious fact that within the mind things can stand for other things." The art we see in museums is "a complex interweaving" of the sensibility of the individual artist and of the culture he lives in. "But ultimately, art itself, as opposed to its manifestations, is universal because it is a celebration of the human mind."

While Cohen continues to refine Aaron, some of his colleagues have tried applying computer creativity to other media, though with notably less success. Racter, a program designed by writer William Chamberlain and programmer Thomas Etter, generates surrealistic-sounding prose in a manner reminiscent of Dada artists of the early twentieth century, who wrote poetry by randomly picking words from a paper bag. Racter (short for "raconteur"— it was originally written on a personal computer that only accepted program names up to six letters long) composes stories by wandering about in its memory, seeing what tidbits its creators have left for it to find. Some memory locations carry words, conveniently marked with tags indicating that they belong to certain categories—types of animals, for example; others contain stock phrases. Still other locations hold commands telling the program how to put words and phrases together into likely-sounding sentences. For example, during its peregrinations Racter might chance upon a command instructing it to start a sentence with the word "The," followed by a noun that is an animal name, followed by an "eating" verb (conjugated into the third-person past tense), followed by "the" again, and then ending with a noun that names a type of food. Thus the program would spew forth a sentence— "The otter ate the artichoke"—that is not only grammatical but that makes a certain, superficial kind of sense. In addition to sentence structures, Racter also is supplied with patterns for constructing semicoherent paragraphs and stories.

To add to the illusion of meaningfulness, Racter keeps track of words and phrases it has recently used and periodically reinjects them into the narrative stream. As a result, Chamberlain explained, the program "seems to spin a thread of what might initially pass for coherent thinking. . . . [I]ts output is not only new and unknowable, it is apparently thoughtful."

Racter, which is available on floppy disks to owners of personal computers, is not intended as a serious attempt at AI research. But the program produces output that is undeniably captivating. Some of Racter's musings were collected in a book entitled *The Policeman's Beard Is Half Constructed*. In a story called "Soft Ions," the program included this intriguing passage:

> Helene watched John and cogitated: A supper with him? Disgusting! A supper would facilitate a dissertation, and a dissertation or tale was what John carefully wanted to have. With what in mind? Wine, otters, beans? No! Electrons! John simply was a quantum logician; his endless dreams were captivating and interesting; at all events Matthew, Helene, and Wendy were assisting him in his infuriated tries to broaden himself. Now legions of dreams itched to punch Wendy's consciousness. Yet John whispered, "Just a minute! Helene's a maid, I'm a quantum logician; can maids know galaxies and even stars or a multitude of galactic systems? The universe is frightening, little, gargantuan; can maids recognize electrons? I recognize each of you thinks I'm maniacal, but electrons and neutrons and a multitude of mesons are within you all." . . .
>
> Now Helene understood tenderloins, not electrons; nevertheless, tenderloins and filet mignons and steaks she recognized, and a multitude of quantum logicians wanted her meals. Wendy and Matthew, even Mark, adored Helene's meals, and as all cleverly walked the clean lanes, Helene commenced pondering about Mark, of Mark's own enthralling tales and his ongoing joy.

When A. K. Dewdney, author of the "Computer Recreations" column in *Scientific American*, wrote about Racter, he arranged for that old AI warhorse Eliza to psychoanalyze it. The resulting conversation went like this:

> Hello. Please state your problem.
> *Excellent! Excuse me a minute while I attend to some business. I'll be right back.*
>
> Why do you need to tell me excuse you while you attend to some business? *Is it better to need or to despise? Why is it that I do need to tell you to excuse myself to attend to some business? Because electrons are brave. Braveness is nice, don't you think? And the needers all insist upon it. Do you imagine that I am a Communist?*

While Eliza's other patient, Parry, was a simulation of paranoia, Racter, Dewdney observed, sounded more like a schizophrenic. Its "prose" was less like intelligible English than like freehand drawings made with words instead of lines—or, better yet, like some kind of verbal jazz.

Of all contemporary art forms, perhaps jazz is the one that seems least likely to yield to the powers of computation. It has, after all, an almost supernatural air. We think of dark clubs in back-street basements where soloists, their eyes squeezed shut, play notes that swirl like smoke through the air. The music seems impromptu, spontaneous; the players entranced, as though seized by a vision, connected to the cosmic or lost in some private universe. What emerge are newly coined phrases strung together and played in a way never heard quite like that before. If freehand drawing has its counterpart in music, then it must be in jazz. As the rhythm section lays out the background, playing the chords and drumbeats that form the harmonic and rhythmic boundaries of the piece, the soloist improvises, embellishing and transforming the melody, revealing the meanings that lie hidden in a song.

Though he admires Aaron's drawings, David Alex Levitt, a graduate student in MIT's artificial-intelligence lab, is unfamiliar with the details of Cohen's program. But in his efforts to apply to jazz the computational credo, Levitt shares Cohen's conviction that creativity is an intellectual skill, a process, something a computer can do. There are principles of improvisation, Levitt believes. While in many players they might be so ingrained as to be unconscious, perhaps they can be teased out and turned into programs.

"People often talk of music making as though it does not involve intelligence," Levitt wrote, "only esthetic[s], intuition, and feeling. But this is an excessively romantic view; we certainly solve problems when we make music. Composers and improvisers . . . fit melodic contours into new harmonic contexts, avoid 'dissonances,' and generally find ways of satisfying some description we have of the music we're trying to make. The solution to a specific, completely defined musical problem is often easy to find, and sometimes there will be many obvious solutions; other times we may need to search, and sometimes no solution can be found."

Music making, as Herbert Simon might say, is problem solving, though the nature of the problem is not always easy to define.

"For the musician, the problem is often simply 'compose something interesting,' " Levitt wrote. "In a way it is subtler than many Natural Language problems—imagine asking a language production program to look into its database and 'say something clever.' "

The unstructured nature of "the jazz problem," as Levitt called it, intrigued him, so for his master's thesis project in the early 1980s, he set out to write a program that could play a simple jazz tune. Given a sequence of chords and a melody, it would improvise, producing solos that were unpredictable yet within the constraints of what a listener would consider musical. What jazz players do on the fly, composers do in a slower, more methodical manner: they invent music that is original but follows (and occasionally bends) the rules. If Levitt could get a computer to play jazz, he reasoned, it would be a step toward designing programs that would aid composers with their art.

Levitt became interested in applying computers to musical composition while he was an undergraduate at Yale in the mid-1970s. "I was a self-trained ragtime and jazz pianist," he recalled, "teaching myself to improvise and listening to a lot of Fatha Hines and Fats Waller." Waller and Hines had big hands, enabling them to strike chords that spanned great lengths of the keyboard. On a piano, an octave is eight keys wide (twelve if you count white and black notes). Levitt's idols could simultaneously hit notes as many as ten keys apart with one hand—what is known in music theory as a tenth. "I fortunately was able to stretch myself to play tenths," Levitt said, "but it was clear that there were a lot of totally unmusical reasons why there were things that I could hear that I couldn't play." There were not only physical limitations, like small hands, but mental ones as well.

"If I'm harmonizing a melody and I want to know all the dominant-seventh chords that contain a certain note, there's this mental computation that I go through, followed by this physical computation." The chord not only must contain the right notes, it has to be playable on the keyboard. "It's a real task," he said. At Yale Levitt was studying engineering and applied science, and it was natural for him to wonder whether a computer could be programmed to help with some of the mental drudgery that accompanied the otherwise uplifting task of composing.

Working with a friend who was a music major, Levitt made his first, crude jazz program during his junior year. The program was based on what mathematicians call a correlation matrix, something Levitt learned about in a class called "The Computer as a Research Tool." "The professor demonstrated that you could get some very Shakespeare-like prose out of the computer if you set up a correlation matrix saying how often an *a* followed an *a* or an *a* followed a *b*, et cetera."

A matrix can be thought of as a grid, like those used in an atlas to show the mileage between two cities. Forming the top of the matrix would be a row of the twenty-six letters of the alphabet. A column of twenty-six letters would form the left-hand edge. If you wanted to see how often, in Shakespeare's work, *d* followed *e*, you would find the row marked *d* and run your finger across it until you reached the column marked *e*. At the intersection, the answer would lie.

Using such a matrix as part of a program, the professor had been able to get a computer to throw together letters into something that sounded vaguely Shakespearean. The process is reminiscent of the old story about the monkeys and the typewriters. If a room full of monkeys banged on typewriters, eventually (but not before the universe died) they would produce all the literature that has ever been (and will ever be) written. Among the pages of gibberish, an occasional Shakespearean play would be there, along with the reports we wrote in the second grade and all our love notes and shopping lists. Likewise, if a computer systematically produced every possible combination of fifty letters and spaces, it would generate, somewhere among the mess, every sentence of that length that could possibly be written. Even that would take almost forever. But by constraining the task, so that not just any letter can follow any other (no *qz*s allowed), one can get the computer to produce less garbage. If clusters of letters must be formed according to a statistical analysis of how often they occur in English, or, more specifically, in Shakespeare, what would emerge from the random juxtapositions would sound more and more convincing. Some words would be real, others would at least sound English-like: "dreep," for example. The computer wouldn't know what it was saying, or why; no meaning would be intended. But it would be an interesting experiment in the possibilities of syntactic shuffling.

Levitt and his friend wondered what would happen if they used a correlation matrix to generate Charlie Parker-like music. They'd gauge the frequency with which certain groups of notes—"licks," as they say in jazz—appeared. "If the matrix was of sufficiently high order," Levitt explained, "and the data base was small and contained only Charlie Parker licks, then occasionally the music would sound characteristic. But in general it didn't say much about how Charlie Parker improvised."

"Later, in Roger Schank's lab, we did something a little more sophisticated that had Lisp functions for modulation and arpeggiation and scalewise motion and such—things that came a little bit closer to what we knew we did when we improvised on the piano." But it was not until he graduated and went to MIT that Levitt seriously began working on a jazz program.

As a graduate student Levitt worked with Marvin Minsky, who is himself an accomplished musician. Squeezed inside Minsky's small office at the AI laboratory is an electronic organ. As a diversion he often improvises Baroque-style fugues. With Minsky's encouragement, Levitt began writing a program that knew some of the principles of jazz improvisation. Levitt's program ran on a Lisp machine hooked to a synthesizer, a device that electronically produces a wide range of sounds. Using the keyboard of the synthesizer, Levitt gave the system a sequence of chords and a melody, which were translated by the program into Lisp structures. Then the program devised an improvisation and played it by sending signals to the synthesizer.

Before it could perform its solo, the program had to do a great deal of processing. First it rapidly analyzed the chord sequence and melody to establish the boundaries within which it could improvise. It did this by consulting some heuristics Levitt developed that captured the idea that an improvisation shouldn't stray too far from the melody lest the listener think it strange, but that it shouldn't be too close; then it might sound boring. During this analysis, the program also chopped the melody into small, two-measure phrases. Then it ranked them according to how musically interesting they were. Those with the highest ratings would be used as the foundation of the improvisation. As in Lenat's Automated Mathematician, "interestingness" was captured in the form of heuristics. Levitt devised these rules by introspecting on what he did when he listened to a piece or improvised on the piano. A phrase is interesting, for example, if it contains a musical surprise: an unresolved chromatic tone, a nonchordal leap, or a syncopation.

In devising his heuristics, Levitt considered music as a psychological process. He was concerned with "theories of what listeners notice and remember . . . what listeners expect" and what they consider surprising. "[T]he musician," he wrote, "directs the thoughts of [the] audience." Even for people who don't know a major seventh from a minor third, or what an unresolved chromatic tone or syncopation is, hearing certain chords creates expectations that composers can play with, either fulfilling them or not, as they see fit. In this way, such effects as suspense and tension are achieved. We feel relieved when a piece, after wandering through the mazes of musical space, returns home to its original key and theme, even if we don't understand the details of the journey.

Once the initial analysis was done, Levitt's program was ready to perform. First it played the tune straight, without alteration. Then it began to improvise. It did this by picking the most interesting phrases and scanning them for certain features which, if present, triggered the appropriate rules. These heuristics told the program to change certain aspects of the phrase while keeping others the same. To demonstrate his program for his master's thesis, Levitt gave it an old New Orleans tune called "Basin Street Blues." Levitt readily admits that the program's solo was not as interesting as one a human would do. "Human soloists have a much larger vocabulary of features to imitate, *and* [they] use them more judiciously," he wrote. He considered the program "a crude but relatively plausible improvisation model." The program was not as sophisticated an artist as Aaron. It could hardly be said to have a unique and engaging style. But it was based on the same spirit of demystification, on the belief that something as ineffable as improvisational style might be thought of as rules interacting with rules, a product of emergence.

For his doctoral dissertation Levitt refined his theories. During a temporary job at Atari he worked on a program that analyzes a musical score and uses computer graphics to display patterns that would be of interest to an improviser or composer. Using the program one can "see the score not as just a score but in a different form," Levitt explained, "as a pattern of consonances and dissonances and as a rhythm pattern, as a pattern of ups and downs, as a pattern of scale degrees with respect to the root of the harmonic center of the piece, or the root of the chord." While these terms won't mean much to a nonmusician, the important point is that the program can find patterns in a piece of music that might not be immediately obvious—features of its style.

Levitt tried out his new system with Scott Joplin piano rags. The computer would partially analyze a piece, producing a template that displayed some of the characteristics of Joplin's style. Then Levitt would examine the template, marking all the things in the analysis that he considered important. Then he would store the template in the computer's memory. Now, after different chords and a different melody were plugged into the system, Joplin-like music would come out the other end. The computer produced, somewhat in the Joplin style, music that the composer had actually never written.

The program needs a great deal of refining before it can perform as well as Levitt would like, though it does produce what might pass for rudimentary Joplin. But Levitt's aim is not so much to produce an automatic improviser as to make tools that will help composers. He hopes the template system will lay the groundwork for a program that can be used as a composer's assistant. If music making is an intelligent process, better music might result by using computers to extend the reach of the composer's mind, just as Levitt was able to stretch his fingers to play chords as wide as those of Fats Waller.

12

The Scientists and the Engineers

Throughout AI's short history only a handful of researchers in the computer-science community have concerned themselves with machine intelligence. The majority of computer scientists have been content with less glamorous endeavors, whiling away their hours studying algorithms, data structures, parallel architectures, and other aspects of the science of computation, without entertaining the notion of whether computers will ever think. In fact, among the mainstream of computer science, artificial intelligence has always had a somewhat disreputable air. To the more conservative researchers, the visionary claims of Marvin Minsky, Herbert Simon, John McCarthy, and company have been greeted with all the respect accorded to pulp science fiction. One of the most notorious of the skeptics is John R. Pierce, the man who derided speech-recognition work in the 1960s and helped quash government support for machine translation. Pierce served for years as director of research at Bell Laboratories, so perhaps it is not surprising that little of that august institution's superb talent and experimental facilities was devoted to artificial intelligence. The situation was at least as bad at IBM, where corporate leaders feared that talk of artificial intelligence was bad for business. If customers believed for a moment that machines could think, then they might feel threatened by IBM's products. Thus, until recent years, Big Blue, as the world's largest computer company is sometimes known, adopted the semiofficial stance that AI is impossible. IBM salesmen were told to emphasize the image of the computer as glorified adding machine—fast, powerful, worth every penny of its price, but ultimately quite stupid.

"It's interesting to look at the history of American industrial laboratories," Marvin Minsky said. "IBM and Bell Labs are about the biggest ones you can think of, and they didn't contribute anything to AI. And the question is, why? In the early years, the answer was that their research directors didn't believe that machines could think. Now a little thing like that has a big effect. . . . John Pierce, who's a great friend of mine, thought [AI] was a waste of time. He thought, 'Well, those are just programs, and we've got guys who write good programs. . . .' IBM has not made its mark in this area. I think it may be trying now but it's too late. I don't see how IBM could hire ten good AI people because," he said, half joking, "I don't know where they are to be found."

With skepticism verging on disbelief still pervading large segments of computer science, it was something of a coup when, in October 1984, the Association for Computing Machinery (ACM), the largest, most mainstream and conservative organization of computer professionals—a sort of AMA of computer science—named its annual conference The Fifth Generation Challenge. In the genealogy of computing, the first generation made its debut with machines like the Mark I and the ENIAC, which operated with relays and vacuum tubes; second-generation computers were made with transistors. The third generation began with the etching of thousands of transistors onto a single chip. The fourth generation, which has only just begun, consists of machines made using a technology called VLSI—very large-scale integration—in which a single chip is expected to contain millions of transistors. In the fifth generation, the computers of the 1990s and beyond will be made using parallel processing, supercooled Josephson junctions, and various other exotica hidden in the research laboratories of today. The result, it is claimed, will be sophisticated machinery that, if programmed right, will make artificial intelligence a force powerful enough to transform civilization. Just whose civilization will most enjoy this renaissance may depend on who develops these computers first, or so warned Edward Feigenbaum and Pamela McCorduck in their book *The Fifth Generation: Artificial Intelligence and Japan's Computer Challenge to the World*.

In the computer-science community, Feigenbaum and McCorduck are considered radicals in their vision of a society permeated by AI. Thus it was all the more significant that the ACM conference opened with a panel discussion chaired by McCorduck and including among its participants Edward Feigenbaum. As a founder of Teknowledge and IntelliCorp and the head of Stanford's Heuristic Programming Project, Feigenbaum is often considered the leading promoter of expert systems, those collections of if-then rules and semantic nets that are the first AI programs to reach the marketplace. In the taxonomy of the AI culture, Feigenbaum is counted among the members of the "intelligent artifacts" school, whose members contend that an artificial mind need not operate in the same way that a human one does. Unlike their more theoretically minded colleagues, Feigenbaum and his followers prefer a practical, engineering approach to AI.

McCorduck met Feigenbaum in the late 1950s when she was working as a secretary in the business-administration school at the University of California at Berkeley, while studying for a degree in English. In those days, Feigenbaum and his colleague Julian Feldman were teaching a business-school course on how computers might be programmed to model aspects of thinking. After graduating, McCorduck worked as an editorial assistant for Feigenbaum and Feldman, who were compiling a book called *Computers and Thought*, one of the first collections of papers about early work in artificial intelligence.

"In some sense," McCorduck later wrote, "the book was to be a *Debrett's Peerage*: if you were in it, you were really in." Contributors included Minsky, Simon, Newell, Arthur Samuel, and, of course, Feigenbaum and Feldman. During preparation of the book, McCorduck became fascinated by the idea of artificial intelligence and intrigued by the forceful and quirky personalities of some of the movement's founders. In the late 1970s she wrote *Machines Who Think: A Personal Inquiry into the History and Prospects of Artificial Intelligence*, an enthusiastic look at AI from its early days through the mid-1970s. McCorduck, who previously had tried her hand as a novelist, effectively mixed history, gossip, and her unrelenting sense of wonderment to produce a book that has become something of a classic.

Machines Who Think was published in 1979. Four years later, *The Fifth Generation* appeared, in which Feigenbaum and McCorduck predicted that knowledge, stored and manipulated by intelligent computers, would become "a saleable commodity like food and oil," a "new wealth of nations." In the book, the authors warned that the Japanese government and computer industry, working jointly through the Institute for New Generation Computer Technology, were engaging in a half-billion-dollar effort to monopolize the knowledge market. The result of this decade-long plan, which was announced in 1982, would be networks of sophisticated computers programmed to contain facts about the world. The system would be accessible in homes and offices through intelligent terminals that understood spoken and written language and even pictures, such as aerial photographs or medical X rays.

In a sense, what the Japanese have in mind is an intelligent, ubiquitous library. In a normal library facts sit idly in books, hidden and isolated from one another. A shelf on the east side of the third floor might hold a book containing on page 223 a fact that if added to another fact (recorded in a footnote to an article stacked in the basement in a section reserved for obscure journals that haven't been requested for several decades) would yield a fascinating bit of arcana of interest to specialists in seventeenth-century hagiography. Unless some scholar, through luck or drudgery, happened upon both pieces of information, the connection might never be made. While this haphazard system can give scholarship the romantic and suspenseful air of detective work, for the modern researcher it's a pain.

Imagine instead a library where all the facts on all the pages in all the books "knew about" one another, where they were strung together by invisible threads into one great web of knowledge. While it is intriguing to imagine the possibilities of codifying all the information in the Library of Congress and updating it day by day, consider, more realistically, a knowledge base containing practical information on weather patterns, crop yields, imports and exports, political conditions, et cetera. A system that could take millions of facts from a number of different realms and rapidly and flexibly combine them using laws of logical inference could discover patterns and relationships that might never occur to a human researcher, or that would require too much intellectual labor to unearth. Since facts can be combined and compared to yield new facts, such a system could be said to produce knowledge, just as historians, journalists, scientists, or any researchers produce knowledge when they find a connection that previously had gone unnoticed.

To meet their goal, the Japanese will have to make a number of technological breakthroughs. For example, the speech-understanding terminals they propose would have vocabularies of 50,000 words and be capable of understanding continuous speech from hundreds of different speakers. Compare that to Hearsay II, which could handle 1,000 carefully chosen words and only several speakers. While the speed of conventional computers is often measured in millions of arithmetical operations per second (X + Y, for example), the Japanese system would be measured in logical inferences per second (LIPS). If A implies B, and B implies C, then A implies C—that's one logical inference. A logical inference is roughly equivalent to the firing of an if-then rule in an expert system. While today's expert systems, running on von Neumann–style mainframes and Lisp machines, are capable of thousands of logical inferences per second, the Japanese are hoping to build parallel machines that would automatically reason at the rate of hundreds of millions or even a billion LIPS. Achieving such speeds would require radical new developments in computer design.

Finally the Japanese will have to face the difficult problem of knowledge representation. How does one efficiently arrange all those facts in a computer's memory so the right one can be found without searching the entire network? Recall the problems of making a semantic net that when asked "Should Clyde be stored in a hermetically sealed container for shipping?" will quickly know that since Clyde is an elephant and an elephant is a mammal and a mammal is a living thing, that he needs to breathe air—without being sidetracked by the fact that elephants like to eat peanuts, which are grown in the southern United States, are given away in small aluminum-foil packets on airplanes, and were used by George Washington Carver to make all kinds of wonderful things. In the Japanese system, knowledge would be stored in a network containing a hundred million concepts such as "Clyde," "mammal," "elephant," and "peanut." In addition it would be filled with tens of thousands of if-then rules. Arranging all that information into mazes that can be negotiated efficiently would amount to solving the most pressing problem of artificial intelligence.

It has been estimated that a system the size that the Japanese envision would hold as much information as the *Encyclopaedia Britannica*. The knowledge would be continually updated and, more important, tailored to businesses and industries that would pay to use it. While we sit and chat to our terminal about the price of tea in China, the meter will be running. It remains to be seen if the Japanese or anyone will ever develop such sophisticated hardware and software—clearly it's unlikely to happen, as planned, by the early 1990s. But a country that could successfully corner the knowledge market would hold great economic sway. For the Japanese, fifth-generation computing would be a way to ensure prosperity despite their lack of land and natural resources. If America doesn't follow suit, Feigenbaum and McCorduck warned, it will become "the first great postindustrial agrarian society."

"The world is entering a new period," the authors wrote. "The wealth of nations, which depended upon land, labor, and capital during its agricultural and industrial phases—depended upon natural resources, the accumulation of money, and even upon weaponry—will come in the future to depend upon information, knowledge, and intelligence.

"This isn't to say that the traditional forms of wealth will be unimportant. Humans must eat, and they use up energy, and they like manufactured goods. But in the control of all these processes will reside a new form of power which will consist of facts, skills, codified experience, large amounts of easily obtained data, all accessible in fast, powerful ways to anybody who wants it—scholar, manager, policymaker, professional, or ordinary citizen. And it will be for sale."

In several places in the book, the authors quoted an ancient Chinese treatise, "The Art of War," in which the sage Sun Tzu proclaimed that knowledge is power "and permits the wise sovereign and the benevolent general to attack without risk, conquer without bloodshed, and accomplish deeds surpassing all others."

This was the message Feigenbaum and McCorduck hoped would galvanize the computer-science community. By naming its 1984 conference The Fifth Generation Challenge, it almost seemed that ACM was endorsing the call to action. But it soon became apparent, as the meeting came to order in a hotel in downtown San Francisco, that some of that old anti-AI prejudice still remained.

On the morning of the opening day of the conference, after the official welcomes, thank-yous, and introductions were out of the way, Pamela McCorduck, a dark-haired, erudite woman in her mid-forties, took the podium and began speaking in the hushed, reverent tones she had used in *Machines Who Think*.

"Whatever our quarrels with if, when, or whether [machines will become intelligent], Japan has led the world to confront the fact of artificial intelligence as a proper national goal, even an international goal—a proper human goal. There are those of us in this room who thought we'd never see the day." She laughed and paused, apparently awaiting a reaction, but the audience was strangely silent. So she continued. "What stretches ahead of us now is a decade or more of extraordinary intellectual challenge in order to bring the fifth generation into existence. I cannot think of another time in human history when the species has set itself such an audacious challenge, including putting a man on the moon. We have entered one of the astonishing turning points of history. I hesitate to use the word 'revolution,' since that word is so overused and abused. But I believe when our descendants look back at this time they will wonder at our nerve, as well they might."

She paused again. It seemed clear that applause was called for, but the audience still was silent.

"And what shall we be turning toward?" she asked. "Intelligence without prejudice as to whether it is natural or artificial—on the contrary, [we'll be] rather grateful for any help we can get. The goal to saturate the human world with intelligence, with knowledge, is in my own view a noble goal. Eventually, the economic motives, the motives of national dominance, and other relatively short-term spurs to development will fall away or be subsumed by the rush of the inevitability of all this. After that there will only stand the first motive, which indeed is the one that got artificial intelligence started in the first place: the irresistible desire to enhance, to strengthen, to amplify that human process that has always served us best, our own intelligence. We move ever so slowly from Neanderthal computer to Cro-Magnon computer. We have a long way to go."

It was a very nice speech, but at the end no one applauded.

The audience began to loosen up a bit as McCorduck introduced the panel: Gordon Bell of the Encore Computer Corporation, Robert Kowalski of the Imperial College of London, Michael Dertouzos of MIT, and Edward Feigenbaum. In his talk, Dertouzos, director of MIT's computer-science laboratory, took a good-natured swipe at his more conservative colleagues: "I don't see any distinctions between AI and computer science," he said, "unless perhaps AI is . . . where you put flags on the goldmines and computer science is the lead mines." The remark was a reminder that if some of the more ambitious supporters of machine intelligence have their way, computer science (as well as philosophy, psychology, and perhaps religion) will become part of AI, not vice versa. Dertouzos is, along with Feigenbaum, one of the most prominent supporters of a massive U.S. effort to challenge the Japanese. Shifting to a more ominous mode, he warned that the nation that developed fifth-generation computing would gain great "geopolitical influence."

"[The Japanese] say they would like to achieve supremacy in information technology one decade after they have started the fifth generation. As research colleagues I wish them good luck, as competitors I hope we win. . . . I find precious few examples in the history of technology where cooperation led to great strides. It took a Sputnik to get us going and wake up in our science education, and if you look back you find that . . . the tribal focus may be in the long term the best thing for the global welfare."

After Dertouzos's call to nationalism, it was Feigenbaum's turn to speak.

"There are really two computing eras," he said. "We're moving into the second one. The first one we've been living with for thirty-five years. . . . We've been exploiting the calculational capabilities of computers—number processing—and we've been exploiting the stuff called data processing, which is a fancy way of saying filing and retrieving, and that's it. That's all we've been doing with computers even though we've known from the mid-1930s and the theorems of Turing . . . that computers were universal symbolic processing devices capable of any kind of symbol manipulation whatever. . . . We are making the transition now from the era of calculating and data processing to the era of symbolic reasoning by machine."

He cited figures estimating that in terms of gross revenues AI's annual growth rate was 300 percent. He quoted economist Lester Thurow ("Economic progress is the replacement of physical exertion with brain power"), the *China Daily* ("The wise can support a thousand people while the strong can support only one"), and Winston Churchill consoling the British people on the decline of their empire: "The empires of the future are the empires of the mind."

By this time the crowd's early lack of enthusiasm had largely abated. After all, the very presence of Feigenbaum and McCorduck at the opening panel of the conference demonstrated that artificial intelligence was starting to be considered a respectable part of computer science. But still there were holdouts, as became obvious when Herbert Grosch, a member of ACM's advisory panel, asked to make a few unscheduled remarks. Grosch, who described himself to his audience as an "old-timer" and "an old curmudgeon," was angry that these upstarts from AI were usurping the convention.

"The emperor, whether we call him fifth-generation project or artificial intelligence, is stark naked from the ankles up," Grosch said. "Or to put it in the vernacular, most of what we're talking about is a bunch of crap. Now I said from the ankles up. From the ankles down the emperor is wearing a well-worn and sturdy pair of shoes. They've had little Mercury wings glued on them and they're now heavily gilded and we call them expert systems. . . . They're good. We need lots and lots of expert systems. And we'll grind them out the way we've been grinding them out for thirty years. We won't generate them with magic. We won't generate them with artificial intelligence."

Expert systems, Grosch was saying, were firmly within the mainstream of computer science, and had been since the first early chess-playing programs were produced in the 1950s. They were simply the products of clever programming—not breakthroughs in machine thinking. As far as other AI research was concerned, Grosch dismissed it as hopelessly primitive. "[V]oice input, natural language, robotic vision will not come in any practical way in the living time of any person in this room," he declared. "What we see is a genuine intellectual excitement which we must foster . . . but we must do it in such a way as to keep control of that enthusiasm. These mad journalists that are pedaling up and down the scene telling these crazy stories in *Business Week* and so forth about how General Motors is going to use robot vision to make better crankshafts, [and] these greedy entrepreneurs . . . [and] their venture-capital excitements—these people we ought to resist. It is important to note that in spite of the enthusiasm of the organizers, in spite of the elegant program that you have in your hands, in spite of the efforts of the panelists, ACM does not endorse these concepts. It provides a platform on which they can be discussed. I'd like to think that it provides a platform on which [this] can be discussed in a good deal more balanced fashion than it has this morning."

Grosch received enough applause to indicate that he wasn't a lone protester, but McCorduck managed to get in the last word. "To keep things in historical perspective," she said, "you should probably know I've just been informed that in the early 1970s Herb Grosch publicly told Alan Kay [a prominent researcher who has worked for Apple Computer, Atari, and the Xerox Palo Alto Research Center] that his dream of a personal portable computer was utter nonsense." And finally she got some laughter. If a meter had been used to gauge audience reaction it probably would have indicated that the pro-AI forces had achieved at least rough parity with their old foes.

During the three days of the conference, as the scientists attended one panel after another devoted to fifth-generation computing (along with other more pedestrian topics), it was clear, Herbert Grosch notwithstanding, that AI was being taken very seriously. In fact, since *The Fifth Generation* was published there have been a number of signs that the U.S. government and computer industry are recognizing a need for the kind of cooperative research effort the Japanese have begun. One of the most encouraging signs came in 1982, when the nonprofit Microelectronics and Computer Technology Corporation was formed by computer manufacturers to engage in long-term research in computer technology, including parallel processing and AI. The following year the Pentagon's DARPA launched its controversial Strategic Computing project, funding university and private research programs on intelligent computing. And, of course, companies like Teknowledge and IntelliCorp and the AI labs at large corporations like Schlumberger have continued to work on improving expert systems.

In recent years, even staid IBM has made tentative steps into the field, devoting its renowned research facilities to such projects as an expert system that would help humans operate large, complex computers. In addition, company researchers are working on voice recognition and a program called Epistle that may be able someday to read and summarize an executive's mail. In a revealing act of revisionism, the company, in a 1984 press release, proudly announced that "IBM has been active in artificial intelligence research since the 1950s, when it did one of the 'classic' AI research projects: a computer program that learned to play the game of checkers at an advanced level." The press release didn't mention the actual inventor of the program, Arthur Samuel, who was indeed working at IBM when he made his famous checker-playing program. Samuel's recollections of those days were recorded by McCorduck in *Machines Who Think*: "IBM never looked with favor upon my working with it really, because it smacked too much of machine thinking, et cetera, and they wanted to dispel any worry people had with machines taking over the world and all that sort of thing." But IBM recognized Samuel's program as a good vehicle for showing off the abilities of the company's machines. "So I continued," Samuel said. "But it was never my main job; it was always by sufferance." Actually, Samuel had been hired by IBM to help them improve the reliability of vacuum tubes, the heart of their first-generation computers. He had a great deal of difficulty convincing the conservative company that transistors were the wave of the future and that it would be a disastrous mistake for IBM to heavily invest in its own tube-making factory.

IBM-bashing is a popular sport among the AI community and academic computer science in general. Many of the jabs seem unfair. It's hard to argue with the company's commercial success, and their research laboratories do remain among the best in the world. As companies become more successful they naturally become more conservative. Consider the case of Teknowledge, one of the only AI companies in Silicon Valley where male employees regularly come to work wearing coats and ties. It is often said that the company hopes to become "the IBM of expert systems." To attract the kind of corporate customers that made IBM successful, Teknowledge has found itself caught in the same dilemma once faced by Big Blue: the company must make its work seem exciting but at the same time ensure that it doesn't come off sounding like science fiction. AI has to be packaged as something executives will buy. In 1984, Jerrold Kaplan, then serving as president of Teknowledge, said that he wished the name "artificial intelligence" had never been invented. "The words were designed more than twenty years ago to get money out of the government," he said. "The name was designed to be flashy, for public-relations use. Now it's hurting the industry." Because of its futuristic connotations, the "AI" trademark has become a public-relations problem, he said, one that he deals with constantly. "I hammer on it ten times a day." He said he would prefer the more conservative-sounding label "symbolic programming."

"People say, 'Gee, artificial intelligence! That means like smart robots and things. Aren't those machines going to replace people? What happens when you have all these autonomous machines running around?' We're not usurping the great chain of being from human beings," Kaplan insisted. AI is just a programming technology. "There's nothing magic about it," he said several times, sounding a little like an IBM salesman from bygone times reassuring a nervous customer that computers aren't really a threat.

So, perhaps, in reaching the point where ACM would devote its annual meeting to the Fifth Generation Challenge, the purveyors of AI were accommodating the mainstream as much as the mainstream was moving to accept AI. Artificial intelligence, it seemed, was the errant stepson come home—clean-shaven, stylishly dressed, ready to take over the family business.

Not everyone in AI has welcomed—or even considered themselves part of—this reconciliation with computer science. Ironically, many AI researchers would find themselves agreeing with Grosch's contention that expert systems are not artificial intelligence. They resent the fact that these relatively primitive programs have prematurely stolen the thunder. In this view, true AI is not yet ready to be dressed and groomed for the marketplace. It is still in the laboratories where it belongs. When it finally emerges, it will be something more subtle and powerful than anything that has been released so far.

The Fifth Generation was scathingly reviewed in the academic journal *Artificial Intelligence* by Johan de Kleer, a prominent AI researcher at Xerox's Palo Alto Research Center, who is not so enamored of expert systems. The book, De Kleer complained, exaggerated their possibilities, as though the shallow if-then form of knowlege were all there is to intelligence: "When Sun Tzu, who is often cited in the book, wrote in 'The Art of War' about the importance of knowledge . . . he didn't mean Mycin-like rules." The book is antiintellectual and self-aggrandizing, De Kleer wrote, giving the impression that Feigenbaum's small corner of the AI empire constitutes the whole field, and that the difficult problems of mechanizing intelligence are on the verge of being solved. "AI researchers have long been viewed as arrogant, and this book only exacerbates this view," De Kleer wrote. Furthermore, he complained, the book was helping provide "a rationalization for flocks of researchers to join new venture companies (some of which were founded by Feigenbaum). The problem with this is that there is no reason to expect that much scientific progress will be made this way. Under the intense pressure of the marketplace there will be extreme pressure to do whatever it takes to work as fast as possible (i.e., good engineering), but in doing so little will be learned."

De Kleer's polemic was one more salvo in the battle between theorists and the pragmatists, the scientists and the engineers. Because he worked for Xerox and not a university, he could hardly be dismissed as an ivory-tower academic bemoaning the corruption of the marketplace. Although Xerox's Palo Alto Research Center enjoys a reputation for doing more basic, long-term research than many universities, the company itself must be ultimately concerned with turning ideas into products. De Kleer's review expressed a genuine concern among a large segment of the AI community, in industry and academia alike, over how the goal of machine intelligence is best pursued. Should researchers forge ahead by building practical systems, learning through experience which methods are useful and which should be cast aside? Or should they concentrate on developing theories of AI—a solid foundation on which systems can be built? The questions are not entirely academic. There may be dangers in filling the world with intelligent machinery that we don't completely understand.

This is not to say that all proponents of expert systems eschew theory, or that they consider their work complete, so that all that remains is to streamline the technology. At Feigenbaum's Stanford Heuristic Programming Project, as well as at MIT and other institutions, practical-minded scientists are doing basic research that eventually will lead to more sophisticated commercial programs. To alleviate the "knowledge-acquisition bottleneck"—the time it takes to work with experts and convert their knowledge into if-then rules—researchers are working on intelligent programs to help with the interviewing process. These programs are, in a sense, expert systems whose rules are about building expert systems. To make medical-diagnosis systems more intelligent, researchers are studying how it might be possible to give a program a model of the body, so that a machine can reason about how a breakdown in the liver might set off a chain reaction that causes the heart to fail. A hardcore engineer might approach the problem by trying to jury-rig a data base (a kidney is-an organ, is-connected-to the bladder, has-as-parts tubules, et cetera) and fine-tuning it until it seems to work. But many researchers are taking a more theoretical approach, stripping the problem to its essentials. Let's start simply, they say: How do you program a computer with a model of an electrical circuit so that it can diagnose malfunctions? Such a program not only would have to know the laws of electricity, but also that resistor A is next to resistor B, so that if one overheats it might very well melt the other. If we can understand the best ways to program models of such basic systems, perhaps we can move on to more complex ones like the body. Some researchers are studying how to give an expert system a model of itself, so that it can introspect on its own knowledge and behavior. Still other researchers are working on how to deal with uncertainty. In any system all rules have exceptions; they are true only some of the time.

So, even among the expert-systems school, some practitioners are more concerned with immediate applications, others with basic research. What is at stake in the argument between the scientists and the engineers is not so much the value of expert systems or whether AI is ready for the marketplace. Bigger, more abstract issues are involved.

The engineers believe that you learn about intelligent systems by building them. You plug them in, click on the switch, and see what they do. Along the way theories will emerge—not necessarily theories of the human mind but of how to make intelligent machinery. To the builders of expert systems it doesn't matter whether knowledge is arranged as it is in an expert's head, or according to some philosophically sound principle. They believe that a program should be judged by its behavior, by how well it performs a task.

According to the opposite view, one should concentrate first on developing theories, using them to guide the development of intelligent machines. Some of the theorists, like Roger Schank and Marvin Minsky, belong to the cognitive-modeling school, contending that programs should be based on theories of how the human mind works. Others, like John McCarthy, believe theory will come from devising a new kind of logic that can be used to capture commonsense knowledge. It's a subtle distinction. While Schank and Minsky concentrate on the nature of the mind, McCarthy is more interested in the nature of knowledge. He is not saying that the mind necessarily works according to the system he is inventing, only that knowledge is best codified that way. Minsky and Schank are motivated more by psychology, McCarthy by philosophy or, more specifically, epistemology.

The theorists are not saying that AI should stop dead in its tracks while we await the answers to what are, after all, some of the most basic questions imaginable. Rather they are saying that AI should be an ongoing quest for fundamental knowledge, and that systems will emerge as by-products. By proceeding this way, we can ensure that we understand what we are creating.

In any field, researchers are often too busy with day-to-day concerns to spend much time philosophizing about what they do. They pursue what they find interesting and leave it to others to ponder questions like, What is Science? But there are always an insightful few, armchair philosophers, who take an interest in how their work fits into the general scheme of things. In the course of conversations about their latest projects, AI researchers will sometimes pause, take a mental step backward, and look at the field as a whole, speculating from direct experience about how a science begins.

Frederick Hayes-Roth of Teknowledge believes AI must become well developed as an engineering discipline before it can blossom into a science.

"AI is prescientific—and very fruitful," he said. "That makes it very different from other prescientific fields—when you use that word you usually think of alchemy. This is more like being the first people in a South African diamond field. There are diamonds lying all over the surface, so you don't need to worry yet about where the veins are." It would be premature—and a wasteful distraction—to ponder the laws by which they formed.

"A hundred years ago the General Electric company was just being formed, and actually it wasn't General Electric then, it was Edison Electric. At that time there was a very poor understanding of the principles of electronics. Now one school, a hundred years ago, might have said, 'We're not going to get very far in the next century until we introspect and theorize and identify the fundamental principles of electricity.' The other school might have said, 'Gee, we're building some motors and some sound-reproducing things, and some glowing filaments—and now, if we could build some bigger turbines where we could get more of this power, maybe we could build some wire that would conduct it farther and, who knows, maybe we could light something.' That took a lot of money and energy, and out of a lot of engineering feats of that sort a context developed in which theory could emerge."

Hayes-Roth began his career as a theorist, at MIT's Sloan School of Management in the late 1960s. Working as a research associate under a Ford Foundation grant to study intelligent systems, he spent several months reading his way through the university's psychology library, learning about the unsuccessful attempts of scientists to develop grand unifying theories of intelligence. In the early 1970s, he went to the University of Michigan, where he studied the mathematics of inductive learning, earning his Ph.D. in mathematical psychology. Then he moved on to Carnegie-Mellon where he worked on Hearsay II, and from there to the Rand Corporation.

By the time he joined Teknowledge in 1981, Hayes-Roth's experience had convinced him that artificial intelligence will come not by discovering elegant theories of the nature of the mind but by building systems, one after the other, seeing what works and what does not.

"The whole notion of 'elegance' is a heuristic that you learn in academia that is of no practical value," he said. Theories, he believes, are a neat way of oversimplifying reality, packaging knowledge for consumption by our limited human brains. "Humans look for simple, elegant explanations for intelligence." But there aren't any, he said. "I'm of the intelligent-artifacts school of AI. My formal background and all of my experience leads me to believe that that is the same camp that human intelligence lives in. Human intelligence is not an example of something that was created by a stroke of brilliant insight into the design of intelligence. It is an artifact of tremendous engineered complexity." And evolution is the engineer. The mind is a kludge, as Minsky would say. "What we need to do is collect hundreds of these artifacts and see what the engineering principles are. . . .

"AI is still a technology today as opposed to a cultural renaissance, but electricity produced a cultural renaissance eventually and so will artificial intelligence."

Patrick Winston of MIT disagrees that engineering must precede science. He believes it works better the other way around. A science must develop to the point where it provides solid theories—foundations on which the engineers can build. AI, he said, must undergo a transition from "alchemy to art to science to engineering." Currently he believes the field is somewhere in the middle of the progression—an art about to become a science, with some pockets of engineering here and there.

"To be sure, there have been applications before there's been a science, but I think there will be more applications after we've managed to find a common thread, and we begin to have robust theories. Right now the applications are based on a fairly primitive technology that we can't say represents anything very deep. And I imagine that the applications will be much more powerful once we have reasonable theories. Before we have a science, we can certainly fool around with things that we believe anecdotally or that we have observed empirically, but I think that the number of applications for electromagnetism weren't very great before we had Maxwell's equations." James Clerk Maxwell, a nineteenth-century scientist, revolutionized physics with his mathematical descriptions of the behavior of electromagnetic fields.

Winston believes that parts of AI are already developing enough theory to qualify as science.

"I think that the people doing computer vision are way into the science stage. The people doing learning are still watching the sparks jump across the room like the early magnetism guys—pre-Maxwell's equations."

John Seely Brown, director of the intelligent-systems laboratory at Xerox's Palo Alto Research Center, worries that without good theory it is impossible to evaluate just what AI has accomplished and what needs to be done. He complains of what he calls a "machoism" in the field displayed by overconfident researchers who plunge ahead designing "gee-whiz types of systems" that purport to demonstrate some aspect of intelligence. "There are a lot of mavericks. It's a young field," he said. In this early stage, it is difficult to judge whether a program lives up to its claims. Is it really a theory of the mind or just fancy engineering? There are no standards to measure it by. To researchers in the intelligent-artifacts school this might not be so much of a problem. After all, they are simply interested in getting systems to perform certain, salable tasks. But to those who hope to use the computer as a window to the mind or to the nature of knowledge, this lack of grounding is a serious problem. Brown explained:

"All too often you will find scientists simply building a program that actually generates some interesting behavior—interesting problem-solving behavior, interesting knowledge acquisition, interesting learning—and saying, 'Aha, this is a model of the inner mind!' " But is the success of the system really due to the scientist's theory about how learning or some other phenomenon works, or simply to his skills as a programmer?

"Basically, in any particular system you have ideas and you have implementations of those ideas. If that system doesn't work it could be because the implementations aren't right and the ideas are right," or vice versa. Maybe the theory is bad or maybe the theorist is a lousy programmer. "If the system does work there is a question of what do you attribute its working to. So, say I write this humongous program of a hundred thousand lines, it does something interesting, and I say it does it because XYZ. There is almost never any crisp argumentation given saying that, in fact, that behavior *necessarily* requires these ideas that I have attributed to the system. How do you know it is those ideas that are really in there? Because what I really have is a gigantic program of millions of variables, metaphorically speaking, that somehow I claim embodies my ideas. And yet for all I know this program really works, if it does, for reasons completely different. So there's a real confusion about sufficiency versus necessity." A programming technique may be *sufficient* to generate a certain behavior but that does not mean that an intelligent system *necessarily* must work that way.

"How do you know that this model is really a serious model of cognition? How do you start to frame those kinds of arguments? There's a whole kind of methodology that has been overlooked, and we've been very sloppy in doing what is usually ad hoc science."

Even the good, thoughtful work is rarely examined as closely as it should be, Brown said.

"You would be surprised if you go around and look at a lot of the famed AI systems how, in fact, most of them don't do much more than the published problems that occur in the original papers. There are some glaring counter-examples to that. We have a few systems that really did a tremendous amount of innovative, honest problem-solving work. But a lot of them are more *Gedanken* exercises [thought experiments] than any reader might at first believe. The classic example, which is Terry Winograd's famous SHRDLU, didn't really handle much more than the sentences he put in his book. It was very far from a major attack on building a robust natural-language interface. That does not mean it's not an interesting piece of work. It just means that people have overextrapolated. And how do you really extrapolate—it's a very real challenge. Because it's very hard to tell what these systems have done—what the ideas really are, and what are their inherent limitations. People have been very romantic in describing the behavior and capabilities of most of these systems."

What does it mean to say that a program understands a sentence? Is putting a simulated green pyramid on top of a simulated blue block really enough? Some AI researchers skirt such questions by invoking the Turing test. Put the computer in one room and a human in the other and interrogate the two with a computer terminal. If you can't tell the difference, then the computer thinks. Brown believes it is time that AI scientists do some harder thinking about the nature of intelligence and computation. In what ways can these phenomena be said to mesh?

In 1984 Brown and Douglas Lenat examined some of these issues in a soul-searching paper for the journal *Artificial Intelligence*. The paper, which was intriguingly entitled "Why AM and Eurisko Appear to Work," examined

Lenat's celebrated discovery systems, which are among the most impressive programs produced thus far by the AI field. What does it mean, they asked themselves, to say that AM *discovered* natural numbers and then went on to reinvent arithmetic? It is an important question to consider, and it's worth the effort of reviewing Lenat's claim in some detail.

As explained earlier, AM started the discovery process with one of the concepts that Lenat had given it in advance: "lists that are equal" (that is, they have exactly the same elements as members). Guided by a heuristic that advised AM to judge a concept's worth by trying to find examples of it, the program took lists at random and tested them, two at a time, to see how many fit the definition. Since not many lists happened to be identical, AM referred to another heuristic that advised it to generalize concepts that have too few examples. Thus it took the idea of lists that are equal and broadened it to form the more useful idea of lists that are the same length.

But what does that mean, generalize?

To understand completely how AM works requires a strong knowledge of Lisp. But it's possible to get the gist of the idea by considering a few more details.

When Lenat says that AM knows the concept "lists that are equal," he means that the program contains a Lisp function called LIST–EQUAL along with some examples of equal lists. Recall that a Lisp function is a little program, a step-by-step procedure that carries out some simple task. LIST–EQUAL, then, is Lenat's name for an algorithm—a few lines of Lisp code—that, given two lists, will compare one against the other, one element at a time, and return the value T (true) if they are identical and NIL (false) if they are not. The number of Ts that LIST–EQUAL produced was very low. It was this simple fact that triggered the heuristic that advised AM to generalize concepts that have few examples. As a result, other heuristics were invoked that knew, in detail, how to carry out the generalization.

In AM "generalizing" simply meant "weakening" a function (in this case, LIST–EQUAL) so that it returned the value T more often—i.e., it was true more of the time. AM was able to make this modification because Lenat had supplied it with very specific rules about how to alter the form of Lisp functions to achieve certain ends, like generalizing or specializing them. Paraphrased, one of these heuristics went like this: "One way to generalize a definition with two conjoined recursive calls is simply to eliminate one of them entirely, or to replace AND by OR."

Again, to understand what that means a grounding in Lisp is necessary. But even those of us who find the technical terms largely opaque still can get a feel for how narrow and specialized is AM's notion of "generalization." It is an algorithm that tells how to modify another algorithm. By making a few syntactic changes in a few lines of Lisp, AM made a new, mutated version of LIST–EQUAL that was "weaker"—it would say T whenever two lists simply had the same number of elements instead of requiring that the pair be identical.

It was Lenat who decided that this new function was equivalent to what we call "same length." Naturally, AM can't name things since it doesn't know English, and many other things. It's not clear that it should. Names are a means for communicating to us in the outside world, a way of sending signals from one kind of system to another.

AM took its next step on the road to discovering arithmetic by using this new concept SAME–LENGTH (along with several other heuristics) to produce examples: a ranked set of lists each with different lengths: ( ) (T) (TT) (TTT) (TTTT) (TTTTT) . . . These, as interpreted by Lenat, were equivalent to the natural numbers: 0, 1, 2, 3, 4, 5, et cetera. Then AM juxtaposed its new playthings in various ways. In Lisp there is a common function called APPEND, which simply takes one list and tacks it onto another. AM found that appending (TT) onto (TTT) yielded (TTTTT). $2 + 3 = 5$. This was a step in the discovery of what we call addition. After that, the program discovered more examples of addition, properties of the examples, et cetera, fleshing out the concept with further experimentation.

So, is there anything inflated about Lenat's claims? Can AM really be said to know how to generalize or what numbers and arithmetic are? These are not easy questions. AM (as well as Eurisko) is a system that takes Lisp code and mutates it to make new Lisp code—according to built-in standards which are also structures of Lisp. Ultimately it is all syntactic symbol shuffling, as is anything in a computer. It takes people to provide the semantics, to interpret the symbols and give them significance. Without a human to attribute meaning to it, the program would be solipsistic, a closed system referring to nothing but itself.

"AM poses a very interesting philosophic question," Brown said. "If a program creates something new, where does the meaning of that new construct lie? In what sense does the system understand it or what it has just done? Or does the meaning lie in the attribution process that we bring to bear in interpreting what it has just done? If so, does the meaning it has coincide with the meaning we attributed to it? To the system the new concept might mean a whole variety of loosely formed ideas, but when we see it we assign a name to it that anchors it in our own conceptual space and that infuses it with all kinds of additional content. And so it's a very interesting issue of where the meaning lies." In some sense, it lies in the eye of the beholder.

"If you open up a computer system, or open up a paper in a classical AI book, you see a network of these big nodes with names on them, little dumb arrows connecting them. If you took the names off those nodes and the names off those links, that network would mean almost nothing." Or, conversely, almost *anything*. You can label it in any way you want. "Because you see those names, like 'prove,' 'disprove,' or 'cow,' 'animal,' 'living,' you say, 'Aha, I can attribute significance to those structures.' But the computer can't attribute significance to them. So basically the meaning that we think is there is again in our attribution."

But what is going on in our brains as we do the attributing? If the AI people are correct, we too are performing some kind of symbol shuffling.

We observe AM's behavior, noting patterns and characteristics that are similar to others we already have stored in our memory. Seeing a structure that takes TTT and TT and makes TTTTT, we call it addition. By giving the structure a name, we absorb it into the nodes and links of our own semantic nets. If these processes we call interpretation—perceiving patterns, matching them with other patterns, adding new structures to memory—can be described as processes, then theoretically a computer can do them. If on some level the brain works like a computer, then AM (or rather some far more advanced version) is the same thing as a mind. Lisp is simply AM's mental language, just as our minds must have some internal language of their own.

AM's functions seem disappointingly simple when we examine them closely, but that is the nature of the computational view of intelligence. If we zoomed in closer for a more microscopic look, we'd find that the Lisp functions themselves are complex shufflings of 1s and 0s. Ultimately everything is reduced to the familiar collection of stupid homunculi that can only tell the difference between on and off, but as they interact in incredibly complex ways interesting behavior emerges, behavior that is qualitatively different from that on the levels below.

And what would we find if we closely examined our own thinking? Incredibly complex patterns of neural firings. But from this electrochemical dance, our higher-level abilities emerge: generalizing, discovering, interpreting, inventing computer programs and philosophizing about what they mean.

Some researchers believe that until programs become more intelligent, their inventors should avoid words like "generalize" and "discover" that are so laden with connotation. In 1976, Drew McDermott, an AI researcher at Yale University, wrote an article called "Artificial Intelligence Meets Natural Stupidity," in which he took the field (himself included) to task.

> As a field, artificial intelligence has always been on the border of respectability, and therefore on the border of crack-pottery. Many critics have urged that we are over the border. We have been very defensive toward this charge, drawing ourselves up with dignity when it is made and folding the cloak of Science about us. On the other hand, in private we have been justifiably proud of our willingness to explore weird ideas, because pursuing them is the only way to make progress.
> . . . In a young field, self-discipline is not necessarily a virtue, but we are not getting any younger. In the past few years, our tolerance for sloppy thinking has led us to repeat many mistakes over and over. If we are to retain any credibility, this should stop.

McDermott was irked at his colleagues' tendency to use what he called "wishful mnemonics."

> If [a programmer] calls the main loop of his program "UNDERSTAND," he is (until proven innocent) merely begging the question.

He may mislead a lot of people, most prominently himself, and enrage a lot of others.

What he should do instead is refer to this main loop as "Goo34," and see if he can *convince* himself or anyone else that Goo34 implements some part of understanding. Or he could give it a name that reveals its intrinsic properties, like NODE–NET–INTERSECTION–FINDER, it being the substance of his theory that finding intersections in networks of nodes constitutes understanding. . . .

As AI progresses (at least in terms of money spent), this malady gets worse. We have lived so long with the conviction that robots are possible, even just around the corner, that we can't help hastening their arrival with magic incantations.

As AI matures, Brown, McDermott, and others who place themselves in the dual role of participant and observer, expect the field to gain high standards—a stronger sense of what it is trying to do.

"It's part of growing up," Brown said. "AI has just begun. As a science we're just getting off the ground, which is all right. It's a very real challenge to try to separate the essence from the hype, and get a sense of clarity of what the issues are. Most of us are often lost in the detail and fail to see the real gem that's lying beneath the surface. To see that gem often requires putting on a variety of eyeglasses and being willing to challenge the catechism, which is easy to do if you understand the multiple catechisms defining AI. You can use one against the other. As a research heuristic, I can usually mimic any one of the schools in AI and play it off against another school dialectically in my own head.

"We're practically entering a new phase of AI which I think is going to be scientifically more respectable," he said. "I think we're beginning to understand some of the issues more deeply. We're going beyond the mere building of systems."

CHAPTER

13

In
the
Chinese
Room

In 1984 John Searle, a philosopher at the University of California's Berkeley campus, was chosen to deliver the Reith Lectures, a series of six thirty-minute talks presented each year by the British Broadcasting Company. The lectures, begun in 1948 by Bertrand Russell, are designed to introduce a general audience to some of the important intellectual and scientific issues of the day. For his presentation, Searle chose to speak about the nature of the mind and what, if anything, it has in common with a digital computer.

Searle, a short, rugged-looking man with a self-confident swagger, believes that artificial intelligence is impossible. He is not merely saying that making thinking computers is insurmountably difficult, requiring vastly better machinery, vastly smarter programmers, and a thousand or more years of progress, but that there are theoretical reasons why it can never be done. No matter how sophisticated a computer eventually becomes—even if it carries on a conversation convincing enough to pass the Turing test—Searle would insist that it can never understand what it hears and says. Therefore it cannot be said to think.

"No one supposes that computer simulations of a five-alarm fire will burn the neighborhood down," Searle has written, in the down-home, commonsense style for which he is known, "or that a computer simulation of a rainstorm will leave us all drenched. Why on earth would anyone suppose that a computer simulation of understanding actually understood anything?" To Searle a program that passed the Turing test would be an excellent simulation of thinking, but he would insist that the map is not the territory, that the computer does not really think. Thinking is something only humans do, rooted perhaps in brain chemistry.

Searle's argument is based on the fact that a computer and its program comprise what mathematicians call a formal system. The essence of a formal system is that it consists of tokens and rules for manipulating them. Chess, checkers, tic-tac-toe, and Go all are formal systems of different levels of complexity. On a more abstract level, arithmetic is a formal system whose tokens are numbers; the rules tell how they can be manipulated using addition, subtraction, division, and multiplication. In all these systems, the nature of the tokens doesn't matter. Tic-tac-toe could be played on a grid of any size using pencil marks, pennies and dimes, or manhole covers and sofa cushions. Arithmetic could be carried out using colored dots in place of numerals. The details are arbitrary. It is the *form* of the games that is important, not the content. That is why they are called formal systems.

Another interesting feature of formal systems is that one can be "mapped" onto another. For example, in the game of chess, letters are often assigned to chess pieces—K for king, KB for king's bishop, Q for queen, QKt for Queen's knight, et cetera. To differentiate white pieces from black, the letters are printed in two colors, or two fonts of type. By also assigning letters and numbers to the squares of the board—QKt8 for the square eight rows in front of the one initially occupied by the Queen's knight—chess players have devised a code for describing the moves of a game.

In fact, an entire game can be translated into this system, as row after row of numbers and letters. If someone who didn't know about chess happened to encounter one of these descriptions, he would be baffled. He would have no way of knowing that it referred to the movement of little plastic statues shaped like horses, castles, and other figures on an eight-by-eight pattern of black-and-white squares. But if he examined the list carefully, he would see that there are syntactic rules for how the letters and numbers can be configured. Many combinations—KQ, QQ, or 3TkO5, for example—are illegal and never occur. As he read through the list of plays, he might notice other, more subtle regularities: While Kkt-KR3 and Kkt-KB3 are legal patterns, Kkt-Kkt2 is not. These esoteric relationships reflect the fact that a knight can make L-shaped moves, but cannot advance to the square in front of it. But our naïve observer wouldn't know that. Thinking that he had found a lengthy proof written in some strange mathematics, he might set out to decipher it, devising his own set of rules—a formal system that specified how to manipulate meaningless tokens like Kkt. Then the patterns of letters and numbers all would make sense. Left in isolation, he could enjoy the intricacies of his abstract world without ever knowing that it can be mapped onto an entirely different formal system: the game of chess.

A computer can be thought of as a hierarchy of formal systems all mapped onto one another. At the highest level is the program—a word processor, for example, in which the tokens are letters of the alphabet, numerals, and punctuation marks. This system, written in some high-level language like Pascal or Lisp, is mapped onto an interpreter or compiler, which is mapped onto the computer's machine language, the system whose tokens are 1s and 0s.

Artificial intelligence is based on the assumption that the mind can be described as some kind of formal system manipulating symbols that stand for things in the world. Thus it doesn't matter what the brain is made of, or what it uses for tokens in the great game of thinking. Using an equivalent set of tokens and rules, we can do thinking with a digital computer, just as we can play chess using cups, salt and pepper shakers, knives, forks, and spoons. Using the right software, one system (the mind) can be mapped onto the other (the computer).

Searle rejects this notion. He believes that formal systems are, by their very nature, incapable of thinking.

"There is more to having a mind than having formal or syntactical processes," he said during the Reith Lectures. "Our internal mental states, by definition, have certain sorts of contents. If I am thinking about Kansas

City or wishing that I had a cold beer to drink or wondering if there will be a fall in interest rates, in each case my mental state has a certain mental content in addition to whatever formal features it might have. That is, even if my thoughts occur to me in strings of symbols, there must be more to the thought than the abstract strings, because strings by themselves can't have any meaning. If my thoughts are to be *about* anything, then the strings must have a *meaning* which makes the thoughts about those things. In a word, the mind has more than a syntax, it has a semantics. The reason that no computer program can ever be a mind is simply that a computer program is only syntactical. . . . Minds are semantical, in the sense that they have more than a formal structure, they have a content."

Perhaps the single most important idea to artificial intelligence is that there is no fundamental difference between form and content, that meaning can be captured in a set of symbols such as a semantic net. Or, to put it another way, semantics can arise from syntax. To represent the meaning of "dog" we can, in effect, draw a box—a meaningless, empty symbol—and arbitrarily call it "dog." Then we can connect that box to other boxes. A dog is-a mammal is-a vertebrate is-a living thing is-a pet; it has-as-parts feet which have-as-parts toes . . . et cetera, et cetera. Then we connect those boxes to other boxes: pets are owned by humans, trained to be friendly, to be protective, to do amusing tricks. If we connect symbols to symbols in one great web, eventually we'll reach a point where the tangle of lines and boxes becomes dense enough to capture the richness and complexity the human mind associates with the word "dog," and, if the network is good enough, "pet," "human," "foot," "trick," and "living thing." The meaning of a word will not reside in any single box; the "dog" box by itself means nothing. Meaning arises from the interaction of all the boxes. It is an emergent quality, just as style arises from the interaction of Aaron's rules. While we don't yet know how to string together adequate semantic networks, most AI researchers assume that there are no theoretical barriers to doing so. If you take the mind and break it into pieces, and break the pieces into pieces, you can turn it into a medley of processes each one precise enough to be computerized.

It is this, the central dogma of artificial intelligence, that Searle refuses to accept.

"Understanding a language, or indeed, having mental states at all, involves more than just having a bunch of formal symbols," he insists. "It involves having an interpretation, or a meaning attached to those symbols." To which an AI enthusiast would reply, "Fine, so attach the meanings." Using is-a links, has-as-parts links, et cetera, you weave the symbols into a structure that is meaningful. Searle, however, would insist that no matter how good the formal system, this elusive thing called "content" will always be missing. To illustrate his point, he likes to tell a story, the parable of the Chinese Room. In this thought experiment a human (in an interesting turn of events) simulates a digital computer. In his lectures for the BBC, Searle described the situation like this:

". . . [I]magine that you are locked in a room, and in this room are several baskets full of Chinese symbols. Imagine that you (like me) do not understand a word of Chinese, but that you are given a rule book in English for manipulating these Chinese symbols. The rules specify the manipulations of the symbols purely formally, in terms of their syntax, not their semantics. So the rule might say: 'Take a squiggle-squiggle sign out of basket number one and put it next to a squoggle-squoggle sign from basket number two.' Now suppose that some other Chinese symbols are passed into the room, and that you are given further rules for passing back Chinese symbols out of the room. Suppose that unknown to you the symbols passed into the room are called 'questions' by the people outside the room, and the symbols you pass back out of the room are called 'answers to the questions.' Suppose, furthermore, that the programmers are so good at designing the programs and that you are so good at manipulating the symbols, that very soon your answers are indistinguishable from those of a native Chinese speaker."

To the programmers outside, the room would appear to understand Chinese. But the human on the inside would understand nothing as he uncomprehendingly shuffled symbols. Likewise, Searle contends, a computer programmed with the very same rules would not understand Chinese, even though it would be capable of passing the Turing test. So, Searle concluded, while a computer might be programmed to simulate intelligence, that doesn't mean that it is actually thinking. Just because something acts as though it is intelligent doesn't necessarily mean that it has mental states, or that it is experiencing the subjective feeling of being aware and conscious.

Upon first hearing it, many people feel that Searle's parable is a convincing argument against artificial intelligence. Naturally, supporters of AI are ready with a number of responses. For example, suppose that we take the room, the human, the baskets of symbols, and the rules for matching squiggles and squoggles and somehow shrink them all down and implant the whole thing in someone's head. Now, when *this* person begins conversing in Chinese how can we say that he does not understand what he is doing? And if we switch the conversation to English (his native tongue) what is it about his behavior now that makes it genuine comprehension, and not just symbol shuffling in an internal Chinese room?

In order to speak English don't we have to have something in our head that is equivalent, on some level, to a Chinese room? If not, then how do we understand? If having uncomprehending symbol shufflers is not enough, then presumably we'd need the equivalent of a homunculus inside us that is somehow capable of "real" understanding. And it, of course, could not understand Chinese unless *it* had something inside that didn't merely shuffle symbols but that *really* understood. And so we fall head first into that infinite regress that has troubled philosophers for so many years.

In his BBC lectures, Searle made it clear that he does not consider himself a mystic who holds that there is something inexplicable about the mind. ". . . [A]ll mental phenomena," he said, "whether conscious or unconscious, visual or auditory, pains, tickles, itches, thoughts, indeed, all of our mental life, are caused by processes going on in the brain." He implied that we should find the philosophers' old mind-body problem no more perplexing than the "digestion-stomach" problem. Both digestion and thinking are natural processes arising from the physical actions of organs. The key word here is "natural." There is something special, Searle believes, about the fact that the brain is biological. Thinking, he told his audience, is produced by something a computer can never have: what he calls "the causal powers of the brain."

Scientists are uncomfortable with such assertions, feeling that they smack of the philosopher's old *élan vital*, the ineffable spirit that supposedly inhabits our bodies and gives us life. But Searle's argument is more subtle. He accepts wholeheartedly that the mind—consciousness, memory, intelligence, love, despair, and all the rest of it—arises somehow from neurons, just as the phenomenon we call digestion arises from the cells and chemicals that make up the stomach and the other organs of the digestive tract. There are two levels of abstraction on which brains can be described: the neurophysiological and the psychological. On the low level all we see is a medley of electro-chemical reactions; on the high level we see the behavior those reactions produce. Likewise, the stomach can be described as muscle fibers, chemicals, et cetera, or, on a higher level, as something that digests food. We know so little about the brain that we can't yet say how chemical reactions cause thinking, as we can say how they cause digestion. But it's premature, Searle believes, to presume that the brain works like a computer.

AI researchers try to circumvent our ignorance about the brain by assuming that it doesn't matter how the "wetware" in our heads actually operates. In between the low level, where neurons interact with neurons, and the high level, where behavior emerges, they interpose a middle level—the information-processing level—on which the brain can be described as a computer running a batch of programs called the mind. If we can use hardware and software to simulate this middle level, the result will be a computer that thinks using silicon instead of brain cells. Both will be species of this thing called information processor, a formal system that thinks.

Searle says that there is no information-processing level in the brain any more than there is in the stomach. We can simulate the stomach with a computer but it won't digest. If we simulate the brain it won't think. The brain only seems like a computer because scientists have been seduced by a metaphor.

"Because we do not understand the brain very well we are constantly tempted to use the latest technology as a model for trying to understand it," Searle said. "In my childhood we were always assured that the brain was a telephone switchboard. . . . Freud often compared the brain to hydraulic and electromagnetic systems. Leibniz compared it to a mill, and I am told that some of the ancient Greeks thought the brain functions like a catapult. At present, obviously, the metaphor is the digital computer."

But there is something misleading about Searle's comparison between simulated stomachs and simulated minds. Of course, a computer simulation of digestion won't digest anything but simulated food. A better comparison would be between a real stomach and an artificial one made with tubes and valves, a supply of digestive acids, and perhaps a microprocessor to control its cycles. If food came in one end and what emerged was indistinguishable from digested food, then is the system merely a simulation, does it lack causal powers of the stomach? One kind of food processor has been used to simulate another. AI people believe that a simulated mind would think because the machine doing the simulation is, like the brain, an information processor.

Ultimately, then, Searle is denying that the brain works by processing information. However we think, he believes, it is not by manipulating symbols. This elusive thing called content or meaning will slip through the cracks of any formal system, not because it is flawed and could, by implication, be fixed, but because there are things about the mind that cannot be described computationally. Not all the world can be formalized.

It is an old lament: by studying the science of rainbows we ruin their beauty somehow. Light diffracting through water vapor is broken into pieces: red, orange, yellow, green, blue, indigo, and violet—each describable as a frequency, a shade on the electromagnetic scale. The opponents of artificial intelligence deny that the mind can be shattered this way. They believe, as Douglas Hofstadter whimsically wrote, that the soul is greater than "the hum of its parts," that you can't explain a thought by breaking it into pieces. Some irreducible essence will always remain—the stuff that makes us human.

Hubert Dreyfus, another Berkeley philosopher, draws on a school of philosophy called existential phenomenalism to argue that thinking cannot be reduced to computation. To Dreyfus, the world of the subjective is more important than that of the objective; reality is defined from within—in terms of the individual and his power to perceive and act, to know truths that are unutterable. Using this kind of argument Dreyfus reaches a conclusion similar to that of Searle: some of the things people do are intrinsically human and cannot be mechanized. To Searle these irreducibles are meaning, content, and the "causal powers of the brain." To Dreyfus they are intuition, insight, and comprehension—the ability to immediately grasp complex situations, resolving ambiguities, weeding the relevant from the irrelevant. All these abilities, he believes, are things that we just do; they cannot be rationally analyzed.

According to Dreyfus, the conviction that we can formalize reality, explaining everything with rules, began as far back as the days of ancient Greece and has become so dominant in the twentieth century that few people question it. With the advent of the computer, we can design formal systems so complex that we stretch their possibilities to the limit. In the ultimate act of hubris we believe that, having formalized the motions of the atoms, planets, and stars, we can now formalize the mind that did the formalizing. Dreyfus is convinced that the effort must fail, overturning the assumptions of the mainstream of philosophy and vindicating those of an opposing strain, based on ideas of Wittgenstein, Heidegger, Husserl, Merleau-Ponty, and others who hold that reality cannot be completely explained by any abstract system. According to this school of thought, our powers of reasoning are derived from the fact that we are at home in the world, that we have bodies, that we are rooted in the situations around us.

"Great artists have always sensed the truth, stubbornly denied by both philosophers and technologists, that the basis of human intelligence cannot be isolated and explicitly understood," Dreyfus wrote in his book *What Computers Can't Do*. "In *Moby-Dick* Melville writes of the tatooed savage Queequeg that he had 'written out on his body a complete theory of the heavens and the earth, and a mystical treatise on the art of attaining truth; so that Queequeg in his own proper person was a riddle to unfold; a wondrous work in one volume; but whose mysteries not even himself could read.' " Then Dreyfus quoted Yeats: "Man can embody the truth, but he cannot know it."

Dreyfus is joined in his crusade against artificial intelligence by his brother, Stuart Dreyfus, a professor of industrial engineering and operations research at Berkeley. He described their position in a presentation to the annual convention of the American Association for the Advancement of Science, which was held in Los Angeles in the spring of 1985. In an abstract of the talk (which, parodying Pamela McCorduck's book *Machines Who Think*, was called "People That (sic) Think"—the "sic" being part of the title), the brothers warned of the dangers that may befall a society whose love affair with the computer causes it to value pure reason above all else.

The mistaken view that human skill and expertise is produced by complicated inferences drawn from masses of facts and beliefs is rooted in the thought of Socrates and Plato, was nurtured by the likes of Hobbes and Descartes, and has flowered in the era of the computer and artificial intelligence. It now permeates our society. Expert legal testimony must take the form of facts and inferences rather than experience-based intuitive judgments, although the latter are superior. Environmental impacts must be modeled, not intuitively assessed based on prior observations. If school children cannot explain why they know something, they are accused of guessing or cheating. Doctors, once trusted and admired for their wisdom, now attempt to rationalize their diagnoses and recommended therapies. Politicians impress voters, not by a record of sound judgment, but with factual knowledge and debating prowess. The list is endless.

Intuitive expertise, acquired through concrete experience, is an endangered species. We must resist the temptation to exalt calculative reason as personified by the computer. Instead, we must recognize that facts, rules and logic alone can produce neither common sense, the ability to go to the heart of a problem, or intuition, our capacity to do what works without necessarily knowing why. Only if we recognize and appreciate the unique ways in which human beings transcend any reasoning device will machines *that* think become what they rightfully are, subservient aides and assistants to people *who* think.

According to the Dreyfuses, only novices use facts and rules. When we take driver-training classes, we learn to signal when we are half a block from the intersection where we want to turn. We learn to calculate the proper distance to leave between us and the car ahead of us and to shift gears at certain speeds. But as we become expert drivers, we forget the rules and act intuitively, automatically adjusting our following distance according to speed and road conditions. We shift unconsciously by reacting to the sound of the engine, the feel of the road. We become an extension of the car. Most scientists assume that these kinds of abilities are based on the unconscious and simultaneous processing of signals coming from the eyes, the ears, and the hands. But the Dreyfuses believe that intuition defies rational powers of description, that it can't be computerized. Like judgment and wisdom it is one of the irreducibles.

In their speeches and writings, Hubert and Stuart Dreyfus raise some interesting points about the possible limits of formalizing reality. For those of us who have been steeped in the scientific tradition, it is difficult to step outside our world view and imagine that everything we believe might be wrong. It is easy for us, the keepers of Western civilization's dominant paradigm, to become smug, dismissing philosophical opponents as charlatans and mystics. It is important to have a minority to force the majority to constantly reexamine its assumptions.

Unfortunately, though, the Dreyfuses, especially Hubert, have diminished their credibility in AI circles because of the rhetoric they often use in their critiques. In 1964 Stuart, who was working for the Rand Corporation, persuaded the research institute to hire Hubert as a consultant to write a report analyzing AI from a philosopher's point of view. The result was a biting paper entitled "Alchemy and Artificial Intelligence," which was expanded into the book *What Computers Can't Do*, published in 1972 and again, in a revised edition, in 1979.

In the book, Hubert Dreyfus tries to show how existential phenomenalism can be used to refute the philosophical foundation of artificial intelligence, and, for that matter, much of Western science. It's a fascinating topic, but Dreyfus seems to spend less effort clarifying his rather obscure arguments than in ridiculing AI researchers. Minsky, whose "naïveté and faith are astonishing," makes "surprising and misleading claims" about a students' programs and engages in "the usual riot of speculation" endemic to the field. While it is instructive (and occasionally amusing) to take the overly enthusiastic predictions of AI's pioneers and compare them with what the field has accomplished so far, Dreyfus overdoes it. He is as guilty of prematurely announcing AI's death as others are of heralding its triumph. He spends page after page deriding programs for their shortcomings—ones that their inventors readily admit.

But AI researchers can be equally intolerant of the opposition. When Minsky's colleague Seymour Papert, of the MIT AI laboratory, wrote a memo about *What Computers Can't Do*, he entitled it "The Artificial Intelligence of Hubert L. Dreyfus."

* * *

Ultimately, when all the details and rhetoric are stripped away, most debates on whether or not AI is possible come down to a standoff between the reductionists and the holists—those who believe that mind can be explained as the sum of its parts, and those who believe that in any such explanation something will always elude analysis. The reductionists are excited by the possibility that what seemed ineffable—life and mind—is accessible to human inquiry. By cutting through the mystical obscurantism that has surrounded thoughts of life and soul, we will be more enlightened creatures; by freeing intelligence from its roots in the brain, we will be able to amplify it, unleash its power to shape the world in a way more beneficial to humankind. In a newspaper, photographs are reproduced by breaking them into dots, each one black or white. As the grain becomes finer and finer, the reproduction approaches a point where it is indistinguishable from the original photograph. By continuing to refine their models of thinking, the reductionists of AI believe they will eventually reach a point where a system becomes so subtle and complex that its behavior will be indistinguishable from human thought.

But perhaps thinking has no grain. Perhaps it cannot be isolated by rules and definitions, skimmed off the brain and transplanted. The holists believe that intelligence and life can never be described simply as the interaction of millions of definable functions. While Searle and the Dreyfus brothers speak philosophically of formal systems, semantics, existential phenomenalism, et cetera, their arguments seem to spring from a deep-seated, gut-level revulsion at the very suggestion that something as wonderful as a human mind might someday inhabit a computer cabinet.

They are not the first people to feel this way. In his essay "Computing Machinery and Intelligence," Alan Turing bemusedly quoted a Professor Geoffrey Jefferson, who proclaimed in a speech in 1949:

"Not until a machine can write a sonnet or compose a concerto because of thoughts and emotions felt, and not by the chance fall of symbols, could we agree that machine equals brain—that is, not only write it but know that it had written it. No mechanism could feel (and not merely artificially signal, an easy contrivance) pleasure at its successes, grief when its valves fuse, be warmed by flattery, be made miserable by its mistakes, be charmed by sex, be angry or depressed when it cannot get what it wants."

Jefferson suggests that the mind's irreducibles include creativity, consciousness, and emotions. But just as the reductionists have ready answers for those who hold that meaning and intuition are beyond the ken of computation, so they argue that there are no theoretical reasons why a machine can't know what it knows or have feelings. A computer will have consciousness as soon as we can program it with a good enough model of itself, so that it can reason about its own behavior and imagine itself in various situations. The simulation would contain its own simulation—not exact in every detail, of course, since that would lead to an infinite regress, an endless hall of mirrors. In his Society of Mind theory, Marvin Minsky shows in rich

detail how the collection of software routines he calls agents—stupid homunculi that are a little like Hearsay II's experts or the "beings" in Douglas
Lenat's early work—might interact to produce, through emergence, human
consciousness. While agents such as SEE and GRASP know how to recognize
and manipulate objects in the outside world, other agents can recognize and
manipulate "objects" in the mind. Thus we can think about thinking.

What then about emotions? Could a computer ever have feelings? Could
it live in fear of having its plug pulled; could it find a problem interesting
or dull? If these are processes, then we should be able to program them.

In the early 1960s, while the field of artificial intelligence was just beginning, psychiatrist and computer scientist Kenneth Colby was already
studying artificial neurosis. One of his early programs roughly simulated the
belief system of a young woman who couldn't accept the fact that she hated
her father because she believed he had abandoned her. Her repertoire of
canned beliefs also included the following: "Mother is helpless," "I am defective," "I descend from royalty," "I must not marry a poor man," "I must
love people," "I must love father." These beliefs, and many others, were
stored in the computer's memory; each was coded with a "charge," or number
describing how emotionally potent and threatening it was. The woman's
overall mental state was also quantified and indicated by several "monitors,"
numerical scales that measured such qualities as self-esteem, well-being, and
anxiety.

Once the program started running it would free associate, trying to
discharge its highly negative beliefs by expressing them and thus reducing
the reading on its anxiety scale. But the most negative beliefs were too
threatening to admit, so the program tried to alter them into milder forms,
which carried lower charges. By employing various neurotic mechanisms, it
created distorted beliefs. Using deflection (as well as a subroutine called
FIND–ANALOG), "I hate father" became "I hate the boss." Or, using other
devices, hating father could be weakened to "I see faults in father" or "I
couldn't care less about father." Through the mechanism of rationalization,
the belief would become "Yes, I dislike father—because he abandoned me
long ago." Using reversal it would become "I love father." Or, through
reflection, "I hate myself" and, through projection, "Father hates me." Which
defense mechanism was chosen depended on the current readings of the
program's various emotional scales. For example, "I dislike father" could be
expressed only if the program was at a fairly low anxiety level. In turn, each
defense mechanism varied in how it affected anxiety, well-being, and self-
esteem. As the program ran, the readings on the scales would rise and fall,
beliefs accumulated charges, dissipated them, spawned distortions—all in a
rough simulation of a person fighting with a mind she can't control.

The artificial neurotic was a forerunner to Colby's more renowned and
sophisticated program, Parry, the artificial paranoid. Both systems were
attempts to use computers to study the structures of mental illness and to
suggest ways that programs might someday serve as "patients" to analysts-
in-training, allowing them to make their mistakes on machines, which are

more easily reprogrammed than people. More important, the programs represented a new kind of psychological theory—a dynamic model that could be run, observed, and refined until it provided a closer and closer approximation to what seemed to be happening in human minds.

Another step in the modeling of emotions and beliefs was taken by Robert Abelson, a social psychologist and a colleague of Roger Schank at Yale. Abelson used AI techniques to study the mechanisms of political belief. In the late 1960s, he wrote a program called the Ideology Machine, a simulation of the belief system of a right-wing ideologue. The program, often referred to as the Goldwater machine, contained a network of concepts such as "Communist nations," "left-leaning neutrals," "Free World Nations," "liberal dupes," and "good Americans." Paraphrased, the ideology Abelson coded into the system went like this:

"The Communists want to dominate the world and are continually using Communist schemes to bring this about; these schemes when successful bring Communist victories which will eventually fulfill their ultimate purpose; if on the other hand the Free World really uses its power, then Communist schemes will surely fail, and thus their ultimate purpose will be thwarted. However, the misguided policies of liberal dupes result in inhibition of full use of Free World power; therefore it is necessary to enlighten all good Americans with the facts so that they may expose and overturn these misguided liberal policies."

When the program was asked what would happen if Communists attacked Thailand, it replied: "If Communists attack Thailand, Communists take over unprepared nations unless Thailand ask-aid-from United States and United States give-aid-to Thailand." The program clearly lacked Goldwater's oratorical skills, but it was an interesting experiment in using computers to simulate the thought processes of the True Believer and study what Abelson called "the human penchant for interposing oversimplified symbol systems between themselves and the external world."

About a decade after Abelson designed his Goldwater machine, Jaime Carbonell, a student of Roger Schank's, wrote a more advanced program called Politics, which could simulate both conservative and liberal points of view. The system was based on Schank and Abelson's work on scripts, goals, and plans as expressed in the PTRANSs, MTRANSs, et cetera, of conceptual-dependency theory. Instead of a restaurant script, Politics contained scripts with such titles as "Confrontation" and "Invade," as well as a knowledge of some of the geopolitical goals a nation might have. It also was armed with if-then rules: "If a new weapon system is built by some agency of the armed forces of country X, then the military power of X will increase"; "To stop actor X from accomplishing his goal $G(X)$ see if there is any goal $G(A)$ which is mutually exclusive with $G(X)$. If so, give high priority to accomplishing $G(A)$."

In one experiment, the program was set to mimic a conservative and told, "Russia massed troops on the Czech border." Then it was asked to explain why. "Because Russia thought that it could take political control of

Czechoslovakia by sending troops," the program replied. "What should the United States do?" it was asked. "The United States should intervene militarily." In liberal mode, the program answered the same question like this: "The United States should denounce the Russian action to the UN."

While it is difficult to decide whether a simulation of thinking really thinks, it seems fairly clear that these simulated emotions don't feel. The programs are, as Professor Jefferson would say, "artificially signaling." Nothing happened during Parry's childhood to make it paranoid; the artificial neurotic doesn't really have a father to hate. The beliefs expressed by Politics aren't rooted in a concern for survival. The programs each contain a crude approximation of a tiny corner of a human belief system. The "emotions" are preprogrammed imitations of those that people have. (And yet, how many ideologues, right and left, are responding to rigid, patterned belief systems programmed into them through books and magazines or by forceful, charismatic leaders?)

Still, these programs suggest that emotions can be thought of as mechanisms, more gears in the machinery of the mind. After all, we can always make the simulations finer, including in the programs a more densely drawn semantic network with more general knowledge of the world. Then the artificial neurotic would know the connotations attached to "father" and "mother" and what it means for a human to love, hate, or feel pain. If we are ever able to make computers sophisticated enough to work with us as companions and colleagues, this kind of knowledge probably would be essential. Still, without a body to be caressed or beaten or to feel hunger or desire, without a social structure in which to feel acceptance or rejection, all that the machine knew about human emotions would be secondhand.

Perhaps a more interesting question is whether a computer could exhibit emotions of its own. Using Schankian structures like goals, plans, scripts, et cetera, a generally intelligent program might be given rules similar to Isaac Asimov's mythical laws of robotics:

1. A robot may not injure a human being, or through inaction allow a human being to come to harm.
2. A robot must obey the orders given it by human beings except where such orders would conflict with the First Law.
3. A robot must protect its own existence as long as such protection does not conflict with the First or Second Law.

Now, what if the machine couldn't get the data it needed to carry out its master's order? Could it be said to feel frustrated? Or suppose that the system was ordered to devise an industrial policy that, according to its own calculations, would raise the nation's Gross National Product by five percentage points annually over the next decade but would indirectly cause, through increased pollution, three more lung-cancer deaths per million people per year. Thou shalt not kill, but on the other hand, improving the economy would increase employment and the general health and well-being of the people, indirectly saving lives. As it thrashed back and forth, weighing costs and benefits (drawing perhaps on preprogrammed moral precepts), could the computer be said to be "pondering" the decision, to be caught on the horns of a dilemma? A reductionist would say yes, provided the program is sophisticated enough. A holist would say no, never, impossible.

Or perhaps computer emotions wouldn't be things that were intentionally put into the machine. Instead, they would be unpredictable, complex interactions—qualities and quirks that arose through emergence, through the combination of millions of different processes. Emotions like these might seem as foreign to us as ours would to a machine. We might not even have names for them.

As one speculates, performing one thought experiment after another, it becomes clear that for any objection a holist poses—a machine can never be intelligent because it can't do X—a reductionist will always have a ready answer: Yes, but X can be simulated. And the holist will reject the answer out of hand. A computer will never have free will. But what do we mean by that? Perhaps free will is simply a term we use to explain decisions so complex or irrational that we have difficulty grasping how they came to be made. From the outside, a complex expert system might seem to exhibit free will when it made a decision based on so many logical inferences that a human couldn't untangle them all. But still, the holist would reply, it makes that decision because it must. It has no choice. Its behavior, no matter how unfathomable, is still predetermined by the architecture of the program and the machine. So, what if we add a random element so the program will occasionally act on a whim? No, the holist would say, that's not what I meant at all. Machines, by definition, cannot have free will—or emotions, consciousness, intuition, wisdom, judgment, understanding, causal powers of the brain. Even if we someday succeed in making a computer that writes symphonies as great as Beethoven's or plays as moving as Shakespeare's, a holist would always object that it is "artificially signaling."

When people argue across a chasm, there is no middle ground.

CHAPTER

14

Calculating Minds

With the reductionists and the holists at an impasse, each claiming victory, MIT computer scientist Joseph Weizenbaum believes that AI researchers should concern themselves with more important issues. The question, he believes, is not what computers can do, but what they should be allowed to do. Whether or not intelligent computers can be programmed with secondhand emotions and values—or develop ones of their own—they are bound to have qualities very different from ours. After all, the systems are expected to be faster and more facile than our lumbering brains, considering more information in seconds than we can in a year. Subjectively it would be very different to be a computer than it is to be a human. Weizenbaum doubts that we should have such an alien intelligence in control of human affairs. "[T]here are some acts of thought," he has written, "that ought to be attempted only by humans."

Weizenbaum, a kind, avuncular gentleman with a walruslike mustache, is the inventor of Eliza, the simulated psychoanalyst. When he designed the program around 1965, he considered it a plaything, a parody of understanding—proof that with a few simple programming tricks people could be fooled into thinking they were conversing with a machine. He started worrying about the implications of artificial intelligence when he saw people becoming emotionally involved with the program, sitting at terminals, telling the machine their secrets.

"Once my secretary, who had watched me work on the program for many months and therefore surely knew it to be merely a computer program, started conversing with it," Weizenbaum wrote. "After only a few interchanges with it, she asked me to leave the room." Considering how quickly the program's semblance of understanding disintegrates into nonsense, it is difficult to imagine someone being so easily deluded, but then we have a tendency to anthropomorphize. Think of how many people carry on lengthy one-sided conversations with their dogs and cats, or, for that matter, with their cars. For Weizenbaum, the greatest shock came when some psychiatrists, such as Kenneth Colby (the inventor of Parry and the artificial neurotic), began seriously discussing the possibility of using a more sophisticated version of Eliza to make psychoanalysis available to the masses.

"Further work must be done before the program will be ready for clinical use," Colby and his colleagues wrote. "If the method proves beneficial, then it would provide a therapeutic tool which can be made widely available to mental hospitals and psychiatric centers suffering a shortage of therapists. Because of the time-sharing capabilities of modern and future computers, several hundred patients an hour could be handled by a computer system designed for this purpose. The human therapist, involved in the design and operation of this system, would not be replaced, but would become a much more efficient man since his efforts would no longer be limited to the one-to-one patient-therapist ratio as now exists." Astronomer and popular prognosticator Carl Sagan has envisioned "the development of a network of computer psychotherapeutic terminals, something like arrays of large telephone booths, in which, for a few dollars a session, we would be able to talk with an attentive, tested, and largely nondirective psychotherapist."

As such science-fiction scenarios proliferated, Weizenbaum became appalled. AI might very well be possible, he conceded, though he has his doubts. Still, that doesn't mean we are required to develop it. Even if making automated analysts is possible, it would be immoral, a sign that we had lost all sense of the value of humanity, that we'd come to see empathy and understanding as mechanical processes, as something a machine can do. Having convinced ourselves that computers are really thinking (and listening and caring) we would forget the "differences between information, knowledge, and wisdom, between calculating, reasoning, and thinking, and finally . . . the differences between a society centered on human beings and one centered on machines."

In the early 1970s Weizenbaum was granted a two-year leave of absence from MIT. He spent the first year at the Center for Advanced Study in the Behavorial Sciences at Stanford and the second year as a Vinton Hayes Research Fellow at Harvard studying the works of Lewis Mumford, Hannah Arendt, Jacques Ellul, Theodore Roszak, and other critics of technology. The result of his studies was a book, published in 1975, called *Computer Power and Human Reason: From Judgment to Calculation*, an eloquent argument against our society's devout belief that science holds the answer to all our problems.

Weizenbaum began the book with some observations, inspired by Mumford's classic work *Technics and Civilization*, about the way life might have been in ancient days, before humankind had become imprisoned by such abstractions as time and space.

> Times of day were known by events, such as the sun standing above a specific pile of rocks, or, as Homer tells us, by tasks begun or ended, such as the yoking of oxen (morning) and the unyoking of oxen (evening). Durations were indicated by reference to common tasks, e.g., the time needed to travel a well-known distance or to boil fixed quantities of water. Seasonal times were known by recurring seasonal events, e.g., the departure of birds.

Our consciousness was deeply rooted in the world around us, in things we could see, touch, hear, taste, and smell.

But then we invented the clock. Time became an abstraction, a never-ending march of imaginary units called seconds, and later, micro-, nano-, and picoseconds. We began to talk about time as though it were some invisible kind of stuff, isolated from the concrete world in a platonic phantom zone of pure idea. Based as it was on the sun's motion through the sky, the clock was, in a sense, an idealized model of the solar system—the first simulation. By causing us to trust the dictates of an abstract system, the clock created a whole new way of looking at the world. To quote Lewis Mumford, it "disassociated time from human events and helped create the belief in an independent world of mathematically measurable sequences: the special world of science."

While this ability to reason abstractly gave us power over nature, we began to lose contact with the material world. Weizenbaum wrote:

> [T]his newly created reality was and remains an impoverished version of the older one, for it rests on a rejection of those direct experiences that formed the basis for, and indeed constituted, the old reality. The feeling of hunger was rejected as a stimulus for eating; instead, one ate when an abstract model had achieved a certain state, i.e., when the hands of a clock pointed to certain marks on the clock's face. . . .
>
> This rejection of direct experience was to become one of the principal characteristics of modern science. It was imprinted on western European culture not only by the clock but also by the many prosthetic sensing instruments, especially those that reported on the phenomena they were set to monitor by means of pointers whose positions were ultimately translated into numbers. Gradually at first, then ever more rapidly and, it is fair to say, ever more compulsively, experiences of reality had to be representable as numbers in order to appear legitimate in the eyes of the common wisdom. Today enormously intricate manipulations of often huge sets of numbers are thought capable of producing new aspects of reality. These are validated by comparing the newly derived numbers with pointer readings on still more instruments that mediate between man and nature, and which, of course, produce still more numbers.

We have numbers on top of numbers on top of numbers, each layer insulating us from the real world.

With the coming of the computer, still more numbers can be stored, compared, and generated. We have come to believe that nothing is real unless we have a number for it, that we don't know something until we can measure it with one of our invisible yardsticks. Our abstract quantities like force, mass, velocity, acceleration, volts, amperes, watts, degrees Fahrenheit or Celsius have become more real to us than the world itself. As a result, science and mathematics are seen as oracles with the answer to every question. We've lost sight of the fact that our science and mathematics and computers and programs are human inventions, and that the data they process so perfectly are still gathered by imperfect senses—whether those of human or machine.

Weizenbaum believes that artificial intelligence will widen this split from reality, intensifying the schizophrenia. With the advent of thinking machines, we will be tempted to abandon our role as decision maker, thus realizing our ultimate aim of removing ourselves from the system—getting the human out of the loop—eliminating the soft, mushy factors that mess up the computations. In this new world everything will be quantified. Calculation will replace judgment. Should we invade country X or develop nuclear power plant Y? The answers will be in the numbers, the cost-benefit ratios. We won't have to make value judgments. Isolated from reality by our machines, we will withdraw into a fantasy world, lulled into passivity and dazzled by our simulations.

A decade after the publication of *Computer Power and Human Reason*, Weizenbaum's view of artificial intelligence is even gloomier. When he speaks, it is often with the air of an Old Testament prophet inveighing against the evils of modern life.

"We've been around on this earth as human beings for thousands of years," he said, "and in the last hundred years almost all of the ancient dreams of mankind have been realized. We can fly in the air, we can send messages at incredible distances, we can even take pictures halfway around the world. We can leave the planet—all these ancient dreams.

"When you think of the ways these incredible feats of genius actually touch the average person today, it's pretty astonishing. For example, look at television. When I contemplate modern television a feeling comes over me as must come over, say, a deeply religious Catholic as he contemplates the saints. When I contemplate television, I know enough detail about what goes on between the transmitter and my television set at home to be absolutely overawed when I consider that it works, and that it works for millions of television sets. It's enormously impressive—and what comes out at the end? Well, just put yourself in front of the television set for twelve hours. And that's what it's all about. This feat of incredible genius—I mean God must be proud to see human intelligence develop to the point that it has—and then look at what comes out. *I Love Lucy*, and stuff like that—*Kojak*, or whatever."

As with television, so with computers.

"I've been in the computer field for thirty years and I think I know what goes on inside computers, and I must say that, in a very real sense, when I contemplate a modern computer I don't believe it. I think of, say, ten million micro-operations per second going on in this little box, and they all work out—they all get there just on time. That's mind boggling. I can design such things, but there's a particular way of looking at it where I really have to say that I don't believe it. And these things run for hours without making a mistake."

Something so wonderful should instill reverence for our ability to create. But how does the computer reach the public? In the form of things like video games.

"Now look at computers. What do you see? You see a young man standing there at these boxes, hitting a button as fast as he can, turning something or another, and in the main, fully engaged in killing exercises— shooting down spaceships. And that's really how the computer comes to the public. It's one of the manifestations of it. That's very sad."

And, he believes, it is dangerous—one more example of the schizophrenia that results when we become so absorbed in our simulations that we forget reality. We forget that this dazzling game with all the colors and lights is about killing people. With television, we've had to worry about the effect of dramatized violence on children. But with video games, Weizenbaum believes, the question is not "how many murders has Johnny witnessed?" but "how many murders has Johnny committed?"

To Weizenbaum even computers in classrooms are suspect, one more example of the technological fix. If Johnny can't read, buy him a computer. In older days, Weizenbaum reminds us, encyclopedia salesmen terrorized parents with the notion that without the latest edition of the books of knowledge, their children would fall behind in school, be rejected by the good universities, be barred from all but the lower echelons of the job market. Now computer salesmen have seized on the term "computer literacy" and reified the words into a thing that children must have to succeed in life. Studies show that our educational system is inadequate, so instead of exploring what might be wrong, we flood the schools with computers. But what is the effect of this computer education? We begin at an earlier age to distance people from reality by immersing them in artificial worlds of abstraction. We teach children to play with computers instead of toys.

"One of the things that the computer is doing . . . is to make the world of abstract birds and trees and falling objects and all the other things that children are asked to do with computers—make that the reality as opposed to what's actually going on outside." What psychological effect might that have? Weizenbaum is unsure, but he doubts that it can be good. "We ought not use an entire generation of schoolchildren as experimental subjects."

If AI becomes as dominant as its advocates predict, Weizenbaum fears that all of society will be guinea pigs. Shortly after Feigenbaum and Mc-Corduck's book *The Fifth Generation* was published, he reviewed it for the *New York Review of Books*. In one chapter, Weizenbaum noted, Feigenbaum and McCorduck enthused over the advantages of using robots instead of humans to care for the elderly. The authors wrote:

> The geriatric robot is wonderful. It isn't hanging about in the hopes of inheriting your money—nor of course will it slip you a little something to speed the inevitable. It isn't hanging around because it can't find work elsewhere. It's there because it's yours. . . . The very best thing about the geriatric robot is that it listens. . . . It never gets tired of hearing [your] stories, just as you never get tired of telling them. . . . Never mind that this all should be done by human caretakers; humans grow bored, get greedy, want variety.

Should we make geriatric robots, even if we can? Must we be driven by the technological imperative? In a reply to the review, in which they called Weizenbaum "the Torquemada of computing," Feigenbaum and McCorduck wrote that they intended the geriatric robot as a joke. But to Weizenbaum, this kind of thinking is an example of how technology is causing us to lose sight of our humanity.

To its critics the idea of artificial intelligence is either threatening or absurd. They find it unsettling to think of inanimate objects that think, and they reject the idea that people are a kind of machine. As Weizenbaum puts it, we are remaking ourselves in the image of the computer. That certainly sounds like a grim development. But is it, really? It is easy to be borne away on rhetoric, driven to indignation by all the moralistic oughts and shoulds.

When sociologist Sherry Turkle joined the MIT faculty in the late 1970s, she found herself surrounded by a culture in which it was widely assumed that people were computers and machines could think. Like an anthropologist studying an aboriginal culture, she began taking field notes.

"People are thinking of themselves in computational terms," she wrote in her 1984 book, *The Second Self: Computers and the Human Spirit*. She told of a computer scientist who said, "My next lecture is hardwired" to emphasize the fact that it was so engrained in his memory that he could recite it as though his mind were on automatic pilot. Another acquaintance called psychotherapy "debugging." At lunch one day she overheard a conversation between two women at the next table. "The hard part," one woman said to the other, "is reprogramming yourself to live alone."

Turkle's field is the sociology of ideas. Previously she had studied the effects of the Freudian revolution on our way of perceiving ourselves. Her interest in the computer culture evolved into a six-year study of the effect the computer has on the way we see ourselves as humans. As she observed children, programmers, college students, and professors interacting with computers, she came to believe that the computational metaphor is largely positive. The computer, she believes, has become a tool that spurs people to ask philosophical questions that might not have occurred to them before—questions about the tension between free will and determinism, the nature of the conscious mind. "The computer," she wrote, "has become an 'object-to-think-with.' It brings philosophy into everyday life." She told the story of an engineering student whose first brush with artificial intelligence "led him to the idea that there might be something illusory in his own subjective sense of autonomy and self-determination." The point is not so much what he decided (one of his classmates reached the opposite conclusion) but that he was moved to consider one of the key issues of philosophy and theology—all because of his encounter with a machine.

Turkle has reservations about the extremes to which some of the students and AI researchers at MIT have taken the idea of mind as program. Several of the undergraduates she interviewed seemed to have absorbed the notions of emergence and Minsky's Society of Mind theory to such an extent that they had elevated the computational metaphor almost to the status of a religion. But by showing the thoughtfulness with which people of all ages confront the difficult questions of mind and machine, Turkle helps allay the fears stirred by those who assume that we are breeding a generation of robots, not in our labs but in our homes and schools.

Weizenbaum warns us of the atrocities he believes have been committed in the name of science. He cites Hitler's extermination of the Jews and the horrors of modern technological warfare as results of the "cold and ruthless application of calculating reason." He insists that he is not arguing against reason per se, but simply reminding us that "rationality may not be separated from intuition and feeling," that there are such things as ethics and morality, even if they can't be quantified.

Ethics, morality, wisdom, judgment, intuition, feeling—these are all fine words. Perhaps they are processes and can be expressed computationally. Perhaps not. As the debate between the holists and the reductionists shows, it all depends on what one is willing to accept as a definition, and that depends on whether or not one believes in irreducible essences—that which can't be explained away, that which simply is. When we make a fetish of numbers and exalt reason—or what we say is reason—to absolute faith, there is a danger that we will get carried away by the power of our tools and wreck the world we live in. But the damage we do might just as easily be in the name of country, patriotism, or God as in the name of science. Hitler didn't order the extermination of Jews because his scientists had performed a cost-benefit analysis. While he may have quoted pseudoscientific "evidence" to support his maniacal belief in the superiority of the Aryan race, he was also fond of citing a forged document called *The Protocols of the Elders of Zion*, which purported to describe a secret Jewish cabal that used extraordinary powers to rule the world. Nazism was partly rooted in a mystical, manichean world view in which forces of light battled forces of darkness. Mixed into this weird philosophy were esoteric ideas drawn from works on the occult. Like anything, the notion of science can be seized and distorted to justify the irrational ends of madmen.

Reason is most likely to be deified and distorted when we treat it as though it were one of those irreducibles the holists embrace. On the other hand, if we believe that thinking is based on processes almost anyone can understand, it loses its mystique. It becomes less likely that we will be able to use it to subjugate ("We have Reason and you do not, so do what we say"), or as justification for wreaking cataclysmic changes ("Yes, but this study says it will be okay").

"Thinking of ourselves as *nonmachines* is really kind of inhuman in a way," said Nils Nilsson, the director of the artificial-intelligence laboratory at SRI International. "That's kind of a twist. But I think it is much more humane to think of ourselves as machines, because look at the trouble that we get into if we don't. We say things like, 'Too bad Johnny can't learn algebra.' And that isn't a very humane way of treating Johnny. It's more humane to think of Johnny as a machine that has some kind of bug in its program for learning algebra. It would help Johnny a lot more.

"When you think of people not as machines but as having ultimate responsibility and all that other kind of stuff, you censure them or you brand them, or you send them to jail. Now, I think that is a rather roughshod way of fixing things. We wouldn't send a malfunctioning television set to jail. We'd fix it. Now nothing could be more dangerous than having a wrong mechanistic model of people and then fixing things in the wrong way. That might be even worse, but ultimately I think there is no substitute for knowing things. Not knowing things is bad. The more we know about ourselves as mechanisms, the more humane we'll be."

John Seely Brown of the Xerox Palo Alto Research Center tells the story of Amy, a girl who didn't know how to subtract. As part of their research on building computer coaching devices, Brown and his colleague Richard Burton studied arithmetic exams, trying to understand the reasons for the errors students make. Amy's answers to subtraction problems seemed completely chaotic—there was no discernible pattern to her mistakes.

"The math specialists and everybody thought she was a random processor," Brown recalled. Speaking of people as computers has become second nature to him. "In fact, I thought she was a random processor. But then one night as I was throwing her paper off my dining room table—literally—I said to myself, *There are a lot of 1s in her answers.* There just shouldn't be that many 1s. I pulled the paper back off the floor and started looking at it again and, lo and behold, something hit me—what Amy's problem was." Amy apparently had an error in one of the subroutines or "microskills" that made up her subtraction program. To use computer jargon, Brown had found a bug in a line of code, one that explained the mistakes Amy had made. Her errors were not random but systematic.

"As soon as I saw the problem, everything she had done was explained. All her subtraction, all her addition, all her multiplication, her word problems—all could be explained with this one simple bug. And it was dramatic, because if you didn't know Amy had a systematic explanation to her, almost anybody looking at her answers would be totally confused. It wasn't just that we were dumb, or that the math specialists were dumb. If you don't see structure, then it really looks like pure noise."

Brown and Burton analyzed thousands of arithmetic tests that had been administered to students from across the country and found that, like Amy, many children were making systematic errors. For example, after learning a procedure for deciding when to "borrow" in subtraction, some students would develop a bug that told them to borrow all the time. Or, if confronted with the problem of borrowing from 0, some students would change the digit to 1 instead of 9; others would borrow from the number below the 0. There were random errors as well. Part of the challenge was filtering out this noise so that a finite number of standard bugs could be identified. Altogether Burton and Brown found about a hundred primitive bugs just for subtraction.

Inspired by this and other experiences, Brown, Burton, and some colleagues embarked on the Buggy project.

"We said, 'Why can't we take a complete theory of all the microskills involved in doing math, look at all the ways in which each microskill can go wrong, and build this giant semantic net?' " Since a student often had more than one bug, the number of ways in which they could interact was enormous. The space of bugs, as Brown called it, was very large. Some bugs would produce the same wrong answers as other bugs. Using the network the researchers could represent all the thousands of ways the various bugs could work together to produce predictable errors. The result was the Buggy program. (Later, a more advanced version was called Debuggy.) Using the network as a sieve, researchers could analyze a student's test results and sift out the bugs. Guided by heuristics about what bugs or combinations of bugs were most likely, the computer searched the network, finding the ones that explained the student's behavior. Then, to confirm the analysis, the system predicted future errors the student would make, down to the last digit of the answers.

Having identified the primitive bugs of subtraction, the Xerox team was faced next with developing a theory of bugs explaining why these particular ones occurred and not others. What they were after was a system, or "grammar," that would generate all the possible bugs—and no others—just as a grammar of English generates all allowable sentences.

"It would be easy to build a theory that would generate some of the bugs," Brown explained. "Or you could build a theory that generates all the bugs and all kinds of others. But what you want is a theory that generates just those bugs and captures the boundary, and if you can do that you're actually going to crack an interesting mystery of the human mind."

The result was "repair theory," devised by Brown and Kurt VanLehn.

"Repair theory starts with an interesting observation," Brown explained. "It says, Suppose that the kid has partially learned a procedure but is missing certain steps because he was out of school that day, or he's forgotten or whatever. So he has a correct procedure which is missing a few lines of code or a few subprocedures. Now if he goes to execute this procedure, this impoverished procedure, what happens? Well, if you do that with a computer what would happen? The computer would go into an error state and halt." But people don't seem to do that. "When he gets into an error state the kid isn't going to stop and say 'Error 145. Halt.' " Instead, he does the best he can to finish the problem. Somewhere in his mind a program is invoked that quickly tries to repair the buggy algorithm. Guided by a set of rules, this repair subroutine patches the holes in the procedure. Then this altered version of the program resumes.

Unfortunately, the patches often don't work right. They introduce new bugs. For example, in trying to repair a defective subtraction procedure, some students developed a bug called "stutter subtract." Given a problem in which the top number had more digits than the bottom number, their subtraction program would go haywire. Consider this example:

$$
\begin{array}{r}
7654 \\
-\ 31 \\
\hline
4323
\end{array}
$$

The student has no trouble subtracting 1 from 4 to get 3, and 3 from 5 to get 2, but when he gets to the 6 in the upper row and sees a blank beneath it he doesn't know what to do. He's missing the part of the subtraction procedure that says how to handle blanks in the bottom row. Instead of halting and saying "Error 203," he tries to patch the hole in the program. In this case he calls on a repair heuristic called Refocus Right. Moving one column in from the blank, he sees a 3. Six minus 3 is 3. Then he moves to the 7 in the final left-hand column. There is a blank beneath it, too, so again he invokes Refocus Right. Seven minus 3 is 4. In repair theory, heuristics such as this (others include Refocus Left, Swap Vertically, Back Up to Last Choice, Skip, and Quit) are accompanied by censors that constrain the choices; i.e., they keep the student from picking just any repair rule. These critics include "Don't leave a blank in the middle of an answer" and "Don't have more than one digit per column in an answer."

By finding the right combination of heuristics and critics, Brown and VanLehn were able to explain how all the various subtraction bugs might be generated. The theory also predicted bugs that had not yet been found— and, more important, a new phenomenon called bug migration, which predicts that some bugs spontaneously transform themselves into other kinds of bugs. The situation was reminiscent of that in subatomic physics, when theorists predict with their equations that a certain kind of particle must exist. Otherwise the formulas won't come out right—conservation of momentum or conservation of energy will be violated. So, spurred by the predictions of the theorists, the experimentalists go to their particle accelerators and bubble chambers and find that, yes, sure enough, there is such a particle. It was here all along. They just didn't know to look for it amid the jumble. After analyzing more data, Brown and VanLehn found the bugs their theory predicted also were real, and that bug migration existed and acted as they had foreseen.

This work on arithmetic bugs is part of a general research project on how to make intelligent computer coaches—not the mindless teaching machines touted in the 1960s, an example of technology misapplied, but coaches that in some rough manner think about the effects of what they are doing. What Brown has in mind would be a simulation of a good teacher, one that would constantly judge whether it should interrupt a student who was stuck on a problem or let him work it out on his own.

"How do you tell when to break in? When you break in how do you know what to say? It's very, very subtle," Brown said. "It's trivial to build a computer-based coach which runs at the mouth. Ironically a lot of the intelligence in these systems is used to keep the coach quiet. For certain demonstrations we often turn down the intelligence so that the coach runs at its mouth more, just so people can see it operating. But when the coach is running at full-blown sophistication it almost never says anything, or it will come in so subtly that you won't even notice it. At any moment it says to itself, 'Why don't you say something?' and, 'Here are the reasons why I should say something. On the other hand, there are reasons for not saying something.' And so, you see, the coach is often engaging in a dialectical process with itself—himself, herself, itself—in order simply to decide, 'Should I step in, and if so, what should I say?' "

A good computer coach would know not to assume that its way is best. "After all, the student might be approaching the problem differently. There might be multiple correct ways to approach the problem. So just because a student's problem-solving path deviates from an expert's doesn't mean that the student's deviation isn't correct. When a student starts to deviate from any one of the correct ways, it would be straightforward to just break in and say 'Stop, you just did something wrong.' Certain educational theories would say that is the optimal way to do learning—we're not going to let him waste any time. But that kind of coaching strategy, I claim, is extraordinarily detrimental, for it never gives the student a chance to learn how to detect his own screwups. It doesn't provide him a chance to do metacognitive learning, learning about learning, learning about his own problem-solving strategies. You have to let him wander around, thrash to some extent. But on the other hand, if eventually he's really thrashing and not getting any-where, you want to step in and jog his imagination a little bit. You have to talk to him in just the right terms. And a brilliant coach is one who senses exactly when to break in and say that simple little thing—and the student says, 'Wow,' and his whole world view is suddenly changed."

The work of Brown and his colleagues assumes that the mind has a set of procedures for doing arithmetic, that it embodies some kind of formal system. Just as he has pondered what it means for a program like AM to discover arithmetic, Brown also wonders what it means for us to have pro-grams in our mind, based on sets of abstractions that somehow refer to things in the world outside. After all, what we have in our heads are simulations of reality, idealized models of the way the world works: laws of physics, biology, finance, human behavior. Laws for how to make friends or dis-courage enemies. Faced with a problem, we run these simulations and come up with answers. By understanding how this mental software works—and the architecture of the processor on which it runs—we can learn how best to teach others basic skills. We can learn how to learn. All this will come because we agree to accept a computational theory of the mind, to think of ourselves as computers.

CHAPTER

15

The Copycat Project

Almost all artificial-intelligence programs—whether they are designed to diagnose diseases or improvise jazz—are based on a common assumption: that it is fruitless to work at too low a level of abstraction, attempting to mechanize intelligence by duplicating the electrochemical flashes of the brain. According to this view, the world experienced a kind of renaissance in the late 1950s when early AI researchers decided to ignore whatever it is that neurons do and concentrate instead on the end result: how people make decisions, understand language, create new ideas from old. Once rules for this information processing were determined, intelligence could be skimmed off the top of the brain and programmed. Implicit in this theory is the conviction that there are, as George Boole called them, laws of thought that are independent of the hardware on which they run.

Cognitive scientist Douglas Hofstadter believes that such high-level rules are a chimera, that in freeing itself from its neurological underpinnings, AI has climbed too far up the ladder of abstraction. The rules, he believes, don't exist at that high a level. Nor do they exist down at the level of the neurons. Rather they lie in an altogether different realm, one that is somewhere below the information-processing level but above the neurological. It is in this subconscious region that ideas are created, though not as part of any methodical, deterministic process. A great deal of randomness is involved. Symbols collide with symbols, joining to form larger symbols—structures that vie for survival like creatures in a primordial sea. From this roiling, chaotic struggle, ideas are born.

For the last four years Hofstadter has been working on programs to re-create what he calls "subcognition," this middle level of the mind. While he agrees with his colleagues in AI that it is not necessary to model neurons, he is convinced that any attempt to mechanize intelligence without taking into account its subcognitive roots is bound to fail. He believes that it is impossible to capture the top level of intelligence by writing explicit rules of thought that can be applied to the objects we think about as one applies rules to the tokens of a game. In creating artificial intelligence you can't ignore the substrate, the subcognitive level from which the rules emerge. Otherwise the programs will be empty shells, simulations of intelligence that are not intelligent.

Hofstadter is not arguing along with John Searle that intelligence is necessarily rooted in brain chemistry, that only things biological can think. Nor is he suggesting a return to the day when scientists tried to imitate brain function by wiring together electronic neural nets. Rather he is saying that what we call rationality is a surface manifestation of something more fundamental. And it is those deeper processes that AI should be studying and trying to synthesize.

Hofstadter's views on artificial intelligence were first described in his book *Gödel, Escher, Bach: An Eternal Golden Braid*. Since it was published in 1979, he has gathered around him a group of students and co-workers who are attempting to turn AI on its head with programs that operate in a manner unlike anything the field has seen. At the University of Michigan, where Hofstadter was appointed to an endowed chair in psychology in 1984, he and his colleagues have embarked on the Copycat Project, an attempt to write a program that will capture the essence of how people appreciate analogies. Another project, called Letter Spirit, seeks to explain how we sense something as subtle as artistic style. All this work involves what Hofstadter calls subcognition, and, moreover, it is rooted in a unique world view that he has been developing since he was a child. To appreciate the flavor of Hofstadter's ideas it helps to know something about the mind from which they sprang.

For as long as he can remember, Hofstadter has been fascinated by what he calls strange loops—mirrors that reflect mirrors, sentences that refer to themselves, the eerie feeling we get when we think about ourselves thinking, then think about ourselves thinking about ourselves thinking. Once, in a dramatic demonstration of this kind of phenomenon, he connected a television set to a video camera and then pointed it at the screen. So the image of the television was picked up by the camera, cycled through the system, and displayed as a picture on the screen. Then this image of a screen displaying a screen was picked up by the camera, recycled, and *it* was displayed on the screen. Then this picture of a screen displaying a screen displaying a screen was picked up by the camera . . . and on and on, nested images of television sets proliferating at the speed of light. Input became output became input, as the television projected an infinite regress of images of itself— screens within screens—a tunnel that seemed to lead to infinity.

"My interest in abstract, twisted structures dates from my earliest childhood," Hofstadter said, reminiscing about his boyhood in the environs of Palo Alto and Stanford, where his father, Robert Hofstadter, is a physicist and Nobel Laureate. "I was so fascinated by things like squares and square roots—the concept of multiplying three by *itself* just thrilled me when I first thought about it. And I thought not only of the idea of three threes but *three* three threes, which seemed to me unbelievably fascinating—just too abstract for words. And then square roots were the same idea—what number when multiplied by *itself* gives two?—that just seemed very exciting to me."

He also loved paradoxes, such as the one named for Epimenides, the ancient Greek: "This sentence is false." But if it is false, then it's true. And if it's true, then it's false—around and around, another strange loop spinning endlessly.

When he was fifteen, Hofstadter came across one of the strangest loops of them all: Gödel's Incompleteness Theorem, which proved that mathematics is not as perfect as many people had imagined. In the early part of the twentieth century, mathematicians dreamed of proving just the opposite: that mathematics was both complete and consistent. For a system to be complete it must have the power to determine whether any given statement is either true or false—nothing can be undecidable. A system is consistent if it contains no errors. Such considerations are not as abstruse as they might sound. For years mathematicians had struggled in vain to prove such statements as Goldbach's Conjecture, which holds that any even number is the sum of two primes. While no one has ever been able to find an exception to this rule, neither has anyone been able to prove it. If mathematics is complete, then it should be possible, in theory, to prove Goldbach's Conjecture, or Fermat's Last Theorem, or any of the other statements whose proofs have eluded mathematicians for centuries.

In 1931, Kurt Gödel, a Viennese mathematician and logician, destroyed the hopes of many mathematicians by proving that any formal system must always be either incomplete or inconsistent. If it is incomplete there will be statements that can't be proved true or false. They will be forever undecidable. Perhaps Goldbach's Conjecture is one of them. Gödel showed that theoretically one can extend such a system to make it complete, but only by introducing inconsistencies, rendering it unreliable. So, one can have completeness or one can have consistency, but never both. The two qualities are mutually exclusive.

What fascinated Hofstadter was the way Gödel constructed the proof for his theorem, using a concept much like self-reflection. In a sense, Gödel demonstrated that any system that is at least as complex as arithmetic has the power to talk about itself. Thus we get strange loops or paradoxes, flaws that render the system imperfect. The crux of the argument is this: any sufficiently complex formal system contains a statement that says, in effect, "This statement is not provable." And so we have a replay of Epimenides' paradox. If the statement is true, then the system is incomplete: it contains at least one true statement that it is incapable of proving. On the other hand, if the statement is false, then it must be provable—so we can prove that it is unprovable. Thus the system contradicts itself.

Gödel's theorem ended the dream of a completely consistent, all-encompassing mathematics, but it opened new, uncharted realms to explore. Formal systems like mathematics and logic are, after all, languages for describing what goes on in the world, instruments for observing reality. Gödel showed that when we use these tools, self-referential statements inevitably will arise— "This statement is not provable"—and so the systems will end up talking not just about the things they are meant to be describing but also about themselves. In 1960, when Hofstadter encountered Gödel's theorem, he was already obsessed by paradoxes and self-reference. Now Gödel seemed to be showing that there was something primal about strange loops.

"I thought about the beauty of the way Gödel turned a system around on itself," Hofstadter recalled. "It's almost like taking a telescope which has always been straight and twisting it into a circle and having it look at itself.

He showed that in some sense the telescope was inevitably looking at itself, and you *couldn't* straighten it. And that fact of the eye that was looking at itself was to me very enthralling. It excited me because it said when you have sufficient complexity—when you study something like numbers which are sufficiently rich—you automatically get something like self-awareness. You have an automatic loop whether you intended it or not. And that seemed to me somehow deeply connected with consciousness."

The mind is a system that can think about itself—perhaps some kind of Gödelian knot is at the heart of it.

Throughout high school, and college at Stanford University, Hofstadter seemed to find strange loops lurking everywhere, in art, music, and science as well as in logic and mathematics. He discovered the drawings of M. C. Escher, such as the lithograph "Ascending and Descending," in which hooded men, monks perhaps, climb a series of winding stairs, marching higher and higher until—through the magic of optical illusion—they find themselves at the bottom again. The monks are like the ants that, in another Escher work, crawl along the surface of a Möbius strip, forever circling but always returning to the beginning. In one of the most striking of Escher's strange loops, a hand is drawing a hand, which is drawing the first hand, around and around, ad infinitum.

Some of the most elegant strange loops were in the music of Johann Sebastian Bach. Much of Bach's work consists of canons, in which one takes a melody, or "theme," and devises variations in which the same notes are played faster, slower, backward, upside down—in some way that is different from but structurally related to the original. By taking one or more of these "voices" and playing them in counterpoint to the main theme, a composer can spin complex melodic webs. In one of Bach's pieces, which Hofstadter nicknamed the Endlessly Rising Canon, three intertwined voices begin in one key, C minor, play all the way through, ending in a slightly higher key, D minor. Then the cycle begins anew, ending this time in E. It continues this way through six steps, climbing higher and higher, returning finally to the original key—but one octave above where the whole thing began. Another strange loop, like Escher's endlessly rising stairs.

By the time he had become a graduate student in physics at the University of Oregon in the late 1960s, Hofstadter had spent a great deal of time playing with computers. And so he added to his collection of strange loops recursion—functions, such as those in Lisp, which are defined in terms of themselves. For his doctoral work he used recursion to describe the range of energy levels an electron could take if it was part of a crystal immersed in a magnetic field. He was delighted to find that the problem could be described by constructing a graph that was made of many tiny copies of itself. And, of course, those copies were made of tiny copies of themselves, and so forth.

But Hofstadter wasn't to become a physicist. By the time he received his Ph.D. in 1975, he realized that his heart wasn't in his work. In a way, he found himself more fascinated by the recursive nature of his graph than by the physics it sought to represent. After much soul searching he realized that he had become captivated by something that was perhaps more fundamental than physics—the nature of formal systems and other languages and what they have to do with consciousness. While he was at Oregon he had begun writing his book, in which he used the drawings of Escher, the music of Bach, and Gödel's Incompleteness Theorem to demonstrate how recursion and self-reference are woven into the fabric of reality, helping to explain how consciousness might spring from mechanism and how computers might learn to think. Just as Gödel, Escher, and Bach used strange loops to create complex, self-referential systems of awesome beauty, so had evolution contrived to produce the strangest loop of them all, the human mind. Now perhaps we could begin to turn our self-referential powers toward the task of understanding intelligence and consciousness and re-creating them in machines.

Hofstadter continued to work on the book after he left Oregon and, in 1977, became an assistant professor—not of physics but computer science—at Indiana University in Bloomington. Two years later, *Gödel, Escher, Bach: An Eternal Golden Braid* was published. Its sub-subtitle was "A metaphorical fugue on minds and machines in the spirit of Lewis Carroll." A fugue, like a canon, is woven from a number of related themes. Richly illustrated with drawings by Escher, chapters explaining Hofstadter's philosophy alternated with dialogues between the Tortoise and Achilles, two characters first used by Zeno of Elea, a Greek philosopher from the fifth century B.C., to pose an interesting paradox. In Zeno's story, Achilles the warrior is engaged in a footrace with the Tortoise. Because the Tortoise is far slower than Achilles, he is allowed a small head start. Achilles quickly catches up with the animal, but in the instant that it takes to close the gap, the Tortoise has advanced slightly farther. Again, Achilles catches up, but in that almost infinitesimal amount of time, the Tortoise has moved ever-so-slightly farther. And so on, ad infinitum. No matter how fast Achilles is, he will never catch up to the Tortoise. In an alternate version of the paradox, Zeno's method is used to prove that motion is impossible. For to travel ten feet, first you must traverse half that distance. But to go five feet, you must first go half that much. To go two and a half feet, you must first go one and three quarters feet, et cetera, et cetera. Since you must traverse an infinity of ever tinier distances, you'll never get off the starting line.

More than two thousand years after Zeno, Lewis Carroll borrowed Achilles and the Tortoise to illustrate a paradox of his own. Hofstadter carried on the tradition with *Gödel, Escher, Bach*. Dialogues involving the two characters (and others, including the Crab, the Anteater, Charles Babbage, Dr. Tony Earrwig—Terry Winograd in disguise—and finally, the author himself) are used to introduce themes that are explored in more detail in the main text. And, to deepen the self-referential nature of the book, the dialogues are patterned after Bach's music, with the voices of the characters corresponding to musical themes, playing against one another in a conversational counterpoint.

"I have sought to weave an Eternal Golden Braid out of these three strands:

Gödel, Escher, Bach," Hofstadter wrote in the Introduction. "I began, intending to write an essay at the core of which would be Gödel's Theorem. I imagined it would be a mere pamphlet. But my ideas expanded like a sphere, and soon touched Bach and Escher. It took some time for me to think of making this connection explicit, instead of just letting it be a private motivating force. But finally I realized that to me, Gödel and Escher and Bach were only shadows cast in different directions by some central solid essence. I tried to reconstruct the central object, and came up with this book."

To illustrate this unity in three dimensions, Hofstadter carved a redwood block so that when a light is shown through it in one direction it casts the shadow of a *G* on the wall. Shine a light on another face of the block and it casts an *E*. Shine it from above and it casts a *B* below. On the jacket of the book is a photograph in which two such blocks are suspended one above the other in the corner of a room. They are illuminated so that on one wall a *G* appears above an *E*; on the other wall an *E* above a *G*. The blocks align just right so that they cast a single *B* on the floor.

Not everyone appreciated Hofstadter's unusual approach. The manuscript was rejected by several publishers, including the press at Hofstadter's own Indiana University, where a reader dismissed the carefully crafted work as "a formidable hodgepodge." When Basic Books published *Gödel, Escher, Bach*, included in the bibliography was a reference to a fictional work called *Copper, Silver, Gold: An Indestructible Metallic Alloy*, written by one Egbert B. Gebstadter and published by Acidic Books. In his description of the imaginary work, Hofstadter quoted the Indiana reviewer.

But by the time *Gödel, Escher, Bach* reached the bookstores, it had gained many influential champions, including Martin Gardner, author of the "Mathematical Games" column in *Scientific American*, and science writer and physicist Jeremy Bernstein. While Basic Books, anticipating a small audience, initially printed five thousand copies, the book has sold more than five hundred thousand copies in hardcover and paperback. In 1980 it won the Pulitzer Prize for nonfiction. Hofstadter, it seemed, had tapped a vast hidden audience fascinated by strange loops, paradoxes, and the nature of human and mechanical minds.

One of the beauties of *Gödel, Escher, Bach* is how, in his whimsical fashion, Hofstadter illuminates such subtle, difficult ideas: the theories of Alan Turing and logicians Alonzo Church and Alfred Tarski; the nature of languages and symbolic logic; the interplay between syntax and semantics, and the various levels in the hierarchy of abstraction. By relating these notions to the music of Bach, the art of Escher, and the mathematics of Gödel, Hofstadter makes the abstractions come alive. One emerges with an intuitive feel for how a formal system, such as a computer program, possibly could be imbued with consciousness and intelligence.

Hofstadter wrote:

Computers by their very nature are the most inflexible, desireless, rule-following of beasts. Fast though they may be, they are nonetheless the epitome of unconsciousness. How, then, can intelligent behavior be programmed? . . . One of the major purposes of this book is to urge each reader to confront the apparent contradiction head on, to savor it, to turn it over, to take it apart, to wallow in it, so that in the end the reader might emerge with new insights into the seemingly unbreachable gulf between the formal and the informal, the animate and the inanimate, the flexible and the inflexible.

Hofstadter plays with these ideas in a key section titled "Prelude . . . Ant Fugue." In this four-voice invention, Achilles, the Tortoise, and their friend the Crab converse with the Anteater, who counts among his friends Aunt Hillary—who, it seems, is an anthill. Recently she and the Anteater were houseguests of the Crab:

> CRAB: Yes, Aunt Hillary is quite eccentric, but such a merry old soul. It's a shame I didn't have you over to meet her last week.
> ACHILLES: I thought anteaters were devourers of ants, not patrons of ant-intellectualism!
> ANTEATER: Well, of course the two are not mutually inconsistent. I am on the best of terms with ant colonies. It's just ANTS that I eat, not colonies—and that is good for both parties: me, and the colony.

In fact, the Anteater explains, he is a trained "colony surgeon" who treats nervous disorders of ant colonies—speech impairment, for example—by removing offending ants, much as one would remove diseased cells from a body.

> ACHILLES: Well, I can vaguely see how it might be possible for a limited and regulated amount of ant consumption to improve the overall health of a colony—but what is far more perplexing is all this talk about having conversations with ant colonies. That's impossible. An ant colony is simply a bunch of individual ants running around at random looking for food and making a nest.
> ANTEATER: You could put it that way if you want to insist on seeing the trees but missing the forest, Achilles. In fact, ant colonies, seen as wholes, are quite well-defined units, with their own qualities, at times including the mastery of language. . . . Ant colonies don't converse out loud, but in writing. You know how ants form trails leading them hither and thither? . . . Actually, some trails contain information in coded form. If you know the system, you can read what they're saying just like a book. . . .
> ACHILLES: There must be some amazingly smart ants in that colony, I'll say that.
> ANTEATER: I think you are still having some difficulty realizing the difference in levels here. Just as you would never confuse an individual tree with a forest, so here you must not take an ant for the colony.

You see, all the ants in Aunt Hillary are as dumb as can be. They couldn't converse to save their little thoraxes! . . .

TORTOISE: It seems to me that the situation is not unlike the composition of a human brain out of neurons. Certainly no one would insist that individual brain cells have to be intelligent beings on their own, in order to explain the fact that a person can have an intelligent conversation.

As the discussion continues, Hofstadter develops the image of an anthill as a complex system, not unlike an organism. While the wandering of each of the ants is largely random, they communicate and interact, joining into teams to build trails, transport food, transmit information. Teams can interact with teams, forming meta-teams. Likewise, in the brain, the semirandom interactions of neurons generate structures or symbols from which thought arises.

Or, to change metaphors, the brain can be thought of as a gas. The pressure of a volume of oxygen doesn't depend on the precise behavior of a single one of its molecules. Viewed individually the molecules seem to wander at random, but when their motions are averaged together they produce predictable phenomena such as temperature and pressure. Just as there are laws of thermodynamics that use statistics to describe the mass behavior of gas molecules, so might there be laws of neurodynamics to predict the mass behavior of neurons. In all these cases—ants, neurons, and gas molecules—high-level behavior emerges from activity on the levels below, and randomness is an important part of the process.

Although the fact was not widely noticed when it was published, *Gödel, Escher, Bach* is more than a brilliant popularization. Woven throughout the book is an approach to artificial intelligence that is very much at odds with the mainstream of the field.

In 1980–81 Hofstadter spent a year at Stanford on a Guggenheim fellowship. Then he returned to Indiana University for three years. All the while he was developing this alternate view. In 1982, he described the theory in more detail in a paper called "Waking Up from the Boolean Dream, or, Subcognition as Computation." To illustrate what he meant by subcognition, Hofstadter described the experience of solving anagrams, the word-jumble puzzles that are often printed in newspapers next to the crossword. One is given "rirleta," for example, and expected to rearrange it to find "trailer." There is nothing very systematic about the way we do this. We don't seem to consciously follow rules to manipulate the letters, methodically rearranging them to find a word. The process is more random, and it seems to occur just below the level of consciousness. Somewhere in the recesses of the mind, we take a few letters and juxtapose them in various combinations, discarding the ones that don't feel right, keeping the ones that do. Then we take these groups of letters and try to build them into structures that feel stable. Some of our structures topple and disintegrate, so we take the pieces and try to join them into more robust configurations. Eventually, from all this shuffling a word gets built. It pops into consciousness, and in a flash of recognition we have an answer.

"When you first read a Jumble in a newspaper," Hofstadter wrote, "you play around, rearranging, regrouping, reshuffling, in complex ways that you have no control over. In fact, it feels as if you throw the letters up into the air separately, and when they come down, they have somehow magically 'glommed' together in some English-like word! It's a marvelous feeling—and it is anything but cognitive, anything but conscious. (Yet, interestingly, *you* take credit for being good at anagrams, if you are good!)"

Consider the Jumble *telkin*. First we might grab onto *tel* and *kin* as units, reversing them to get *kintel*. It's not a word, but it has a wordlike feel. So we might keep it around awhile and do some surgery on it, swapping the *l* and the *e* to get *kintle*, then the *t* and the *k* to get *tinkle*—the answer to the puzzle. Then again, we might not notice that possibility, abandoning our path of inquiry and starting anew. *Lint* is a likely combination, which leaves either *ke* or *ek* as the other syllable. *Lintek? Kelint?* Those are no good. Maybe something with *tin*. *Keltin, lektin, tinlek, tinkel, tinkle!*

Now imagine scores of these shufflings occurring simultaneously in an alphabet soup where letters, syllable fragments, and syllables swim about. Three letters coalesce to form *elk*, which migrates to where the combination *tin* has arisen, fusing with it to yield *elktin*, which reshuffles itself into *tinelk* and eventually perhaps into *tinkle*. But if it does not succeed all is not lost, for there are dozens of other experiments going on. Meanwhile, in another part of the soup, the unsuccessful combination *inklet* has disintegrated into its constituent symbols *ink* and *let*, which quickly mutate into *kin* and *tel*. Because the system knows which kinds of combinations to encourage, and which to discourage, the right word eventually will emerge.

"The part of this process that I am interested in," Hofstadter wrote, "is the part . . . that involves experimentation, based only on the 'style' or 'feel' of English words—using intuitions about letter affinities, plausible clusters and their stabilities, syllable qualities, and so on."

It is because of this sense of "style" or "feel" that we don't waste much time playing with low-level structures like *ktl* or *nkt* or high-level ones like *kltnie* or *lketi*—they don't feel like words. On the other hand, *linket* does seem wordlike—it just doesn't happen to be a word. While the shuffling of fragments is random, it is guided by this feeling for plausible patterns. As in evolution, mutations are random, but in the long run only the best structures survive.

In fact, Hofstadter believes, the subcognitive process is akin to what goes on in a living cell, with molecules in place of letters, syllables, and words. He wrote:

> In a cell, all activity is carried out by enzymes. Enzymes of various sorts are distributed at random throughout the *cytoplasm* (the cell's interior), and because of random motion taking place inside the cytoplasm, they

encounter all sorts of molecules in a very short time. Each enzyme has one or more (usually two) active sites—physical slots that fit a specific type of substrate, or molecule. When an enzyme encounters a molecule that fits one of its active sites, it latches onto that molecule and fills that site. When all of its sites are filled, the enzyme then performs its function, which may be constructive (combining two substrates into a larger molecule), reconstructive (changing the structure of a substrate), or destructive (reducing substrates into their components on a lower level of molecular structure). Usually one enzyme's action is but a small link in a long *chain* of enzymatic actions whose collective result is the buildup of some complex product, such as an amino acid, a nucleic acid, a protein, a chain of DNA or RNA, and so on. It is to be emphasized that the cell relies on the random peregrinations of molecules inside it for these activities to be carried out; there is no Director General who observes all and shunts all pieces to their proper places at the proper times. This is simply because a cell is at too low a biological level to have such a centralized intelligent agent. A cell's "intelligence," such as it is (and it is astonishing!), must emerge from the interplay of thousands of small, independent processes whose outcomes have effects on the further activities to take place. A cell's "intelligence" is of necessity highly distributed, in short, with wave after wave of enzymatic activity creating order out of chaos. In particular, the products made by one set of enzymes become the substrates to another set of enzymes. One remarkable feature of the cell is that enzymes themselves are produced, altered, and destroyed by other enzymes, so that the enzyme population of a cell is incredibly sensitive to the "needs" of the cell: it is constantly adjusting itself according to the types of substrates present and absent.

If there is too much of substrate A, then an enzyme will appear to decompose it. If there is a lack of substrate B, then an enzyme that encourages its production will arise.

Just as this kind of self-controlled randomness is fundamental to life, so Hofstadter believes it is basic to such subcognitive processes as solving word jumbles. As in the cell, procedures are not imposed from the top down in a bureaucratic manner. The letters and syllables are not passive symbols, tokens to be manipulated from above according to a set of formal rules. Rather, the symbols seem to manipulate themselves. They are active players, swimming around, sniffing at other symbols, searching for mates that will make them happy. *T*, *i*, and *n* feel good together; *t*, *k*, and *n* do not. If one set of reactions fails to produce the proper syllable or word, another set will. Unlikely combinations will occasionally arise—*sck* or *eei*—but if we fine-tune the system, with the proper "enzymes," wordlike fragments and wholes will be statistically more likely to emerge. Give the computer a set of robust, active symbols, and an arena in which they can play, and intelligent behavior will arise.

Hofstadter wrote:

The brain itself does not "manipulate symbols," the brain is the medium in which the symbols are floating and in which they trigger each other.

There is no central manipulator, no central program. There is simply a vast collection of "teams"—patterns of neural firings that, like teams of ants, trigger other patterns of neural firings. The symbols are not "down there" at the level of the individual firings; they are "up here" where we do our verbalization. We feel those symbols churning within ourselves in somewhat the same way as we feel our stomach churning; we do not *do* symbol manipulation by some sort of act of will, let alone some set of logical rules of deduction. We cannot decide what we will next think of, nor how our thoughts will progress.

Thus, according to Hofstadter, there are no "laws of thought," in the manner that Boole intended.

"Not only are we not symbol manipulators," Hofstadter wrote, "in fact, quite to the contrary, we are manipulated by our symbols!"

In 1982, Hofstadter wrote a program in which symbols seemed to take on a life of their own. Guided by little enzymatic programs or "codelets," the system, called Jumbo, combined letters into syllables and syllables into words. In a sense, the enzymes were like the experts in Hearsay II. In place of a blackboard, Hofstadter had a central working area called, of course, the cytoplasm.

"There are codelets for combining consonants into clusters, vowels into vowel groups, consonants and vowels into syllables or syllable fragments, syllable fragments into full syllables, and finally syllables into polysyllabic structures, or word-like objects, " he wrote. "These are the constructive, or entropy-decreasing operations. . . . There are likewise codelets for operating on structures from the inside and transforming them internally—the entropy-preserving operations." These included enzymes that knew how to swap syllables within words and letters within syllables. "Then there are destructive, or entropy-increasing, codelets, which break bonds established by earlier constructive codelets." Along with a collection of enzymes, the program was provided with standards for which letter combinations seem wordlike—it knew, for example, that clusters with a vowel in the middle and a consonant on either end are "happier," (i.e., more stable) than ones made of three consonants; that *ee* is a happier vowel cluster than *ii*; that *nk* is happier than *kn*. Thus *linket* would be more likely to arise than *ktlnei*. And when it was discovered that *linket* was not a word after all, it could be broken into smaller components and reshuffled.

At the same time that this main activity was taking place, another set of enzymes called "musing" codelets would "imagine" what would happen if, say, this syllable was substituted for that, and these two letters were swapped. Without actually making changes in the cytoplasm, the musing codelets considered alternative hypotheses, exploring several paths at once. In this way, the system exhibited parallelism.

When first exposed to a set of letters, Jumbo engaged in a great deal of random shuffling. Structures were continually shattered and rearranged. But as large, stable structures began to evolve, the randomness slowly decreased, so there was less likelihood of destroying what had already been made. Or, to use another metaphor, the "temperature" of the system was lowered. Heat, after all, is the result of randomly vibrating molecules. Steam cools from a diffuse cloud, condenses into a slightly more structured liquid, then freezes into the lattice of molecules called ice. Similarly, Jumbo started with a hot steam of letters that slowly cooled, condensed, and froze into plausible structures.

"While the choice of Jumbo's domain might on the surface seem frivolous," Hofstadter wrote, "actually it was motivated by a lifelong fascination with the unconscious processes of rapid assembly, disassembly, and regrouping of letters that seem to take place at lightning speed in the unconscious mind. These phenomena are not restricted to the manipulation of letters, of course. They take place in the manipulation of ideas of all sorts, particularly in creative activities such as writing, composing music, making mathematical discoveries, tossing ideas about in search of a new way to understand them. . . ."

So far, Hofstadter's notion of subcognition, or "statistically emergent behavior," has received an unenthusiastic response from the mainstream of the AI community. When "Waking Up From the Boolean Dream" was published, Allen Newell complained that it was "somewhat polemical and diffuse" with an "abundance of strong opinion and argumentation from general conceptual considerations and the absence of concrete scientific data or theory to build on. There is an abundance of attacks on the general opinions of others, with a corresponding promotion of the general opinions of self." When quoted in a profile of Hofstadter written by James Gleick for *The New York Times Magazine*, Newell was more succinct: "[Hofstadter is] trying to make the case that intelligence is somehow emergent out of the lower-level stuff. But I don't think he has produced a technical sort of proposal there to support the rhetoric." In AI, Newell said, programs are the "coin of the realm." If you don't have an acceptable program to show, philosophers may take your ideas seriously, but AI researchers will not. Because Hofstadter's ideas are so radical, a preliminary program like Jumbo hasn't been enough to gain his opponents' respect. He finds it frustrating that few of his colleagues seem to have taken the time to seriously study his work—they either consider it too weird or are unaware that it exists.

Other leaders of the field, such as Edward Feigenbaum, agree with Newell. Until Hofstadter produces a program to compete on the same turf with those forged by more orthodox researchers, he won't be taken seriously by the AI community.

"There *is* a Dendral. There *is* a Mycin. There *is* a General Problem Solver," Feigenbaum said. "Since Hofstadter . . . is just speculating, we view him as an outsider, a philosopher. We love him for his book, for his ideas. He can help clarify our thinking, but we can't use his stuff. Newell is absolutely right. He's expressing the view of all of us."

It's not only the old guard that is skeptical. Richard Granger, a young protégé of Schank who heads the AI program at the University of California at Irvine, characterized Hofstadter as "a physicist turned philosopher who now has something to say about AI.

"His AI work is far from the mainstream. He's a loner. His opinions are one man's view. It's not clear that we should throw our hands up and change the course of what we're doing." But Granger said he loved *Gödel, Escher, Bach*. "You have to understand that Hofstadter has recognition because he won the Pulitzer Prize. He's a good writer. He's a smart, very clever person. But that doesn't mean that he's right about AI."

Much of the criticism seems unfair. After all, Minsky has been producing theories for years without offering programs to substantiate them. His *tour de force*, the Society of Mind theory, will come to the world in the form of a book, written for a general audience, not as a few hundred thousand lines of Lisp code. Minsky is a provider of ideas, all of which serve to energize the field. No one would dismiss him as an outsider with no programs to his credit.

Hofstadter has gained some influential supporters, including Minsky, who invited him to spend a sabbatical year in 1983–84 as a visiting scientist at MIT's artificial-intelligence laboratory. While he was there he wrote a paper called "The Copycat Project: An Experiment in Nondeterminism and Creative Analogies," in which he proposed a program that would do analogical thinking, again using subcognition. Building on the work he did with Jumbo, Hofstadter hopes to produce a system that will challenge his critics by showing that subcognition can lead to programs that think in a fluid, creative manner that the top-down approach has been unable to achieve.

Copycat's domain is also letters. Consider this problem: ABC is to ABD as PQR is to what? To draw the analogy, we examine the relationships between ABC and ABD and formulate a rule, "Change the last letter to its successor in the alphabet," which we apply to PQR yielding an answer: PQS. Then again, we might decide that the answer is PQD, on the theory that the rule is "Change the third letter—whatever it is—to D." What if the question was, ABC is to ABD as CDE is to what? Using the previously mentioned rules we might chose CDF, or CDD, or we might decide that the rule is simply change C to D, regardless of its position, yielding DDE. Or consider ABC is to ABD as XYZ is to what? Is the answer XYA (assuming a circular alphabet) or XYD? A better answer, perhaps, is to recognize XYZ as a kind of mirror image of ABC. So instead of operating on the right-most letter, we operate on the left-most one instead. The answer then would be YYZ. But if we are dealing with mirror images, then for purposes of symmetry perhaps we should change the left-most letter to the one that is *before* not after it in the alphabet. The answer then would be WYZ.

Analogies don't have to involve groups with the same number of letters. ABC is to ABD as PPPQQQRRR is to what? PPPQQQRRS? That seems weak, somehow. If PPP, QQQ, and RRR are each units, then the best answer might be PPPQQQSSS. The rule "Change the right-most letter" has been adapted to "Change the letters in the right-most group."

In his proposal for the Copycat Project, Hofstadter described a program that would be constructed much in the manner of Jumbo, using enzymelike codelets to guide random shuffling. Using such subcognitive processes, the program would come up with the one answer to an analogy problem that had the best "feel." The program would know about "copy groups" such as PPP and QQQ, "successor groups" such as ABC, and "predecessor groups" such as CBA. It would know about the alphabet as a succession of letters, and about right and left edges, right and left neighbors, et cetera. In a limited sense, it would know about symmetry: its network of concepts would be arranged so that it was clear that changing the last letter of a group to its successor was symmetrical to changing the first letter to its predecessor; or that changing a right-most letter was close in flavor to changing a right-most group.

Hofstadter recognizes that he is embarking on a mammoth undertaking. Fortunately he will have some help. In 1985, after leaving Indiana to set up a lab at Michigan, he and his colleagues began programming Copycat. They are also sketching out proposals for the Letter Spirit project, which would explore the way we subcognitively perceive letters. How does one sense the "spirit" of a typeface—what do all the letters in Bodoni have in common with one another? What is the spirit of Bodoni, or of Baskerville, Helvetica, Italia, Times Roman, Optima, Palatino, and the infinite number of type styles that exist or can be imagined? Fundamentally this is another analogy problem: Baskerville A is to Baskerville B as Optima A is to what?

In choosing his problems, Hofstadter has purposefully sought to work in very simple domains. To understand analogies he looks at patterns of letters; to understand "spirit," or style, he works with letterforms. He believes that it is only by stripping a problem to its essence that one can get at the heart of intelligence.

"That's what physicists do, and I was trained that way—maybe because I grew up in a physics family, but also because I studied physics," Hofstadter said. "I don't know for certain where that aspect of my approach to AI came from. I have a feeling it was already in place by the time I was an adolescent. But it is in marked contrast to what most people in AI seem to do. I find it very perplexing. My approach has me dealing with extremely idealized, purified, simplifed worlds where I've tried to isolate things to the maximum degree possible. I've tried to say, 'Here is a phenomenon, here is its most refined form, where you've gotten rid of all extraneous detail, and there's nothing left but this phenomenon pure and simple'—when so many other people almost have the opposite approach." Instead of studying letterforms and simple analogies, they try to make fancy expert systems.

"I even avoid the word 'AI' these days. I tend to say that my research is cognitive science. I just don't want to call it AI anymore, because I think that AI has come to mean something more commercial, despite its original flavor coming from that meeting in Dartmouth with McCarthy and Minsky and Simon and Newell. Nowadays there's a kind of pollution by the industrial component of AI, a commercial component that is extremely driven by this pragmatic, product-oriented kind of approach. And also the fact is that many people believe that all the 'simple' problems have been solved. I think they're fooling themselves. . . . They believe that simple-seeming questions have all been resolved and the real essence of AI is 'How do you manage gigantic data bases with huge amounts of knowledge?'

"Originally the term 'artificial intelligence' was something that was like science fiction, and it conjured up images of giant electronic brains and thinking machines and probes into the very nature of thought. Nowadays, though, it's like, 'You want a fancier product? You want a smart terminal? Here, we'll throw some AI at you.' It doesn't sound anymore the way it did. It used to have a meaning; now it just seems devoid of meaning. It seems to mean fancy programming. And so I just tend to use another word, because 'cognitive science' is more bland. It doesn't seem to excite people, so that's good. It excites the people who are more interested in the philosophical aspects but it doesn't draw all the commercial people."

Since Hofstadter wrote the subcognition paper he has found several groups of researchers who have been independently exploring the kinds of basic mechanisms he is interested in. He counts as spiritual allies those scientists who are researching ways to achieve massive parallelism—computers in which millions of processors interact something like the neurons in a brain. At Carnegie-Mellon University, researchers such as Geoffrey Hinton and Scott Fahlman are working on such a massively parallel computer called the Boltzmann machine. Like Hofstadter they have developed the idea of computational temperature and statistically emergent intelligence. At the University of California at San Diego researchers such as Paul Smolensky, David Rumelhart, and James McClelland are working on other projects with this kind of flavor, as is a group led by Jerome Feldman of the University of Rochester. In a way these efforts are more sophisticated versions of the old neural-net research of the 1940s. In recognition of this heritage, some AI researchers speak of what they call the New Connectionism.

Hofstadter takes these efforts as a sign that the field is ready to move beyond the old top-down, deterministic dogma.

"I think that there is a lot of momentum. It may not be overwhelming, but it's growing towards a new view of what AI could be."

He tells the story of a Chinese American student whom he met at Stanford in 1980–81. The young man had read *Gödel, Escher, Bach* and was interested in studying artificial intelligence. But when Hofstadter saw him again four years later at MIT, he had become disillusioned and decided to get out of the field. As Hofstadter recalls, the student explained his objections to mainstream AI like this:

"Suppose you had said to the Greeks that there was such a thing as television—that you could see images at a great distance of hundreds or thousands of miles. Now supposing that the Greeks had said, 'Aha, then let's go out and build one. We have these things called mirrors. Let's put together a bunch of mirrors and send the images that way.' The goal is to get images somewhere, and mirrors get images somewhere, so you just take something that you already know that sort of does what you want to do—vaguely—and you figure out some fancy way to use them.

"But it's obvious that television is not a bunch of mirrors linked together. It actually involved thousands of years of work—not directly aiming at television. It actually involved something that the Greeks already knew about, namely the fact that if you rub something with something else you get some crazy kind of static, and it also involved magnetism, and it involved this combination of electricity and magnetism—electromagnetic waves. And it took two thousand years before Maxwell wrote down Maxwell's equations and did some mathematics on them and found that there were waves that propagated at the speed of light, and then Marconi put it together and made radio, and then people realized that you could have visual signals carried along with the sound. It was totally indirect. It involved unbelievably fundamental things. If the Greeks had tried to make a TV out of mirrors that would be like what the AI people are trying to do."

Then, Hofstadter said, the student switched to another analogy. "He likened the current AI to alchemy. The alchemists said, 'We want to transmute lead into gold so let's just do fancy chemical things and maybe we'll get it,' when in fact the answer again was this extremely subtle thing. You have to bombard the lead with a certain number of protons and neutrons, and you have to know that matter is made of atoms, and atoms have nuclei, and nuclei contain protons and neutrons, and that's what makes the difference between lead and gold. And you'd have to know something about nuclear physics, not just chemistry. And once again it involves going to a deeper level and postponing the gratification and saying, 'There must be something here that's a little deeper, that's below the surface, that is not direct.' "

Hofstadter's work remains on the fringe of the developing science of artificial intelligence, as do the theories of the New Connectionists. As their contributions are added to the marketplace of programs and ideas, they will compete for survival with both the established and the new. And from the bubbling on this lower level, the nature of the field will continue to emerge and grow.

Perhaps we are like the ancients in the story, tricking ourselves with mirrors—this technology that seems so shiny and new—but still lacking a sense of what is fundamental. Sometimes it seems we try to take one step only to find that we must first take half a step, and before that a quarter step. But, unlike with Zeno's paradox, we hope that our small steps will eventually take us somewhere. Rather than letting ourselves become paralyzed by the seeming infinitude that stretches before us, we must steel ourselves for a long period of basic research—a quest for fundamentals. Then slowly we'll begin moving off the starting line.

EPILOGUE

In August 1985, computer scientists from around the world gathered in Los Angeles for the International Joint Conference on Artificial Intelligence. The event, which was cosponsored by the American Association for Artificial Intelligence, was held amidst the palms of the University of California's Los Angeles campus, an island of higher learning surrounded by the opulence of Beverly Hills. To the north was the enclave of mansions known as Bel Air; to the east Rodeo Drive, which vies with New York's Fifth Avenue and Palm Beach's Worth Avenue as one of the most fashionable shopping districts in the world.

Considering how much the AI business had prospered in the year since the Austin convention, the setting seemed altogether appropriate. While some three thousand devotees had attended AAAI–84, IJCAI–85 (pronounced by the cognoscenti as "idge-kigh") drew more than five thousand. Those who had been bothered by the hype and commercialization at the previous year's fête must have been appalled by what they saw at UCLA.

If the exhibition hall at the Austin conference was like a carnival, at IJCAI–85 it was a full-scale circus—or, considering all the high-tech glitz, a midway at some futuristic state fair. In addition to old hands like Teknowledge and IntelliCorp, exhibitors included companies called Exper-Telligence, Perceptronics, Artelligence, Logicware, and Neuron Data. Information also was available on the Computer Thought Corporation, Forethought Systems, Intelliware, and Silogic, maker of such sturdy-sounding products as the Knowledge Workbench. One man was seen sporting a tag identifying him as a representative of something called Cognitech. It seemed that the heuristic for naming new AI companies went something like this: take a word like "intelligence," "knowledge," "perception"—one that distills the quintessence of what we think of as human—and graft it onto another word with a sharp, technological edge. One company, in deference to the ancient philosopher who reputedly invented the syllogism, proclaimed that "Aristotle would be proud" of their new product: a version of Prolog (short for "logic programming"), a language that has been competing with Lisp for use in the AI world.

While the smaller companies were content with booths in the exhibit area—which occupied a basketball court—the more prosperous firms also rented space at nearby Beverly Hills hotels. Hewlett-Packard set up its "Technology Gallery" in the Monte Carlo Room of the Beverly Hilton. Next door, in a chandeliered ballroom of its own, was IntelliCorp. Teknowledge, not to be outdone, hosted an afternoon reception in the hotel's Royal Suite. In one corner, an elegantly gowned young lady plucked a harp, playing such favorites as "Lara's Theme" from *Dr. Zhivago*, while white-jacketed waiters served wine and hors d'oeuvres. Symbolics, the Lisp machine company, held a party on the grounds of a mansion overlooking the ocean, entertaining guests with mariachi music and a margarita fountain.

Throughout the conference, companies issued one press release after another charting AI's march into the mainstream of the computer industry. Teknowledge announced that it had decided to rewrite its software in a popular language called C, so it would run on a wide range of conventional computers. Symbolics emphasized that their Lisp machines were good not only for Lisp—they also could be made to run less exotic languages such as Pascal and even clunky old Fortran. As a sign that the industry was becoming more consolidated, several companies announced cooperative marketing agreements, a trend that was already in evidence at the Austin convention. In most of these pacts, a hardware and a software firm joined forces to boost each other's products. Symbolics, for example, announced such arrangements with ExperTelligence and the Carnegie Group, supplementing agreements it already had with the Inference Corporation, IntelliCorp, and Teknowledge. And then there was IBM. In a move that seemed to indicate how serious Big Blue was becoming about AI research, it proudly announced that two of its researchers had won the MIT Press Publisher's Prize for the best paper presented at IJCAI. The title: "Belief, Awareness, and Limited Reasoning."

As at Austin, there was science going on in the background. Two fat volumes of conference proceedings testified to the fact that knowledge rarely advances with cataclysmic breakthroughs, but rather through the slow accretion of small details: "An Efficient Context-Free Parsing Algorithm for Natural Languages," "Determining 3-D Motion of Planar Objects from Image Brightness Patterns," "Weighted Interaction of Syntax and Semantics in Natural Language Analysis," "Judgmental Reasoning for Expert Systems," "Splicing Plans to Achieve Misordered Goals," "The Notion of Adventurousness and Some Implications for Searching," "RHINOS: A Consultation System for Diagnosis of Headache and Facial Pain," "Daydreaming in Humans and Computers," "A Common Sense Theory of Time."

Altogether more than 250 papers were presented, most of them by relatively unknown researchers—a reminder of how much important work goes unheralded. But many well-known faces also were at IJCAI. In one panel discussion, Stuart Dreyfus praised the glories of intuition. In a special presentation, John McCarthy was honored as the first recipient of the IJCAI research excellence award.

And, like a familiar presence hovering in the background, was the Defense Department's DARPA. In an announcement released at the conference, Teknowledge boasted that as part of the Strategic Computing program its Federal Systems division had received a $1.75 million contract to develop software that would help programmers build sophisticated expert systems for national defense. If the research went as planned, giant military "knowledge bases" containing tens of thousands of rules would make inferences at a rate a thousand times faster than was possible now. General Electric's

Research and Development Center announced that it had received $1 million from DARPA to begin development of "a novel 'expert system'—one designed to help military field commanders make fast and accurate decisions based on reams of incomplete and sometimes conflicting intelligence reports." With chilling self-confidence GE described the project:

"Expert systems are based on software that allows a computer to mimic the reasoning process of one or more human authorities on a given subject—in this case, tactical warfare. . . .

"The GE/DARPA program brings cutting-edge computer technology to bear on an age-old military challenge—the interpretation of intelligence data. This has never been easy—whether for the handful of Greeks who, in 480 B.C., defended the pass at Thermopylae from invading Persians, or for the U.S. infantrymen who, in 1944–45, struggled to contain the German breakthrough in the Battle of the Bulge.

"With the development of today's high-tech weapons systems—from 'eye-in-the-sky' reconnaissance satellites to laser-aimed bombs delivered by 2,500-miles-per-hour tactical fighter planes—the challenge has become more severe than ever."

The answer, of course, was artificial intelligence. G.E.'s system would enable a computer "to 'think' through various hypotheses and weed out the ones that prove to be false [and use] probabilistic reasoning strategies including 'fuzzy logic' that enable a computer to mimic common sense. With these software strategies, the system will be able to make sense of relative terms such as 'almost' and 'probably' as opposed to strictly 'yes' and 'no' thought patterns necessary with conventional expert systems." In addition the system would be capable of "reasoning by analogy—e.g., by weighing the similarities and differences of a current situation [against] a previous one."

According to G.E., developing this superhuman intelligent warrior was expected to take four years.

Not everyone at the conference was so enthusiastic about the way the Defense Department continues to dominate the field. Away from the main exhibit area, in an annex used to accommodate the overflow of displays, a group called Computer Professionals for Social Responsibility distributed literature opposing the use of computers as tools of war. The organization was founded in 1981 by a group of computer scientists at Xerox's Palo Alto Research Center, who, via their computer message system, engaged in a discussion about computing and nuclear war. By the time of the IJCAI conference, the group had grown to include seven hundred members from across the country and was beginning to establish international chapters.

In the AI community, DARPA is a very touchy subject. It is hard not to be loyal to the Defense Department when it has been responsible for nurturing not only artificial intelligence but most of computer science. For all their interest in exploring the vistas of the mind, amplifying our humanity, et cetera, almost all AI researchers are working indirectly for the Pentagon. In case after case, what would seem on the surface to be pure research turns out to be funded by the military. Marvin Minsky's company's Connection

Machine is partly funded by DARPA, as is much of Roger Schank's work. Jaime Carbonell's Politics, Douglas Lenat's AM and Eurisko, Patrick Langley and Herbert Simon's Bacon, Patrick Winston's learning programs—all have received DARPA funds. Because all the major university AI labs get money from the Defense Department, it is difficult to find a thesis, dissertation, or article in an AI journal that does not acknowledge the largesse of DARPA. Donald A. Norman, one of the leading cognitive psychologists in the United States, has written a wonderful, thoroughly humanistic book called *Learning and Memory*, in which he uses information-processing theories to speculate about the workings of the mind. One turns to the acknowledgments and finds that he thanks not only his family, friends, students, and colleagues, but DARPA as well.

Supporters argue that DARPA takes an enlightened attitude toward basic research, funding projects whose practical uses are remote to say the least. A program that learns if-then rules from a Shakespearean précis is unlikely to find immediate military application. Among AI researchers, the standard rationalization is this: the Defense Department may be giving us money, but it is not telling us what to do. However, with the advent of the Strategic Computing program, far more money is being spent on research for specific applications—the automatic intelligent copilot, the autonomous robot tank, and real-time battle management.

"Look," said Roger Schank, "the Defense Department funds AI because the Defense Department is the only serious funder of research in the United States. The Defense Department is the only part of the United States government with any money. I mean, what else is there to say? Certainly the problem is not whether AI people take Defense Department money, the problem is whether or not the United States has an organization that is concerned about the health of the economy and technological development. Until we have some sense that we had damn well better be doing that as a country—building new technologies because we're competing in world markets—we are in trouble.

"Right now the only one who is bailing us out of any of that is the Defense Department. I think it's a matter of economic defense rather than military defense. But I still think it's damned important. The people in the Defense Department happen to be very enlightened, sensible people vis-à-vis AI and other advanced research projects. The fact that we live in a peculiar country that thinks that's defense—well, okay. In my younger days I was offended by that. In my older days [Schank is thirty-nine] I'm resigned to the fact that the world is inconsistent and idiotic on some occasions."

A few scientists resist the allure of DARPA money. Terry Winograd refuses to work on defense-related projects, as does Douglas Hofstadter, whose Copycat Project is supported by the University of Michigan, the National Science Foundation, and the Lotus Corporation, maker of the popular accounting spreadsheet program Lotus 123. Some AI research has been funded by other government organizations like the National Institutes of

Health. But it is very difficult to find funding that is not related to national defense.

"I don't know what to make of all the Defense Department involvement," Hofstadter said. "It makes you think about why this whole society of 250 million people is supporting science at all. Why are we interested in science? One reason is to make life more comfortable, to develop things—like televisions and washing machines and cars and Lotus 123s—that make life easier, and to remove burdens from humans, nasty chores that computers or other machines can do better. That's one thing. Of course the other thing is to support some sort of overarching society with its own higher-level goals, which are to protect its own membranes—the national boundaries—and the national this and the national that, and all these higher-level entities that spring up and have their own momentum, whether they're corporations or nations or whatever.

"Just as organisms composed of cells seem to transcend the cell and function as wholes, it seems like these corporations have their own goals and transcend their members. Corporations interact with each other, and nations interact with each other, and they become very, very high-level forces that are dealing with each other and combating each other, and coopting their members. And so we little pawns—the human beings—are somehow trapped in it. We are almost forced to go along with these high-level forces, and very few people resist it because they don't even see the forces. They say, 'I'm doing what I want out of my own free will.' "

We are like the ants in *Gödel, Escher, Bach* that wander at random, unaware that they are acting as parts of teams, meta-teams, and meta-meta-teams— the higher-level structures of the anthill.

"I talked to somebody recently who was explaining why he had Symbolics Lisp machines," Hofstadter said. "He had four Symbolics Lisp machines at his university. He was just an assistant professor. He was barely out of MIT, and yet he has fancier machines by a factor of five than I do, and much more equipment, and here I am a full professor with a chair. He had gotten his money through the Defense Department, and I said, 'I wouldn't do that,' and he sort of smiled and said, 'Well, you know, I really want those machines.' I mean it was just like that. That's where the money is, so if you really want good machines, then that's it. There was really no more questioning of it than that."

To the members of Computer Professionals for Social Responsibility deciding whether to work for the military is more than a personal moral dilemma. They believe that if computers take charge our nuclear arsenal will become more dangerous than it already is, that we will surrender control to systems so complex that we can't possibly guarantee their reliability.

Conventional software is already so intricate that in many cases no single person can completely understand how an entire system works. Programs are generally designed by teams of programmers. The project is divided into pieces, and each team is given a set of specifications: "For a certain input X, design a program that will produce an output Y." When each subsystem is finished, they are linked together into one large program and tested. At this stage of the process, flaws or "bugs" inevitably appear. It is important to realize that these are not only sins of commission, such as a misplaced comma, but sins of omission as well. Something is left out of the program because the programmer had no way of knowing that it was necessary. Researchers Brian Smith, Severo Ornstein, and Lucy Suchman described the problem in a report issued by the Computer Professionals for Social Responsibility:

"[C]omputers are maddeningly literal-minded; they do exactly what we program them to do. Unfortunately, except in trivial cases, we cannot anticipate in advance all the circumstances they will encounter. The result is that, in unexpected situations, computers will carry out our original instructions, but may utterly fail to do what we intended them to do.

"Such failures are very real. The ballistic missile warning systems of the U.S. (and presumably those of the U.S.S.R. as well) regularly give false alarms of incoming attacks. Although most of these alerts are handled routinely, on a number of occasions they have triggered the early stages of a full-scale reaction. These false alerts stem from causes as varied as natural events (in one case a moonrise, in another a flock of geese), failures in the underlying hardware (such as a failing integrated-circuit chip that started sputtering numbers into a message about how many missiles were coming over the horizon), and human errors (such as an operator who mounted a training tape onto the wrong tape drive, thereby confusing the system into reacting seriously to what was intended to be a simulation)."

The programmers hadn't foreseen these kinds of situations, thus the computer contained no rules for dealing with them.

"The system had no way to say *Oh, yes, I forgot about the moon.* . . . [C]omputer systems don't 'know' [when] they are encountering an event outside the scope of the assumptions on which they were built; they merely sort every event into the prespecified set of categories." The moonrise and the geese fit into a category called "Soviet missile attack."

Eventually AI systems may contain something like commonsense knowledge, a feeling for how the world works. Then they might react in a more flexible, sensible manner. And yet, as software becomes complex enough to exhibit such humanlike intelligence, it will be that much more susceptible to bugs. If a system has a mere 1,000 parts—hardware or software—that can interact one with another, then there are a million ways ($1,000^2$) in which any two parts can combine, a billion ways in which any three can combine, and a trillion ways in which any four can combine. It would be impossible to test all the states in which a complex computer system conceivably could find itself. A program might run well for years until an unexpected situation occurred, causing a hidden bug to pop out.

Or perhaps it would not be bugs that kept a humanlike system from properly waging war, but rather its own intelligence. As David Rogers, an associate of Douglas Hofstadter, observed: "Humans are undependable, not because of programming or hardware errors, but because we're intelligent! . . . If a truly intelligent system were placed in charge of the nuclear arsenal, it might not be willing to fire on command. Is that a bug, or an unavoidable manifestation of intelligence?"

Scientists such as McCarthy are studying methods of "proving" programs—guaranteeing that they meet their specifications. But the work is preliminary, and possibly beside the point. Even if we can show that a program meets its specifications, there is no way to prove that whoever did the specifying has taken into account all the situations that the system might encounter. Furthermore, as David Rogers pointed out, "Building an intelligent system guaranteed to behave in a specified manner seems a contradiction in terms."

For any computer system, the ultimate test is reality. It is standard practice to debug a program as much as time allows, then put it into service and wait for the problems that inevitably arise. Even such relatively simple programs as word processors for personal computers often come with disclaimers absolving the maker from damages caused by bugs. In determining the price of a program, the manufacturer will figure in the cost of maintaining a mailing list of owners so they can be periodically apprised of recently discovered flaws.

Intelligent programs complex enough to operate the automatic copilots, autonomous vehicles, battlefield experts, and other weapons systems that DARPA envisions are likely to be hundreds of thousands to millions of lines long. The Department of Defense has estimated that President Reagan's Strategic Defense Initiative—the network of killer satellites and beam weapons that critics call Star Wars—will require programs containing some ten million lines. And, if artificial intelligence continues to develop at the pace that its supporters predict, such enormously complex programs might someday control not only our weapons systems but our cities, our economy, and perhaps even our national policy.

Edward Fredkin of MIT worries that, as with nuclear physics, artificial intelligence may develop faster than our ability to control it.

"Eventually there will be programs that are intelligent," he said. "I don't know when that will be exactly, but there's a problem with such programs. They can be very dangerous. If you apply to some important global task this very intelligent system that happens not to work correctly, the consequences are likely to be unforeseen and very bad. It takes intelligence to get us into trouble, very high intelligence to get us into great trouble, and super intelligence to get us into more trouble than we can imagine. If we were dumber we couldn't have made intercontinental ballistic missiles or hydrogen bombs, so we'd have to kill ourselves off more slowly. But as we get more intelligent there are all kinds of ways to cause mischief. The difficulty of mankind coping with something that's smarter than itself—even though it's presumably doing our bidding—is not something you learn in fifteen minutes. But there is almost no one in the world concerned with this issue."

He imagines a predicament involving a very sophisticated advice-giving program, an expert in foreign relations.

" 'What if we stopped aid to El Salvador?' you say to this advanced system, and it says, 'Well, the Salvadoran government will fall in seven and a half months.' And you say, 'What if we do this and what if we do that?' and it gives you this kind of advice. So say that on the basis of that you formulate a policy and start carrying it out. It says if you do this—a, b, c, d, e, f—then what will happen is that there will be a spontaneous revolution in Nicaragua, they'll throw the Sandinistas out, blah, blah, blah, blah. The only problem is that somewhere along the way the computer may have created a situation of such complexity that people will be unable to deal with it. It may set events into motion that can't be stopped. A good example of that kind of circumstance was World War I. In World War I a whole set of alliances, agreements, conditions, and events propelled everyone into a war that basically no one wanted, a very senseless war. But they got pushed into it against their will and the events took over. That kind of thing can happen in a much worse way because of the complexity of the kind of scenarios a computer will dream up and try to carry out.

"The question is, 'Why would a computer do something like that?' The answer is that it may have bugs in the program. So how do you know whether an intelligent thing has bugs? How do you tell if a program that is smarter than you is working the way you think it's supposed to work? It can be done, but it's very difficult. It takes time. So what's needed is to create these programs under such circumstances that they can be so tested, and you can find out that they work and certify them. An airplane gets a type certificate. The government says you can go fly in this machine and it has passed all these tests, and the wings aren't going to fall off and it's a safe airplane. To get this certificate requires lots and lots of work. You have to bend the wings so they break and you have to do all kinds of things. Something like that— except even more so—is going to be needed for AI: a procedure for certifying that this program is doing what it's supposed to do. The rate of progress here is so great that it's an urgent matter."

To guard against the perils of AI run amok, Fredkin proposes the establishment of an international artificial-intelligence laboratory "to get the best advanced work out of the competitive arena where it's very dangerous. If you're competing with someone, you don't have the time to certify. Just like in wartime. If you want a new airplane fast, you don't have the time to go through all the testing you do for a civilian airliner, because that takes longer to do than it does to fight the war. AI can be an instrument of national policy, just as are weapons."

In the movie *War Games*, the mythical supercomputer in the subterranean war room was so much more intelligent than the humans who ran it that it finally achieved a state of electronic enlightenment in which it recognized the futility of trying to win the game of thermonuclear war. By removing emotional factors such as paranoia, aggression, and hyperpatriotism from defense considerations, can computers make war rational and less likely? Or will they increase the horror by removing the last vestiges of human control?

As AI begins to move out of the laboratory and into our lives, the political and moral implications of thinking machines will become as important as the scientific questions. When we live in a world where artificial systems make decisions, who will take responsibility for bad judgments? Can a computer program be held legally and morally accountable? One afternoon midway through the IJCAI conference, a panel of experts explored these questions. Philosopher Margaret Boden of the University of Sussex opened the discussion:

"Hackers and laymen alike constantly refer to programs . . . in psychological terms. We speak of their *reasoning, judgments, evidence, knowledge, ignorance,* and *mistakes.* We speak of what they are *trying to do,* and what *priorities* are *guiding* their *decisions.* Is this simply sentimentality," Boden asked, "a sloppy way of speaking which can and should be avoided—above all, in the law courts? If it is not, if people as a matter of fact do not or cannot avoid using such terms in conceptualizing AI systems, then what implications follow? If we are allowed to use some psychological words when describing AI programs, why not all? If we use the language of knowledge and inference, and even choice, then why not the language of purpose, effort—and even blame?"

For something to be blamed, it must, in some sense, be considered a person. Over the years, societies have extended personhood to previously excluded groups such as blacks and women. Some people would like to see it granted to fetuses. In many ways corporations are considered persons in the eyes of the law. So why not intelligent machines as well? As attorney Marshal Willick pointed out, whether a computer is responsible for its actions is as much a legal as a philosophical question:

"Decision makers have used various rationales over the years in extending legal recognition to new groups. The individual decisions tend to reflect the values of their times and do not shed much light on the essence of legal personality. Each such extension, however, constituted an acknowledgment that the individual entities being considered were more like the persons doing the considering than like the property belonging to those persons."

Ironically, for all the philosophical discussions about the validity of the Turing test, the limits of formal systems, or the difference between a simulation and reality, the question of whether a program is intelligent might be decided by a judge and jury, as the result of a lawsuit filed by someone who feels damaged by a negligent machine. This might happen sooner than we think, Willick said. After all, for a machine to be held responsible in a court of law, it probably wouldn't have to be of superhuman intelligence.

"Courts seeking a definition of 'person' might look to the abortion decisions," he suggested, "which draw distinctions based on the degree of individual development." In the *Roe* v. *Wade* decision, the Supreme Court held that one may legally abort a fetus before the first trimester—at that point it is not developed enough to be considered a person. "[B]y analogy," Willick explained, "any individual computer *exceeding* a minimum behavioral capacity roughly equating fetus 'viability' would be *presumed* to be a person. As with the abortion decisions, a single such decision concerning computer personality could affect many more persons than the parties before the court."

Proving that a computer should be legally considered a person might simply be a matter of showing that it is not dead.

"When a human person dies, he loses all of his rights," Willick explained. "The law in this area tends to set an overinclusive minimum, so that any human *but* one who can be shown to have died tends to be defined as 'alive.' Given the recent emergence of 'brain death' as a critical factor, and since many computers today can exhibit far more 'intelligent' behavior than that of comatose human beings (who do enjoy legal recognition), a legal minimum standard test of personality could probably be satisfied by a computer system in the proper circumstances.

"The emergence of the modern corporation provides the most subtle means by which computer systems might achieve legal recognition," Willick continued. "Corporations have names, can buy and sell property, and can commit crimes, but they cannot be drafted, be married, or vote. They are persons, but they are owned."

Corporations, Willick explained, demonstrate the concept of "partial personality."

"[This] concept is applied in many ways in modern society. Minors, for example, slowly accrete rights and obligations as they grow older . . . while rights are removed from the retarded and the insane. . . . The legal system is thus equipped with a variety of approaches with which to decide the extent and variety of rights that should be given to computers that are recognized as persons.

"Computer systems that perform increasingly complicated tasks in an increasingly competent manner will be thrust onto these drifting sands of constitutional presumptions, tests, and standards. Since there does not seem to be an analytically sound test of 'personality' that will exclude computer systems which behave intelligently, the question of legal recognition will remain one of 'when' and not 'if,' until and unless some absolute limitations on the abilities of such machines can be demonstrated. Once computer systems can satisfy established legal tests of personality, either a valid ground of distinction between them and humans will have to be found, or the distinction will have to be abandoned as mere prejudice."

As the minds we make become increasingly sophisticated, it is tempting to wonder how long we will be sitting in judgment of them, rather than vice versa. If computers become more intelligent than people, then perhaps the opinions of men and women won't matter. A machine with the power to consider more data in a second than a human could in a lifetime might very well be assumed to have the better answer. Machine-made decisions would become elevated to the status of absolute truth, as unquestionable as decrees and dogmas.

It will always be unsettling, this idea of systems more complex than their makers. But is it really so unique a phenomenon? Over the centuries, working piece by piece, humans have created a world economy, a vast, barely fathomable machine that runs us as much as we run it. Economists study this great artifice as though it were an autonomous organism whose behavior can be charted but never completely understood. Nor do we understand the individual gears in the machine, the minds of the consumers and sellers. Each is in itself a complex system, not precisely understandable but pre-dictable enough, in a statistical sense, that we can enjoy a certain amount of order. People made and make up the economy, but it doesn't depend on our understanding in order for it to run.

So it is likely to be with artificial intelligence. The image of the silicon oracle and the obedient human servants is a fantasy. It's not very likely that we'll suddenly be presented with a giant conglomeration of hardware and software and told, "Here is your new leader." Gradually, over the years, intelligence will be injected into the systems we have already built. Our economy, politics—even our psychology and philosophy—will give way to ones in which intelligent machinery also has a role. At the same time, a system of checks and balances might very well evolve, a web of contracts and laws—controls imposed from the top down or generated from the bottom up by two kinds of minds, natural and artificial, attempting to keep each other in line. Perhaps our idea of what constitutes humanity will evolve as well. Looking down from a higher plane of abstraction, we—machines and humans—might see ourselves as two kinds of ants in an anthill with a mind of its own.

If the day comes when we share the world with another intelligence, the age-old problems of philosophy won't be solved. Even if computers are writing prize-winning novels and discovering new mathematical theorems, we'll still argue over who should get the credit, us or them. If computers join in the discussion, the issue will become that much more interesting, but still not resolved. There always will be holists and reductionists, who debate whether a formal system can be genuinely intelligent—just as people continue to debate whether a fetus is a person, or a brain-dead man has a soul. As we watch our systems become more intelligent—even if they gain indepen-dence and seem to develop a culture of their own—we'll still be left wondering if they're *really* thinking.

Can a purely formal system—a symbol shuffler—capture this thing we call meaning? Can it have feelings and lead a mental life of its own? The great questions don't have final answers. But given our tendency to anthro-pomorphize, most of us probably wouldn't require philosophically rigorous definitions before we accepted, on an emotional level, that a machine we were talking to seemed alive. If it responded to us in a manner that was interesting and coherent, in a style consistent yet surprising enough to seem like a personality, then some kind of bonding probably would occur. We'd enjoy the machine's company. We'd miss it if it was gone.

And yet there would always be those moments, late at night, when we'd wonder. After an evening spent in stimulating conversation, we would be left with an uncomfortable feeling: To the computer, all this enjoyable banter and witty repartee consists of tokens—words made from letters, each of which is arbitrarily assigned a binary code. It's all 1s and 0s that have been produced by manipulating other 1s and 0s. And all this symbol shuffling is triggered by yet another string of 1s and 0s, which at some level is all our side of the conversation is. As we sat in the dark, disturbed by these questions, perhaps the machine would be pondering them too: "Are these people just formal systems, like me? Do they also shuffle symbols, according to another arbitrary code—one written by evolution instead of humankind?"

So there we'd both be, sitting at the boundary between the natural and the artificial, each wondering if there really is a boundary at all.

Although artificial intelligence is only some thirty years old, it already has its classics—books that should be considered by anyone wishing to explore the subject in more depth. The early days of AI are described in Pamela McCorduck's wry and amusing *Machines Who Think* (W. H. Freeman), an informal history which is on its way to becoming a standard reference. McCorduck concentrates on the people of AI rather than the programs, so her book is best complemented by *Artificial Intelligence and Natural Man* (Basic Books), in which British philosopher Margaret Boden examines the details of some early AI work and considers the philosophical implications. For an even closer look at the older AI programs, see the following anthologies: Edward A. Feigenbaum and Julian Feldman's *Computers and Thought* (McGraw-Hill), Marvin Minsky's *Semantic Information Processing* (MIT Press), and Roger Schank and Kenneth Colby's *Computer Models of Thought and Language* (W. H. Freeman). More recent AI work is described in the *Machine Intelligence* series (Edinburgh University Press), edited by Donald Michie, Bernard Meltzer, and others; in the two-volume *Artificial Intelligence: An MIT Perspective* (MIT Press), edited by Patrick Winston and Richard Henry Brown; and in the encyclopedic *The Handbook of Artificial Intelligence* (William Kaufmann), edited by Avron Barr, Paul Cohen, and Feigenbaum. The articles in this three-volume set are clearly written and surprisingly accessible, especially if one has read one of the simpler technical introductions such as Bertram Raphael's *The Thinking Computer* (W. H. Freeman), or, on a more sophisticated level, Winston's textbook *Artificial Intelligence* (Addison-Wesley). For a stronger sense of what Lisp is about, spend an evening with Daniel P. Friedman's brief and entertaining *The Little Lisper* (Science Research Associates). For more details, see Winston and Berthold Horn's *Lisp* (Addison-Wesley).

Many of the founders of the AI field lead such interesting lives that they each deserve a book of their own. So far we've had to settle for shorter expositions: Jeremy Bernstein's excellent piece on Marvin Minsky in *The New Yorker* (December 14, 1981) and Philip J. Hilts's well-wrought profile of John McCarthy in *Scientific Temperaments* (Simon and Schuster). A fine article about Douglas Hofstadter was written by James Gleick for *The New York Times Magazine* (August 21, 1983). Two scientists whose work helped lay the foundations for artificial intelligence are artfully profiled in Steve J. Heims's *John von Neumann and Norbert Wiener: From Mathematics to the Technologies of Life and Death* (MIT Press). Andrew Hodges's biography *Alan Turing: The Enigma* (Simon and Schuster) provides a detailed look at one of the most influential theorists (and fascinating characters) in the early history of artificial intelligence and computer science. Howard Rheingold's *Tools for Thought* (Simon and Schuster) also contains useful and interesting profiles of computer scientists, including many who had been largely ignored. Frank Rose ably profiles an entire AI research project in his book *Into the Heart of the Mind* (Harper and Row).

For those interested in a broader look at computers, a number of popular books have been written. My favorites are Tracy Kidder's *Soul of a New Machine* (Little, Brown), Steven Levy's *Hackers* (Anchor Press/Doubleday), Jeremy Bernstein's *The Analytical Engine* (William Morrow), Dirk Hanson's *The New Alchemists* (Little, Brown), and the *Scientific American* special issue on software (September 1984), which has been reprinted as a book.

Readers who wish to plumb the philosophical depths of computation, formal systems, and intelligence should read, first and foremost, Douglas Hofstadter's *Gödel, Escher, Bach* (Basic Books). His ideas are further developed in *Metamagical Themas* (Basic Books). Other fine philosophical works include J. David Bolter's *Turing's Man* (University of North Carolina Press), Pamela McCorduck's *The Universal Machine* (McGraw-Hill), Daniel Dennett's *Brainstorms* (MIT Press), and Hofstadter and Dennett's *The Mind's I* (Basic Books). Sherry Turkle's *The Second Self* (Simon and Schuster) is an intriguing sociological study of the effect of computers on our image of ourselves. In *The Sciences of the Artificial* (MIT Press), Herbert Simon discusses the fascinating implications of a science based on the study of artificial (as opposed to natural) creations, whether they be computers or the economy. During my research, one of the most interesting books I read was Jeremy Campbell's *Grammatical Man* (Simon and Schuster), which is about information theory, language, entropy, chaos, and many other things. Jagjit Singh's delightful book *Great Ideas in Information Theory, Language and Cybernetics* (Dover) is also well worth considering.

Reading about artificial intelligence naturally arouses curiosity about related fields. To learn more about cognitive psychology, in which researchers use information-processing ideas in their theories of the mind, see Morton Hunt's *The Universe Within* (Simon and Schuster). In *The Mind's New Science* (Basic Books), Howard Gardner describes how ideas in psychology, artificial intelligence, philosophy, linguistics, anthropology, and neuroscience are coming together to form the new field of cognitive science. In *The Conscious Brain* (Vintage Books), Steven Rose provides an excellent account of the brain's "wetware." For a more detailed look, see *Scientific American*'s special issue on the brain (September 1979), also republished as a book. To get a sense of how the concepts of information processing might apply to biology, read Jacques Monod's *Chance and Necessity* (Vintage Books).

To keep up with the very latest AI research, it is necessary to go to the articles and papers from which later books will be written. Some of the best work is published in the journal *Artificial Intelligence*, *The AI Magazine*, *The SIGART Newsletter*, and the proceedings of the conventions of the American

Association for Artificial Intelligence and the International Joint Conference on Artificial Intelligence (William Kaufmann). For even more up-to-date information, see the technical reports available from the various AI laboratories. The magazine *High Technology* also provides timely—and very readable—coverage of the field.

NOTES

CHAPTER 1. The State of the Art

PAGE

12 The 1984 convention of the American Association for Artificial Intelligence was held from August 6 to 10 at the University of Texas in Austin.

13 "Things have been slower": interview with John McCarthy; Stanford University, June 18, 1984.

14 For details on the history of Lisp, see John McCarthy, "History of LISP," *ACM SIGPLAN Notices*, August 1978, pp. 217–23.

17 "I would get several," et cetera: interview with Edward Feigenbaum, Stanford University, May 7, 1984.

19 For details of McCarthy's commonsense reasoning project, see "How Can Computers Get Common Sense?" by Gina Kolata, *Science*, September 24, 1982, pp. 1237–38.

21 "When Schlumberger," et cetera: Feigenbaum interview.

22 *Business Week* estimated forty companies: July 9, 1984, p. 55.

23 "greening of AI": interview with Daniel Bobrow, Palo Alto, California, May 7, 1984.

23 "the threshold": *Business Week*, March 8, 1982, p. 66.

23 "Artificial Intelligence: It's Here!": *Business Week*, July 9, 1984.

23 "the people in suits": Bobrow interview.

23 The Society of Mind theory is described in volume 1 of Winston and Brown, *Artificial Intelligence: An MIT Perspective*, and in Minsky, *Society of Mind*.

24 "the set of things," et cetera: Minsky speaking at the tutorial "An Overview of Artificial Intelligence" at the annual conference of the American Association for Artificial Intelligence, August 6, 1984, Austin, Texas.

24 "a hundred years of hard work," et cetera: interview with Marvin Minsky, Massachusetts Institute of Technology, December 12, 1984.

25 "Bell Labs would hire": Bobrow interview.

25 "Firms are using money": Feigenbaum interview.

26 "Businesses are constantly," et cetera: interview with Richard Granger, University of California at Irvine, May 24, 1984.

26 "You'd think that artificial intelligence": interview with Douglas Hofstadter, AAAI conference in Austin, Texas, August 1984.

27 "What are the letters": Hofstadter, "Artificial Intelligence: Subcognition as Computation," Indiana University Computer Science Department, Technical Report Number 132, November 1982, p. 2; reprinted in Hofstadter, *Metamagical Themas*, as "Waking Up From the Boolean Dream, *or*, Subcognition as Computation."

28 Restak interview with Schank: Restak, *The Brain: The Last Frontier*, pp. 372–78.

28 *Psychology Today* cover story on Schank: April 1983.

28 *Esquire* piece on Schank: December 1984, p. 46.

28 "In college I was studying": interview with Randall Davis, Massachusetts Institute of Technology, July 26, 1984.

29 "I'm not aware of any," et cetera: interview with Frederick Hayes-Roth, Palo Alto, California, June 11, 1984.

30 "I just imagine," et cetera: interview with Edward Fredkin, Brookline, Massachusetts, July 25, 1984.

CHAPTER 2. Thinking Without a Brain

36 "This statement—that computers can do": quoted in Feigenbaum and Feldman, *Computers and Thought*, pp. 3–4.

37 Gelernter's theorem prover, Logic Theorist, General Problem Solver, and Samuel's checker-playing program are described by their creators in Feigenbaum and Feldman, *Computers and Thought*.

37 "not had such competition": ibid., p. 104.

38 "I have so many ideas": quoted in Bell, *Men of Mathematics*, p. 117.

38 The full title of Boole's book is *An Investigation of the Laws of Thought on Which Are Founded the Mathematical Theories of Logic and Probabilities*.

39 Shannon's thesis was published as "A Symbolic Analysis of Relay and Switching Circuits" in *Transactions of the AIEE*, 1938, p. 713.

41 Shannon's papers on information theory were published in *Bell System Technical Journal*, volume 27, 1948, pp. 379–423, 623–56.

41 "has perhaps ballooned": Shannon, "The Bandwagon," *IEEE Transactions on Information Theory*, 1956, volume 2, number 3, p. 3, quoted in Campbell, *Grammatical Man*, p. 17.

41 "Behavior, Purpose and Teleology" was published in *Philosophy of Science*, volume 10, 1943, pp. 18–24.

42 "A short, stout man": Heims, *John von Neumann and Norbert Wiener: From Mathematics to the Technologies of Life and Death*, p. 205.

42 "a new interpretation of man": Wiener, *I Am a Mathematician: The Later Life of a Prodigy* (Cambridge, Massachusetts: MIT Press, 1966), p. 325, quoted in Rheingold, *Tools for Thought*, p. 110.

42 McCullough and Pitts's paper was published in *Bulletin of Mathematical Biophysics*, volume 5, 1943, pp. 115–33.

43 Turing's proof is in a paper titled "On Computable Numbers with an Application to the *Entscheidungsproblem*," which was published in the *Proceedings of the London Mathematics Society*, second series, volume 42, 1936, pp. 230–65.

44 The Turing test is described in his essay "Computing Machinery and Intelligence," originally published in *Mind*, October 1950, pp. 433–60, and reprinted in Feigenbaum and Feldman, *Computers and Thought*, and more recently in Hofstadter and Dennett, *The Mind's I*.

45 For a detailed description of the Perceptron, see Chapter 15 of Singh, *Great Ideas in Information Theory, Language, and Cybernetics*.

46 Minsky and Papert's critique of perceptrons was made in their 1968 book *Perceptrons*, published by MIT Press.

49 Levy's reaction to Chess 4.7 is described in Evans, *The Micro Millennium*, pp. 192–93.

51 Weizenbaum introduced his program in "ELIZA—A Computer Program for the Study of Natural Language Communication Between Man and Machine," published in the *Communications of the ACM*, January 1965, pp. 36–45. It is also described in Boden, *Artificial Intelligence and Natural Man*, pp. 106–7.

53 The workings of Parry are nicely analyzed in Boden, *Artificial Intelligence and Natural Man*, pp. 97–106. Parry's encounter with Eliza is described in Vinton Cerf, "Parry Encounters the Doctor," *Datamation*, July 1973, pp. 62–64.

55 Feigenbaum's EPAM program is described in *Computers and Thought*. Dendral is described in *Machine Intelligence 4*, pp. 209–54.

56 "I've always thought," et cetera: interview with Herbert Simon, Carnegie-Mellon University, July 30, 1984.

CHAPTER 3. A Symphony in *1*s and *0*s.

60 Dennett writes on AI and homunculi in *Brainstorms*, pp. 119–25.
60 "homunculi so stupid": ibid., p. 124.
61 "weaves algebraic patterns": quoted in Bernstein, *The Analytical Engine*, p. 50.
66 "like a roomful of ladies": ibid., p. 64.

CHAPTER 4. The Art of Programming

77 The Game of Life is described in more detail in Poundstone, *The Recursive Universe*, and Gardner, *Wheels, Life and Other Mathematical Amusements*.
80 Von Neumann described his automaton in his book *Theory of Self-Replicating Automata*, published in 1966 by the University of Illinois Press.
80 "given a large enough 'Life space' ": quoted in Gardner, *Wheels, Life, and Other Mathematical Amusements*, p. 254.
80 "In a sense, nature": quoted in Brian Hayes, "Computer Recreations," *Scientific American*, March 1984, p. 21.
81 "the elaborate symmetries," et cetera: ibid., p. 12.
81 Packard's snowflake model is described in Stephen Wolfram, "Computer Software in Science and Mathematics, *Scientific American*, September 1984, p. 188.
82 "passing the wool *over* the needle": Boden, *Artificial Intelligence and Natural Man*, p. 9.
92 "a castle built on air," et cetera: Minsky, "Why People Think Computers Can't," *Technology Review*, November/December 1983, p. 69.
94 "We're building systems": interview with Cordell Green, Palo Alto, California, June 15, 1984.

CHAPTER 5. The Meaning of Meaning

99 Woods's letter to his colleagues is dated November 8, 1983.
100 "Philosophers didn't have": interview with William Woods, Cambridge, Massachusetts, July 24, 1984.
100 "They came to me," et cetera: interview with William Woods, Cambridge, Massachusetts, December 11, 1984.
100 The Lunar program is described in Woods, "Progress in Natural Language Understanding—An Application to Lunar Geology," *AFIPS Conference Proceedings*, volume 42 (1973 National Computer Conference and Exposition), pp. 441–50.
101 The Student program is described in Minsky, *Semantic Information Processing*.
102 Bobrow's BBN incident is described in McCorduck, *Machines Who Think*, pp. 225–26 (footnote).
102 "I went to Harvard": Woods interview, December 11, 1984.
102 For details of the machine translation project, including Bar-Hillel's critique, see his book *Language and Information*.
104 "If you discovered," et cetera: Woods interview, December 11, 1984.
109 Woods's Augmented Transition Network is described in his paper "Transition Network Grammars for Natural Language Analysis," *Communications of the ACM*, October 1970, pp. 591–606.
110 Hofstadter's ATN experiment is described in *Gödel, Escher, Bach*, pp. 621–23.
110 "I attacked the problem," et cetera: Woods interview, December 11, 1984.
110 Woods's work on procedural semantics is described in Woods, *Semantics for a Question-Answering System*.
111 "If you believe": Woods interview, December 11, 1984.
112 "is immediately circular": Woods, *Semantics for a Question-Answering System*, p. 7–1.

112 "People presumably learn," et cetera: ibid., pp. 7–1 to 7–3.
113 "I was coming up," et cetera: Woods interview, December 11, 1984.
115 SHRDLU is described in Winograd, "A Procedural Model of Language Understanding," in Schank and Colby, *Computer Models of Thought and Language.*
117 " . . . [P]eople are able," et cetera: ibid., pp. 184–85.
118 "[C]ommunicating in natural language," et cetera: Hendrix and Sacerdoti, "Natural-Language Processing, Part One: The Field in Perspective," SRI International Technical Note 237, July 13, 1981, pp. 37–38.

CHAPTER 6. Listening Intelligently

123 For more details on Hearsay I, Hearsay II, HWIM, Harpy, the DARPA speech-understanding project, et cetera, see the articles in Wayne Lea's definitive anthology, *Trends in Speech Recognition.*
123 "the most popular letter": Lea quoted in *Trends in Speech Recognition,* p. 67.
123 "mad inventors," et cetera: Pierce, "Whither Speech Recognition?" *The Journal of the Acoustical Society of America,* November 1969, pp. 1049–51. (The letter was received by the journal on June 20, 1969.)
125 Ronald A. Cole on hidden words: Cole, "Navigating the Slippery Stream of Speech," *Psychology Today,* April 1979, pp. 77–87.
125 "When we listen": quoted in Pierce, "Whither Speech Recognition?" p. 1050.
126 The University of Michigan and the Harvard experiments are described in Cole's *Psychology Today* article.
128 Reddy's early speech-understanding system is described in Newell, et al., *Speech Understanding Systems,* pp. 9–12.
129 "It felt a lot": Woods interview, December 11, 1984.
130 "Not just DARPA": telephone interview with Frederick Hayes-Roth, February 1985.
130 The "dijahititatahm" example is based on one used by Dennis H. Klatt in Lea's *Trends in Speech Recognition,* pp. 251–52.
132 Hearsay II is described in Lee Erman, Frederick Hayes-Roth, Victor Lesser, and Raj Reddy, "The Hearsay-II Speech-Understanding System: Integrating Knowledge to Resolve Uncertainty," *Computing Surveys,* June 1980, pp. 213–53, as well as in Lea, *Trends in Speech Recognition.*
133 "There were a lot of surprises," et cetera: Hayes-Roth interview, February 1985.
136 BBN's method of using people to simulate a speech-understanding machine is described in William Woods and J. Makhoul, "Mechanical Inference Problems in Continuous Speech Understanding," *Artificial Intelligence,* 1974, volume 5, pp. 73–91.
138 "From my point of view," et cetera: Woods interview, December 11, 1984.
139 "Our strength was that we never," et cetera: Hayes-Roth interview, February 1985.

CHAPTER 7. Planning and Seeing

143 The Hayes-Roths' planning program is described in Barbara Hayes-Roth, "A Blackboard Model of Control," Report Number HPP-83-38, Heuristic Programming Project, Stanford University, June 1983.
144 The sonar analysis program is described in H. Penny Nii, Edward A. Feigenbaum, John J. Anton, and A. J. Rockmore, "Signal-to-Symbol Transformation: HASP/SIAP Case Study," Report Number HPP-82-6, Heuristic Programming Project, Stanford University, April 1982.
144 Crysalis and AGE are described in H. Penny Nii, "An Introduction to Knowledge Engineering, Blackboard Model, and AGE," Report Number HPP-80-29, Heuristic Programming Project, Stanford University, March 1980.

145 VISIONS is described in Hanson and Riseman, *Computer Vision Systems*.
146 For more information on blocks-world programs such as See, Obscene, and Poly, and on the origami world and the Play-Doh world, see Boden, *Artificial Intelligence and Natural Man*; Winston, *The Psychology of Computer Vision*; Barr, Cohen, and Feigenbaum, *The Artificial Intelligence Handbook*, volume 3; and Michael Brady, "Computational Approaches to Image Understanding," AI Memo Number 653, MIT Artificial Intelligence Laboratory, October 1981.
150 "Today's robots have to be told," et cetera: interview with Michael Brady, Massachusetts Institute of Technology, December 13, 1985. Brady's ideas on AI and robotics are further developed in his paper "Artificial Intelligence and Robotics," AI Memo Number 756, MIT Artificial Intelligence Laboratory, February 1984.
151 "One theory is that," et cetera: Simon interview.

CHAPTER 8. Learning About the World

156 "Instead of trying to produce": Turing, "Computing Machinery and Intelligence," in Feigenbaum and Feldman, *Computers and Thought*, p. 31.
158 "I've always been interested," et cetera: interview with Patrick Winston, Massachusetts Institute of Technology, July 26, 1984.
158 Winston's *Macbeth* program is described in his papers "Learning New Principles from Precedents and Exercises: The Details," AI Memo Number 632, MIT Artificial Intelligence Laboratory, May 1981; "Learning by Augmenting Rules and Accumulating Censors," AI Memo Number 678, May 1982; and in his textbook, *Artificial Intelligence*, pp. 419–29.
161 Winston's program that learns about cups is described in "Learning Physical Descriptions from Functional Definitions, Examples, and Precedents," by Patrick H. Winston, Thomas O. Binford, Boris Katz, and Michael Lowry, AI Memo Number 679, MIT Artificial Intelligence Laboratory, November 1982, and in *Artificial Intelligence*, pp. 429–37.
163 "systems that can chain-react": Winston interview.
164 The diabetes world is described in Winston, "Learning New Principles from Precedents and Exercises: The Details."
164 "Right now, there's no way," et cetera: Winston interview.
165 Berwick's work is described in his book *The Acquisition of Syntactic Knowledge*, pp. 4–45.

CHAPTER 9. Labyrinths of Memory

170 Schank's theory of dynamic memory is detailed in his book *Dynamic Memory*.
171 "I say what I think": interview with Roger Schank, Yale University, December 10, 1984.
171 FRUMP, written by Schank's former student Jerry De Jong, is described in Schank, *The Cognitive Computer*, pp. 151–53.
171 CYRUS, written by former student Janet Kolodner, is described in Schank, *The Cognitive Computer*, pp. 156–63.
171 "This was an attempt," et cetera: ibid., pp. 160–63.
172 Conceptual-dependency theory is described in Schank's article "Identification of Conceptualizations Underlying Natural Language," in Schank and Colby, *Computer Models of Thought and Language*, and in *The Cognitive Computer*, pp. 96–109.
173 MARGIE, written by Schank, Christopher Riesbeck, Chuck Rieger, and Neil Goldman, is described in Boden, *Artificial Intelligence and Natural Man*, pp. 161–65, and in *The Cognitive Computer*, pp. 140–43.
174 SAM, written by Richard Cullingford and Wendy Lehnert, and PAM, written

by Robert Wilensky and Richard Granger, are described in *The Cognitive Computer*, pp. 143–48.

175 Scripts, goals, and plans are described in *The Cognitive Computer*, pp. 110–33.

175 BORIS is described in Wendy G. Lehnert, Michael G. Dyer, Peter N. Johnson, C. J. Yang, and Steve Harley, "BORIS—An Experiment in In-Depth Understanding of Narratives," *Artificial Intelligence*, volume 20, 1983, pp. 15–62, and in *The Cognitive Computer*, pp. 154–56.

176 "I have a kid," et cetera: Schank interview.

179 "Suppose I tell you": Fahlman, *NETL: A System for Representing and Using Real-World Knowledge*, p. 4.

181 "In addition to being": ibid., p. 19.

CHAPTER 10. The Light of Discovery

185 Eurisko and the Automated Mathematician are described in three papers by Lenat published in *Artificial Intelligence*: "The Nature of Heuristics," volume 19, 1982, pp. 189–249; "Theory Formation by Heuristic Search," volume 21, 1983, pp. 31–59; and "EURISKO: A Program That Learns New Heuristics and Domain Concepts," volume 21, 1983, pp. 61–98.

186 "I never did actually play": interview with Douglas Lenat, Stanford University, June 12, 1984.

187 "At first, mutations": Lenat, "EURISKO: A Program That Learns New Heuristics and Domain Concepts," p. 80.

188 "Thus the final crediting": ibid.

188 "literally unhittable by any": ibid., p. 81.

189 "They changed the rules," et cetera: Lenat interview.

189 "I got far enough," et cetera: ibid.

190 Lenat's "Beings" program is described in Lenat, "Beings: Knowledge as Interacting Experts," *Advance Papers of the Fourth International Joint Conference on Artificial Intelligence*, 1975, pp. 126–33.

191 "There was one subroutine," et cetera: Lenat interview.

193 "AM went off and discovered": ibid.

193 "the cell can be realized": Lenat, "The Nature of Heuristics," p. 245.

194 "even stranger": Lenat, "EURISKO: A Program That Learns New Heuristics and Domain Concepts," p. 90.

194 Lenat's ideas on evolution are described in Lenat, "Learning by Discovery: Three Case Studies in Natural and Artificial Learning Systems," in Michalski, Mitchell, and Carbonell, editors, *Machine Learning*, pp. 287–302.

194 "smaller, whiter, lighter-boned," et cetera: ibid., pp. 294–302.

197 "the mystique of the all-seeing I's": ibid., p. 249.

198 Bacon is described in two articles by Gary Bradshaw, Patrick Langley, and Herbert Simon: "Studying Scientific Discovery by Computer Simulation," *Science*, December 2, 1983, pp. 971–75, and "Rediscovering Chemistry with the Bacon System," in Michalski, Mitchell, and Carbonell, editors, *Machine Learning*.

199 Simon's research on chunking, et cetera, is summarized in his book *The Sciences of the Artificial*.

200 "Viewed as a geometric figure": ibid, p. 64.

200 "A man, viewed as a behaving system," et cetera: ibid., pp. 126–27.

200 "Scientific discovery is problem solving," et cetera: Simon interview.

CHAPTER 11. The Finer Arts

205 "This extraordinary sight," et cetera: telephone interview with Harold Cohen, May 22, 1985.

206 "Harold Cohen built up a reputation," et cetera: quoted in *Harold Cohen*, a

pamphlet published for a showing at the Tate Gallery, London, England, June 8 to July 24, 1983.

207 "Right through the '60s": interview with Harold Cohen, La Jolla, California, May 13, 1985.

208 "From the beginning," et cetera: interview with Harold Cohen, May 13, 1985.

208 Cohen's earlier work with Aaron is described in his paper "What Is an Image?" *Proceedings of the Sixth International Joint Conference on Artificial Intelligence*, 1979, pp. 1028–57.

209 "the paradox of insistent meaningfulness," et cetera: Cohen, "What Is an Image?" p. 1039.

210 "I am proposing": ibid.

212 "As human beings do," et cetera: Cohen interview, May 22, 1985.

219 "At the moment, the knowledge," et cetera: Cohen interview, May 13, 1985.

220 "The hope is that somewhere": Cohen interview, May 22, 1985.

220 "After nearly thirty years": Cohen, "The Material of Symbols," *First Annual Symposium on Symbols and Symbol Processes*, University of Nevada, Las Vegas, August 1976, p. 6.

220 "Like any other cultural function," et cetera: personal communication, August 5, 1985.

221 "[A]rt is an elaborate": Cohen, "What Is an Image?" p. 1046.

221 "seems to spin a thread": Introduction, *The Policeman's Beard Is Half Constructed: Computer Prose and Poetry by Racter* (New York: Warner Books, 1984).

222 For information about Racter, see A. K. Dewdney, "Computer Recreations: Artificial Insanity: when a schizophrenic program meets a computerized analyst," *Scientific American*, January 1985, pp. 14–20.

223 Levitt's jazz program is described in his master's thesis, "A Melody Description System for Jazz Improvisation," Massachusetts Institute of Technology, June 1981.

223 "People often talk," et cetera: ibid., p. 6.

223 "I was a self-trained," et cetera: interview with David Levitt, Cambridge, Massachusetts, December 12, 1984.

225 "theories of what listeners notice": Levitt, "A Melody Description System for Jazz Improvisation," p. 40.

225 "[T]he musician directs the thoughts": ibid., p. 6.

226 "Human soloists have a much larger": ibid, pp. 34–40.

226 "see the score": Levitt interview.

CHAPTER 12. The Scientists and the Engineers

229 "It's interesting to look": Minsky speaking at the tutorial "An Overview of Artificial Intelligence" at the annual conference of the American Association for Artificial Intelligence, August 6, 1984, Austin, Texas.

229 "The Fifth Generation Challenge" was held October 8 to 10 at the San Francisco Hilton Hotel.

230 "In some sense, the book": McCorduck, *Machines Who Think*, p. 279.

231 "a saleable commodity," et cetera: Feigenbaum and McCorduck, *The Fifth Generation*, p. 2.

232 Estimate that the Japanese system would hold as much information as the *Encyclopaedia Britannica*: ibid., p. 114.

232 "the first great postindustrial": ibid., p. 3.

232 "The world is entering," et cetera: ibid., p. 14. (Italics deleted from original.)

233 "and permits the wise": ibid., p. 9.

236 "IBM never looked with favor": quoted in McCorduck, *Machines Who Think*, p. 151.

237 "The words were designed," et cetera: interview with Jerrold Kaplan, Palo Alto, California, May 9, 1984.
237 "When Sun Tzu," et cetera: De Kleer, review of *The Fifth Generation*, *Artificial Intelligence*, volume 22, 1984, pp. 222–26.
240 "AI is prescientific," et cetera: Hayes-Roth interview, June 11, 1984.
241 "alchemy to art to science," et cetera: Winston interview.
241 "machoism," "gee-whiz types of systems," et cetera: interview with John Seely Brown, Palo Alto, California, June 11, 1984.
242 "Why AM and Eurisko Appear to Work" appeared in *Artificial Intelligence*, volume 23, 1984, pp. 269–94.
244 "AM poses a very interesting," et cetera: Brown interview.
245 "As a field, artificial intelligence," et cetera: McDermott, "Artificial Intelligence Meets Natural Stupidity," in Haugeland, editor, *Mind Design*, pp. 143–45.
246 "It's part of growing up," et cetera: Brown interview.

CHAPTER 13. In the Chinese Room

249 Searle's Reith Lectures are reprinted in Searle, *Minds, Brains and Science*.
249 "No one supposes": Searle, "Minds, Brains, and Programs," in Hofstadter and Dennett, *The Mind's I*, p. 370. The original article appeared in *The Behavioral and Brain Sciences*, September 1980, along with a number of rebuttals.
250 "There is more to having": Searle, *Minds, Brains and Science*, p. 31.
251 "Understanding a language": ibid., p. 33.
252 "[I]magine that you": ibid., p. 32.
252 "[A]ll mental phenomena": ibid., p. 18.
253 "Because we do not understand": ibid., p. 44.
254 "the hum of its parts": Hofstadter and Dennett, *The Mind's I*, p. 191.
255 "Great artists have always": Dreyfus, *What Computers Can't Do*, pp. 65–66.
255 "The mistaken view that": Hubert L. Dreyfus and Stuart E. Dreyfus, "People That (sic) Think," pp. 2–3.
256 "naïveté and faith": Dreyfus, *What Computers Can't Do*, p. 36.
256 "surprising and misleading," "the usual riot": ibid., p. 135.
256 Papert's memo on Dreyfus: McCorduck, *Machines Who Think*, p. 186.
257 "Not until a machine": quoted in Turing, "Computing Machinery and Intelligence," in Feigenbaum and Feldman, *Computers and Thought*, p. 22.
258 Colby's artificial neurotic is described in Boden, *Artificial Intelligence and Natural Man*, pp. 21–33.
259 The Ideology Machine is described in Abelson, "The Structure of Belief Systems," in Schank and Colby, *Computer Models of Thought and Language*, pp. 287–93.
259 "the human penchant": ibid., p. 287.
259 The Politics program is described in Carbonell, "POLITICS: Automated Ideological Reasoning," *Cognitive Science*, volume 2, 1978, pp. 27–51.
260 Isaac Asimov's Laws of Robotics are described in his 1950 book, *I Robot*.

CHAPTER 14. Calculating Minds

265 "[T]here are some acts": Weizenbaum, *Computer Power and Human Reason*, p. 13.
265 "Once my secretary": ibid., p. 6.
265 "Further work must be": K. M. Colby, J. B. Watt, and J. P. Gilbert, "A Computer Method of Psychotherapy: Preliminary Communication," quoted in Weizenbaum, *Computer Power and Human Reason*, p. 5.
266 "the development of a network": quoted in Weizenbaum, *Computer Power and Human Reason*, p. 5 (footnote).

266 "differences between information": Weizenbaum, "The Computer in Your Future," *New York Review of Books*, October 27, 1983, p. 62.
266 "Times of day were known": Weizenbaum, *Computer Power and Human Reason*, p. 21.
267 "disassociated time from": quoted in Weizenbaum, *Computer Power and Human Reason*, p. 23.
267 "[T]his newly created reality," et cetera: Weizenbaum, *Computer Power and Human Reason*, p. 25.
268 "We've been around on," et cetera: interview with Joseph Weizenbaum, Massachusetts Institute of Technology, July 25, 1984.
269 Weizenbaum's comments on computers in the schools were made in a presentation entitled "Are Computers Really Good for Children?" at the Annual Meeting of the American Association for the Advancement of Science, Los Angeles, California, May 30, 1985.
269 "One of the things that," et cetera: ibid.
269 Weizenbaum's review of *The Fifth Generation:* "The Computer in Your Future," *New York Review of Books*, October, 27, 1983, pp. 58–62.
269 "The geriatric robot": Feigenbaum and McCorduck, *The Fifth Generation*, p. 93.
269 Feigenbaum and McCorduck's reply to Weizenbaum's review: *New York Review of Books*, December 8, 1983, p. 52.
270 "People are thinking of themselves," et cetera: Turkle, *The Second Self*, pp. 17–23.
271 "cold and ruthless application," et cetera: Weizenbaum, *Computer Power and Human Reason*, p. 256.
271 For more information on Nazi conspiracy theories, see George Johnson, *Architects of Fear: Conspiracy Theories and Paranoia in American Politics* (Los Angeles: Tarcher, 1983).
271 "Thinking of ourselves as *nonmachines*," et cetera: interview with Nils Nilsson, Menlo Park, California, June 14, 1984.
272 "The math specialists and everyone," et cetera: Brown interview.
272 Some of the work of Brown and his colleagues is described in Sleeman and Brown, *Intelligent Tutoring Systems*, in Brown and Richard R. Burton, "Diagnostic Models for Procedural Bugs in Basic Mathematical Skills," *Cognitive Science*, volume 2, 1978, pp. 155–92, and in Brown and Kurt VanLehn, "Repair Theory: A Generative Theory of Bugs in Procedural Skills," *Cognitive Science*, volume 4, 1980, pp. 379–426.

CHAPTER 15. The Copycat Project

280 "My interest in abstract": telephone interview with Douglas Hofstadter, August 1985.
281 "I thought about the beauty": ibid.
282 Hofstadter's Ph.D. work is described in his paper "Energy Levels and Wave Functions of Bloch Electrons in Rational and Irrational Magnetic Fields," *Physical Review B*, September 15, 1976.
283 "I have sought to weave": Hofstadter, *Gödel, Escher, Bach*, p. 28.
284 "Computers by their very": ibid., p. 26.
285 "Prelude . . . Ant Fugue": ibid., pp. 275–84 and 311–36.
286 "Waking Up From the Boolean Dream" is reprinted in Hofstadter, *Metamagical Themas*.
287 "When you first read," et cetera: ibid., p. 641.
287 "In a cell, all activity": Hofstadter, "The Copycat Project: An Experiment in Nondeterminism and Creative Analogies," AI Memo Number 755, MIT Artificial-Intelligence Laboratory, January 1984, p. 12.

288 "The brain itself does not," et cetera: Hofstadter, "Waking Up From the Boolean Dream," p. 648.
289 "There are codelets," et cetera: Hofstadter, "The Copycat Project," pp. 12–13.
290 "While the choice": ibid., p. 11.
290 "somewhat polemical and diffuse," et cetera: Newell, "Endnotes to the Papers on AI," in Machlup and Mansfield, editors, *The Study of Information: Interdisciplinary Messages*, pp. 291–92.
290 "[Hofstadter is] trying": James Gleick, "Exploring the Labyrinth of the Mind," *New York Times Magazine*, August 21, 1983, p. 83.
290 "There *is* a Dendral": Feigenbaum interview.
291 "a physicist turned philosopher": Granger interview.
292 "That's what physicists do," et cetera: Hofstadter interview, August 1985.
293 For more information on the New Connectionism, see Hinton and Anderson, editors, *Parallel Models of Associative Memory*.

EPILOGUE

295 IJCAI-85 was held from August 18 to 23 at UCLA.
298 "Look, the Defense Department," et cetera: Schank interview.
299 "I don't know what to make," et cetera: Hofstadter interview, August 1985.
300 "[C]omputers are maddeningly," et cetera: Severo M. Ornstein, Brian C. Smith, Lucy A. Suchman, "Strategic Computing: An Assessment," June 21, 1984, p. 3. The report is available from Computer Professionals for Social Responsibility, P.O. Box 717, Palo Alto, California 94301.
300 "Humans are undependable," et cetera: personal communication, October 1985.
301 For more information on the problems of verifying software, see Brian C. Smith, "The Limits of Correctness," prepared for Symposium on Unintentional Nuclear War, Fifth Congress of the International Physicians for the Prevention of Nuclear War, Budapest, Hungary, June 28 to July 1, 1985.
301 "Eventually there will be programs," et cetera: Fredkin interview.
303 "Hackers and laymen alike": Boden, "Artificial Intelligence and Legal Responsibility," summary statement, *Proceedings of the Ninth International Joint Conference on Artificial Intelligence*, 1985, pp. 1267–68.
303 "Decision makers have used," et cetera: Willick, "Constitutional Law and Artificial Intelligence: The Potential Legal Recognition of Computers as 'Persons,' " *Proceedings of the Ninth International Joint Conference on Artificial Intelligence*, 1985, pp. 1271–73.

BIBLIOGRAPHY

Bar-Hillel, Yehoshua. *Language and Information: Selected Essays on Their Theory and Application* (Reading, Massachusetts: Addison-Wesley, 1964).

Barr, Avron, Paul R. Cohen, and Edward A. Feigenbaum, editors. *The Handbook of Artificial Intelligence*, three volumes (Los Altos, California: William Kaufmann, 1981, 1982).

Bateson, Gregory. *Mind and Nature: A Necessary Unity* (New York: Bantam Books, 1980).

Bernstein, Jeremy. *The Analytical Engine: Computers—Past, Present and Future*, revised edition (New York: William Morrow, 1981).

———. *Three Degrees Above Zero: Bell Labs in the Information Age* (New York: Scribner's, 1984).

Berwick, Robert C. *The Acquisition of Syntactic Knowledge* (Cambridge, Massachusetts: MIT Press, 1984).

Boden, Margaret. *Artificial Intelligence and Natural Man* (New York: Basic Books, 1977).

Bolter, J. David. *Turing's Man: Western Culture in the Computer Age* (Chapel Hill: University of North Carolina Press, 1984).

Campbell, Jeremy. *Grammatical Man: Information, Entropy, Language, and Life* (New York: Simon and Schuster, 1982).

Davis, Philip J., and Reuben Hersh. *The Mathematical Experience* (Boston: Houghton Mifflin, 1982).

Dennett, Daniel C. *Brainstorms: Philosophical Essays on Mind and Psychology* (Cambridge, Massachusetts: MIT Press, 1978).

Dreyfus, Hubert L. *What Computers Can't Do: The Limits of Artificial Intelligence*, revised edition (New York: Harper Colophon, 1979).

Eigen, Manfred, and Ruthild Winkler. *Laws of the Game: How the Principles of Nature Govern Chance* (New York: Harper Colophon, 1981).

Ernst, George W., and Allen Newell. *GPS: A Case Study in Generality and Problem Solving* (New York: Academic Press, 1969).

Evans, Christopher. *The Micro Millennium* (New York: Viking, 1979).

Fahlman, Scott E. *NETL: A System for Representing and Using Real-World Knowledge* (Cambridge, Massachusetts: MIT Press, 1979).

Feigenbaum, Edward A., and Julian Feldman, editors. *Computers and Thought* (New York, McGraw-Hill, 1963).

———, and Pamela McCorduck. *The Fifth Generation: Artificial Intelligence and Japan's Computer Challenge to the World* (Reading, Massachusetts: Addison-Wesley, 1983).

Friedman, Daniel P. *The Little Lisper* (Chicago: Science Research Associates, Inc., 1974).

Frude, Neil. *The Intimate Machine: Close Encounters with Computers and Robots* (New York: New American Library, 1983).

Gardner, Howard. *The Mind's New Science: A History of the Cognitive Revolution* (New York: Basic Books, 1985).

Gardner, Martin. *Wheels, Life and Other Mathematical Amusements* (New York: W. H. Freeman, 1983).

Goldstine, Herman H. *The Computer: From Pascal to von Neumann* (Princeton, New Jersey: Princeton University Press, 1980).

Graham, Neill. *Artificial Intelligence: Making Machines "Think"* (Blue Ridge Summit, Pennsylvania: Tab Books, 1979).

Hanson, Allen R., and Edward M. Riseman, editors. *Computer Vision Systems* (New York: Academic Press, 1978).

Hanson, Dirk. *The New Alchemists: Silicon Valley and the Microelectronics Revolution* (Boston: Little, Brown, 1982).

Haugeland, John, editor. *Mind Design: Philosophy, Psychology, Artificial Intelligence* (Cambridge, Massachusetts: MIT Press, 1981).

Hayes, J. E., and Donald Michie, editors. *Intelligent Systems: The Unprecedented Opportunity* (Chichester, West Sussex, England: Ellis Horwood Ltd., 1983).

Heims, Steve J. *John von Neumann and Norbert Wiener: From Mathematics to the Technologies of Life and Death* (Cambridge, Massachusetts: MIT Press, 1980).

Hilts, Philip J. *Scientific Temperaments: Three Lives in Contemporary Science* (New York: Simon and Schuster, 1982).

Hinton, Geoffrey, and James A. Anderson, editors. *Parallel Models of Associative Memory* (Hillsdale, N.J.: Lawrence Erlbaum Associates, 1981).

Hodges, Andrew. *Alan Turing: The Enigma* (New York: Simon and Schuster, 1983).

Hofstadter, Douglas. *Gödel, Escher, Bach: An Eternal Golden Braid* (New York: Basic Books, 1979).

———. *Metamagical Themas: Questing for the Essence of Mind and Pattern* (New York: Basic Books, 1984).

———, and Daniel Dennet. *The Mind's I: Fantasies and Reflections on Self and Soul* (New York, Basic Books, 1981).

Hunt, Morton. *The Universe Within: A New Science Explores the Human Mind* (New York: Simon and Schuster, 1982).

Kent, Ernest. *The Brains of Men and Machines* (New York: McGraw-Hill, 1981).

Kidder, Tracy. *The Soul of a New Machine* (Boston: Atlantic-Little, Brown, 1981).

Kline, Morris. *Mathematics in Western Culture* (London: Oxford University Press, 1953).

———. *Mathematics: The Loss of Certainty* (New York: Oxford University Press, 1980).

Kosslyn, Stephen Michael. *Ghosts in the Mind's Machine: Creating and Using Images in the Brain* (New York: Norton, 1983).

Lea, Wayne A., editor. *Trends in Speech Recognition* (Englewood Cliffs, N.J.: Prentice-Hall, 1980).

Levy, Steven. *Hackers: Heroes of the Computer Revolution* (Garden City, New York: Anchor Press/Doubleday, 1984).

Machlup, Fritz, and Una Mansfield, editors. *The Study of Information: Interdisciplinary Messages* (New York: Wiley, 1983).

McCorduck, Pamela. *Machines Who Think* (New York: W. H. Freeman, 1979).

———. *The Universal Machine* (New York: McGraw-Hill, 1985).

Michalski, Ryszard S., Jaime G. Carbonell, and Tom M. Mitchell, editors. *Machine Learning: An Artificial Intelligence Approach* (Palo Alto, California: Tioga Publishing Company, 1983).

Minsky, Marvin, editor. *Semantic Information Processing* (Cambridge, Massachusetts: MIT Press, 1968).

———. *Society of Mind* (New York: Simon and Schuster, 1986).

Monod, Jacques. *Chance and Necessity: An Essay on the Natural Philosophy of Modern Biology* (New York: Vintage Books, 1972).

Nagel, Ernest, and James R. Newman. *Gödel's Proof* (New York: New York University Press, 1958).

Newell, Allen, et. al. *Speech Understanding Systems: Final Report of a Study Group* (Amsterdam: North-Holland Publishing Company, 1973).

Norman, Donald A. *Learning and Memory* (San Francisco: W. H. Freeman, 1982).

Papert, Seymour. *Mindstorms: Children, Computers, and Powerful Ideas* (New York: Basic Books/Harper Colophon, 1980).

Poundstone, William. *The Recursive Universe: Cosmic Complexity and the Limits of Scientific Knowledge* (New York: William Morrow, 1984).

Raphael, Bertram. *The Thinking Computer: Mind Inside Matter* (San Francisco: W. H. Freeman, 1976).

Restak, Richard. *The Brain: The Last Frontier* (New York: Warner, 1979).

Rheingold, Howard. *Tools for Thought: The People and Ideas Behind the Next Computer Revolution* (New York: Simon and Schuster, 1985).

Rose, Frank. *Into the Heart of the Mind: An American Quest for Artificial Intelligence* (New York: Harper and Row, 1984).

Rose, Steven. *The Conscious Brain*, revised edition (New York: Vintage Books, 1976).

Schank, Roger C. *Dynamic Memory: A Theory of Reminding and Learning in Computers and People* (Cambridge, England: Cambridge University Press, 1982).

———, with Peter G. Childers. *The Cognitive Computer: On Language, Learning, and Artificial Intelligence* (Reading, Massachusetts: Addison-Wesley, 1984).

———, and Kenneth Mark Colby, editors. *Computer Models of Thought and Language* (San Francisco: W. H. Freeman, 1973).

Searle, John. *Minds, Brains, and Science* (Cambridge, Massachusetts: Harvard University Press, 1984).

Shurkin, Joel. *Engines of the Mind: A History of the Computer* (New York, Norton, 1984).

Simon, Herbert A. *The Sciences of the Artificial*, second edition (Cambridge, Massachusetts: MIT Press, 1981).

Singh, Jagjit. *Great Ideas in Information Theory, Language and Cybernetics* (New York: Dover, 1966).

Sleeman, Derek, and John Seely Brown, editors. *Intelligent Tutoring Systems* (London: Academic Press, 1982).

Sloman, Aaron. *The Computer Revolution in Philosophy: Philosophy, Science and Models of Mind* (Hassocks, Sussex, England: Harvester Press, 1978).

Sobel, Robert. *IBM: Colossus in Transition* (New York: Times Books, 1981).

Steen, Lynn Arthur, editor. *Mathematics Today: Twelve Informal Essays* (New York: Vintage Books, 1980).

Turkle, Sherry. *The Second Self: Computers and the Human Spirit* (New York: Simon and Schuster, 1984).

Von Neumann, John. *The Computer and the Brain* (New Haven, Connecticut: Yale University Press, 1958).

Watzlawick, Paul. *How Real Is Real? Confusion, Disinformation, Communication* (New York: Vintage Books, 1977).

Weizenbaum, Joseph. *Computer Power and Human Reason* (San Francisco: W. H. Freeman, 1976).

Wiener, Norbert. *Cybernetics*, second edition (Cambridge, Massachusetts: MIT Press, 1961).

Winograd, Terry. *Language as a Cognitive Process. Volume 1: Syntax* (Reading, Massachusetts: Addison-Wesley, 1983).

Winston, Patrick Henry. *Artificial Intelligence*, second edition (Reading, Massachusetts: Addison-Wesley, 1984).

———, editor. *The Psychology of Computer Vision* (New York: McGraw-Hill, 1975).

———, and Richard Henry Brown, editors. *Artificial Intelligence: An MIT Perspective*, two volumes (Cambridge, Massachusetts: MIT Press, 1979).

———, and Berthold Klaus Paul Horn. *Lisp* (Reading, Massachusetts: Addison-Wesley, 1981).

Woods, William A. *Semantics for a Question-Answering System* (Cambridge, Massachusetts: Aiken Computation Laboratory, Harvard University, 1967).

INDEX